D1434302

THE DEAD STRAIGHT GUIDE TO
THE VELVET UNDERGROUND

PETER HOGAN

This edition © Red Planet Publishing Ltd 2017
Text © Peter Hogan 1997–2017

This first edition published October 2017 by
Red Planet Publishing Ltd
www.redplanetzone.com

Email: info@redplanetzone.com
Previously published as The Rough Guide to The Velvet Underground

Printed in the UK by CPI

Publisher: Mark Neeter

Picture Credits
See web for details

A catalogue record for this book is available from the British Library

ISBN: 978 1 9113 4646 3

www.redplanetzone.com

CONTENTS

THE STORY

THE MUSIC

VELVETOLOGY: FURTHER EXPLORATIONS

ACKNOWLEDGEMENTS

This book began life as *The Complete Guide To The Music Of The Velvet Underground* in 1997, and was then vastly expanded into *The Rough Guide To The Velvet Underground* in 2007. Since I seem to revisit this territory every ten years, I'm glad that Mark Neeter of Red Planet talked me into writing this new edition, which has been completely revised, expanded and updated, and is as complete as I could make it; if there are errors or omissions here, it's not for the want of trying.

But we ran out of time on a couple of things. There've been numerous Lou Reed live albums released in recent years. Most of these are taken from Seventies radio broadcasts, and are of dubious legality and quality, so I decided not to include them. In other words, buyer beware... but if there was anything fantastic about any of these, I'm sure I would have heard about it. Also, there's been a small avalanche of books about Lou Reed published since his death, and I simply didn't have time to read or review the books by Mick Wall, Chris Wade or Adrian Levy. They may all be great; they also may not, so trust your own judgement. Again, I doubt if I've missed any important information that I didn't find elsewhere.

I'm also indebted to the writings of those who have explored this territory before me, notably Lester Bangs, Victor Bockris, John Cale, Diana Clapton, Peter Doggett, Nat Finkelstein, David Fricke, Mary Harron, Joe Harvard, Clinton Heylin, Nick Kent, M.C. Kostek, Olivier Landemaine, Gerard Malanga, Legs McNeill, Tim Mitchell, George Plimpton, Lou Reed, Chris Roberts, Howard Sounes, Jean Stein, Dave Thompson, Lynn Tillman, Andy Warhol, Steven Watson, Gillian Welch, Mary Woronov, Michael Wrenn, Richard Witts, James Young and Albin Zak III (and apologies if I missed anybody). Many of these accounts contradict each other – as do the faulty and selective memories of the story's protagonists. In every instance, I've opted for the version that seemed the most plausible.

Special thanks to: Ken Clark and Bill Allerton, who tracked down quite a few rarities for me; Patrick Humphries and Sue Parr, who let me raid their library and provided the occasional moment of sanity; Lou Reed's number one fan Glen Marks, who provided useful info and insight and let me raid his collection; William Higham and Mailan Henning, who both helped with early research.

I'd also like to thank the following for sharing their thoughts about the Velvets with me down through the decades, which has undoubtedly influenced the way I've viewed the band: Lawrence Ball, Michael Bonner, Peter Buck, Chris Carr, Stephen Dalton, Fred Dellar, Steve Ehrenberg, Neil Gaiman, Charles Hayward, Markus Holler, Allan Jones, Nick Kent, Michael McDonough-Jones, Bill MacCormick, Phil Manzanera, Dave Marsh, Alan Moore, Charles Shaar Murray, Nico, Ruth Pitcher, John Tobler, and Pete Townshend. And a few more, sadly no longer with us: Tim Broadbent,

Mick Farren, David Ferguson, Debbie Geller, Susan Hill, Sean Hogan, Ian MacDonald/
MacCormick, Vanessa Morgan, John Platt, Steve Whitaker and Carol Whitaker.
Special thanks go to Chris Charlesworth of Omnibus Press and Andrew Lockett of
Rough Guides, for commissioning the earlier versions of this book.

Finally, I'd like to thank Ellie, Quinn and Hal, for being my mirrors — and for
putting up with hearing a lot of music they'd probably rather have avoided.

This one's for Stephanie Jones.

Peter Hogan, September 2017

ABOUT THE AUTHOR

Peter Hogan has written about music, film and other aspects of popular culture for
numerous British magazines, including *Melody Maker*, *i-D*, *Vox* and *Uncut*. He is also
the author of the critically acclaimed graphic novel series *Resident Alien* and lives in
Tunbridge Wells with his wife and sons, and numerous imaginary friends.

INTRODUCTION

"ROCK AND ROLL IS AS VALID AS ANY OTHER ART FORM" – JOHN CALE

Fifty years on from the year it was recorded, The Velvet Underground & Nico sounds as fresh, as dazzling and as socially relevant as ever – a claim that very few other records of that era could make.

As the late Lester Bangs once observed: "Modern music begins with the Velvets, and the implications and influence of what they did seem to go on forever." Yet Andy Warhol's 'Peel Slowly And See' slogan on the cover of that first album proved to be a prophetic phrase, since it took literally decades for the Velvets to become what Lou Reed would accurately describe in the early Nineties as "a big cult band".

Brian Eno once famously quipped something to the effect that although not many people had bought the Velvets' debut album, those who did all promptly formed bands of their own. There's more than a grain of truth in that, and the Velvets' influence visibly extends through glam-rock and punk to grunge and beyond. The timelessness of their appeal is almost certainly related to the fact that back in the Sixties the Velvet Underground were completely and radically out of step with their times, and usually ahead of them. For example, when Lou Reed met John Cale at the beginning of 1965, he had already written 'Heroin' and 'I'm Waiting For The Man'. It's worth noting that at this point the Beatles were just starting to record their *Help* album, and Bob Dylan was still thought of as simply a 'protest singer'.

But the social and musical movements of the Sixties largely passed the Velvet Underground by. They had no interest in protest, or folk-rock; they thought the whole hippie movement was shallow and absurd, and while most of their contemporaries were extolling the virtues of psychedelic drugs, the Velvets (apart from Moe Tucker) embraced narcotics that were much harder and darker. They had far more in common with the beat generation that had preceded them, and with the punks who would follow a decade later; they almost fit the profile of what Danny Fields called 'Mole People': "they only seemed to come out at night; they all wore black – black turtlenecks, pants. Some leather. Their skins were light, and they were very intense." Visually, John Cale had a fashion sense that verged on the bizarre – while the other Velvets have usually dressed in basic black throughout their career(s), Cale has frequently been seen in garments that lead you to believe he's just wandered in from another dimension. For a man to wear a rhinestone necklace in public in 1965 – as Cale did – was, to put it mildly, extremely unusual for the time.

INTRODUCTION

Artistically, the Velvet Underground was a place where widely differing ideas collided – and whatever Lou Reed may have later claimed, there's no doubt at all that the Velvets were a true collaboration, a synthesis of four very talented people. Lou Reed's love of doo-wop, and his and Sterling Morrison's grounding in the blues were by no means unusual for the time – but they became something far greater when wedded to the ingredients brought to the table by Cale (a man later described by Brian Eno as "a fountain of musical ideas... and very original ones, too"). Cale's background in both classical and avant-garde music made him a unique figure in rock at this time, and no other rock band in 1965 would even have dreamt of using as unusual an instrument as the electric viola. Nor should the input of Morrison and Moe Tucker – as musicians and as people – be underestimated.

But perhaps most importantly, the band provided an outlet for Lou Reed's literary ambitions. More than any other contemporary songwriter, Reed has explored the possibilities of fiction, with lyrics that he'd later describe as "personalized short stories". These were often peopled by characters from the darker side of the tracks: junkies, transsexuals, drunks and losers. People about whom, as Lester Bangs once observed, "nobody else gives a shit" – but Reed did, and his work is steeped in that compassion. That anybody should write rock songs about this territory was deemed outrageous at the time, since pop music was still almost universally thought of as merely entertainment for empty-headed teenagers. As Reed told Barney Hoskyns in 1996: "That's why, in a sense, it was so easy to do. It was like uncharted waters. Which made it so absurd to be told you were doing something shocking, with *Howl* and *Naked Lunch* and

Last Exit To Brooklyn already out. There was such a narrow-minded view of what a song could be ... And ironically, now we have rap and stuff, people say to me, 'Oh, your stuff's not so shocking.' And I'm saying, 'I never said it was.' The point is, I wanted those songs really to be *about* something that you could go back to thirty years later. And in fact, you can: they're not trapped in the Sixties, they're not locked into that zeitgeist." In fact, Reed's lyrics took a factual, reportage approach to their subject matter. 'Heroin' is neither explicitly for nor against the drug, merely descriptive – but the fact that there was a song called 'Heroin' at all still caused waves.

All of these ingredients were wrapped up in three chords and an attitude, and overlaid with the sensibility and lessons they learned from Andy Warhol. At least some of the Velvets' long-term intellectual cachet springs from their association with Warhol – a man who was either a great artist or a great con-artist, and probably both. Today, Warhol's talent is still somewhat overshadowed by his image as 'party Andy', a seemingly shallow creature dazzled by celebrity and puzzled by pretty much everything (Gore Vidal once acidly described him as "the only genius with an I.Q. of 60"). Yet it was Warhol's unquenchable curiosity, and his uniquely childlike view of the world, that led him to experiment constantly in his art – and to encourage others to do likewise.

While he may not have known much about music, and had little to do with what the Velvets actually produced, there is no doubt that they all took Warhol's opinions extremely seriously. Andy undoubtedly knew about style, and recognised it in others. Not only did he gain the Velvet Underground exposure on a scale undreamt of by most of their contemporaries (even if it also backfired on them), but he also

THE VELVET UNDERGROUND

paired them with Nico for their debut album – against their wishes, but to their ultimate profit. Would that first album have attracted as many people *without* those wistful ballads, sung in that breathless voice? If only for making them more user-friendly, Warhol's role in this story should not be underestimated. "It seemed almost fated," commented Gerard Malanga on the marriage of the Velvets and Warhol. Certainly, no other band of that era would have fitted so well into Warhol's half-formulated plans for a multi-media spectacle – compared to most of their rock contemporaries, the Velvets looked like fine artists in the first place. It was also Warhol's death which instigated the coda to the Velvets' career, inspiring Reed and Cale to patch up their differences with a masterful tribute to their mentor... which in turn led to the unexpected 1993 reunion of the band.

But back in the Sixties the Velvet Underground were pretty much ignored, and what little success they had came mainly via word of mouth. They attracted few reviews, got little or no radio airplay. They weren't invited to play at Woodstock (and if they had been, they probably wouldn't have gone), and few mourned when they broke up after recording just four studio albums. This may have been at least partly because there were many who identified the Velvets band with their subject matter – which for many others was of course part of their appeal – but confusing the teller with the tale is usually a foolish thing to do. In later years Reed's material has become more confessional,

seemingly more personal, but even there the lines blur. "I'm interested in writing a book, but not about me," he once asserted.

It is true that Reed's sexuality was more than somewhat fluid, and that both Cale and Reed inflicted an enormous amount of damage on themselves through alcohol and hard drugs ("I was really fucked up. And that's all there is to it," Reed candidly admitted in 1989). However, it's also true that both Reed and Cale – and the vast majority of the Factory crowd – gave up drugs for good in the Eighties. Even Nico, the queen of the junkies, was seriously attempting to quit heroin and methadone at the time of her death (which was not drug-related).

Surprisingly, the Velvets managed to survive the weight of their own legend, resulting in solo careers that have been – at the very least – interesting. Some of that solo work is truly great, some of it truly awful – but for all of their excesses and failures, the output of both Reed and Cale mainly displays intelligence, craft, maturity and compassion. Throughout, both followed the dictates of art and conscience rather than those of the marketplace, and – to paraphrase Reed – grew up in public.

After half a century, the Velvet Underground's stature remains undiminished. The *NME*'s Mary Harron once called them "the first avant-garde rock band, and the greatest." And as Lou Reed pointed out in 1993: "The proof is in the work, and the work is on record".

Peter Hogan, 2017

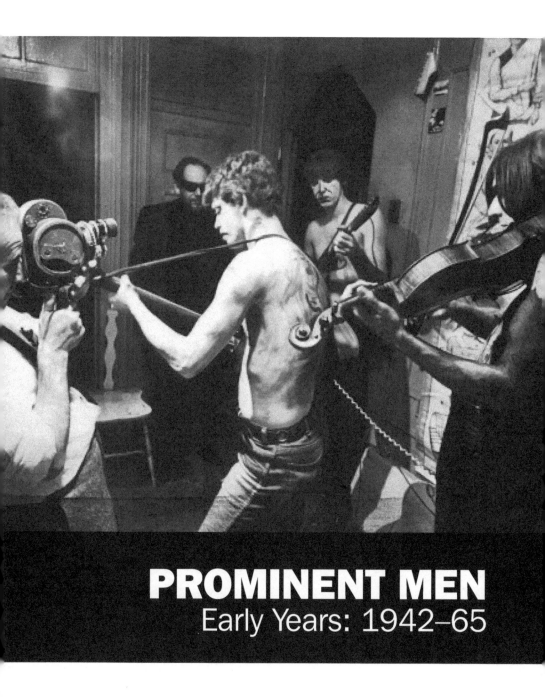

PROMINENT MEN
Early Years: 1942–65

1

"*What we did was unique. It was powerful*"

JOHN CALE

PROMINENT MEN

EARLY YEARS 1942–65

Born during World War II and raised during the Eisenhower years of the 1950s, the four core individuals who formed the Velvet Underground were an unusual collection by any definition: three suburban New Yorkers and one Welshman; three men and a woman; a poet, two rockers and a classicist. They were the last flare of the Beat Generation before the hippies turned up, drawn to nightclubs and drugs and the bright lights of New York City, where they played their first club gigs and met an artist named Andy.

Lewis Alan Reed was born on 2 March 1942 in Brooklyn, New York. His father Sidney Reed (originally Rabinowitz) was a tax accountant, his mother Toby a former beauty queen; a few years later they had a daughter. The family moved to Freeport, Long Island when Lou was eleven years old – at which point he discovered rock'n'roll, via the radio. As a child he'd trained in classical piano, and had demanded that his guitar tutor show him the three chords necessary to play a Carl Perkins song, rather than learn 'Twinkle Twinkle Little Star'.

By twelve he'd mastered enough guitar to begin writing his own songs, and his first single came out when he was still only sixteen; he played rhythm guitar on a recording of two of his songs, 'So Blue' and 'Leave Her For Me' by the doo-wop group the Jades (who changed their name to the Shades when another group surfaced called the Jades). He later claimed his total royalty earnings from the record amounted to 78 cents. Reed had a suburban middle-class upbringing, attending public school in both Brooklyn and Long Island; like most

Jewish boys, he was bar mitzvahed at age 12. But Lou hated his school education, and had a problem with authority from the very beginning. He told others he was "routinely" beaten up after school by tougher kids. This was the reason the family moved to Long Island, but the bullying continued there.

After Lou's death, his sister Merrill 'Bunny' Reed Weiner – herself a psychotherapist – penned a revealing portrait of the Reed family life that showed a very different aspect to previous accounts. She recalls that in his teens Lou became "anxious, avoidant and resistant to most socializing". Prone to panic attacks and social phobias, he'd sometimes hide under desks and refuse to come out. Music provided a refuge for him, but it was the only one he had. He also suspected he might be homosexual, but that was the least of his troubles. He was subject to violent mood swings, and argued with his father frequently; he'd already begun experimenting with drugs, and much of the time was obviously depressed and acting very weirdly.

In September 1959, Lou escaped his family by going to college, at NYU's campus in the

THE VELVET UNDERGROUND

Bronx, where he studied music theory. But living alone for the first time proved too much for him, and according to his sister the Reeds were forced to bring their son home in November after he suffered a nervous breakdown.

The Reeds sought medical advice, though Bunny insists her parents' concern had nothing to do with Lou's sexuality. A psychiatrist delivered a verdict of suspected schizophrenia, and prescribed medication. When it didn't work, the then-popular solution of a course of electroshock therapy was prescribed for Lou, three times a week for eight weeks, at Creedmore Psychiatric Center. Reluctantly, the Reeds agreed, feeling they had no other choice. Lou later described the treatment he received at the mental hospital as being "like a very prolonged bad acid trip with none of the benefits".

The electroshock failed to cure the mood swings, but caused memory loss – Lou would struggle with memory problems all his life – and also badly affected Lou's sense of empathy and identity, and his ability to concentrate. All of which may well explain some of his more antisocial personality traits, and his destructive behaviour towards anyone with whom he became closely involved. It certainly didn't help his family situation – he felt betrayed by his parents, and the relationship took decades to heal. In truth, most witnesses feel that the Reeds were nice people who only wanted the best for their son, and had trusted the medical advice they were given. Still, Sterling Morrison has said that while they were at university together Lou's parents were constantly threatening to have him "thrown in the nut-house", though that may well have been just Lou's version of events. Even so, the anger and sense of betrayal he felt towards his parents would fuel his work for years.

Lou Reed's high-school yearbook photo, 1959

One good side-effect of this episode is that it may have saved Lou from being drafted to serve in Vietnam. When he attended the army draft board five years later, Lou's medical record and prescription medicine meant that he was classified 1-Y, which meant he would only be drafted in an emergency.

In September 1960 Lou returned to college, this time enrolling at Syracuse University in the fall of 1960, where he joined his childhood friend Allen Hyman (with whom he'd form a band called L.A. And The Eldorados to play bars and parties). At Syracuse, Reed studied journalism for one week before moving over to Liberal Arts to study music, philosophy and literature, as well as taking courses in directing and the history of theatre. He was expelled from the (compulsory) Reserve Officers' Training Corps after a few weeks, having refused to obey orders from his commanding officer. He cultivated the image of a rebel-cum-poet, one who had been through electroshock treatment and was (to quote a fellow student) "very shocking and evil".

Lou also contributed to a quarterly poetry magazine and operated as a DJ three nights a week for the college radio station, calling his show 'Excursion On A Wobbly Rail' after an improvisational Cecil Taylor piece. He played everything from doo-wop, soul and rockabilly through to Ornette Coleman, but his show was too radical for the times and was cancelled within months. As well as his band with Hyman, Reed – heavily influenced by Bob Dylan – took up the harmonica, and played in at least one folk group.

Reed also became friends with another musician, a student from Long Island who'd discovered the guitar at age 12 (after already being a proficient trumpet-player), and who shared his passion for electric blues and streetcorner doo-wop: Holmes Sterling Morrison (born 29 August 1942). Morrison recognized Reed as a kindred spirit, part of the college's "one percent lunatic fringe". Morrison had played in numerous Long Island bar bands (which he described as "some of the shittiest bands that ever *were*"); he and Lou occasionally jammed together, but neither took the association too seriously. Morrison soon transferred from Syracuse to New York's City College and he and Reed lost touch; they would meet again in 1965, by accident.

Another big influence on Reed was his roommate, Lincoln Swados, who was highly intelligent, witty and literary – but also agoraphobic, hygienically challenged and socially inept. Like Reed, he'd been given electroshock treatment and – though no one realized it at the time – Swados was actually schizophrenic, and was later hospitalized. In a failed suicide attempt in 1964 Swados threw himself under a subway train, losing an arm and a leg in the process. Lou continued to visit him after this, and through Lincoln met Bettye Kronstad, who would eventually become his first wife. Lincoln died in 1990.

Reed had an active sex life at Syracuse, and had several girlfriends, of whom Shelley Albin was the most important. Their relationship lasted several years, but Reed eventually drove her away. He was frequently unfaithful with other women, and had also begun to experiment with gay affairs. 'I'll Be Your Mirror' is said to have been written for Shelley, though it would be Nico who supplied the title. After Shelley, Lou took up with her friend Erin Clermont, but there were no ill feelings between the girls, who both knew that Lou was not someone who could make a serious relationship work.

At the end of his first year at Syracuse Lou was placed on academic probation – partly for achieving low grades, partly because the college knew he was smoking marijuana (and had been for years). In addition to this, Lou was being prescribed the tranquilizer Placidyl, and imbibing alcohol; while at Syracuse he also reportedly tried peyote, LSD, magic mushrooms, cocaine, the codeine-laced cough syrup Turpenhydrate and, finally, heroin. Shelley Albin and others have suggested that Lou was also supposedly dealing marijuana to other students.

According to Sterling Morrison, prior to the Velvets discovering speed through Angus MacLise (and later Andy Warhol's Factory crowd), they were primarily "pill people",

THE VELVET UNDERGROUND

1

using downers like Seconal and Thorazine. Reed's drug of choice for many years – in the mid-Seventies specifically – was amphetamine (injectable liquid methedrine). He also claims to have injected himself in 1966 with "a drug" that made all his joints freeze (doctors suspected that he had terminal lupus).

But in one of his professors at Syracuse, Lou found a mentor. Delmore Schwartz was a born storyteller who spent as much time teaching in the local Orange bar as he did in the classroom. Lou, who studied creative writing under Schwartz, later called him "the first great man that I had ever met."

Schwartz taught his students the value and beauty of language, and in Lou he found an eager student, and a talented one, who he encouraged to write.

But Reed would never show Schwartz his writing, because the poet hated rock music, and although Lou was writing poetry and short stories (and had been since high school), Reed was most interested in writing rock songs. He wanted to see if the medium could be combined with the kind of literary writing he loved, his favourite authors including William Burroughs, Allen Ginsberg, Raymond Chandler, Hubert Selby Jr and Edgar Allan Poe (Reed was often known to

DELMORE SCHWARTZ

Delmore Schwartz was a poet, short story writer and essayist, whose Kafkaesque short story 'In Dreams Begin Responsibilities' earned him praise from T.S.Eliot. A larger-than-life figure, Schwartz was sadly prone to serious alcohol and amphetamine abuse, and his teaching days were then numbered. Reed tried to contact him a few years after leaving college, but was refused entry to Schwarz's apartment as by this time the poet was suffering from an acute case of paranoia. Schwartz died of a heart attack in a cheap hotel in July 1966, aged 53. The failed poet Von Humboldt Fleisher in Saul Bellow's novel *Humboldt's Gift* is said to be based upon Schwartz. "The smartest, funniest, saddest person I ever met," was how Reed later described him. When Lou married Sylvia Morales in 1980, their wedding vows were adapted from two of Schwartz's poems, and much later Reed helped found the Delmore Schwartz/Lou Reed Scholarship Program for young writers at Syracuse.

1

register in hotels as 'Joe Salinger' and 'Philip Marlowe'). Much of Lou's writing was dark, and had been from his earliest attempts; sex and violence were the major themes. Oddly, one of Reed's fellow students in Schwartz's class was Garland Jeffreys, who also later became a rock musician.

The subject matter of Reed's short stories included dysfunctional families and gay subculture. The Velvets later accompanied one of his stories, 'The Gift', with music at the suggestion of John Cale. Before leaving college Lou had also written both 'Heroin' and 'Waiting For The Man', subjects about which he obviously knew a great deal. It's

worth noting that there were no overt pop songs about drugs at all at this point – even the Byrds 'Eight Miles High', from a few years later, is very vague – and there were certainly none about addiction outside of old blues songs.

Reed graduated from Syracuse in June 1964 with a BA in English, and two weeks later found himself facing the draft board and a possible trip to Vietnam. He avoided military service, probably on medical grounds (having just had his first bout of drug-related hepatitis), but would later claim to have been judged psychologically unfit for the army after requesting a gun and telling the board

REED AT PICKWICK RECORDS

Songs known to have been co-written by Lou Reed while at Pickwick include:

'You're Driving Me Insane' by The Roughnecks
'This Rose' by Terry Phillips
'Flowers For The Lady' by Terry Phillips.
'Wild One' by Ronnie Dove
'Johnny Won't Surf No More' by Jeannie Larimore
'I've Got A Tiger In My Tank' by The Beechnuts
'Cycle Annie' by The Beechnuts
'I've Got A Tiger In My Tank' by The Intimates (has different lyrics to the Beechnuts version)
'The Ostrich' b/w 'Sneaky Pete' by The Primitives
'Tell Mama Not To Cry' b/w 'Maybe Tomorrow' by Robertha Williams

'Why Don't You Smile' b/w 'Don't Put All Your Eggs In One Basket' by The All Night Workers
'Don't Turn My World Upside Down' – artist unknown
'Oh No, Don't Do It' – artist unknown
'Help Me' – artist unknown
'Baby You're The One' – artist unknown
'What About Me' – artist unknown
'Bad Guy' – artist unknown
'Say Goodbye Over The Phone' – artist unknown
'I'm Gonna Fight' – artist unknown
'Love Can Make You Cry' – artist unknown
'Maybe Tomorrow' – artist unknown
'Soul City' – artist unknown
'Teardrops In The Sand' – artist unknown
'Ya Runnin' But I'll Get Ya' – artist unknown

According to Reed, another song, titled 'Let The Wedding Bells Ring', ended with the hero dying in a car crash.

THE VELVET UNDERGROUND

1

he was "ready to kill", which seems unlikely.

Music was still important to him. He'd gone through a folkie stage a year or so earlier, and became very influenced by Bob Dylan before heading in a totally different direction and attempting to write simple pop songs. At the end of summer 1964, Lou got a job at Pickwick International Records, based in their office on Staten Island, as one of the label's in-house songwriters – "a poor man's Carole King", as he later put it.

Basically, Pickwick was a copycat label. Whatever the hit vogue of the time was –

be it surf music, girl groups or motorcycle songs – Pickwick would churn out a string of records in that style until the fad passed, and Lou Reed was one of a small team employed to write the material. In retrospect it seems strange that he would embrace a posture so cynical, but Lou genuinely enjoyed the job and gained a lot of studio experience in the process.

He was happy to be working in the music business at all, and hoping it might lead to something more serious. One of the numerous songs Reed co-wrote for

LA MONTE YOUNG

One of the leading lights of avant garde music in the Sixties, La Monte Young had been a jazz saxophonist in California in the late 1950s before returning to New York and discovering Arabic and Indian music at the turn of the decade.

He'd had an affair with Yoko Ono, and was one of the first musicians to destroy an instrument onstage. Prior to Cale's joining Young's ensemble, the Theatre Of Eternal Music, the members included Young, Angus MacLise on percussion (sculptor Walter De Maria also occasionally drummed), Tony Conrad on violin and Young's wife Marian Zazeela on vocals (she also provided "calligraphic light art projections"). This line-up's major piece was entitled Second Dream Of The High Tension Line Stepdown Transformer, which experimented with both drone and extremely loud volume. The key piece they worked on after Cale joined was titled The Tortoise (His Dreams & Journeys), an improvisation the parameters of which were set each time by Young. One of these was the time factor – the group would already be playing before the audience was

allowed to enter the auditorium. Cale does not appear on Young's Theatre Of Eternal Music LP, but the Young archives contain tapes of 18 months of daily rehearsals, all featuring Cale.

Throughout 1965 Cale continued to play with Young, as well as rehearsing with Reed and making his own experimental tapes. He played his last performance with the Theatre Of Eternal Music in December 1965, the same month the Velvets went public. After Cale's departure, Terry Riley joined Young's group. Cale also formed a spin-off duo with Young's violinist Tony Conrad, nicknamed the 'Dream Syndicate' (and not to be confused with the Eighties rock group of the same name).

Cale and Conrad both experimented with adding electric pickups to their instruments. Cale went a step further, adding electric guitar strings (Conrad followed suit, with metal strings) and flattening the viola's bridge to allow three or four strings to be played simultaneously – in short, a drone... and one that could sound like an airplane taking off.

1

Pickwick was a dance number titled 'The Ostrich' (inspired by a fashion revival of ostrich feathers), which was released in late 1964 under the name 'The Primitives'. Pickwick thought the song could be a real hit (the lyrics are great: "you put your head on the floor and have someone step on it"), but they needed to form an actual band that could promote the record for an *American Bandstand* TV performance. At a party in January 1965, Pickwick executive Terry Phillips met two people with long hair he thought might fit the bill: avant-garde

musicians Tony Conrad and John Cale.

John Cale

John Cale was born one week after Reed, on 9 March 1942 in the mining village of Garnant, South Wales. He was a classical music student and child prodigy – he'd started on piano at the age of seven, and gave his first performance on the radio at the age of twelve. At home Cale and his mother Margaret spoke Welsh, though his father Will spoke only English; as a result,

The ideal of Young's group was, as Cale later explained, "to sustain notes for two hours at a time." Young's drone-inspired experiments would have a lasting impact on Cale, who would employ similar techniques with the Velvet Underground: "If they were three-chord songs, I could just pick two notes on the viola that really fit for the whole song. It would give a dream-like quality to the whole thing." Young's group rehearsed seven days a week, six hours a day for the duration of Cale's involvement (approximately 18 months). The newly amplified instruments forced Young to abandon his saxophone in favour of amplified vocals, and the music moved away from its blues/raga direction towards something much louder and harsher. At a private party for Metropolitan Museum curator Henry Geldzahler, the Theatre Of Eternal Music played for an audience that included Jackie Kennedy and Andy Warhol. Cale and Conrad also worked on soundtracks for underground films by their friend, director Jack Smith. According to Cale,

La Monte funded his music by dealing marijuana – an enterprise that Cale was briefly involved in, and which led to his arrest. He spent one night in prison, but nothing could be proved and charges were dropped. He also narrowly avoided having to go to Vietnam, since his Green Card status also made him eligible for the draft. Fortunately, at his examination in spring 1964 he was dismissed as unsuitable on medical grounds (hepatitis, according to biographer Tim Mitchell).

La Monte Young and Yoko Ono, 1960

THE VELVET UNDERGROUND

1

John always thought of his mother as warm and his father as distant. He eventually learned English in school. Will Cale was a miner in the local colliery, Margaret a schoolteacher who stressed education as a means of avoiding having to work in the mines. She wanted John to be a doctor or lawyer when he grew up; he preferred music. John practiced piano every evening, played the organ in the village church and discovered the viola – "the saddest of all instruments" – at grammar school, simply because it was the only instrument free. At the age of 12 he was molested by his organ tutor in the local church, and at around the same age also discovered heterosexual sex with a local girl. At 12 he was also recorded playing one of his own compositions by BBC Radio Wales; at age 13 he toured Wales and Holland playing with the Welsh Youth Orchestra.

At night he educated himself in other kinds of music by listening to Alan Freed playing rock'n'roll on the *Voice of America*, as well as to Radio Moscow and Radio Luxembourg; his heroes were John Coltrane and John Cage, yet he dressed like a Teddy Boy. He'd experienced serious childhood bronchial problems, for which he was given an opium-based sedative (possibly the cause of future problems), and suffered a nervous breakdown at the age of 16. His ambition was to become an orchestral conductor – anywhere but Wales, and preferably in New York.

The first stop was London. Having failed to gain a place at a musical academy, Cale gained a scholarship to Goldsmiths Teacher's College, which he accepted even though he had no plans to become a music teacher. Frustrated by the formal classical approach, Cale found himself drawn to more experimental composers such as Karlheinz Stockhausen and began corresponding with John Cage and

Aaron Copland. He left Goldsmiths College in the summer of 1963, having won a Leonard Bernstein scholarship to study for eight weeks at the Berkshire Music Center in Tanglewood, Massachusetts, under the tutorship of Iannis Xenakis. As his farewell performance at Goldsmiths, Cale performed an experimental piece by La Monte Young.

Arriving in New York, Cale was miraculously granted a Green Card by the immigration department, which allowed him to stay in the USA indefinitely – and also to work there. Inevitably, when his eight week scholarship was over, Cale gravitated towards Manhattan, cashing in his return air ticket to pay for a lease on a loft apartment, and working in a bookshop called Orientalia.

On 9 and 10 September 1963 Cale was one of a relay team of pianists taking part in a 18-hour marathon event of John Cage's, each pianist playing the 180-note Erik Satie piece 'Vexations' for a total of 840 times (Cale later learned that Andy Warhol had been in the audience for part of the concert, perhaps attracted by the idea of repetition, which echoed his own work). Days later, a studious looking Cale appeared on the TV quiz show *I've Got A Secret*, his secret being the fact that he'd played in the marathon. He then played a short extract from the piece, putting his glasses on to read the music.

At the marathon, Cale and John Cage were photographed together (which did much for Cale's reputation when the photo appeared in the *New York Times*), and Cage suggested Cale get in touch La Monte Young. A few days later Cale took his viola along to a meeting with Young, and was promptly invited to join Young's ensemble, the Theatre Of Eternal Music.

Artistically, Cale quickly grew frustrated with the avant garde, and liked the sense of urgency he had discovered in modern rock 'n' roll via Tony Conrad's record collection once the two began sharing an apartment on Ludlow Street (Angus MacLise and underground actor Mario Montez lived in the same building, and underground filmmaker Piero Holiczer lived next door). Cale also avidly listened to Murray the K's radio shows, being especially impressed by Phil Spector's 'Wall of Sound'. It was the time of the British Invasion, and the Beatles and the Stones were already rocking America. When he met Lou Reed, Cale was ripe and ready.

Pickwick's Primitives

The day after meeting Pickwick executive and future Spector collaborator Terry Phillips (real name Philip Teitelbaum), Cale and Conrad turned up at the offices of Pickwick Records in Queens together with sculptor Walter DeMaria, who they had recruited to play drums. DeMaria was actually a jazz drummer on the side, but was to gain greater acclaim as a sculptor for his 1977 piece *Lightning Field*. It was then that Cale and Lou Reed met for the first time.

Cale was amazed to discover that the open-tuning of 'The Ostrich' – with all the instruments tuned to one note – was effectively the very same approach he'd been using with Young. Cale, Conrad and DeMaria refused to sign the slave-labour contracts they were offered by Pickwick, but agreed to play a few East Coast promotional gigs with Reed as the Primitives, drafting in Jimmie Sims as well. They played the gigs, but the *American Bandstand* appearance failed to materialise and the record flopped.

Meanwhile, Reed had played Cale some of the songs he'd already written that Pickwick *wasn't* interested in, including 'Heroin' and

'Waiting For The Man'. Cale was initially sceptical, since Reed used an acoustic guitar and the songs sounded to Cale's ears like folk music – something in which he had no interest. But he couldn't help but be impressed by both Reed's lyrics and by his ability to improvise intelligent ones on the spot. "They were very different, very literate," he noted, "and he was writing about things other people weren't". Cale and Conrad had quickly worked out that Reed was the most talented person they'd met at Pickwick, Conrad observing that rock'n'roll "came out of him like sweat".

Though Tony Conrad wasn't really interested in playing rock in the long-term himself, he sensed the potential of this meeting and was aware that both Reed and Cale were deeply impressed with each other. For Reed, the discovery that a classical musician from the avant garde would take him seriously was a vindication, and it was clear that the duo's association would last beyond the Primitives.

At this point Reed was still living at home, under strict parental discipline. He was still taking the tranquilizer Placidyl, subject to bouts of depression and still indulging in 'shocking' behaviour – like trying to provoke drunks into fights. Cale tried to boost Reed's confidence, assuring him that they could make groundbreaking music together. Shortly afterwards, Tony Conrad moved out of the Ludlow Street apartment, and Reed moved in. The two men began to create more music that Pickwick wouldn't have touched with a bargepole, funding themselves with (very) odd jobs – like modelling for photographs of supposed criminals to illustrate sensational and fictitious stories in the supermarket tabloids – and by selling their blood. Reed continued working at Pickwick until

THE VELVET UNDERGROUND

September, even though the pay wasn't great.

Ludlow Street – just off of Canal Street – was then a rough, drug-dealing neighbourhood, and the landlord carried a gun when collecting the rent. Electricity came via an extension cable to another apartment. Cale and Reed scavenged the streets for wood to burn as fuel, and lived on oatmeal – and occasionally, chicken giblets – for weeks on end. Reed was given to experimentation with what Morrison termed "mad diets" anyway, which may well have had as big an effect on his mental state as any drugs.

Falling Spikes and Warlocks

Cale had early on rejected the possibility of a sexual relationship with Reed, and was soon beginning to suspect that sharing an apartment with him wouldn't work out either. Meanwhile, Reed had introduced Cale to heroin, giving him his first injection (since Cale was too squeamish to shoot up alone). Soon the pair were both suffering from hepatitis as a result of sharing dirty needles, and decided to christen their act the Falling Spikes. For both of them, poverty made heroin a weekend pastime only – though both would have recurring bouts of hepatitis over the years.

Improbably, the duo had some success performing Reed's songs as buskers up in Harlem, in front of the Club Baby Grand on 125th Street. Reed played acoustic guitar, Cale his viola and recorder. In the course of these adventures they recruited a female vocalist named Electra, but it didn't work out (she was unstable, and Cale had an affair with her). Cale claimed that Electra played the sarinda (a bowed Indian lute) so hard that her knuckles bled, because she enjoyed the pain. She was soon replaced by another female vocalist named Daryl, who was another disaster (a junkie, who had affairs with both Cale and Reed), and the pair were consequently wary of working with women again – something that would overshadow their initial meetings with both Moe Tucker and Nico. It did not, however, deter both Reed and Cale from later having affairs with Nico and also with Warhol superstar Susan Bottomley, aka International Velvet.

In April 1965 Reed ran into Sterling Morrison on the D train of the subway, and soon persuaded him to join the band, renaming it The Warlocks in the process. Cale now played bass guitar as well as viola. Shortly afterward, they added Angus MacLise on drums. MacLise was very interested in Asian music and the possibilities of tablas and hand drums and had, according to Morrison, "radically different ideas about rhythm and percussion". From the sound of it, MacLise would have made the band sound jazzier and more beatnik-oriented. Regardless, it was clear from the start that the music they were making was *not* ordinary pop music, and despite Reed and Morrison's blues grounding they were determined not to rely on standard blues riffs if they could avoid it.

Reed later cited his main guitar influences as being Carl Perkins, Ike Turner and James Burton; the only one of his contemporaries he'd admit to admiring was the Byrds' Roger McGuinn. Reed wasn't much given to compliments, but many years later he'd pay tribute to Sterling Morrison's playing: "Sometimes I think his guitar playing is very much like his first name – sterling. It's involved. And yet it has a grace and elegance to it, even in the fast-note runs. You could play me a hundred guitars, and I could spot Sterling."

They made a demo tape with MacLise

(long since lost) of 'Heroin', 'Venus In Furs', 'The Black Angel's Death Song', 'Wrap Your Troubles In Dreams' and an otherwise unknown song titled 'Never Get Emotionally Involved With Man, Woman, Beast Or Child'. On a brief return to London that year, Cale tried to generate interest in the tape – without success – via Marianne Faithfull (who declined to pass a copy on to her boyfriend Mick Jagger) and Miles Copeland. Cale returned to NYC laden with new records by the Kinks and the Who.

There's also a tape from this era made without MacLise (which would eventually be released on the *Peel Slowly And See* boxed set), simply because Angus had forgotten to turn up that day. MacLise had a particularly fluid concept of time, and was apparently incapable of following any kind of schedule.

According to Sterling Morrison, at one gig MacLise carried on playing for half an hour after the rest of the band had left the stage, which to his mind compensated for the fact that he'd arrived onstage half an hour late. What is most striking about the Ludlow Street demos on the boxed set is how folky they are. Despite Cale's avowed hatred for folk music, the versions of early Velvets songs here sung by him all sound like old English ballads and laments... and the influence of Bob Dylan on Reed's vocals is also undeniable.

Throughout 1965 the band practiced (and experimented) almost constantly, working on arrangements for the songs that would comprise their first album. There was no doubt in Cale's mind that this material "was going to last. What we did was unique, it was

ANGUS MACLISE

A native New Yorker, Angus MacLise graduated from high school in 1956 and went on to study Geology at New York University. During vacations he played bongos with jazz groups at resort hotels in the Catskills 'Borscht Belt'.

After a short period in the army he moved to Paris, and founded a small publishing company – The Dead Language Press – with friends Piero and Olivia Holiczer. This published their own poetry – including several books of MacLise's, as well as some by celebrated beat poet Gregory Corso.

MacLise returned to New York in 1960, and the following year joined the La Monte Young Trio as a drummer, being particularly drawn towards oriental music. He was also a member of New York's neo-Dadaist group Fluxus – a loose collective of experimental artists of all types – and collaborated with fellow Fluxus member Yoko One on her piece 'Music For Dance'.

THE VELVET UNDERGROUND

1

Performing for 'Venus in Furs', an underground film by Piero Heliczer, New York, November 1965: Lou Reed, Sterling Morrison and John Cale (left–right)

1

THE VELVET UNDERGROUND

powerful". It would later surprise him that Reed would claim sole composing credit, as if Cale had been merely an arranger. This would cause many arguments in the years to come. Sterling Morrison maintained that the Velvets' music "evolved collectively. Lou would walk in with some sort of scratchy verse and we would all develop the music. It almost always worked like that. We'd all thrash it out into something very strong. John was trying to be a serious young composer, he had no background in rock music, which was terrific – he knew no clichés. You listen to his bass lines, he didn't know any of the usual riffs, it was totally eccentric." Cale wanted to see if Spector's 'wall of sound' approach could be recreated with a four-piece band – but in fact, the music they were beginning to make was like no rock music ever heard before.

They were also idealistic, intending that no performance should be the same, and that any records they might make should all be recorded live. Throughout this year Cale had also been playing with La Monte Young, and making his own experimental tapes, sometimes with Tony Conrad and MacLise (and, on at least one occasion, Sterling Morrison).

As a band they also played live behind the screen at arthouse cinemas like the Lafayette Street Cinemathèque, providing improvised film soundtracks for the silent underground movies of director Piero Heliczer, as well as Kenneth Anger's *Scorpio Rising* and Barbara Rubin's *Christmas On Earth*. At the Cinemathèque they also performed in two mixed media 'ritual happenings' – 'The Launching Of The Dreamweapon' and 'The Rites Of The Dreamweapon' – which involved movies, slide projections, poetry and music, with the group playing stripped to the waist with their chests painted. In

WHAT ANGUS DID NEXT

After leaving the Velvets, Angus MacLise remained involved with La Monte Young for some years, as well as creating his own music. With his wife Hetty and son Ossian, MacLise travelled to India in 1971, moving to Kathmandu in Nepal in 1973. Here he started another small publishing company – Dreamweapon Press – to produce his poetry. He and Hetty also provided the music for a film titled *Invasion Of The Thunderbolt Pagoda* by photographer Ira Cohen (best known for the cover photographs on Spirit's album *Twelve Dreams Of Dr Sardonicus*).

MacLise had long been interested in the kabbalah, and the works of Aleister Crowley. One of his last projects was to write a film adaptation of Crowley's book *Diary Of A Drug Fiend*. He spent most of his last year alive in New York, recording a soundtrack to Sheldon Rochlin's film *Hymn To The Mystic Fire*. MacLise then returned to Kathmandu, where his health worsened; an "intestinal malady" exacerbated by years of drug abuse led him to be hospitalized, but he reportedly ripped out his feeding tubes in the last days of his life. He died of malnutrition on 21 June 1979. In what may well be the strangest footnote to the entire Velvet Underground story, MacLise's son Ossian (a.k.a. O.K.) was recognised at a young age as being a tulku, the reincarnation of a Tibetan lama. He is now known as Sangye Nyenpa Rinpoche.

short, the band were well versed in multi-media presentations long before they ever met Andy Warhol.

They gave each other nicknames (Reed was 'Lulu', Cale was 'Black Jack'), but collectively they were still called the Warlocks, until they found a better name on the cover of a cheap paperback that Tony Conrad had found in the street. *The Velvet Underground* was the title of a 1963 book by Michael Leigh; the cover would lead one to assume it concerned sado-masochism, but according to Morrison it was about "wife-swapping in suburbia". The cover blurb boasted, "It will shock and amaze you. But as a documentary on the sexual corruption of our age, it is a *must* for every thinking adult". Much the same could be said of the band who adopted its title – but they did so because the word 'underground' resonated with the world they inhabited in New York, of underground films and art, not because of the S&M connotations. A less romantic version of their discovering the book simply has it that Angus MacLise owned a copy.

Late that year, journalist Al Aronowitz – the man who had introduced Allen Ginsberg to Bob Dylan, and Dylan (and marijuana) to the Beatles – became interested in managing the Velvets, and managed to book them what would become their proper debut gig (on December 11 1965, at Summit High School in New Jersey, as support for band called The Myddle Class). Shortly before the gig, Angus MacLise, dismayed to learn that they were going to be paid (albeit a mere $75 for the whole band) and that his art would thus be corrupted by capitalism, quit the group.

The Velvets found a last-minute replacement drummer for the Summit gig in the sister of one of Morrison's college friends, Jim Tucker. Her name was Maureen

Anne Margaret Tucker (born August 26 1944). She had grown up with Morrison in his hometown of Levittown, New York, and had known him since the age of 10. Having studied clarinet and guitar, she eventually decided to try her hand at drumming, and had first played with Sterling Morison as early as 1963. When the Velvets approached her, the local band she'd been drumming with – the Intruders – had just broken up. "At that point I was the only one they could grab - the only one with a drum kit," she later recalled. As it turned out, the group had lucked out – Maureen (or 'Moe', as she soon became known) had a solid rhythmic approach, inspired by Bo Diddley, Charlie Watts and the Nigerian drummer Babatunde Olatunji. Throughout the early days of the Velvets she continued to work as a data-entry clerk, living in Levittown and commuting into the city to play music in the evenings.

In 1998 Reed called Tucker "one of the greatest drummers in the entire world", but at the time he had his doubts about her ability, as did Cale. They were nervous about having a woman in the band again – and female drummers were a distinct rarity in rock at this point – but the self-confessed "tomboy" Tucker felt totally at home playing pool and drinking beer in all-male company. The fact that she could drive and had the use of her parents' car were also factors in her favour – and the fact that many people who saw the band early on were unsure whether Moe was a boy or a girl added some real novelty value, according to Warhol film director Paul Morrissey.

Supposedly it was Cale who insisted on the need for continued experimentation by making Moe discard the cymbal from her drum kit and play standing up – which gave her a striking visual presence onstage. Her simple

THE VELVET UNDERGROUND

1

John Cale and Lou Reed on stage at the Cafe Bizarre, New York, December 1965

THE VELVET UNDERGROUND

but unorthodox approach to rhythm radically affected the Velvets' sense of timing, and was as important a factor as any other in the Velvets' creation of a totally new kind of beat music. In the end, even Cale was convinced; the Velvets had found their drummer.

Moe would also become their emotional anchor, a calm centre around which the three men could argue and rage and storm without actually killing each other. In the years after the band broke up, when the others were barely speaking to each other, all of them stayed in touch with Moe. As Lou Reed later put it: "Maureen Tucker is so beautiful. She has to be one of the most fantastic people I've ever met in my life. She's so impossibly great."

The Summit gig went badly. They played 'Venus In Furs', 'Heroin' and 'There She Goes Again'. There was a lot of booing, two girls fainted and, according to Cale, the crowd "fled screaming out of the room". Later that month Al Aronowitz, their then-manager, got them a two-week residency playing the Café Bizarre on West 3rd Street in Greenwich Village. The building had once been Aaron Burr's livery stable, but was now a beer and wine joint with a small stage in the back where folk singers would play – as Bob Dylan had done a couple of times when he was

THE FACTORY

At the end of 1963 Andy Warhol rented a former hat factory on New York's East 47th Street to use as his studio. The 50' x 100' loft space was originally known as the Silver Dream Factory (doubtless because of its all-silver decor, created by Billy Name), its name soon shortened to simply the Factory. It would have four different homes over the next two decades.

Here Warhol worked on his silkscreens and paintings, and also made his movies. Billy Name lived there (as did Gerard Malanga, briefly), and many of the initial visitors came specifically to visit Billy – a crowd that was mainly homosexual, and mainly amphetamine users ("fags on speed", as one catty observer put it).

Through the Factory's doors also came Warhol's 'superstars': Baby Jane Holzer, Edie Sedgwick, Ultra Violet, Viva, Ingrid Superstar and many more, all of them desperate to be in Warhol's movies or simply just to hang around. Doubtlessly they were attracted by Warhol's fame, but the fact that he was totally non-judgemental about others' lifestyles meant that he was genuinely loved. According to Warhol, the crowd came not to see him, but to see each other: "They came to see who came." They also came to see what would happen, in the certainty that something would, even if it was only dinner.

Despite the sign that read DO NOT ENTER UNLESS YOU ARE EXPECTED, the Factory also had pretty much an 'open house' policy, and attracted more than its fair share of those with alternative lifestyles besides drug-addicts: drag queens, hustlers and all-purpose exhibitionists all rubbed shoulders with the celebrities and European aristocrats visiting Andy. "Nobody normal would go near the Factory," Cale would later comment. "It was a protective environment for kooks – quite dangerous for your sanity."

1

first starting out. The club had an anti-rock group policy, which meant that Tucker wasn't allowed to use a drumkit, just a tambourine. The Velvets played six sets a night (at $5 per member), performing Chuck Berry and Jimmy Reed covers as well as their own material; just before starting the residency they wrote 'Run Run Run' to pad out their set.

They played right through Christmas, but deliberately got themselves booted out shortly afterwards in order to avoid having to endure playing New Year's Eve there. Having been told not to play another song like 'Black Angel's Death Song' or else they'd be fired, they played it again to open their

next set, and got fired. During the residency underground filmmaker Barbara Rubin made plans to film the Velvets playing live, and asked her friend Gerard Malanga to assist her. Malanga drafted in filmmaker Paul Morrissey to help as well; after both men had been duly impressed by seeing the band play, they returned the next night with Malanga's boss, one Andy Warhol. The Velvets were about to become a key part of Warhol's universe.

Andy Warhol

Andy Warhol (born Andrew Warhola – or Varchola – on August 6 1928) was already a

In the mornings Warhol worked; in the afternoon visitors began to show up and, to quote Henry Geldzahler, the Factory became "a sort of glamorous clubhouse with everyone trying to get Andy's attention". The soundtrack was operatic arias, played loud.

It seems strange that the workaholic Warhol surrounded himself with so many people who seemed to lack a sense of purpose. As Mary Woronov noted: "Andy thought if people didn't work they were broken, something was wrong with them."

But since Warhol the film-maker preferred to work with people who weren't professional actors, talent was not a prerequisite for admission; indeed, it sometimes seems pure accident that artists of the stature of the Velvets showed up in the throng as well. Inevitably, one day there would also be a psycho with a gun among the crowd. Casual sex was rife among the

Factory crowd, as was hard drug use – and with so many drugs and so many people with serious problems, casualties were inevitable; there was violence and paranoia and more than a few overdoses and suicides among them. Photographer Nat Finkelstein somewhat harshly summed the Factory scene up thus: "Andy bestrode his world like a bleached blond colossus. I witnessed the birth of a monster: a silver sprayed black widow spider: fucking them over, sucking them dry and spitting them out."

That's not a unique view... but how much Andy Warhol ever really knew about what was going on at this non-stop party is debatable. The explanation for Warhol's open-door approach was simple: he liked company (to the point that he was apparently terrified of being alone), and was interested in what would come of all this energy, hoping to serendipitously capture it on film or tape.

THE VELVET UNDERGROUND

highly successful and celebrated artist at the time he met the Velvets. The son of Czech immigrants from Ruthenia (now a part of the Ukraine), Warhol suffered numerous childhood ailments, including rheumatic fever and scarlet fever. At the age of eight his already pasty complexion grew worse when his skin lost pigmentation; combined with the dark glasses necessary for his poor eyesight and his fair hair, he appeared practically albino. This was heightened further when he started to go bald at the age of 25 and began wearing a wig: the first one was brown with grey streaks; later on they ranged through grey and silver to pure white.

Warhol graduated from the Carnegie Institute of Technology in 1949, and quickly found work in New York as a commercial artist, illustrating stories for magazines and record covers. This in turn led to work for the advertising world, much of it fashion-related – though Warhol's artfully downtrodden apparel caused him to be known as 'Raggedy Andy' on Madison Avenue. His first gallery show took place in 1952, but the fine art world didn't take Warhol seriously until he stopped imitating the Abstract Expressionists and – inspired by the emergence of Jasper Johns and Robert Rauschenberg – began to develop his own style (circa spring 1960), at which point he quickly attracted the attention of collectors and gallery owners. By late 1962 – when he had his first New York show – Warhol was producing the work for which he'd become most famous: silkscreened paintings of Campbell's soup cans, Elvis Presley and Marilyn Monroe – in short, Pop Art.

His choice of such iconic images was no accident: Warhol was fascinated by celebrity, and in his youth had become obsessed with author Truman Capote, to the point of virtually stalking him. Ironically, Warhol soon became as famous as the icons he'd painted. At the opening of his 1965 retrospective exhibition in Philadelphia, he and his entourage were mobbed by a crowd of screaming fans, to the point that all the paintings had to be removed from the museum's walls before it even opened, thus making it an art exhibit without any art. Eventually, Warhol and retinue had to escape the mob via a fire exit to the floor above. The Pop Artist had become a pop star.

In the spring of 1963, Warhol bought a 16mm camera and started making movies. His early films were usually plotless and unedited – experimental celebrations of the mundane created by simply training a camera on the subject and leaving it running. Thus *sleep* showed someone sleeping, the *Kiss* series portrayed various couples kissing and *Empire* showed the same view of the Empire State Building over an eight-hour period. Warhol grew enthusiastic about the possibilities of film, and talked of leaving painting behind.

As a person, some found Warhol manipulative, cold and downright bitchy; yet he inspired enormous affection and loyalty in others. His writings reveal a man of genuine wit, warmth and charm, who loved life and people. And there's no doubt at all that he was a hugely talented graphic artist, who was constantly experimenting with new media (hence the films) though not always successfully. Many (me included) find his movies unwatchably dull. Warhol's credo at this point was that: "The Pop idea, after all, was that anybody could do anything, so naturally we were trying to do it all. Nobody wanted to stay in one category, we all wanted to branch out into every creative thing we could." And that included rock music.

ALL TOMORROW'S PARTIES
The Warhol Years 1965–67

2

"What happens when the Daddy of Pop Art goes Pop Music? The most underground album of all! Warhol's new hip trip to the subterranean scene"

VERVE PROMOTIONAL COPY FOR
THE VELVET UNDERGROUND AND NICO

ALL TOMORROW'S PARTIES

The Warhol Years 1965–67

In meeting Andy Warhol, the Velvets acquired what very few fledgling bands have been lucky enough to find: a wealthy patron. In addition, Warhol's Factory, with all its weird and wonderful denizens, provided the Velvets with a fertile cross-pollination of ideas, while also operating as a powerful PR machine.

Warhol was keen to diversify his talents and get involved with anything under the sun, both for artistic stimulus and for fun. In 1965 he'd placed an idiosyncratically punctuated ad in New York's *Village Voice* that read: "I'll endorse with my name any of the following: clothes, cigarettes, tapes, sound equipment, ROCK 'N' ROLL RECORDS, anything, film and film equipment, Food, Helium, Whips, MONEY – love and kisses, Andy Warhol."

For John Cale, Andy Warhol's Factory was a fountain of ideas, with "new things happening every day"; for Lou Reed it was "like landing in heaven". Everywhere they turned there were odd characters and odd situations, and Reed would write down in a notebook fragments of what he heard and overheard. Many of these fragments would end up in songs; others would suggest a title or a story situation. The Factory crowd also certainly noticed Reed as well, and according to Factory regular Danny Fields, "everyone was certainly in love with him – me, Edie, Andy, everyone. He was so sexy. Everyone just had this raging crush... he was the sexiest thing going."

Warhol and Morrissey had recently been approached to get involved with setting up a new discotheque in Long Island. The plans would come to nothing (after seeing the Velvets, the club owner hired the Young Rascals instead), but at this point Warhol was actively looking for a rock band to play there. Bizarrely (according to Victor Bockris), Warhol had actually contemplated forming his own rock band three years earlier, with La Monte Young and Walter DeMaria.

Seeing the Velvet Underground at Café Bizarre, Warhol liked the fact that Lou Reed looked "pubescent", and that the audience left the gig looking "dazed and damaged" (according to Reed, Warhol saw them the night they were fired). Paul Morrissey claims that it was his idea to marry underground films to rock 'n' roll, but that it was a purely commercial decision to work with the Velvets, rather than an artistic one. At the time, Morrissey also felt that Reed and Cale lacked presence – none of the band were that active onstage, and

THE VELVET UNDERGROUND

2

Lee Childers once remarked that Sterling Morrison "just kinda stood there looking awkward and tall." Morrissey thought that what the Velvets really needed was a singer with "a bit of charisma". He suggested someone who was already attached to the Warhol camp...

A girl called Nico

At the time she joined the Velvets, Nico had only recently come under Warhol's wing. She was a German model, actress and singer – or, as Warhol preferred to put it, "chanteuse" – born Christa Päffgen on 16 October 1938 in Cologne. In 1940 she moved to Lubbenau near Berlin with her mother Grete, a tailor; in 1945 they moved into the rubble of bomb-ravaged Berlin. Christa spent the rest of her childhood there; she called it "a desert of bricks", and the image of "the fallen empire" was one she would return to often in her work.

Much of Christa's background is hazy, since she was a self-confessed (and inventive) liar, inventing fantastic credentials for her father: he was a Turkish archaeologist, a friend of Gandhi, a Sufi and a spy. In reality, Christa was illegitimate, and her father Wilhelm was a German soldier who was shot in the head by a French sniper in 1943, and then killed by his commanding officer (a standard Nazi treatment for wounded troops).

Life was hard for Christa and her mother, and they were often hungry. There are no existing records to confirm it, but Nico has claimed that at the age of thirteen she was raped by an American sergeant. When her mother reported the crime, Christa was forced to testify at the sergeant's trial on multiple rape charges.

The sergeant was convicted and executed.

When she was fifteen the six-foot tall Christa began a career as a fashion model, which took her to Berlin, Paris, Ibiza (where she lived the beatnik life) and Rome. She was extremely successful, appearing on the covers of *Esquire* and *Elle*, and – unlikely as it seems – posing as a housewife to advertise a dishwasher. En route she dyed her dark hair blond, which she claims was at the suggestion of Ernest Hemingway. She allegedly had an affair with the actress Jeanne Moreau.

In 1958 Christa made her first movie appearances, in the Italian film *La Tempesta*, in Mario Lanza's last movie *For The First Time*. In Paris she made a one-minute appearance in the German film *Montparnasse*. The following year she made her most famous appearance, in Fellini's *La Dolce Vita*, flirtatiously giggling with the movie's star, Marcello Mastroianni. Christa's role would have been larger than it was if she hadn't been so unreliable about timekeeping.

But by now she was no longer Christa, having adopted the name Nico Otzak. She later gave many versions of how she came by the name, but the most likely account seems to be that she named herself after Nico Papatakis, a Parisian nightclub owner with whom one of her gay friends was in love. Christa/Nico subsequently lived with Papatakis for several years in New York, where she took singing lessons and attended acting classes with Lee Strasberg; she later claimed to have been in the same class as Marilyn Monroe.

In 1962 a moody photo of her appeared on the cover of *Moon Beams*, a jazz album by the Bill Evans Trio. She also made another film appearance, in Jacques Poitrenard's

Strip-Tease. For the role she appeared nude, having beaten newcomer Ursula Andress to the part. She also sang a version of the film's theme song, written by Serge Gainsbourg, which was only released in 2001 in a box set of Gainsbourg's film music.

That year she gave birth to her only child, a son named Christian Aaron Paffgen (born 11 August 1962), better known as Ari. Nico claimed that the boy's father was the French actor Alain Delon; the resemblance between Delon and the grown-up Ari is remarkable though he has always denied paternity; . Unfortunately, Nico was far too wayward and unreliable to take to motherhood; although Ari spent some of his childhood with her (including the Factory years), for the most part he was raised by his paternal grandmother (Edith Boulogne) and aunt (Didi Soubrier). Meanwhile, Nico went to London, where she dated Brian Jones of the Rolling Stones.

Impeccable credentials, thought Gerard Malanga when he and Andy Warhol met her in Paris in spring 1965. Malanga told Nico to come and visit the Factory if she was ever in New York. Returning to London, Nico recorded a single for Immediate Records: a cover of Gordon Lightfoot's 'I'm Not Saying' b/w 'The Last Mile', written by Andrew Loog Oldham and Jimmy Page. She'd also demoed a version of 'I'll Keep It With Mine' with Bob Dylan on piano; he'd written the song for her several years earlier, when they'd had an affair.

But Nico's musical career failed to really ignite, and so she travelled to Manhattan with the three-year-old Ari that November. She gave Warhol a copy of her Immediate single, which gave Paul Morrissey the idea of wedding her to the Velvets. Meanwhile, Warhol immediately cast Nico in one of his films, *The Closet*. She'd go on to make five more films with him, including *Chelsea Girls* later that year.

Personality-wise, Nico was what was known as 'difficult'. Dour and brooding and a confirmed nihilist, she was often both depressed and depressing. Strange and untalkative, she might take five minutes to answer a question. Yet she could also be, as Warhol observed, oddly fascinating: "mysterious and European, a real moon goddess type." Morrissey thought her "the most beautiful creature that ever lived."

GERARD MALANGA

A poet and photographer in his own right, Gerard Malanga met Andy Warhol while still a student at Wagner College on Staten Island.

He soon became Warhol's assistant in silkscreening (where he probably did most of the actual physical work and originated at least some of the ideas), also introducing him to New York's literary, theatrical and movie crowds. Malanga also eventually assisted Warhol in his own moviemaking. His habit of carrying a leather bullwhip everywhere led to his 'whipdance' routine on stage with the Velvets during 'Venus In Furs' (Malanga had earlier been a dancer on DJ Alan Freed's *Big Beat* TV show, and had first performed his whip dance onstage with the underground group The Fugs). In 1983 Malanga co-wrote (with Victor Bockris) *Up-tight: The Velvet Underground Story*, the first book to appear on the Velvets.

THE VELVET UNDERGROUND

2

Nico meets the Velvets

The suggestion that Nico should join the band didn't go down too well with the Velvets, to put it mildly. Morrissey played them her Immediate single, and according to him Reed was "hostile to Nico from the start." What changed Reed's mind was the fact that Warhol was offering them an enticing management and recording deal (plus the recognition that his patronage would bring) but *only* if Nico was on board; in the end, it was too good a deal for the Velvets to turn down. According to Nico, Reed agreed simply because he lacked the confidence to refuse – or perhaps, lacked enough confidence in himself as a vocalist.

Still, at his insistence the billing would distance Nico from the group, making it crystal clear that she was *not* a band member. They would be the Velvet Underground *and* Nico. So Al Aronowitz was ousted as manager: he'd only ever had a "handshake deal", something he subsequently regretted.

Morrissey and Warhol officially became joint managers of the Velvet Underground. In return for 25%, Warhol would invest in new equipment, get them gigs and a recording contract. In fact, after buying two instruments from Vox, Warhol got them to supply further equipment for free, having arranged an endorsement deal; the band would later endorse Acoustic, and then Sunn.

But a problem remained. Nico wanted to sing *all* the songs, which Reed refused point blank to allow. But since her presence meant that some gentler songs were now needed, Reed wrote three ballads for her: 'Femme Fatale', 'All Tomorrow's Parties' and 'I'll Be Your Mirror'. They suited her unique, breathy singing style:"like an IBM computer with a German accent," as Warhol put it. The gentler songs contrasted interestingly with Cale's experiments in drone-like repetition. According to Cale, Nico was deaf in one ear from a perforated eardrum, which caused her to go off-pitch from time to time, much

EDIE SEDGWICK

A Californian debutante from a rich but troubled Bostonian socialite background, Edith Minturn Sedgwick (born 1943) had spent her late teens in a mental institution, as had several of her brothers, two of whom committed suicide. In 1964, at the age of 21, she moved to New York and met Andy Warhol in early 65; for the next year, they were virtually inseparable. She dyed her hair silver to match Warhol's wig and became a kind of mirror image of him, escorting him to society parties and appearing in a dozen of his movies. "She had more problems than anybody I'd ever met," Warhol later said. Perhaps that

was the appeal of their relationship, which was certainly not sexual (Truman Capote thought that Andy wanted to be Edie).

She became the 'face' of young Manhattan; *Vogue* magazine dubbed her a 'youthquaker', and she seemed the archetypal poor little rich girl. Reed wrote 'Femme Fatale' about her (at Warhol's request) and, according to some, Bob Dylan's 'Just Like A Woman' and 'Leopard Skin Pillbox Hat' are both about her. But though undeniably beautiful and pursued by innumerable suitors Edie was not so much a femme fatale as a 'femme catastrophique'. Though she became a mainstay of Warhol's movies and danced to the band's amusement. "Lou never really liked me," Nico later complained, although that's hard to believe when you listen to 'I'll Be Your Mirror'. She and Reed were lovers early on, and even lived together for a while. Recalling this period, Nico described Reed as "very soft and lovely. Not aggressive at all. You could just cuddle him like a sweet person when I first met him". Sterling Morrison was more cynical: "You could say Lou was in love with her, but Lou Reed in love is a kind of abstract concept." The relationship lasted eight weeks, and was supposedly ended by Nico.

Cale, meanwhile, had been seduced by Edie Sedgwick within 48 hours of arriving at the Factory, and moved in with her for the duration of their relationship (six weeks). Edie had also had a brief affair with Nico.

John Cale has described the material Reed wrote for Nico as "psychological love songs", and even Reed acknowledged her strengths as a performer. Yet after Nico left

the Velvets, Reed would write no more songs for her – despite being asked to by both Cale and Nico herself.

But Nico had little to do onstage when she wasn't singing except stand stock still and play tambourine (usually out of time); at times things could get a little tense between her and the band. Even so, she was a striking vision: dressed all in white in contrast to the Velvets' black attire. Her modelling days had taught her how to strike a dramatic pose, and she was also taller than all the men surrounding her. Inevitably, she captured most of the media attention. As Maureen Tucker said, "She was this gorgeous apparition, you know. I mean, she really was beautiful." Critic Richard Goldstein described Nico's stage presence as "half goddess, half icicle."

However little Andy Warhol knew about music, even he must have sensed that in the Velvet Underground he'd found more than just another rock band. Lou Reed: "Andy told

onstage with the Velvets during their first couple of gigs, most of the time she was out of her head on a cocktail of drugs of every description, many prescribed by the legendary 'speed doctor' Dr Roberts, who was immortalized by the Beatles in their song 'Dr Robert'.

She later blamed Warhol for her condition: "Warhol really fucked up a great many people's – young people's – lives. My introduction to heavy drugs came through the Factory. I liked the introduction to drugs I received. I was a good target for the scene. I bloomed into a healthy young drug addict." "Edie never grew up," Warhol responded,

probably accurately, though his statements such as "a girl always looks more beautiful and fragile when she's about to have a nervous breakdown" don't show him in too sympathetic a light. When Edie left him in 1966, Warhol joked bleakly to playwright Robert Heide: "When do you think Edie will commit suicide? I hope she lets us know so we can film it." After leaving the Factory, Edie attempted to carve a career as an actress (but didn't really have the talent) and model (though her reputation as an unreliable druggie preceded her), without much success. She died in 1971 of a barbiturate overdose, at the age of 28.

THE VELVET UNDERGROUND

Cale, Warhol, Nico and Malanga (from left)

me that what we were doing with music was the same thing he was doing with painting and movies, i.e. not kidding around." Reed was bowled over by Andy's way of looking at the world ("Sometimes, I would go for days thinking about something he said") and impressed by his work ethic. "I'd ask him why he was working so hard and he'd say, 'Somebody's got to bring home the bacon.' Then he'd look at me and say, 'How many songs have you written today?' I'd lie and say, 'Two'. Andy was incredibly hard-working and generous. He was the first to arrive for work at The Factory and the last to leave. And then he would take us all to dinner. He gave everyone a chance". Lou certainly absorbed Andy's work ethic, and would frequently

quote his saying: "Work as hard as you can, for as long as you can."

But the exact nature of the group's relationship to their new manager remains vague. As Sterling Morrison admitted: "It *is* a hard thing to pin down. Was the Velvet Underground some happy accident for him, something that he could work into his grandiose schemes for the show? Would another band have done just as well? I don't think another band would have done just as well. At that time we seemed uniquely suited for each other."

John Cale described Warhol as "a catalyst" for the Velvets. "He understood exactly what we were about, and what our creative side was all about, and how best to bring that out, and gave us a lot of support. I doubt that Lou would have continued investigating song subjects like he did without having some kind of outside support for that approach other than myself. I think it was just basically Andy and I who really encouraged that side of a literary endeavour." Morrison echoes the fact that Warhol gave them "the confidence to keep doing what we were doing."

It's probable that Reed and Warhol each saw echoes of themselves in the other. But Warhol had well earned his nickname of 'Drella' – a combination of Cinderella and Dracula – that Ondine from the Factory had given him. He had an acid wit that Reed could seldom match, and his jibes were less malevolent than Reed's – they could be bitchy and funny at the same time, whereas Lou was often just bitchy. But as Gerard Malanga stated, Warhol also

had his dark side: "he could slice a person with a glance". In the end, the Velvets' relationship with Warhol is best summed up by Mary Woronov: "They were with Andy and Andy was with them and they backed him absolutely. They would have walked to the end of the earth for him." All of the Velvets spoke highly of Warhol ever after, Cale perhaps most succinctly of all: "He was magic".

At this point the Velvets had been ordered by police to stop rehearsing in their West 3rd Street apartment (above a firehouse), and told to rehearse in the country if they were going to make that kind of noise – Cale was experimenting with an electronic 'thunder machine' at the time. The same cop had also accused them of throwing human excreta out of their window. Warhol thought the apartment looked like a stage set – its

ONDINE

Real name Bob Olivo, he was also nicknamed 'the Pope'. Ondine was a manic and charismatic actor and writer, the hub of the amphetamine-driven 'Mole People' gay crowd at the Factory. He had nothing to do with the fashionable New York nightclub Ondine's; Olivo had adopted the name of the lead character in Jean Giraudoux's play *Ondine*, which had been played on Broadway by the iconic Audrey Hepburn. He appeared in numerous Warhol movies, and Warhol's *A: A Novel* was simply a transcription of tape-recordings of Ondine's speed-fuelled rantings over a 24-hour period. He toured the college lecture circuit during the Seventies, talking about Warhol and screening his performances in Warhol's *Vinyl*

and *Chelsea Girls*. In the Eighties he appeared in numerous off-off-Broadway plays, until ill health forced him to retire. After Ondine's death from liver failure in April 1989, his mother burnt all his writings.

THE VELVET UNDERGROUND

furniture included a big black coffin and a 15-foot ceiling heater shaped like a gold dragon.

So now they began to rehearse at the Factory every day, accompanying Warhol in the evenings to art openings, cocktail parties, dinners and nightclubs, as part of his permanent retinue. It's doubtful if the drug-free Moe Tucker tagged along, and she must have been somewhat bemused by the Factory's denizens – photographer Nat Finkelstein once observed that the Factory was "like a sort of human zoo." They, however, liked the fact that Moe looked boyish, which fitted right in with all the blurring of gender going on there. Later on, Tucker worked at the Factory briefly, transcribing tapes of Ondine's rantings for Warhol's book *A: A Novel*. However, she refused to type any of the swear words, substituting asterisks instead.

Meanwhile, Ondine had turned Reed on to methedrine, which then became his main indulgence for years to come. Speed was the drug of choice at the Factory – the workaholic Warhol allegedly took amphetamine pills named Obetrol – one a day – to help him paint. Everybody else shot up methedrine

PAUL MORRISSEY

Underground filmmaker Morrissey (born 1938) had made his own movies ever since his teenage years. As well as managing Warhol's business affairs for many years, from 1966 Morrissey worked closely on numerous movies with him, eventually making several of his own movies under the Warhol banner. The best known of these are the trilogy of *Flesh* (1968), *Trash* (1970) and *Heat* (1972), all of which starred hustler Joe Dallesandro. Morrissey parted company with Warhol in the early Seventies, He continued to make movies into the late Eighties.

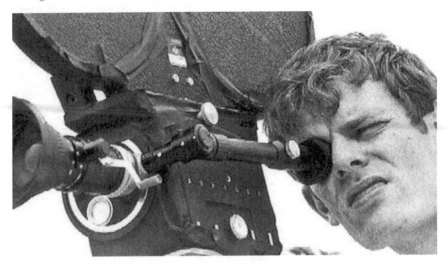

Nico and Sterling Morrison of the Velvet Underground perform on stage at the New York Society for Clinical Psychiatry annual dinner at the Delmonico Hotel, New York, 13 January 1966

on the stairs, according to witnesses. Mary Woronov described the general Factory ambience as being "very grim".

Reed relished the idea of the mayhem they might create in a large venue like the proposed disco, and spoke of using hundreds of car horns and playing in the dark, and persuading Morrison to play the trumpet. But it never happened. The Velvet Underground played their first gig with Nico – while Warhol's movies played behind them and Gerard Malanga and Edie Sedgwick danced onstage – a few weeks later, at the

New York Society of Clinical Psychiatrists' annual banquet at the Delmonico Hotel. "It seemed like a whole prison ward had escaped," one of the nation's top 100 psychiatrists commented, while another described the event as "decadent Dada". A week or so later the Velvets played at the Cinematheque (now on 41st Street), again providing a soundtrack to Warhol movies, including one of themselves. That month the Velvets also recorded improvisational soundtracks for two of Warhol's short movies, *Hedy The Shoplifter* and *More Milk Yvette*.

THE VELVET UNDERGROUND

2

The Exploding Plastic Inevitable

The live events were the prototype for Warhol's touring 'total environment' show, of which the Velvet Underground were the core. Between February and April 1966 the ensemble went through a succession of names: Andy Warhol's Up Discotheque soon became Andy Warhol's Uptight (a word with positive connotations at this point, as in the Stevie Wonder song). This was finally renamed the Exploding Plastic Inevitable or simply E.P.I. by Paul Morrissey (it was very nearly the Erupting Plastic Inevitable, which sounds a lot more painful).

Apart from the Velvets, the show also featured projections of Warhol's films by Paul Morrissey (including footage of Nico and the Velvets), "interpretive dance" by Factory mainstays Gerard Malanga with Ingrid Superstar and/or Ronnie Cutrone and Mary Woronov. For 'Venus In Furs' Malanga and Woronov – dressed in matching black leather trousers – would play out a mock S&M scenario, with Malanga grovelling at his partner's feet, kissing the whip she held and her leather boots. For 'Heroin', Malanga would give mock injections with a huge pink plastic syringe (as used for icing cakes). The Velvets themselves were completely impassive, ignoring the audience completely.

A key ingredient of the E.P.I. was its light show – a mixture of liquid slides and strobe lights. In all there were five movie projectors (to show Warhol's movies),

BRIGID POLK (BERLIN)

Brigid Berlin (born 1939) and her sister Richie (who also hung out at the Factory) were heirs to the Hearst publishing empire. Brigid appeared in several Warhol movies, and also created montage "trip books" – scrapbooks of anything that took her fancy, the most extraordinary containing the impressions of the scars, genitalia, breasts or navels of anyone willing to contribute. She also tape recorded pretty much everything she encountered, from phone calls to orgies. This led to her taping Lou Reed's last concert with the Velvet Underground – eventually released commercially as *Live At Max's Kansas City*. Her 'Polk' nickname evolved from Factory slang – 'taking a poke' meant shooting up with a needle. She gave up amphetamines and alcohol in the Eighties.

2

five carousel slide projectors, and various spotlights and coloured strobes. Added to this was a silver mirrored ball brought from the Factory, which had once hung in a speakeasy and had been bought in an antique shop; the ball hung over the Velvets' heads, and when spun it caught and fragmented the strobe lighting. Within a month, every discotheque in New York had one like it, and the disco glitterball was born. According to Reed, all this was Warhol's idea. He's also claimed that both he and Cale started wearing dark glasses onstage simply to defend themselves against the effects of the strobes (which can induce epilepsy in some and have also been known to cause heart attacks). Danny Williams, who ran the E.P.I. light show, would subject himself to watching strobes for hours on end, as an experiment. Williams subsequently committed suicide, though whether the strobes had anything to do with it remains a matter for speculation. Whatever money the E.P.I. earned from a gig was always divided equally i.e. you got the same amount whether you were a guitarist, a dancer or the projectionist.

According to Morrison, "We just played and everything raged about us, without any control on our part." The effect of all this mixed media many found overwhelming – though it might well look tame by today's standards, back then audiences had never seen anything like it. "At the Plastic Inevitables it is all Here and Now and the Future," wrote underground filmmaker Jonas Mekas in the *Village Voice*. Marshall McLuhan included a photo of the E.P.I. in his book *The Medium Is The Massage*, as an example of the evolving world.

The show took to the road in March (with Nico driving them all in a microbus, much to everyone's general terror) to play two more 'rehearsal' gigs at Rutgers College (where the Velvets all wore white and Malanga danced while twirling lit flashlights) and the University of Michigan (where Warhol discovered the strobe lights). That month fashion designer Betsey Johnson asked Warhol to come up with something for the opening of her hip clothes boutique Paraphernalia. Warhol provided floating (helium-filled) silver pillows, with music courtesy of the Velvets.

The Exploding Plastic Inevitable made their 'official' debut in April 1966 at a club called The Polsky Dom Narodny (or simply 'The Dom' – 'home' in Polish), in the old Polish National Social Hall on St Mark's Place in the East Village. At the time this was a very unfashionable neighbourhood, nicknamed 'Babushkaville' on account of its largely East European population. Warhol took a month's lease on the club and had the place completely repainted and hung with screens for the movies and light show. "Do you want to dance and blow your mind with the Exploding Plastic Inevitable?" asked the ad in the *Village Voice*. 750 people came the first night; while he was onstage, Lou Reed's collection of 1950s doo-wop singles was stolen from his apartment. Within days, Maureen Tucker's tom-toms were also stolen from the Dom, so she miked up two garbage cans and played those for a week. Tucker was still holding down a day job, and living with her parents.

At this time Warhol was riding high. His film *My Hustler* was showing uptown, and his exhibition of floating silver pillows and yellow and pink cow wallpaper was showing at the Castelli Gallery – this being supposedly his farewell to fine art. Additionally, Nico was attracting a lot of media coverage. So all of New York's celebrities – from Jackie Kennedy on down – came to the Dom to check out

THE VELVET UNDERGROUND

2

what Warhol and this chic new singer were up to. On most nights the place was packed, and the Warhol coffers accordingly swelled with cash. For four performances avant-garde violinist Henry Flynt substituted for Cale while the latter was sick. Salvador Dali joined the E.P.I. on stage several times. One night Lou Reed was almost electrocuted by a live microphone (and would have been, if not for a shouted warning from Morrison). On another occasion, Allen Ginsberg joined the Velvets onstage and chanted Hare Krishna mantras. All of this countercultural activity at the Dom was a catalyst for change around St Mark's Place and the East Village, transforming it in the process from cultural wasteland to hip hangout.

As Andy Warhol later commented: "We all knew something revolutionary was happening. We just felt it. Things couldn't look this strange and new without some barrier being broken." But many were appalled by the Velvets' seeming flirtation with decadence. Critic Richard Goldstein

described their sound as "the product of a secret marriage between Bob Dylan and the Marquis de Sade." Reviews of the shows were almost uniformly negative (some were included on the inner sleeve of the first Velvets album, which is indicative of the fact that the band were perversely proud of them).

The following month the E.P.I. went down like a lead balloon when they played a month-long stint in Los Angeles. At their first night at The Trip on Sunset Strip they were supported by Frank Zappa's Mothers of Invention and attracted a celebrity crowd including Sonny & Cher, Mama Cass, several Byrds and Jim Morrison – who Gerard Malanga would later accuse of stealing his leather-trousered image. But by the second night the crowd had dwindled greatly and the club was closed down by police on the third night for disturbing the peace with the Velvets' "pornographic exhibition". It stayed closed because of a lawsuit between the owners, and in order to get paid at all Warhol

MARY WORONOV

Mary Woronov (born 1943) was an art student at Cornell University when she met Andy Warhol and became involved with the Factory. She was one of the principal dancers with the Exploding Plastic Inevitable, accompanying Gerard Malanga's whip dance to 'Venus In Furs'. Having appeared in Warhol's movies *Hedy The Shoplifter* and *Chelsea Girls*, Woronov moved to Los Angeles and acted in a zillion B-movies, of which the most notable is probably Roger Corman's *Death Race 2000* (1975). She revealed herself as a talented comedy actress in

Rock And Roll High School (1979), and Paul Bartel's black comedies *Eating Raoul* (1982) and *Scenes From The Class Struggle In Beverley Hills* (1989), as well as making cameos in mainstream Hollywood movies. Liver damage caused her to give up all drugs and alcohol in the Eighties. She has been a writer-director for the TV show *The Women's Series* and is the author of four volumes of fiction (*Snake*, *Niagara*, *Blind Love* and *Wake For Angels*, which also contains some of her paintings) and *Swimming Underground* (a memoir of her time with the Factory).

2

and the whole E.P.I. had to fulfil Musicians Union conditions and wait out the rest of the month in Los Angeles. As it was, it took them three years to get the money.

The E.P.I. then played two nights at San Francisco's Fillmore, which confirmed that the East Coast crowd had nothing in common with the Haight-Ashbury scene, and where Malanga was arrested for carrying his whip in public. It was also in San Francisco that Reed injected himself with the drug that caused him to be wrongly diagnosed with terminal lupus (it turned out to be hepatitis).

Reviews continued to be bad, while the singer Cher famously remarked that the Velvets "won't replace anything... except maybe suicide." Years later, Reed would claim that the Velvets' favourite of all their reviews was the one that read: "The flowers of evil are in bloom. Someone has to stamp them out before they spread." Returning to New York Warhol discovered that they'd missed the chance to buy the lease of the Dom, which had been snapped up instead by Dylan's manager Albert Grossman. The Dom was renamed the Balloon Farm (later becoming the Electric Circus) and went on to make a fortune. The Velvets played there once grudgingly, resenting the fact that the Dom had been stolen out from under them.

The debut album

By this point the first album had already been recorded. In April 1966 Andy Warhol approached a 27-year-old Columbia sales executive named Norman Dolph who he'd met when the latter acted as DJ at a Warhol exhibition in Philadelphia. Warhol asked Dolph to find a studio for the Velvets, produce a session and help get them a record deal. Dolph rented the 4-track studio

belonging to the small independent New York label Scepter Records for three nights during the week of 18–23 April. Scepter were based in the same building on West 54th Street that would later house the disco Studio 54. The engineer at Scepter was John Licata, a seasoned professional. Dolph claims to have overseen the session, but has given credit for most musical decisions made there to John Cale and Sterling Morrison.

According to Moe Tucker, the sessions lasted for a total of eight hours, which was all they could afford: "We pooled our money with Andy." According to Norman Dolph, they had four working days, which included playback time and mixing; in total, probably less than sixteen hours, of which the actual recording time was more like ten hours. Dolph also invested money of his own for the sessions (and was repaid with a Warhol painting). Total studio costs, probably including those in California, have been estimated at between $1,500 and $3,000. Whatever the amount was, it seemed scandalously high to Warhol, according to Morrissey – but then Warhol was accustomed to making movies that only cost a couple of hundred dollars apiece. In 1966 the *average* cost of making an album was $5,000, and many other masterpieces of the era cost considerably more.

According to John Cale, the studio was not Scepter, but Cameo-Parkway on Broadway, which he claims was practically a building site. One explanation for this discrepancy in memory is that the group may have tried Cameo-Parkway before moving to Scepter, having found the former unacceptable. Then again, Cale thought Dolph was a shoe salesman, so he's not all that reliable a witness.

Nominally, the album was produced by

THE VELVET UNDERGROUND

Andy Warhol – but in reality there *was* no producer – just Dolph, Licata and the band. So why is Warhol credited? According to Reed, "The advantage of having Andy Warhol as a producer was that because he was Andy Warhol they left everything in its pure state. They would say, 'Is that okay, Mr Warhol?', and he'd say, 'Oh ... yeah.' And so they didn't *change* anything. And so, right at the very beginning we discovered what it was like to be in the studio and record things our way, and have essentially total freedom." Given Reed's controversial lyrics, this freedom was necessary: "Andy made a point of trying to make sure that the language remained intact. I think Andy was interested in shocking, in giving people a jolt and not to let them talk us into taking that stuff out in the interest of popularity or easy airplay. He said, 'Oh, you've got to make sure you leave the dirty words in'. He was adamant about that. He didn't want it to be cleaned up and because he was there, it wasn't." According to Dolph, Warhol sat quietly in the back of the control room, "observing, making the occasional wry comment... he was more of a presence, really."

Warhol's initial idea had been to get a manufacturing and distribution deal and market the record himself. But in 1966 this approach was virtually unheard of (certainly when applied to fine artists without any music biz experience), so instead he attempted to interest an established label in the album. But Reed's lyrics and the band's image were too daunting for both Atlantic and Elektra, and no deals were forthcoming. Then Tom Wilson, a young black producer at Columbia, heard the record. He'd worked with many old jazz artists and young folkies, producing groundbreaking tracks like 'Sounds Of Silence' for Simon & Garfunkel

and 'Like A Rolling Stone' for Bob Dylan. Wilson was leaving Columbia to set up a rock division for the jazz label Verve (whose only other rock signing was the Mothers Of Invention) and he offered the Velvets a deal, buying the tape outright. At Reed's insistence, all money went directly to the Velvets, who would pay Warhol his percentage later on (which upset Warhol, who saw it as a betrayal – he also always claimed he never earned a penny from the record).

But Wilson wanted some changes. After the group eventually signed to Verve, they re-recorded three or four songs at T.T.G. Studios in California, where producer Wilson was assisted by engineer Omi Haden (sometimes credited as Ami Hadani). Wilson also felt there was "not enough Nico"; for him, she was the star attraction, and probably the reason why he signed the band in the first place. So a third session took place in New York, which Wilson produced and MGM paid for, which yielded one more track: 'Sunday Morning'. The song was written after one all-night Saturday party, with Cale tinkering about on a small pump-organ while Reed improvised the lyrics. Though Wilson wanted Nico to sing the song, once in the studio, Reed insisted that he sing it instead.

Although Wilson would go on to produce her first solo album, Nico parted company with the Velvets long before the first Velvets album's release – which was delayed and delayed until the following spring. This was due to three main factors: Verve's nervousness about the subject matter, production problems with the cover's peelable banana sticker; and the fact that Herb Cohen, manager of the Mothers of Invention, made sure *their* album was the

2

THE VELVET UNDERGROUND AND NICO   EXCLUSIVELY ON MGM/ VERVE RECORDS R-1499

first rock album to come out on Verve. At one point Verve even claimed to have lost the master tapes. In 1966, the year they were 'hot', the only Velvet Underground product actually made available to the public would be 'Noise' and 'Loop' (one live and one improvisational, feedback-based piece given away free with – respectively – the *East Village Other* and *Aspen*

Verve Records' promo photo for the Velvets

THE VELVET UNDERGROUND

2

magazine) and two edited singles taken from the forthcoming album ('All Tomorrow's Parties' b/w 'I'll Be Your Mirror' and 'Sunday Morning' b/w 'Femme Fatale') which Verve failed to promote at all. If they'd had a more aggressive manager, who would have pressured Verve for results, things might have been different – but Warhol wasn't that kind of manager, and he had no experience of how the music business worked. He did, however, create one of the best album covers of all time for them.

When the album *was* finally released, Verve spent very little on promotion, and what promotion there was touted the album as a Warhol artefact. One Verve ad read: "What happens when the Daddy of Pop Art goes Pop Music? The most underground album of all! It's Andy Warhol's new hip trip to the subterranean scene." Another featured a large photo of Warhol and ran "So far underground... you'll get the bends!" Far from giving them credibility, their association with Warhol meant that many critics refused to take them seriously at the time, assuming the whole thing was just a camp put-on. As Sterling Morrison put it, "We gained all his enemies – the people who thought he was a faker thought we were fakers."

It was also widely assumed that all the Velvets were gay, or else S&M sex maniacs. Or both. What few reviews they got were bad, regarding the band's songs about drugs and sex as proof of true evil; the fact that Reed had used a first-person narrative caused many listeners to assume the songs were autobiographical, rather than simply using a literary perspective.

Then came what Morrison has called "the crowning moment of doom". Eric Emerson, one of the Factory crowd, sued Verve for using a photo of him without his permission on the album sleeve (he was part of a crowd scene). Emerson had been arrested for possessing a large amount of LSD, and needed money for legal costs – and suing Verve seemed an easy way of getting it. Instead, Verve responded by recalling some copies of the album, stickering others, and reprinting the cover with Emerson's face airbrushed out – all of which caused a further delay in distribution. Eric Emerson died of a drug overdose shortly afterwards.

What with one thing and another, the record sank without trace (comparatively speaking), though its time would eventually come. Between the recording of the first album and its release, the Velvet Underground continued to tour, while growing increasingly frustrated. In June 1966 they played a series of dates at a club in Chicago called Poor Richards while Lou Reed was laid up with that bout of hepatitis. Angus MacLise was briefly re-recruited on drums, with Moe Tucker switching to bass and guitar, freeing Cale for keyboards and viola. He also took all the lead vocals – the first time he'd ever sung in front of an audience, and it built up his confidence.

For obvious reasons, Reed wasn't too happy with this line-up (captured on film by Ron Nameth), but Sterling Morrison felt it had real potential. The gig itself took place in 106-degree heat, and the lack of Reed and Warhol (who was busy elsewhere) infuriated the local media. Despite this, the band were asked to stay on for an extra week, much to Reed's annoyance.

The E.P.I.'s most bizarre gig came in November 1966, when they took part in the highlight of Detroit's 'Carnaby Street Fun Festival': the 'Mod Wedding' of Gary Norris (an artist) and Randi Rossi (an "unemployed go-go dancer"). Warhol gave the bride away, while the Velvets improvised (though Tucker denies the rumour that they actually played 'Here Comes The Bride'). The couple also won a screen test at the Factory. But Warhol rapidly lost interest in touring with the E.P.I., and a distance grew between them and the band. When Warhol went to Cannes to promote his *Chelsea Girls* film, he didn't even consider taking the Velvets along for the ride; instead, they were left to play to confused (and occasionally hostile) teenage audiences in middle America.

An improvisation piece conceived during this period called 'Searchin' would eventually metamorphose into 'Sister Ray' (sometimes performed live with an improvised prelude titled 'Sweet Sister Ray', both parts being of indeterminate length). In April 1967 the Velvets played a benefit gig where their support act was Tiny Tim; that month they also played a new New York club on the Upper East Side called the Gymnasium, where they were supported by a group that included future Blondie guitarist Chris Stein. But hopes that the Gymnasium could become another Dom fell flat, and the following month the E.P.I. played their last gig at the Scene club. In fact, the Velvets didn't play New York again until 1970 – local radio stations had ignored the first album, so Reed decided to withdraw their presence from the city.

Partings of the ways

In this period their world also went through some major changes. Firstly, Nico was elbowed out. She'd gone to Ibiza (to model), then Paris (to visit Ari) and then London (where she outstayed her welcome as Paul McCartney's houseguest). Returning to the States, she travelled to Boston to

rejoin the Velvets – but when she arrived late for the gig, the band simply refused to let her onstage. According to some accounts, the band had already played all the songs Nico might have sung, and had only a couple of numbers left in their set. It's also been claimed the gig in question was in Cincinatti. Regardless, this was basically the end of Nico's involvement with the band, and Warhol for one felt she had been treated badly.

Nico then travelled briefly to California, where she attended the Monterey Pop Festival with Brian Jones (and had a fling with Jimi Hendrix). In Los Angeles she resumed an affair with Jim Morrison she'd begun in New York earlier in the year. Nico and Morrison were together for about a month. They took peyote together in the desert, but fought loudly when they were both drunk. Morrison showed her how he wrote lyrics, and encouraged her to write her own songs; she dyed her hair red to please him. In San Francisco she bought herself an Indian harmonium, and began to teach herself how to play (after a fashion). Supposedly Ornette Coleman gave her her first lessons.

Returning to New York, Nico played a series of gigs downstairs at the Dom. In the earliest of these gigs Nico sang along to a backing tape of Reed playing, until someone finally took pity on her and pulled out a guitar; she was subsequently accompanied by various guitar players including Cale, Reed, Morrison, Tim Hardin, Tim Buckley, Ramblin' Jack Elliott and the 18-year-old Jackson Browne (with whom she had an affair). According to some accounts, Warhol films were also shown, and the gigs had the umbrella title of 'Andy Warhol's Mod Dom'. According to Morrison, these gigs coincided

THE VELVET UNDERGROUND

2

with a period of Velvets inactivity; when they resumed touring, Nico was still booked for three more weeks at the Dom, and chose to go solo rather than rejoin the band. Relations seemed to remain good, however, and just after the first Velvets album was released, Nico was recording her first solo album *Chelsea Girls* with the aid of Browne and producer Tom Wilson, plus Lou Reed, John Cale and Stirling Morrison. But with Nico's departure, the band felt less musically compromised, and Tucker for one was glad to see her go: "To me she was just a pain in the ass," Tucker admitted.

More painfully, in late summer 1967 the Velvets parted company with Andy Warhol. As far as Warhol had taken the band, he had no experience of the wider rock world and Reed decided Warhol could not take the Velvets where they needed to go now: "When he told me I should start making decisions about the future, and what could be a career, I decided to leave him. He did not try to stop me, legally or otherwise. He did, however, tell me that I was a rat. I think it was the worst word he could think of." Until the writing sessions for *Songs For Drella*, more than two decades later, John Cale wasn't even aware that it was Reed who had instigated this parting of the ways: "I thought Andy quit."

I CAN'T STAND IT
Falling Apart 1967–1970

3

"You can't walk around with anger in your heart. It causes very negative things"

LOU REED

I CAN'T STAND IT

3

Falling Apart 1967–1970

The Velvet Underground now needed to quickly find someone to assume Andy Warhol's role as manager (and hopefully improve upon it). Recognizing that they needed a businessman – rather than a creative artist – to talk to the music business, in the summer of 1967 they appointed Steve Sesnick, a fast-talking Boston club owner, to look after their affairs.

A new manager

Sesnick had already worked on the band's behalf in California, and was thus a known quantity. One of his first moves was to contact the Beatles' manager, Brian Epstein, in the hope of landing a deal for the Velvets' songs with Epstein's publishing company – but despite Epstein liking the Velvets' album, nothing resulted from it. Epstein did supposedly set up a European tour for the Velvets later on in 1967, but he died just before the contracts were signed and so the tour fell through.

But Sesnick did produce some immediate results. He persuaded Verve/MGM to underwrite the Velvets' tour expenses by paying for transportation and hotels, which meant that the band were able to keep more of the cash they earned by playing live – a vast improvement on their situation with Warhol, where they subsisted on per diem allowances. As a result of Sesnick's Boston connections, they frequently played his club, The Boston Tea Party, over the next few years, where they acquired a fanatical local devotee in one Jonathan Richman.

The most bizarre gig they played in Boston came in October 1967, when they spent one entire weekend opening for each screening of the Roger Corman LSD movie *The Trip*, starring Peter Fonda and conceived by Jack Nicholson.

Touring provided the Velvets' only income, since they were receiving no record royalties at all. Even if they had been, their album wasn't selling brilliantly and certainly wasn't getting much airplay – 'Heroin' was widely banned, and so the rest of the album was mostly ignored by DJs. So the band had to tour almost constantly and would do so for the rest of their brief career, despite often playing to tiny audiences. Touring was also confined to the USA. Plans to go to Europe the previous year with the E.P.I. had come to nothing, and another chance fell through when the film director Antonioni decided that flying the Velvet Underground to London to appear in his film *Blow-Up* would be too expensive, and used the Yardbirds instead.

Though the Velvets were all happy with the choice of Sesnick at the time,

THE VELVET UNDERGROUND

3

that was something that would change, and drastically. Suffice it to say that John Cale later called Sesnick "a snake", and Lou Reed subsequently placed the blame for "destroying" the Velvet Underground squarely on Sesnick's shoulders. Cale claims that Sesnick drove a wedge between Reed and the rest of the band, by inflating Reed's position as 'the' songwriter, and thus the most important member of the group. Morrison claimed that he had his doubts about Sesnick's handling of the band's finances, while Tucker thinks Sesnick simply had unrealistic goals for the Velvets, wanting them to be the next Beatles and so turning down offers that he should have accepted.

Reed and Cale also drifted further apart as Cale became involved with the successful fashion designer Betsey Johnson, who he met again in May 1967. Soon they were living together – for a short while they lived at the Chelsea Hotel. Johnson was a successful businesswoman who spoke her own mind, which may well have not gone down very well with Lou Reed. Then again, Reed's coolness may have been simple jealousy, since he had no serious relationship of his own.

Cracks begin to show

The Velvets had written very few (if any) new songs during their time with the E.P.I., and the material they eventually came up with for their second album is certainly not as immediately user-friendly as their debut. Cale was keen to keep the Velvets' edge sharp. "I had no intention of letting the music be anything other than troublesome

JONATHAN RICHMAN

Jonathan Richman (born 1951) was an avid Velvets fan, who saw them on their every visit to his native Boston. He claims to have attended over 100 live shows, as well as watching the group rehearse, and both photographed the band and made a short colour home movie. Richman would later form his own group, The Modern Lovers, whose first album was partly produced by Cale. Richman's first professional music gig would be supporting the Velvets (while using Morrison's guitar), and during his first sojourn in New York he slept on Steve Sesnick's couch. He later recorded with Moe Tucker, and penned the tribute song 'Velvet Underground' on his *I, Jonathan* album.

to people," he stated and he later admitted that – creatively speaking – he and Reed were "at each others throats" during this period, something he blames largely on the stress of the touring life. The band were virtually under siege: no Andy Warhol patronage, no radio airplay and pretty much no direction, watching bands who'd once supported them overtake them on the road to success.

Amazingly, although touring gave them little time for rehearsal (let alone experimentation), they still managed to write enough material for their second album – though as Cale admits, "The incoherence of our thinking about where the band should go started laying claim to a lot of our time." On another occasion he complained that the band "lost our patience and diligence. We couldn't even remember what our original precepts were."

Quarrels about musical direction would lead to Cale's departure within the year. They were protracted, and loud, and occasionally turned into fist-fights between Cale and Reed. Tucker, according to Morrison, "always said there was no reasoning with any of us, that we were all crazy, and there was no sense in arguing. I think basically the band had three uncontrollable personalities, and if you throw drugs into the confusion, then you really have problems." One of these problems, Morrison explained, was that the others never knew how Lou Reed was going to react. His mood could range unpredictably from "boyishly charming" to "vicious", depending on what drugs or diet he was using: "He was always trying to move mentally and spiritually to some

BILLY NAME

A photographer and lighting designer who subsidized his artistic work with hairdressing, Billy Name (real name Billy Linich) had decorated his entire apartment with silver foil. Warhol liked the look so much ("Silver makes everything disappear") that he asked Linich to decorate his new studio – the original Factory – in the same way. Billy also worked with Gerard Malanga as an assistant on Warhol's silkscreens, designed the cover for *White Light/ White Heat*, and claims to have been one of Reed's lovers. Also a musician, Linich was in LaMonte Young's group for a year, leaving them just before the arrival of John Cale. A genuinely eccentric character, Name was effectively the

Factory's caretaker, living in one of its black-painted toilets (which he used as a photographic darkroom) for years, studying astrological charts and books on the occult given him by Reed; when the Factory moved home, Billy simply moved into the equivalent space in the new one. In 1968 he sealed himself into this room, and was seldom seen at all between then and the time he finally left the Factory (in the middle of the night) at some point in spring 1970, leaving a note behind telling Warhol not to worry. Linich subsequently gave up amphetamines, moved back home to Poughkeepsie and pursued his own individualistic spirituality. Today, his photographs of the Factory era are much in demand. He died in July 2016.

THE VELVET UNDERGROUND

place where no one had ever gotten before."

Reed was deeply interested in astrology during this period, under the influence of Billy Name (an occasional lover of Reed's, with whom he would go to gay bars).

Other areas of interest for Reed at this time included auras and reincarnation and the teachings of the sometime Theosophist Alice Bailey. Her 1934 book *A Treatise On White Magic* made frequent references to 'white light', a phrase Lou would soon make his own. Reed supposedly actually joined Bailey's Church Of Light; during this period, Rob Norris recalls discussing with Reed the topics of "angels, saints, the universe, diet, yoga, meditation, Jesus, healing with music, cosmic rays and astrology". Though Lou's interest in all things mystic wore off fairly quickly, it would return to him in later life.

Meanwhile, in September 1967 the group began recording *White Light/White Heat*, their second album. Other influences that would

BETSEY JOHNSON

Betsey Johnson had been at Syracuse University with Lou Reed and Sterling Morrison (who she had also dated in 1966 – though not seriously, according to Cale). She became the fashion designer for the hip clothes boutique Paraphernalia, at the opening of which in early 1966 the Velvets played, with a scaled-down version of the E.P.I.

She eventually designed suits for all four Velvets (grey suede for Lou, dark green and maroon velvets for Sterling and Moe, sober black for Cale), but after she and Cale became involved she designed numerous clothes for him, with the result that he now cut a much more stylish figure than the other Velvets – which may also not have gone down well with Reed. She and Cale married in 1968 but divorced three years later. In 1969 she opened her own boutique, Betsey Bunki Nini, on the Upper East Side, where Edie Sedgwick was briefly her house model. She went on to build a retail fashion empire with over 45 stores around the world.

Betsey with John Cale (on the back cover of his Vintage Violence album)

come to bear on the music and lyrics were literary (William Burroughs) and musical (jazz, notably the works of John Coltrane, Ornette Coleman and Cecil Taylor), married to an avant-garde sensibility and driven by the tensions between Cale and Reed.

All of their energetic antagonism gave birth to a record that M.C. Kostek accurately described as sounding like "sonic war", with Cale, Reed and Morrison challenging each other at every turn.

Though it stays in the same urban reality that Reed had been exploring for years, that reality now sounded a lot more menacing. The album is distinctly uneasy listening, delivered at loud volume and high speed, like heavy metal with brains (and a lot of problems). As John Cale later admitted: "It was a very rabid record. The first one had some gentility, some beauty. The second one was consciously anti-beauty." Cale also admitted that the album had been fuelled by "a great deal" of drugs, including heroin.

The angst level was high. Looking back on that period in 1994, Sterling Morrison told David Fricke: "Our lives were chaos. Things were insane, day in and day out. The people we knew, the excesses of all sorts. For a long time, we were living in various places, afraid of the police. At the height of my musical career, I had no permanent address."

That month also saw the completion of Andy Warhol's film **** (aka *Four Stars*), in which John Cale made a cameo appearance. John and Betsey spent the Christmas period travelling – first to the Virgin Islands and Spain (where Cale bought both a swordstick and his first gun), then on to Wales so that Betsey could meet his parents. The couple were due to marry in February 1968, but the wedding had to be delayed until April, as

Verve records' promotional poster for the White Light/White Heat album

Cale was quarantined in hospital for four weeks with suspected hepatitis. After John's liver was finally pronounced healthy, the Cales' wedding was attended by Reed, Nico, Billy Name and Andy Warhol.

Shortly before his illness, Cale played a one-off gig in January 1968 with La Monte Young's group, and also made some recordings with Tony Conrad a few weeks later. Cale had created a home studio of sorts, stocking it with not only his bass, viola and organ, but also Indian stringed instruments such as the sarinda, sarangi and dilruba. Some of the home recordings he'd made the previous October (eventually released as *Sun Blindness Music* in 2000) seem to move further along in the same direction as *White Light/White Heat*.

THE VELVET UNDERGROUND

3

Cale spoke of creating music that could control the weather, and thought that albums should come with free colouring books (a notable pastime of speedfreaks) and toys.

Andy Warhol claimed that Reed had confessed to him in early 1968 that he was concerned about his own speed habit, and was trying to stop using the drug. The reason may have been Shelley Albin, who had moved to New York that spring with her new husband. She and Reed had begun seeing each other – probably only platonically, since she claims that was the sole extent of their relationship then – but Lou never gave up on the idea of winning

THE SHOOTING OF ANDY WARHOL

A wannabe playwright and a radical lesbian feminist, Valerie Solanas had written a manifesto for a proposed extremist feminist group called SCUM (the Society for Cutting Up Men, of which Solanas was the only member). Solanas was dangerously psychotic – Andy Warhol later recalled that she "would talk constantly about the complete elimination of the male sex." Pretty much homeless, Solanas survived by begging, prostitution and selling copies of her SCUM manifesto on the street. In late 1966 she met Warhol, and saw in him a chance for recognition of her work. She demanded that he produce one of her plays, titled *Up Your Ass*; but Warhol wasn't interested. When she continued to pester him for money, Warhol gave her a small role in his film *I, A Man* to shut her up.

On 3 June 1968 Solanas decided to take drastic action against one of the central figures of her paranoid delusions. Her initial target was publisher Maurice Girodias, but he was out of town, so instead Solanas switched her attentions to Warhol. She made half a dozen visits that day to the new Factory offices at 33 Union Square West, only to be told that Warhol was not present. When the artist arrived at four o'clock that afternoon, Solanas followed Warhol into the Factory, waited until he had finished a phone conversation, and then pulled out an automatic pistol and fired three .32 calibre bullets into his chest and abdomen at point-blank range. She also shot art dealer Mario Amaya in the leg before leaving. There had been two earlier gun incidents at the Factory, and even though no one had been hurt on those occasions, it's amazing that Warhol's security precautions had remained non-existent.

Warhol was rushed to Columbus-Mother Cabrini Hospital, and pronounced clinically dead six minutes after his arrival there – he was 'dead' for 90 seconds before a doctor cut his chest open and massaged his heart back into action. Four doctors spent the next five hours operating on Warhol's lungs, liver, gallbladder, spleen, intestines and pulmonary artery. Miraculously, Andy survived – though his chest was crisscrossed with scars and he would suffer problems with digestion and sleeping for years to come, and had to wear a corset (to keep his stomach muscles in place) for the rest of his life.

Earlier that year Warhol had made his most famous (and most misquoted)

3

her back again. The Velvet Underground spent most of 1968 on the road, promoting *White Light/White Heat*; but its lyrical content (and the lack of ballads) ensured that it received zero radio airplay. This time there was no Warhol angle to attract the media, and the album got virtually no reviews. It was not distributed properly, stalling on the *Billboard* chart at #200. But live, the

band were in their element, as Sterling Morrison recalled: "Our touring was successful and our playing was excellent. Perhaps the possibility of real success suddenly became so tangible that we pursued it into megalomania and ruin". The group's energy turned inwards again, with destructive force.

The basic problem was that Cale

remark: "In the future everybody will be world famous for fifteen minutes." Ironically, his own shooting garnered not much more than fifteen minutes of press attention, since Presidential candidate Robert Kennedy was assassinated the next day, pushing Warhol out of the headlines. Though Andy was forgiving towards his attacker, most observers agreed with Nico that he was visibly never the same after the shooting: "He was never Andy again. He was like a silkscreen of himself". Nor was Warhol left unguarded or unprotected any more; security video cameras were installed at the Factory, where the 'open house' policy finally came to an end.

As for Solanas, she surrendered to police several hours after the shooting, and was remanded to mental hospital. Released on bail in December 1968, she made several threatening phonecalls, including one to the Factory. A mandatory pre-trial psychiatric evaluation diagnosed Solanas as a chronic schizophrenic, and recommended she be placed in closed-ward psychiatric care. But the court ignored this, and sentenced her to three years in state prison for "reckless assault with intent to harm" in

January 1969 ("You get more for stealing a car," Lou Reed observed). Solanas was released in September 1971, and spent much of the Seventies either homeless or in mental hospitals. She died of bronchial pneumonia in a welfare hotel in San Francisco on 25 April 1988, fourteen months after Andy Warhol.

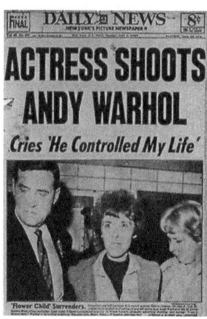

DEAD STRAIGHT GUIDE TO **THE VELVET UNDERGROUND 59**

THE VELVET UNDERGROUND

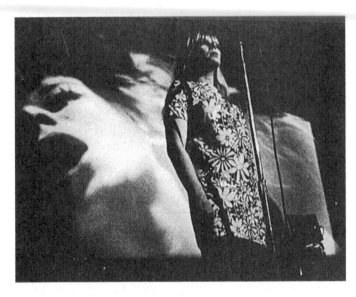

Nico, onstage in front of a film projection, at an Exploding Plastic Inevitable event at Ann Arbor University in Michigan, 1968

wanted the band to go further in the same direction as *White Light/White Heat*, while Reed wanted to do something radically different. Probably at the prompting of Steve Sesnick – and inspired, perhaps, by his relationship with Albin – Reed was now writing gentle love songs. Cale was "trying to develop these really grand orchestral bass parts. I was trying to get something big and grand and Lou was fighting against that. He wanted pretty songs."

Reed maintained that he didn't want to repeat the *White Light/White Heat* formula: "I thought it would be a terrible mistake, and I really believed that. I thought we had to demonstrate the other side of us. Otherwise, we would become this one-dimensional thing, and that had to be avoided at all costs." Morrison tended to side with Cale: "Lou placed heavy emphasis on lyrics. Cale and I were more interested in blasting the house down." Cale would later state that Reed "wanted to keep it

pure. He was right. I wanted to push the envelope and fuck the songs up. That's why we split. He wanted me to be a sideman in my own fucking group."

Matters worsened because Reed and Cale were barely talking to each other. Much of their communication was routed through Steve Sesnick, who may well not have passed messages on – or not passed them on accurately. Intrigue and machinations now became the order of the day – and would eventually cause Reed as much angst as they now did for Cale. Two recording sessions took place in February and May, with an eye to a possible single (resulting in 'Mr Rain', 'Stephanie Says' and 'Temptation Inside Your Heart', which would finally become available on *VU* and *Another View*) but ended up not being released – probably because of these tensions between Reed and Cale. They were unable to reconcile their differences; Cale subsequently blaming Reed's drug intake.

3

While the Velvets were busy touring and scrapping over musical direction, their former manager was lying in hospital. On 3 June 1968, Andy Warhol became the victim of a near-successful assassination attempt by Valerie Solanas. Though deeply shocked when he heard of the incident, for some reason Lou Reed did not go to visit Warhol in hospital – something which would cause him guilt pangs for years to come. Reed later wrote a song inspired by the shooting, 'Andy's Chest' (the Velvets' version of which would finally be released on the *VU* album).

Then in September 1968 the Reed/Cale crisis finally came to a head. Reed convened a meeting in the Café Riviera in Greenwich Village with Morrison and Tucker, and informed them that he wanted Cale out of the group, for good. This didn't go down too well, especially with Morrison, who found the idea "unthinkable". But Reed told them he'd rather dissolve the Velvets completely than continue with Cale, and so – because they both wanted the band to continue – the others eventually acquiesced. Reed left it to Morrison to break the news to Cale, who later observed that Lou "always got other people to do his dirty work for him".

A new bass player and a different sound

John Cale went quietly, and with as much dignity as he could muster, playing his last gig with the group that month. He would subsequently state his opinion that the Velvet Underground had never really fulfilled their potential, blaming "drugs, and the fact that no one gave a damn about us, meant we gave up on it too soon." In the late Eighties Lou Reed conceded he had a point: "I think he's right, in a way."

In the process of ousting Cale, Reed had seriously alienated Sterling Morrison, who remained angry at him for years (and possibly decades). The fact that Morrison continued to socialise with Cale only increased Reed's paranoia. Maureen Tucker reluctantly accepted Cale's departure, though she wasn't happy about it – she later stated that she wished the band had done at least one more album with Cale, and that without him the constructive "lunacy" that had fuelled their first two albums was lost.

As Cale's replacement, the band brought in Doug Yule, a 21-year-old bass player from Boston. Born 25 February 1947, Yule had been in several local cover bands, including the Argonauts, then the Argo, before joining

THE VELVET UNDERGROUND

3

a professional outfit called the Grass Menagerie. Later on, his organ playing would go some way to becoming a worthy substitute for Cale's viola drone-effects. He made his live debut with the band in October, after less than a week's rehearsal with them.

Yule had been discovered by Morrison via the Velvets' road manager Hans Onsager, but Lou Reed was thrilled with the choice, finding the new bass player's "innocence" a refreshing change. The astrology-obsessed Reed was also delighted to discover that Yule was a Pisces, like himself. With Morrison and Tucker both Virgos, the band was now astrologically balanced.

But the other two had reservations. Morrison liked Yule and thought him a good bass player, but missed the sparks that flew from Cale: "Bands that fight together make better music." When Reed began flattering and praising Yule at length, Moe Tucker feared that all the attention would go to Yule's head and cause yet more problems – thus adding the gift of prophecy to her other talents. Yule soon became so influenced by Reed that he began to dress and sound like him.

The time was fast approaching for the Velvets to record again, but this time the group ran into a technical hitch en route to the studio in California. According to Sterling Morrison, all the band's guitar effects boxes were stolen at the airport: "We saw that all our tricks had vanished, and instead of trying to replace them, we just thought of what we could do without them." Doug Yule has since poured scorn on this story, pointing out that if it were true, these boxes could easily have been replaced in L.A. Yule thinks that Reed simply wanted a gentler sound, and a new direction. Regardless, Morrison and Reed kitted themselves out with twin Fender 12-string

guitars. The new album would be as quiet as its predecessor was loud, and be comprised of totally new material, most of which had never been performed live.

In fact, much of it hadn't even been written. According to Yule, at this point Sesnick was still managing to get MGM to foot the bill for first-class travel and accommodation. So, in November 1968 the group stayed at the Chateau Marmont in L.A., where they wrote and rehearsed during the afternoons; they would then record the songs at night. Maureen Tucker was so shy about performing the vocals for 'Afterhours' that she made all the others leave the studio before she would sing it.

Inevitably, without Cale the mania and the menace were gone, and the music was much more orthodox. All the new songs were by Lou Reed. Many of them were personal-sounding. And all of them dealt with love – from the adulterous to the religious – and sex. Many were clearly about Shelley Albin, and Reed later stated that the songs can be seen as one large story cycle. But his voice was shot from playing live, and so Doug Yule took the vocals on several tracks. This may well have planted a seed for the future in Steve Sesnick's mind. Yule was good-looking, had the kind of teen appeal that Reed never would or could have, *and* he could sing. In short, Lou Reed might not be as essential to the band's survival as he seemed.

Sterling Morrison has described his own attitude on the third album as one of "acquiescence", but he was nevertheless pleased with the finished product: "The songs are all very quiet and it's kind of insane. I like the album." But both he and Tucker were annoyed by the fact that – after the album was mixed – Reed went back into the studio and did his own mix. He'd gone behind their backs, and they resented it. Once again, once released the album received little promotion and was badly distributed.

The 'lost' album

On various dates between May and October 1969, the group were in the studio again, this time recording what would come to be regarded as their 'lost' MGM/Verve album at the Record Plant in New York. But whether the tracks were ever actually intended for an album is a little unclear, and Doug Yule was under the impression that these recordings were nothing more than "work tapes", in preparation for more polished recordings that were never made. Still, the group *were* trying to get free from MGM, who were no longer giving them much support, financial or otherwise – and they did contractually owe the label one more album. It seems unlikely they were recording just for the hell of it, but on the other hand their first three albums had been badly-promoted and ineffectively distributed. As Maureen Tucker points out, "We weren't that interested in giving them another one to just let it die."

The material they recorded then would subsequently surface on bootlegs and – much later – on the albums *VU* and *Another View*. In the end – and quite probably *before* they had finished what they set out to do in the studio – MGM dropped them from their roster. At that time MGM President Mike Curb issued a statement, which read in part: "Groups that are associated with hard drugs ... are very undependable. They're difficult to work with, and they're hard on your sales and marketing people." This new company policy not only explains why MGM dropped the Velvets from the label, but also why they chose not to release the 'lost' album.

Crossing to Atlantic

Amazingly, it took the group several months to find a new record deal, before they eventually signed a two-album contract with Atlantic's Ahmet Ertegun, on the strict condition that there would be no drug songs. So, the Velvet Underground returned to New York, to record at Atlantic Studios. Recording took about ten weeks (between April and July 1970), mainly in the evenings after the group had finished playing live at Max's Kansas City, where they had a residency that summer, playing five nights a week. Originally a two-week booking, the residency was extended to ten weeks.

Mysteriously, with the exception of 'Rock & Roll' the Velvets chose not to re-record the songs from the 'lost' album; instead, the finished *Loaded* album would include an additional nine *new* songs. This may have been because they believed that MGM might still release the earlier recordings (which the label refused to return to the band), or because they were legally prevented from re-recording that material. The latter seems unlikely – quite apart from 'Rock & Roll' they *did* also re-record 'Ocean' (though it wouldn't surface until 1995's *Peel Slowly And See*), and Reed was certainly free to re-record much of the material for his first solo album in 1972. It seems more likely that the group were just disenchanted with the 'lost' songs, or found them tainted by the move from MGM, and wanted a fresh start. Whatever the reasons, the songs on *Loaded* were intentionally designed to be as commercial as possible.

But from the start, the Velvets were beset with problems. Firstly, Sterling Morrison had taken a step back from band politics, and seems to have been largely unaware of the arguments that would soon boil over. Having

THE VELVET UNDERGROUND

dropped out of college in 1966, he'd taken advantage of the group's prolonged stay in New York to take some academic courses at City College, and had his head stuck in Victorian novels for most of that summer. Consequently, as he later noted: "It wasn't really apparent to me that we were falling apart."

Secondly, the band had been touring fairly constantly and, during the course of recording, their gruelling summer residency at Max's Kansas City took its toll on Lou's voice. As a result, the group were forced to let Doug Yule sing lead once again on several tracks. Morrison explained: "We either had to stop the production or let Doug take over. But no one preferred to have Doug sing." The result, according to Reed, was that "the sense that the songs were handled and interpreted in got changed", because Yule didn't understand Reed's sense of humour on songs like 'New Age' and 'Sweet Nuthin'.

Worst of all, the group lost Moe Tucker. Though she gets a credit on the sleeve of *Loaded*, she was actually absent throughout recording from March onwards, because of her first pregnancy; her daughter Kerry was born in June. Sesnick insisted that the band not wait for Moe's return, but go ahead and record without her – something Yule later admitted the band should have vetoed. Tucker was replaced on drums for the sessions by Yule's younger brother Billy, who was still at school and who had never heard the Velvets play live until he actually joined them onstage at Max's (his conventional playing style was dismissed by Tucker as "too normal"). The album sleeve credits "percussion assistance" to session drummer Tommy Castanaro and engineer Adrian Barber, and Doug Yule also claims to have played some of the drums.

To this day, Tucker is annoyed that she didn't get to play on the record. Had she been there, she might have been a calming influence. One had certainly been needed, because of their fourth major problem: manager Steve Sesnick. Sesnick had been pushing Reed to become more of a showman, and Morrison later complained that Reed had started to adopt clichéd rock posturing in his live performances. At the same time Sesnick had also been encouraging Doug Yule to take a more prominent role in the group. Whether he intended it or not, the result was that Sesnick drove a wedge between the two. With Tucker elsewhere and Morrison seemingly uninterested, Reed felt not only betrayed by the people he had relied on as allies (who appeared to be conspiring against him), but totally isolated as well.

Lou himself was in rougher shape than his voice. Apart from his paranoia about the band situation, his relationship with Shelley Albin had finally come to an end in the spring of that year. She'd become pregnant by her husband, and had consequently broken up with Lou – this time for good. Most witnesses blamed Lou's obviously distraught mental state on drugs, but according to Morrison, Reed was drug-free at this point; he was, however, experimenting with strange diets and sleeping hardly at all, which may well have exacerbated his paranoia.

Reed told Tucker that he'd been levitating several feet above his bed while trying to get to sleep. According to Geoff Haslam, everyone in the studio was aware of Reed's frailty. Lou later squarely blamed Sesnick for what was to follow, claiming the manager had "destroyed the group. He took two or three years, but he destroyed it and made it so it wasn't fun any more, so I quit."

Moe Tucker later placed more blame on Doug Yule than on Sesnick, recalling that

THE STORY **FALLING APART 1967–1970**

when Doug had joined the band "we all thought he was great – a great guitar player, bass player, singer. But within a year he'd become an asshole". Yule had a tendency to put himself forward, creating guitar parts for songs (to the annoyance of Morrison) without being asked to.

Tucker couldn't understand why Reed put up with this, and thinks Yule was the main reason for Reed's eventual departure, not Sesnick. "But, yes, the moment Lou was gone, Steve clearly picked out Doug as the next 'star'. He took over the vocals and started writing some songs. There seemed to be a lot of ego-petting. Maybe he felt Doug would simply be a lot easier to manipulate."

The atmosphere in the studio must have been pretty terrible. Sesnick even briefly brought in John Cale, in an attempt to reignite former glories, a fact which didn't even surface until 1995 (see *Peel Slowly And See*). This would probably only have increased Reed's paranoia, but Yule thinks it entirely possible that Cale's part might even have been recorded without Reed's knowledge. The situation grated upon Reed, particularly towards the end of their residency at Max's Kansas City: "I never in my life thought I would not do what I believed in, and there I was, not doing what I believed in, that's all, and it made me sick."

On 23 August – the same night that Brigid Polk made the cassette recording of the Velvets that would later appear as *Live At Max's Kansas City* – Lou Reed quit the band. Moe Tucker had come to see her old band in action several nights before. "I didn't hate it," she later said, "but it wasn't the Velvets. To me, there were only two Velvets there, Lou and Sterling. And it didn't work. It was a nice, tight little band. But it wasn't the Velvets." After the show, Lou told her

of his intention to quit the group: "I was heartbroken. But I knew something had gone terribly wrong, that he had to leave in order to survive the thing." She tried to persuade him to reconsider, but Lou's mind was made up.

After his final gig, Reed called his long-estranged parents and asked them to come and get him. When he introduced them to Sterling Morrison, the guitarist was baffled, and knew *something* very strange was occurring – but he would officially hear the news later from Steve Sesnick: "He said, 'Lou's gone home and quit the band.' We finished the week at Max's without him." And that was that. Reed's later comments seem to indicate that Sesnick had smelled impending success with the new record, and was greedily pushing the group places Reed wasn't too sure he wanted to go. Shortly afterwards he said: "I gave them an album loaded with hits, and it was loaded with hits to the point where the rest of the people showed their colours. So I left them to their album full of hits that I made." Sesnick selected the rear cover photo – of Doug Yule alone, presumably to indicate that he was now of far more importance to the band than Reed.

Loaded's release

The following month, *Loaded* was released – though Lou Reed had had no say in the running sequence, and was far from pleased with the production and mixing, citing in particular the "severe" editing of 'Sweet Jane' and 'New Age'. To his ears, the finished product was concrete proof of a "conspiracy" against him. But Sterling Morrison later defended the mixing, and the engineers involved: "*Loaded* is incomparably the best mix

DEAD STRAIGHT GUIDE TO **THE VELVET UNDERGROUND 65**

THE VELVET UNDERGROUND

of any of our albums. Lou had no control over the mix, and if Geoffrey Haslam and Adrian Barber were involved in such a 'conspiracy', why did the work come out sounding better than anything else?"

Ironically, despite all the obstacles stacked against it, *Loaded* is a bright and breezy collection of outright pop songs, and easily the most commercial record the Velvet Underground ever made. And it paid off – the record even got radio airplay, and reviews were uniformly positive. Lenny Kaye wrote in *Rolling Stone*: "Easily one of the best albums to show up this or any other year."

All of this Lou Reed must have found bitterly ironic. Worse, the album sleeve credited "song composition" to Reed, Morrison and Yule, and "lyrics" to Reed and Yule, crediting Reed last each time (almost certainly another Sesnick decision – he had asked Yule which songs he had in any way helped with). Lou Reed later sued, claiming the songs were entirely his work; he (eventually) won back the rights to them and legally freed himself from his management contract with Sesnick. But he was denied control of the 'Velvet Underground' name, enabling Sesnick to continue using it long after the event. Doug Yule later stated that Lou "was doing the writing. I was arranger, musical director. I was handling my half, he was handling his. Many said Lou was the Velvet Underground, and in a sense that it was his brainchild. He was the main force behind it, but it was a band, and like any band its totality is made up of all its members, not just one person with side musicians."

As Sterling Morrison later pointed out, "Lou really did want to have a whole lot of credit for the songs, so on nearly all of the albums we gave it to him. It kept him happy. He got the rights to all the songs on *Loaded*,

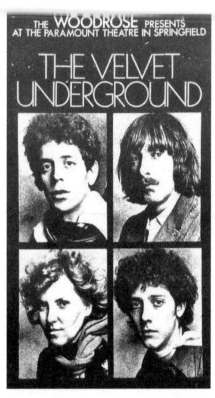

Poster for a 1970 Velvet Underground gig at the Woodrose

so now he's credited for being the absolute and singular genius of the Underground, which is not true. There are a lot of songs I should have co-authorship on, and the same holds true for John Cale. The publishing company was called Three Prongs, because there were three of us involved. I'm the last person to deny Lou's immense contribution and he's the best songwriter of the three of us. But he wanted all the credit – he wanted it more than we did, and he got it, to keep the peace."

I'M SET FREE
The Solo Years 1970–1987

4

"Very few people can leave a group and survive"

LOU REED, 1996

I'M SET FREE

4

The Solo Years 1970–1987

While Cale and Nico had already begun their post-Velvets solo careers – and already achieved some degree of success – for Lou Reed his departure was cathartic, and involved a great deal of artistic frustration and heartache. This was made all the worse for Reed by the fact that his former bandmates were continuing to tour as the Velvet Underground.

The 'Velveteen Underground'

"It was a process of elimination from the start," Lou would later claim. "First no more Andy, then no more Nico, then no more John, then no more Velvet Underground." But Reed's departure was not *quite* the end of the Velvets as a functioning (if dysfunctional) band. The remaining trio played out the rest of their residency at Max's Kansas City, adding Walter Powers on bass (from Doug Yule's old band Grass Menagerie), then continued to tour. Sterling Morrison stayed on for another year, during which period Moe Tucker also returned to the Velvets' drumstool.

Morrison finally quit in August 1971 upon being offered a job as a teaching assistant at the University of Texas, which would also enable him to finish his PhD; he learned he'd got the job while playing some gigs in Texas, and announced at the airport that he wouldn't be getting on the flight back to New York with the rest of the band.

With Morrison gone, Doug Yule attempted to keep the Velvets going by adding Willie Alexander (also from Grass Menagerie) and continuing to tour. Moe Tucker stayed on board, basically because she "didn't feel

like getting a job". Danny Fields nicknamed this version of the band "the Velveteen Underground".

The line-up toured Europe, Tucker tagging along because she thought it might be her only chance to see England. She took her baby daughter Kerry with her on the road, and quit the band at the tour's end at least partly because she felt that they were "cheating the people" by using the Velvet Underground name. She was replaced by Billy Yule. George Kay, Billy's bandmate from Red Rockets (a group put together by Sesnick) also joined on bass. This line-up toured and made studio recordings of at least two tracks – 'Friends' and 'She'll Make You Cry' – but these were never released. Instead, Steve Sesnick supposedly persuaded Yule to break up the band and record an album entirely by himself, though still using the Velvet Underground name.

Yule has since been criticized for this, but has subsequently pointed out that he was still very young at the time (24), and that he simply went along with whatever his manager suggested. The album, titled *Squeeze*,

THE VELVET UNDERGROUND

was recorded in London in the summer of 1972 and featured only Yule, plus session drummer Ian Paice (of Deep Purple) and an unidentified female vocalist (thought to be possibly Yule's girlfriend).

Squeeze was due to be released in October 1972, but was delayed until February 1973 – probably because of legal action by Lou Reed over the use of the Velvet Underground name. No singles were released from the album, and it was never released in the US. Yule did play some American gigs with a band consisting of some of the other 'Velveteens' in 1973, but according to him, these gigs were never supposed to be billed as the Velvet Underground. When he discovered that they were, Yule decided to call it a day. The last gig took place in Vermont early that year.

Doug Yule

Both Yule brothers subsequently quit the music business. Doug Yule was dragged out of retirement by – of all people – Lou Reed, who recruited him to play on his 1974 album Sally Can't Dance, and also to tour Europe with him the following year. In 1975 he played on Eliott Murphy's album Night Flights, before joining a countryish band called American Flyer, with whom he recorded two albums – American Flyer and Spirit of a Woman – in the late Seventies. After that he retired, busying himself with fatherhood and his own cabinet-making business. On occasion he still played music for fun, jamming with friends, and with his brother Billy (about whom little else is known).

Maureen Tucker

Maureen Tucker got married to her boyfriend Steve sometime in the early Seventies. She

moved to Phoenix and had another four children after Kerry: Keith, Kate, Richard and Austen. She also worked for decades as a computer operator, resurfacing musically in 1980 with a single, a version of 'I'm Sticking With You' she'd recorded with Jonathan Richman six years earlier. She followed this with a cover of Chuck Berry's 'Around and Around', and then a solo album, Playin' Possum, in 1981 (on which she played all the instruments). The following year she began to occasionally play live. She and Steve divorced in the early Eighties.

In 1985 Moe travelled to New York to be interviewed for the South Bank Show, in the course of which she was reunited with Morrison, Cale and Reed for the first time in over a decade. That year she released another EP, Another View, and she continued to perform live in concert over the next few years.

Sterling Morrison

After Sterling Morrison finally left the group in 1971, he returned to full-time academia, teaching English Literature at the University of Texas in Austin while studying for his doctorate in Medieval Literature. He married a girl named Martha that both he and Moe had known since childhood. Sterling and Martha had two children, Tommy and Mary Anne. In 1972 he declined an invitation from Lou Reed to hitch up with him in a new band. "Maybe I should have done it," he admitted years later.

Instead, Morrison worked away on his PhD, writing a dissertation entitled 'Historiographical Perspectives in the Signed Poems of Cynewulf.' Once that was completed and he'd gained his PhD in 1986, Morrison then commenced an improbable-but-true new career as a tugboat captain

4

on the Houston Ship Channel. He'd been occasionally working on tugboats as a deckhand since the mid-Seventies; in the Eighties he got himself licensed as a master mariner and then certified as a tugboat captain. According to Martha, it was a job he really enjoyed, even though the work was really hard. However, the waterway Sterling sailed every day was an extremely polluted one – to the point that it once actually caught fire – and John Cale for one suspects that exposure to this may have been the cause of Morrison's eventual cancer.

After the Velvets, Morrison occasionally played live with local bands in Austin, most notably with a band named the Bizarros, which he briefly joined. When that failed to work out, Morrison simply stopped playing music outside of his own house. "I didn't want to play with anybody else. So I didn't," he explained in 1990. However, he did join John Cale onstage for some encores when the latter played Austin – and in the late Eighties Moe Tucker persuaded him to join her onstage with her band for the occasional gig. Morrison evidently enjoyed it, and began to tour with her.

Nico

Her album *Chelsea Girl* had largely been ignored by the critics. And so the blonde who always wore white reinvented herself in black, dressing "like a Russian" in the heavy leather boots that now became a permanent part of her wardrobe. She became a vegetarian, dyeing her hair with henna and surrounding herself with candles (Warhol maintained that a candle shop on Nico's block would be a good business proposition). She became a kind of prototype Goth, but according to her sometime roommate Viva,

she was not the cleanliest of people – Viva accused her of smelling "like a pig farmer."

Although Nico was weary of her own beauty and the way others reacted to it, the changes she now initiated were more than just cosmetic. Much to everyone's amazement, she now proved herself to be an inventive and intriguing songwriter, creating on her Indian harmonium what critic John Rockwell described as "dirge-like songs full of girlish Gothic imagery and a spacey romanticism". Nico's poetry – and her life – would from now on follow what John Cale defined as "a solitary dream."

She managed to get a record deal with Elektra, recording *The Marble Index* in October 1968. The label suggested that John Cale be brought in as an arranger; in the end, Cale did the bulk of the actual work, although Elektra's house producer Frazier Mohawk was nominally the album's producer. Cale and Nico had had a very brief affair in early 1967, and perhaps because of this were able to transcend the problems posed by Nico's impossible timekeeping and general unreliability, and forge a solid working partnership. According to Cale, Nico's harmonium was "not exactly in tune with itself or with anything else", so he recorded her performing the songs solo first. He then carefully chose instruments that would fit in alongside, and used vari-speed tape effects to make it all hang together. Cale spent four days arranging, recording and mixing the album, and when Nico heard it she cried, because of the beauty of what they had made together. The crying/fighting cycle would repeat itself with every album they made together from then on, and sometimes the fights were physical. Yet Cale would consistently praise Nico's "professional attitude" to work.

THE VELVET UNDERGROUND

4

1968 was also the year in which Nico first used heroin. She began by smoking it, but by 1970 had switched to injecting. In 1969 she met the French underground film director Philippe Garrel in Paris. The couple's relationship would last for nine years, with Nico appearing in many of his films. She also got Garrel hooked on heroin (according to him), while he in turn influenced her sense of fashion, and gave her a truly bizarre concept of what an artist should be. Their initial involvement was brief, as Nico soon returned to New York to join John Cale, who was producing Iggy Pop and the Stooges' first album. Nico promptly became involved with Iggy, a relationship which lasted for several months.

In 1970 Nico's mother – whom she had virtually abandoned when she developed Alzheimer's – died in Berlin. Riddled with guilt, Nico refused to attend the funeral, saying "If I go to my mother's grave, I will never leave it." Nico's remark proved prophetic, as her own ashes were eventually interred there; her guilt she would attempt to exorcize on her next album.

That year – after playing a few European gigs to mystified reviews – she moved in with Philippe Garrel, sharing an apartment with him in Paris. Both were now junkies. Nico also starred in Garrel's film *La Cicatrice Intérieure (The Inner Scar)*, for which she wrote the dialogue. Filmed in Egypt (in the middle of the Israel-Egypt war, to which the couple were oblivious), the film is ponderous, pretentious and dull. It received terrible reviews, but Garrel announced it would be the first in a trilogy.

Nico again went to New York, briefly, to visit John Cale, who was attempting to get her another record deal – but then she got into a fight in a restaurant, and had to leave

town in a hurry. As retribution for some remark Nico found offensive she'd smashed a young black woman in the eye with a glass; the woman was supposedly a friend of Valerie Solanas and also had connections with the militant Black Panthers. Nico – scared the Panthers would seek revenge – fled back to Paris. Meanwhile, Cale did succeed in getting Nico a deal with Warners, and produced the resulting album *Desertshore*, recorded during spring and summer 1970 in New York and London. Cale was impressed by Nico's progress, both lyrically and musically, but the record received largely negative reviews.

Back in Paris, Nico claims she was walking down a street on 3 July 1971, when a black car passed her; on the back seat sat Jim Morrison, now bearded and fat. She tried to attract his attention, but without success. Morrison died that night – two years to the day after the death of Brian Jones – and Nico believed that his spirit (or a part of it) had entered into her. She also had a premonition that she herself would die in the month of July (as proved to be the case). It would seem that Nico had a breakdown of sorts shortly after her 'encounter' with Morrison, as a result of which kleptomania was added to her other shortcomings. Around this time she met a 22-year-old blonde German guitarist named Lutz 'Lüül' Ulbrich, and began an ongoing affair with him – though she was still living with Garrel, who didn't seem to mind.

In January 1972, Nico was reunited with both John Cale and Lou Reed for a one-off live performance at Le Bataclan theatre in Paris. Plans to repeat the concert in London fell through, and this was the last occasion Nico and Reed would ever share a concert stage. Over the next few years Nico made two more films with Garrel: *Athanor* and *Les Hautes Solitudes* (the latter co-starring Jean Seberg,

with whom Nico had also once had an affair).

By 1974 John Cale was signed to Island Records, and he managed to get Nico a deal there as well. *The End* was recorded back-to-back with Cale's album *Fear*, and featured the same personnel (Brian Eno and Phil Manzanera). The album included not only the title track – Nico's version of Jim Morrison's Freudian melodrama – but also her version of the old German national anthem 'Das Lied Der Deutschen' (or 'The Song Of The German People'), which had been banned in that country since 1945. Though written in 1922 in the days of the Weimar Republic, the song's associations with the Third Reich

Reed, Cale and Nico at the Bataclan in 1972

were so strong that Nico would be accused of having Nazi sympathies from then on. When she performed the song in Berlin (backed by Cale and Eno), it nearly caused a riot. *Melody Maker*'s review dismissed the album as being "as miserable as ever,"

Island Records promptly dropped Nico from their roster after she allegedly made some racist remarks ("I said to some interviewer that I didn't like negroes"); Island being Bob Marley's record label, her comments hadn't gone down well. According to Lutz Ulbrich, Nico's bias was real and

THE VELVET UNDERGROUND

4

personal, springing from the fact that she had been ripped off many times by black heroin dealers (and if the tale of her teenaged rape is true, that might add another reason). After this, John Cale attempted to get Nico a record deal with another label, but failed. As a result the two argued, and relations were severed for many years. In the meantime, in late 1974 Lou Reed offered to help, even suggesting that he'd write and produce for her. He paid for an airline ticket to New York, and put her up in his apartment. But the promise was empty; instead, Reed constantly belittled and humiliated Nico, and she fled to a hotel after three days, fearful of actual violence. Cale savagely berated Reed over the phone for his behaviour.

Nico spent the next few years dividing her time between Lutz Ulbrich in Berlin (who she had also talked into becoming a heroin user) and Philippe Garrel in Paris, with side trips to Amsterdam to acquire more heroin. She'd stopped dyeing her now brown hair, and dressed totally in black. She made four more films with Garrel in fairly rapid succession (*Un Ange Passe, Le Berceau De Cristal, Voyage Au Jardin Des Morts, Le Bleu Des Ongines*) as their relationship slowly ground to an end, but she recorded no music. In 1976 she finally lost all legal claim to her son Ari, as Edith Boulogne (Delon's mother) formally adopted him as her own son. This was necessary simply to provide Ari with French citizenship; he was actually stateless up until this point, since Nico had never bothered to register his birth.

In the late Seventies Nico returned to live performance, as she began to get bookings in England on the burgeoning punk circuit, supporting bands like the Adverts and the Banshees, many of whom considered her a heroine and a pioneer (when Nico's harmonium was stolen in 1978, Patti Smith insisted on buying her a new one). Sadly, the punk audiences often felt very differently, and Nico was chased from the stage by a rain of spit and beer cans on countless occasions.

In Paris, post-Garrel, Nico took up with a group of Corsicans: photographer Philippe Quilichini, his fiancée Nadett Duget and Antoine Giacomoni. They persuaded her to return to the studio to record an album with a proper rock band – at which point the story becomes very confusing.

Giacomoni claims that Aaron Sixx of Aura Records effectively stole the tapes by bribing Nico and the studio engineer, while Sixx claims that he had an agreement to release the album but was double-crossed by Duget (who was a drug dealer), and had a legal right to the tapes. Nico then re-recorded the whole album. The upshot is that there are two versions of the album *Drama of Exile*, one released in France and one in Holland, each featuring different recordings of exactly the same songs. Quilichini and Duget died shortly afterwards in a car crash, and Nico was informed of their deaths while in hospital, recovering from heroin-related septicaemia.

On *Drama of Exile* Nico had covered Reed's 'Waiting For The Man', the subject of buying heroin being one she now understood only too well: "I find it something to occupy yourself with, running up and down the city." The search for a reliable and steady supply of the drug led her to finally settle in Britain, where imported Iranian heroin was readily available. Nico ended up in Manchester, where she was discovered by local rock entrepreneur Alan Wise. She was homeless, alone and generally messed up; Wise undertook the lengthy, difficult and somewhat unrewarding task of rejuvenating her career, as her new manager.

He sent her to New York, where she played two gigs in 1979 (at CBGBs) with Lutz and John Cale before returning to Manchester, where Wise had put together the first of her many touring bands. These were mainly comprised of young and impoverished Mancunian musicians. Line-ups changed frequently, but over the coming years included keyboard player James Young (who wrote a riveting memoir of his time with her), trumpet player Andy Diagram (later of James) and Henry Laycock (later of Primal Scream).

The biggest problem Wise faced was Nico's drug addiction. It's estimated that between 1980 and 1988 Nico performed over 1,200 gigs – a harsh pace, but Nico was by no means a high-earning act, and even with her record royalties included, Nico still spent much more on heroin than she earned. Plus, there were the problems and expenses of acquiring the drug while on the road; on numerous occasions she was cheated (with sugar, salt or scouring powder) and had to endure withdrawal symptoms. And as Wise points out, "If Nico suffered, everyone suffered."

Wise badgered Nico for years to downgrade her habit to methadone before she finally did, in 1983. She became a registered methadone addict at Manchester's Prestwich Hospital – but methadone alone was not enough, and she took to drinking beer heavily (which tended to make her violent). She also still took heroin, when she could surreptitiously acquire it, but it does appear that she was genuinely trying to quit. She rode her bike, played pool in the local pub, watched TV and slept. She was frequently bored, constantly poor, and didn't even own copies of her own albums. And heroin had caused most of her teeth to rot away.

Nico at Lampeter University in November 1985

Her son Ari returned to her life, tracking her down when he was 22. There was blame and reconciliation, and an uncomfortable intimacy (to the point where some even suspected incest), though the pair also fought frequently. As might perhaps have been predicted, Nico gave her son heroin, apparently making sure it was of the finest quality. Ari became a roadie for her – or, to put it another way, her errand boy for drugs. He left, and returned, frequently. In 1984 she went to visit him in

THE VELVET UNDERGROUND

New York, and attempted to use this break to write some songs. But nothing would come.

The following year she moved down to London, sharing a house in Brixton with fellow junkie and punk poet John Cooper Clarke (also managed by Wise). Clarke had just been through expensive rehab, but in Nico's company quickly started using heroin again. Meanwhile, Wise had managed to get her a record deal with Beggar's Banquet, and somehow persuaded John Cale to produce her once again. Nico had managed to scrape together a handful of songs, plus a couple of cover versions, and the resulting *Camera Obscura* album was far better than might have been predicted.

In 1987 Ari suffered a nervous breakdown, and was committed to mental hospital. Over the next few years he would return to hospital many times, enduring electroshock, a brain lesion and a coma. As with her mother, Nico felt responsible and guilty. No one argued with her.

Her talent aside, it's hard to know what to make of Nico. "Socially difficult," was how someone who knew her in Brixton put it. Viva called her "a helpless, adult kid." Nico

herself stated her belief, in 1983, that "a true artist must self-destruct".

Yet most of those who knew her remained fond of her, despite the fact that she was a nightmarish junkie. Iggy Pop perhaps summed her up most memorably: "I never would call her *responsible*. Nobody ever said, 'Here comes Nico. Everything's gonna be alright now!' She didn't inspire confidence, but she was a great sport. She was very cute, charming, and a hell of a lot of fun. She was a little crazy, too."

John Cale

John Cale's first paid work after leaving the Velvet Underground came in October 1968, when he acted as arranger for Nico's *Marble Index* album, at the invitation of Elektra's Jac Holzman. Over the coming decades Cale would be in steady demand as an arranger and record producer, often helping new artists to make memorable debuts.

In June 1969 Cale produced The Stooges' first album, recorded at New York's Hit Factory in two days. Nico turned up for a visit during the recording, and Iggy Pop remembers her and Cale sitting in the

ARI BOULOGNE

Ari Päffgen spent most of his childhood being raised by Alain Delon's mother (which caused the charmless Delon to sever relations with her, never to be restored). At the age of four Ari had contracted jaundice – the result, some said, of being allowed to drink the dregs of wine glasses downstairs at the Dom, while his mother sang onstage. It was also rumoured that in those days she'd rub his gums with heroin, to keep him quiet. After dumping her son on relatives, Nico rarely

visited him – and there was a period of four years when she didn't even write or call him at all. As with her Alzheimer's-ridden mother, she simply abandoned him.

After Nico's death, Ari spent his mother's royalty payments on heroin, travelled the planet and ended up homeless in New York. More stints in psychiatric hospital followed, and in 2010 it was rumoured that he had died – but apparently he is alive and well, and working as a photographer.

4

recording booth, "looking like they were in the Addams Family."

Meanwhile, encouraged by his wife Betsey, Cale had been attempting to write songs of his own, and at the end of 1968 five of his poems were published in *Aspen* magazine. In February 1969 Cale recorded the piece 'Dream Interpretations' with Tony Conrad, and the duo also reunited very briefly with La Monte Young.

In early 1970 Cale signed a two-album deal with CBS producer John McClure, on the condition that one of these records be a collaboration with the minimalist composer Terry Riley. *Church Of Anthrax* was recorded before (but released after) Cale's first solo collection of songs, *Vintage Violence*. In the end, the songs that would make up that album were written quite quickly, and displayed a real talent for epic pop. But CBS failed to market the album – its title and cover photograph both suggested that the record was in the same general vein as *White Light/ White Heat*, and CBS did nothing to alter that perception. Cale's refusal to tour in support of the record probably didn't help matters.

In the summer of 1970 Cale moved to London to finish production work on Nico's *Desertshore* album (begun in New York that spring) and there resumed a friendship with producer Joe Boyd, the man who had persuaded Warners to sign Nico in the first place (with the proviso that John Cale was producer). Through Boyd, Cale met engineer John Wood, with whom he would often work; he also played on numerous recording sessions for Boyd's stable of acts, including Mike Heron and Nick Drake. By late 1970 Cale had separated from Betsey. Reasons for the break-up seem to have been her wealth and success, and their differing lifestyles – she claims to have been completely drug-free,

and worked by day, while Cale still used drugs and had become increasingly nocturnal. He was working through the night for Sony, remixing tapes from the CBS back catalogue into quadraphonic sound (then thought to be a musical development to rival/replace stereo). Pressure and boredom drove Cale's occasional heroin use upwards, until he forced himself to go cold turkey.

In early 1971 Cale moved to Los Angeles to work as an in-house producer for Warner Brothers at the invitation of Joe Boyd, by then head of Warners' film and music department. Cale was part producer, part A&R man, listening to tapes of new bands and going to their gigs. Newly divorced from Betsey, Cale soon became involved with Cindy Wells, a.k.a. 'Miss Cindy' of the Frank Zappa-sponsored group the GTOs, who had broken up the year before. Wells was a former groupie, who had had a child with Jimmy Page in her teens. She and Cale married but the marriage was a disaster almost from the start; Cale later described it as "the most destructive relationship I ever had". After her bandmate Miss Christine died from a drug overdose in 1972, Cindy plunged into serious depression and hysteria, to the point where she was committed for mental treatment on the recommendation of a psychiatrist. Meanwhile, Cale developed new substance problems himself, this time with alcohol and cocaine.

While at Warners, Cale recorded two albums for the subsidiary label Reprise: the semi-classical *The Academy In Peril*, and the song-oriented *Paris 1919*. Despite the fact that *Paris 1919* was loaded with memorable tunes, neither album fared well commercially. Cale also produced some promising demos for Jonathan Richman's group The Modern Lovers (which included future Talking Head

THE VELVET UNDERGROUND

Jerry Harrison). In March 1973, he took the Modern Lovers to Bermuda to record a proper album, with Warners offering them not only a recording contract but a management deal as well. At this point Richman announced he no longer liked those songs and wanted to record something else instead, and the whole deal fell through. Cale did produce two albums for the Reprise label, one by Jennifer Warren and one by Chunky, Novi and Ernie (a.k.a. songwriter Ilene Rappaport).

In late 1973 Cale signed a deal with Island Records to record six albums over three years, and decided to move to London in the following spring. Just before leaving LA he recorded a soundtrack for Roger Corman's girls-in-prison romp *Caged Heat*, improvising the music on viola as he watched the movie. Cale took Cindy to London with him, but she never forgave him for having had her institutionalized, and her behaviour became increasingly erratic. Cale's drink and cocaine problems also spiralled upwards, and he was now occasionally using heroin again (one bout being prompted by a visit from Lou Reed, accompanied by his transsexual lover Rachel).

Island asked Roxy Music guitarist Phil Manzanera to produce Cale's first album for the label, and Manzanera recruited his former cohort Brian Eno to add special electronic effects, thus beginning the long-standing relationship between Eno and Cale. The resulting album *Fear* (the title track perhaps inspired by the agoraphobia Cale was suffering while trying to quit heroin again) earned rave reviews from both *Melody Maker* and the *NME*.

Several members of former Soft Machine bassist Kevin Ayers' band had also played on *Fear*, which led to a one-off gig on 1 June 1974 at London's Rainbow theatre by ACNE

John Cale in 1973

(Ayers, Cale, Nico and Eno). Ayers took the second half of the evening (with a band that included Mike Oldfield and Robert Wyatt), the other three the first half. Cale performed 'Buffalo Ballet', 'Gun' and a radical reworking of Elvis Presley's 'Heartbreak Hotel'. Cale was suffering the humiliation of knowing that Ayers had slept with Cindy the night before the concert; on the upside, performing in public did a lot for his confidence, and soon afterwards he began making plans for an elaborate solo live show in London. It was

4

to feature St Paul's Cathedral Boys Choir performing the Beach Boys' 'Surf's Up', among other things, but the plans all came to nothing. Supposedly the choir and Cale did record a reggae version of 'God Only Knows' as part of a planned album of cover versions (shortlisted were 'Eight Miles High', 'I Can See For Miles' and the hymn 'Jerusalem'), but the track was never finished and the proposed album was abandoned.

Since Manzanera had returned to active duty with Roxy Music, Cale recruited session guitarist Chris Spedding for his follow-up album *Slow Dazzle* (released April 1975) which once again garnered good reviews. Most of the album was written in the studio; although Cale had a half dozen songs up his sleeve prior to then, he'd become bored with them by the time the studio date came around – which became a recurring problem for him. Spedding and the other musicians on the album became Cale's new backing band as he embarked on major tours of Britain and France. Touring would become increasingly important to Cale – he thrived on the uncertainty of it all, and the income was vital. Live, he adopted a range of costume disguises that included ski goggles and a hockey mask (which may well have influenced the look of the villain in the *Friday The 13th* movies). Some nights he appeared swathed in bandages, looking like the Invisible Man. His performances became more theatrical and improvised, conjuring up an atmosphere of seething violence and paranoia. One night Cale broke some fake blood capsules concealed in the crotch of a human dummy, and played the remainder of the gig covered in bloodstains.

Cale had always been fascinated by gore, and even in his youth had paid visits to the local abbatoir; the fascination reached a peak at a gig in Croydon in early 1977, when Cale hacked the head off a chicken he'd killed earlier, and tossed its carcass into the audience. Half his band quit in protest.

Much of this was genuine mania, fuelled by Cale's collapsing marriage to Cindy, as well as by his own booze and cocaine intake. The couple finally parted in late 1975, after Cindy was arrested for shoplifting; Cale bailed her out of jail, and she flew back to Los Angeles for good. Cale himself went to New York, to produce Patti Smith's first album, *Horses*. When she'd first approached him about the project, Cale was unsure whether he was being offered work or asked out on a date. The first thing Cale did was to replace the entire band's instruments, since they were all out of tune. Cale worked on the record for six weeks, which he later described as "a battle". Sometimes the fights with Smith got physical.

Cale had taken on the Smith project at least partially for money; he was spending vast amounts on cocaine at the time. But Island were annoyed that he seemed to be neglecting his own career. Cale went straight from working with Smith into the studio to mix his own *Helen Of Troy* album. After several days there he had to leave to go off on tour again, and while on the road he discovered that Island were planning to release the album as it was. Cale hit the roof, and although the label allowed him to finish mixing the record to his satisfaction, his relationship with them was fatally soured by the incident. *Helen Of Troy* came out in November 1975, and Island released Cale from his contract the following year even though he still owed them three albums (though Cale would not record again until 1979). Several unreleased tracks from the

THE VELVET UNDERGROUND

Cale performing in Toronto, 1977

Island years remain in their vaults, including a cover version of 'Willow Weep For Me'.

In 1976 Cale returned to New York, where he became romantically involved with Patti Smith's manager Jane Friedman, who would also manage his business affairs. As a result, Cale missed out on the explosion of punk energy that was about to erupt in London, something he'd surely have been a part of – if only as a producer – if he'd stayed in England (both Spedding and Chris Thomas would work with the Sex Pistols). Cale toured with Patti as a solo support act, and in July played several solo shows at New York's Ocean Club, where he was visited one night by Andy Warhol. On another night, he was joined onstage by Patti Smith, Lou Reed and David Byrne of Talking Heads. He was given to increasingly bizarre drunken/drugged behaviour on the road, much of it self-destructive. Cale subsequently toured France supporting Patti Smith, and also played at London's Roundhouse – though his new American band had long hair and beards, which failed to resonate with image-conscious, leather-clad punk Britain.

Cale remained in London through the rest of 1976 and 1977, recording his *Animal Justice* EP and doing production work for Miles Copeland's Illegal Records, working with (among others) Squeeze and Sham 69. He also recorded two tracks – 'Jack The Ripper (In The Moulin Rouge)' and 'Ton Ton Macoute' – for a single, but decided not to release it as he was already bored with the songs (the first song would surface on the *Seducing Down The Door* anthology, but the second never did). 1978 was spent in more production work and also in founding a record label, Spy, with Jane Friedman and Michael Zilkha in New York. No new music was produced.

Throughout 1979 Cale toured the US almost constantly, resulting in a live album for Spy, *Sabotage Live*. One of the many guitarists Cale worked with during this time was Davey O'List, formerly of The Nice and Roxy Music. Judy Nylon also joined the band for a while, adding her ad-lib scat poetry to the proceedings. On two different tours, Cale was joined onstage in Austin, Texas, by Sterling Morrison. Cale's songs from this era displayed an obsession with war, terrorism and global politics, and he'd also developed a passionate interest in the workings of the CIA. Cocaine-induced paranoia would eventually lead Cale to believe the agency was following him.

Spy released very few other records, but among them was a single by rock critic Lester Bangs. Cale and Friedman eventually gave up their interest in the label to Michael Zilkha, who rechristened it Ze. In late 1979

4

Cale broke up with Friedman after four years together, having accused her of mismanaging his affairs, something he later learned was untrue. In October he demoed two new songs with David Bowie, which remain unreleased; Bowie joined him onstage at a benefit concert in Carnegie Hall, playing violin on a version of 'Sabotage'.

Early in 1980 Cale became involved with Risé Irushaimi, an actress and art gallery worker he'd met at CBGBs. The couple were soon living together, and married in October 1981. Through Risé's sister Judy (who was involved with Chris Spedding), Cale met Sylvia Morales (later to become Mrs Lou Reed), and had a one-night stand with her – which probably didn't help his relations with Lou Reed in years to come. Professionally, things weren't going that well. Cale's next album *Honi Soit* attracted mixed reviews; the one after that, *Music For A New Society*, got great reviews but zero sales. By now Cale's drink and drugs problems had become extremely serious, and though Risé stayed with him she was undoubtedly worried about him – especially after witnessing the occasion when Cale swapped his guitar for cocaine. In 1983 Cale's father died, and he was deeply affected.

The following year Cale released a below-par studio album, *Caribbean Sunset*, and a weak live album, *John Cale Comes Alive*. On a European tour in February 1984, he collapsed while in Berlin and the doctor who treated him (with a massive injection of vitamins) warned Cale that if he persisted in his substance abuse, it would soon kill him. Between 1984 and 1986 the Cales were also victimised by a deranged female stalker, who physically attacked Risé and made countless nuisance calls. Eventually Cale was able to have her successfully prosecuted.

Travelling to London in spring 1985 to produce Nico's *Camera Obscura* album Cale found himself surrounded by numerous junkies, and was soon using heroin again himself. He next recorded an album of his own at the same studio, *Artificial Intelligence*, which was co-written with cult journalist Larry 'Ratso' Sloman. The record didn't go down that well with the critics or the public, but Cale liked it. Even so, the process of recording it had left him "physically and emotionally exhausted."

Although Cale had received a fair amount of critical acclaim throughout his solo career, commercial success eluded him, and he had remained determinedly maverick. As critic Mary Harron once observed, throughout Cale's solo career he had "not simply avoided success, but tried to throttle it with both hands." This was at least partly due to Cale's drink and drug problems, but the birth of his daughter Eden in July 1985 planted the seed for a realization that the time had finally come to sober up. It would take many months to bear fruit – during which Cale recorded another album, *Even Cowgirls Get The Blues* – but he eventually gave up drugs and alcohol for good in early 1986.

He began playing squash regularly, underwent a course of Interferon injections to combat liver damage (as Lou Reed had also done several years earlier) and began to repair himself. Cale took a year off work to be a full-time father, and decided to avoid touring for a while. Instead, he worked on classical pieces on his home computer, many of which would later appear on record from the French label Crepescule. Some were soundtracks for films (including a contribution to the soundtrack of Jonathan Demme's film *Something Wild*); others were commissions from dance companies. After

THE VELVET UNDERGROUND

decades of chaos, John Cale was finally putting his house in order.

Lou Reed

After Lou Reed quit the Velvet Underground in August 1970, he went to live with his parents in New Jersey, and spent the next year "realigning" himself. He was broke and depressed, and when he suggested to Sterling Morrison that they reform the Velvets without Yule, Morrison turned him down. To many, Reed seemed confused, and possibly on the brink of a nervous breakdown. It was, as he'd describe it shortly after, a time of "exile and great pondering."

He did, however, successfully sue to establish copyright ownership of some of the Velvets' songs (but failed to acquire the rights to the name the Velvet Underground). He was working as a typist in his father's accountancy firm for $40 a week, and had seemingly given up on music completely. Instead, he developed aspirations of becoming a writer instead. He wrote poetry for *Fusion* and *Harvard Graduate* magazines, and even took part in a poetry reading at St Marks Church on the Bowery (where he was joined in the pulpit by John Cale). But Lou's material went down badly, seemingly too sincere and personal to gain the approval of a hip crowd that included Gerard Malanga and Patti Smith. Lou licked his wounds and retreated back to his guitar.

During this period Reed also started seeing Bettye Kronstad, a 20-year-old English student at Columbia University with acting ambitions, whom he'd met through Lincoln Swabos. Lou pursued her casually for over a year, and they started dating seriously after he moved to Long Island.

Lou Reed makes his mark.
Lou Reed, supermusician and legendary city poet. On his own now, with a new album "Lou Reed" LSP-4701.
Songs and secrets from the phantom of rock

RCA's advert for Lou Reed's debut album

They'd soon begin living together, and soon after that she became his first wife. But she was aware from the start that Lou drank heavily, and although he didn't seem to be using drugs at that time it wasn't long before he started using cocaine again, and that would soon be joined by valium, speed and heroin. Bettye warned him she'd leave him if she ever saw him using a needle.

They briefly shared an apartment on East 73rd Street with *Rolling Stone* writer

Ed McCormack and his wife Jeannie, but according to Bettye this arrangement came to an end when a drunken Lou suggested they all have a foursome. After that, Lou and Bettye got their own apartment on East 78th Street and were mostly happy, despite Reed apparently being controlling, competitive and insecure.

Meanwhile, Lou was still writing songs, and taping acoustic demos at home. Having heard these tapes, Lou's friends Lisa Robinson (a rock critic) and her husband, record producer Richard Robinson (who had worked with the Flamin' Groovies, among others), persuaded Reed that he should start making records again. They introduced him to RCA's A&R man Dennis Katz, who had signed David Bowie to the label, and who duly came up with a record contract offer. Lou Reed was to make two albums, the first with Richard Robinson on board as producer. Within a year, Katz – brother to Steve Katz of Blood, Sweat and Tears – would leave the label to become Reed's manager. Reed described his new material as being "all love songs", and he rehearsed it by taking it on the road, backed by a high-school garage band from Yonkers, the Tots. Reed thought them competent but too ugly. At Lou's insistence Bettye went on the road with him – as she would throughout their relationship

The album would be recorded in London, since at that time British studios and engineers were thought to be not only more adventurous and more technically advanced than their American counterparts, but also cheaper. So in December 1971 an enthusiastic Lou – accompanied by Bettye and the Robinsons – arrived in London. Recording commenced at Morgan Studios a few weeks later with a motley collection of session musicians – partly because Reed was having to settle for whoever he could get. No one could have really expected Reed to come up with his best work in those circumstances – and the Velvets' stunning *Loaded* was a particularly hard act to follow – but even making these allowances, Reed's first solo album was a huge let-down for performer and audience alike. RCA Records were allegedly horrified when they heard it.

After completing the album, Reed flew to Paris to reunite with John Cale and Nico for a gig at the Bataclan Theatre in Paris, rehearsing for several days beforehand. Afterwards, he allegedly suggested to the others that they form a new band, but they also turned him down. It was perhaps, an indication of how desperate he'd become that he'd even asked them. When *Melody Maker* asked about the chances of a Velvets reunion, Reed replied, "You couldn't recreate what went on then. It's dead." Plans to repeat the Bataclan concert in London came to nothing.

Lou was aware that something drastic had to be done. *Lou Reed* was released in May 1972 and bombed commercially, to the point that there was serious talk at RCA of dropping Reed from the label. Then David Bowie entered the picture. Another RCA artist, at this point Bowie was the hottest rock act on the planet, riding high on the success of his *The Rise And Fall Of Ziggy Stardust* album. His offer to act as Reed's next producer undoubtedly persuaded RCA to give Reed another chance.

Interviewed in 1997, Bowie praised Reed's generosity towards him, and admitted to being a little awed by Reed's back catalogue and his talent for lyrical economy when they first met. The admiration was

THE VELVET UNDERGROUND

4

seemingly mutual: Reed later spoke of their creative simpatico, and said that their collaboration "reminded me of when I was with Warhol." High praise indeed, since Reed has always given Andy Warhol due credit for his input on the Velvets' early career (and beyond). But it wasn't all smooth sailing, with both parties given to moods and tantrums in the studio. Still, most people would agree that the results more than achieved Bowie's stated ambition for *Transformer*: that it should be "a *memorable* album, that people wouldn't forget."

Marrying Reed to the English glam-rock scene seemed to make a lot of sense, although Reed was tougher than the English glam dandies, and possessed of New York grit and streetsmarts. But Reed was obviously aware of the fact that Bowie had gained enormous press coverage with his admission of bisexuality – and he was willing to play the controversy card himself, for all it was worth. Responding to a journalist's query as to whether his boss was 'bi', one of Reed's roadies once gave the eminently quotable answer: "Bi? The fucker's *quad*!". Since alternative sexuality was now fashionable, this was the time to exploit his own.

Much of the work of arranging the album was done by Mick Ronson, to whom Reed would first play the songs on an acoustic guitar. Reed himself played very little guitar on the actual album – in fact, he'd play very little guitar on any of his solo records until 1975's *Coney Island Baby*. Reed found Ronson's Hull accent impenetrable; he was thus somewhat bemused the first time Ronson removed Reed's out-of-tune guitar and started tuning it. Ronson in turn later admitted that some of Reed's more artistic explanations of his lyrics went

straight over his head.

When the finished *Transformer* was released in August 1972 Lou was seemingly overjoyed with the results, and showered praise on his collaborators, saying of Bowie simply: "The kid's got everything... *everything.*" But later on, he'd be deeply resentful that David Bowie received much of the credit for the commercial and artistic success of *Transformer*, and would bitchily dismiss Bowie's input. The Reed/Bowie relationship would have its ups and downs, but this wouldn't be the end of it.

The album became a hit and, even more surprisingly, the single 'Walk On The Wild Side' made the top ten in the charts. In less than a year Reed had gone from abject failure to having the biggest success of his career. He and Bettye celebrated by getting married in December – though neither his parents nor hers attended the wedding – and spent a honeymoon in Jamaica. The man who was selling sexual ambivalence to the world was at this point happily married to a woman. At Lou's insistence, Bettye went with him when he started touring again; to keep herself sane, Bettye took on the roles of stage direction and lighting person, while trying – without much success – to keep Lou away from the bottle. Having had a massive hit in 'Walk On The Wild Side', he was struggling to cope with its success and the shadow that it cast.

Since his position with RCA was now much stronger, Reed flexed his muscles, refusing to work with Bowie again, or to simply repeat the *Transformer* formula for his next album. Instead, he apparently reached an agreement with RCA over his next project, *Berlin*, which was originally conceived as a double-album: in return for complete artistic control over this 'serious'

4

album, Reed would subsequently deliver two further 'hit' albums. One was to be a live album, the other a studio album in the *Transformer* mould, as consciously commercial as he could make it. But with *Berlin* he would make no compromises.

Berlin was to tell the story of the disintegrating relationship of Jim and Caroline, two American junkies living in Berlin. The fact that the story ended in suicide meant that everyone knew in advance that this wouldn't exactly be cheery. Many thought the character of Caroline was modelled on Nico (and there are certainly some biographical elements that match), but Reed wasn't saying. Nico would later claim Reed "wrote me letters saying *Berlin* was me." For his producer, Lou chose Bob Ezrin, a 24-year-

old Canadian who'd masterminded Alice Cooper's successful career turnaround. Though Reed would later claim that the album was already mapped out, according to Ezrin, Reed only had a few fragments ready when they first met. Ezrin suggested Reed strengthen the storyline and approach the project as if it were a film. There was even talk of making the album the basis for an actual movie at some point, with Reed having Roman Polanski in mind to direct, but it came to nothing. Once the songs were written, Ezrin worked on orchestral arrangements with the help of fellow Canadian Allan Macmillan. Unusually, no violins were to be used in the string section; instead, Ezrin substituted violas and cellos, to evoke "a Kurt Weill/Bertold Brecht atmosphere which would suit the

DAVID BOWIE

David Bowie had been a Velvet Underground fan ever since his manager Ken Pitt had visited the Factory in 1966 and had returned to Britain with an acetate copy of the Velvets' first album ("I'd never heard anything quite like it – it was a revelation to me"). The influence showed on Bowie's 1970 album *The Man Who Sold The World*, and the following year's *Hunky Dory* had contained not only a song about Andy Warhol, but also a Velvetish pastiche song, 'Queen Bitch', dedicated to the "VU". In 1972 Bowie leapt from being a cult figure to being a superstar, as his *The Rise And Fall Of Ziggy Stardust* album propelled him into the pop stratosphere overnight, and gained him an enormous teen following.

Bowie decided to expand into record production, and who better to start with

than one of his heroes? He and Reed had already met several times, and had got on well (it probably didn't hurt that Bowie had publicly called Reed "the most important writer in rock and roll in the world"), so when Bowie offered to produce Reed's second solo album, both Lou and RCA readily agreed. This might not have been an entirely selfless act on Bowie's part. According to his ex-wife Angie, "David was very smart. He'd been evaluating the market for his work, calculating his moves and monitoring his competition. And the only really serious competition in his market niche, he'd concluded, consisted of Lou Reed and – maybe – Iggy Pop. So what did David do? He co-opted them. He brought them into his circle. He talked them up in interviews, spreading their legend in Britain."

THE VELVET UNDERGROUND

Poster for Lou Reed gig, 1973

Ezrin confessed, "all of us were messing around with things we shouldn't have been messing around with." Specifically, Lou was drinking "constantly", by his own admission, and also using valium and methedrine, while Ezrin himself was using heroin (which he'd discovered in London). Reed and Ezrin were also putting in 14 and 20 hour-long days while working on the record, and came close to psychological meltdown as a result.

When the tapes were finally delivered, RCA were appalled by what they heard. While Reed was holidaying in Portugal, Ezrin was summoned to a meeting and informed that they would not release the record as a double-album. Ezrin was instructed to cut the hour-long record's length by fifteen minutes so that it could be squeezed onto one vinyl disc. Ezrin refused to cut any of the songs and since the album sleeve and booklet had already been printed, that wasn't really an option anyway. Instead, Ezrin trimmed the tracks, cutting 14 minutes "of endings, solos, interstitial material, digressions inside songs". Soon after making the cuts, Ezrin was hospitalized following "a heroin rebound". The album was mastered in Ezrin's absence by Jack Richardson and Paul King in Nashville.

Understandably, Reed hit the roof over the fact that his work had been mutilated without his even being consulted. When the record finally came out it received almost universally bad reviews, *Rolling Stone* calling it "patently offensive". Reed pointed out that adults liked the record, even if younger listeners had trouble relating to it. It didn't matter. Sales were terrible – it stalled at No 98 in the charts. "I knew I wasn't writing for a majority," Lou would

lyrics."

The album was recorded in June 1973, shortly after Lou was briefly arrested and detained in Miami for publicly performing a song that referred to oral sex. Meanwhile Reed's marriage to Bettye was falling apart amid stormy scenes of domestic violence, with Bettye occasionally seen sporting a black eye. According to Reed, Bettye attempted suicide during this period by cutting her wrists in the bathtub, but this seems utterly groundless.

All this seemed to mirror the lives of the fictional Jim and Caroline, which probably made it fairly difficult for Reed to deal with recording the album at all. As

comment decades later. "I was writing about pain, and I was writing about things that hurt."

But if Reed hadn't expected a commercial success, he hadn't expected a flop either; nor did any of this help his relationship with his record label. Years later, Reed stated: "There are people I'll never forgive for the way they fucked me over with *Berlin*. The way that album was overlooked was the biggest disappointment I ever faced." At this point it was as if something fundamental switched off within him, and it would take many years before it switched on again. In 1997, Ezrin proudly spoke of *Berlin* as having been "a *seminal* work, that digs deeper into the soul of the artist than any other work that had been released, certainly into the American music scene, for fifty years." Perhaps so, but in 1973, the world clearly wasn't ready for it.

Bettye left Lou shortly afterwards. Her account has it that she was furious with him for using details of her family's history in songs like 'The Kids'. Then she caught him shooting up heroin backstage, and that was more or less the end of their relationship. She flew to the Dominican Republic for a quickie divorce before, weirdly, returning for a month before finally leaving Lou for good. She eventually remarried happily, had several children, and evenutally became a grandmother.

Still reeling from the fallout from Bettye and *Berlin*, Lou Reed kept himself busy touring. Two New York dates were recorded for a live album, *Rock 'N' Roll Animal*, which proved to be a sound commercial move. Despite the album's musical quality being pretty grim, the heavy quotient of Velvets material reminded reviewers and Reed's new post-*Transformer* audience of

Reed's startling image in 1974 (above and overleaf), all black leather and bleached crew cut

his pedigree. Reviews were almost all extremely good, as were the sales: the album reached No 45 on the US charts, remaining in the Top 100 for over six months.

Image-wise, Reed now seemed to be exploiting his reputation as a bad boy – he didn't play guitar at all now, and was allegedly injecting vast quantities of speed. Having gone through a long period of being bloated and fat, he was now skeletally thin, strutting manically round the stage in chains and leather, with a severe crewcut and facial make-up that made him look like a refugee from *The Rocky Horror Show*, which

THE VELVET UNDERGROUND

he'd probably inspired in the first place, to be fair.

The image was not a good sign. Reed's next album, *Sally Can't Dance*, was written in the studio during June 1974 by a road-ragged Reed, who was also flat broke and reeling from his divorce the previous autumn. He was skeletally thin, had shaved Iron Crosses into his bleached-blond crewcut, and his use of amphetamines appeared to be out of control. Decisions were largely left to producer Steve Katz (brother of Dennis), who produced the album because most of the time Reed "was in the bathroom shooting up". Reed meanwhile became involved with Barbara Hodes, a successful businesswoman who worked in the fashion industry, and who he'd known since 1966; inevitably, the relationship didn't last for long.

Recording the album, Reed couldn't even remember the words to 'Ride, Sally, Ride' at all; Katz had to sing the song into a cassette player, then send Reed home with the tape to learn the song. But if Reed trusted Katz to come up with the goods, he hated what Katz actually produced. Though at the time Reed played along with the publicity machine, later on he got vitriolic, describing *Sally Can't Dance* as "a piece of shit". But ironically, Lou had kept the promise he'd made RCA before making *Berlin: Sally Can't Dance* became his biggest commercial success, reaching the top ten and staying on the charts for 14 weeks. Lou commented sarcastically: "This is fantastic – the worse I am, the more it sells."

To keep the ball rolling, RCA promptly released *Lou Reed Live* the following spring, drawn from the same 1973 concert as *Rock 'N' Roll Animal*. Unremarkable as this album is, it's probably better than any new live

material Reed could have recorded during this period. His live act now included him pretending to shoot up onstage; offstage he was doing it for real and was definitely not in good shape. He was hanging out with a crowd of hardcore methedrine users, barely eating or sleeping, and seemingly living on a diet of ice cream and cigarettes.

In the first week of January 1975, Reed went into the studio with Michael Fonfara on keyboards, Bob Meday on drums and, surprisingly, former Velvet Underground bassist Doug Yule. Steve Katz was nominally the producer for these sessions, but was not actually present in the studio. Five songs were recorded before manager Dennis Katz hit the roof, claiming the songs were far too negative and uncommercial. As Reed later recalled, "A lot of fighting took place. I fired him. Then, typically, there was a money crunch, so I went on tour."

When he returned from touring a few months later, Reed discovered that he was knee-deep in legal problems with Katz, and also both broke and homeless. RCA paid for him to stay at the Gramercy Hotel while he put his life back together – which gave added urgency to their demand that Reed should deliver a new album. So he gave them one, called *Metal Machine Music*. Reed was contractually obliged to deliver an album, but wasn't yet ready to record one; instead, according to Michael Fonfara, Reed "went and hooked up all these amplifiers with his guitar in his loft and got it feeding back and made that record. They were so horrified when they heard it. They said, 'Oh my God'. He said, 'This is it, you asked for product, you got it. I've lived up to my part, now you've got to release it'." A double album of electronic music created with guitar feedback was not exactly what RCA

THE VELVET UNDERGROUND

4

had been expecting.

Having made the record, Reed sold it – to RCA and to the world – as a serious piece of art. This involved a great deal of hyperbole, with Reed listing all the (completely fictional) equipment he'd used on the back of the album. He also claimed that it contained "frequencies that are dangerous... they're illegal to put on a record", and that within it there were also "symphonic rip-offs" from the likes of Beethoven and Mozart. Reed also later claimed that the head of RCA had wanted to put the album out under the label's classical division, but that he'd refused on the grounds that it would be pretentious. In fact, the record caused RCA some problems on the classification front, and Reed claimed: "They don't know how to copyright it. How do you take musical notation on it? I said, 'Look, don't worry. Nobody's gonna cover it.' I can't see The Carpenters doing their version of it."

Was Reed really serious about this? Either way, critics were divided. Lester Bangs said,

"Just because it's an amphetamine-head playing around with electronics and tape recorders doesn't mean it isn't valid," going on to call it "the greatest album of all time". But the majority of reviews were extremely negative. John Rockwell dismissed it as "sheer self-destructive indulgence".

Reed was unrepentant. He told *Creem* magazine, "They should be grateful I put that fucking thing out, and if they don't like it, they can go and eat ratshit. I make records for *me*." Today the record is generally referred to as having been years ahead of its time, and hailed as a major influence on everyone from Philip Glass to Sonic Youth, and there now seems little doubt that Reed did intend the work to be taken seriously (whatever his other motives might have been).

Mastering engineer Bob Ludwig confirmed in 1997 that "Lou was extremely interested in every detail of it, and that it be just right. There was never a *hint* that this was anything that he wasn't one hundred per cent serious about." As Reed admitted

RACHEL

Rachel (real name Richard or Ricky, last name possibly Humphries) was a sultry and inscrutable drag queen that Reed met in a bar. According to him she was "completely disinterested in who I was and what I did. Nothing could impress her. He'd hardly heard my music and didn't like it all that much when he did." Rachel was half Mexican and/ or Indian, and though she often appears extremely glamorous in photographs, those who met him/her speak of the illusion dissolving into heavy stubble at close quarters. Though Reed's relationship with Rachel was

occasionally stormy, the couple were clearly devoted to each other, and she provided him with some badly needed stability. They moved in together almost immediately; she toured the world with him, and they were virtually inseparable for the duration of their relationship (over three years). When it ended, Reed missed her terribly – then seldom mentioned her ever again. Rachel's current whereabouts are unknown, but many think she may now be dead and that she was the model for the dying character 'Rita' on Reed's *Magic and Loss*.

with refreshing honesty in 1997: "I was serious about it, y'know? I was also really stoned."

Regardless of the work's musical merit, there's no doubt at all that it was also Reed's revenge on the executives who'd insisted on cutting the length of Berlin and made Sally his biggest hit. It certainly wasn't the kind of Lou Reed record people were expecting, though amazingly it sold nearly 100,000 copies. RCA issued a statement in which Lou Reed seemingly apologised for Metal Machine Music, though he later denied he'd been involved in the apology at all, and claimed that the album had achieved "what it was supposed to do".

In October Reed finally felt ready to re-enter the studio and give RCA the album of songs they'd been waiting for. Strangely, given Lou's legal problems with his brother, Steve Katz was briefly re-enlisted as Reed's co-producer, but the arrangement didn't last. Katz later claimed that by this time Reed's drug problem was markedly worse, to the point that he had to quit the project: "I felt that Lou was, at the time, out of his mind. So I had to stop the sessions. I had someone in authority from RCA come to the studio and verify that I could not make an album with the artist – that was that."

As Katz's replacement, Reed brought in Godfrey Diamond, an engineer in his early twenties. The relationship worked out well, probably because Lou largely got his own way... though Diamond also boosted Lou's confidence in his own guitar playing. At the time Reed stressed the importance of spontaneity, writing most of the songs for Coney Island Baby on the spot in the studio.

But Dennis Katz attempted to halt the album even while it was being recorded, and Reed was served three times with three

A pistol-packing Lou Reed in 1977

separate subpoenas, as the lawsuits and counter lawsuits flew back and forth. Some of them took eleven years to settle.

But at least Lou's emotional life had reached calmer waters. He'd been involved since late 1974 in a steady relationship with a transsexual named Rachel.

Reed's relationship with Rachel is a recurring motif on Coney Island Baby. In Rachel, Reed had obviously found a muse, and his happiness and confidence were clearly evident. That said, according to

THE VELVET UNDERGROUND

4

Diamond he was also snorting crystal meth, and his suite at the Gramercy was seemingly a non-stop party. The record is a minor artistic triumph given Reed's circumstances at the time; sadly, the critics didn't agree, and it garnered largely bad reviews. It sold comparatively well, hitting Number 41 on the *Billboard* chart. Still, Reed had finally had it with his record company. In the summer of 1976 he switched record labels, moving from RCA to Arista. Lisa Robinson asked Lou what Arista could do for him that RCA couldn't. "Sell records," Reed quipped.

Two other projects from this era never saw the light of day: a book of Reed's collected poetry, to be titled *All The Pretty People*, and a musical based on the book *The Philosophy Of Andy Warhol*, for which Reed had apparently written all the songs. He'd also won an award for one of his poems – 'The Slide', about homophobia – from the American Literary Council of Little Magazines.

Reed's first album for Arista was recorded almost immediately. Most of the songs were written in the studio, and the entire album took 27 days to record and mix. Sadly, *Rock And Roll Heart* was as awful (in its own way) as *Sally Can't Dance* – and this time around it

didn't even sell.

Reed was almost constantly broke during this period, and most of his earnings went on speed. The following year Reed recorded his next album, *Street Hassle*, using a 'revolutionary' technique for stereo sound called binaural, and Reed was evangelistic about the system's 360-degree sound: "There is no stereo, there's no left and right, it's total. You've never heard anything like it in your life. And it is spectacular." The system had been invented by a German, Manfred Schünke. Reed was so enamoured of binaural recording that he would also use it for his next two albums, recording his next album, *The Bells*, in Germany with Schünke himself. Though it never caught on with the music industry, Reed still believed in the system's merits in 1990: "I do believe that binaural or virtual reality sound will eventually become the standard for recordings, replacing stereo in the same way that stereo replaced mono. While various technical problems mitigated the success of the effect, I believed then and believe now that I'd heard the sound of the future."

But *Street Hassle* was beset by problems. Reed had recruited Richard Robinson to

SYLVIA REED

Sylvia Morales was half-Mexican, an artist and designer, and part of the CBGBs punk crowd. She was also studying writing, and – according to Victor Bockris – funding herself by stripping and working as an S&M dominatrix. She met Lou in a club in 1978, and from then on the couple were inseparable. They married on Valentine's Day 1980. He was nearly 38, she was 24. The relationship was

described by some as a punk version of a traditional 1950s marriage, and Reed seemed to confirm that: "I like to look at centuries past, when knighthood was in flower, I'm still a great one for that. I think I've found my flower, so it makes me feel more like a knight." Sylvia Reed would also become Lou's manager, some of her decisions greatly increasing his commercial worth.

4

produce it but Robinson soon walked out. At the album's end Reed complained about having been "betrayed by all the evil people around me," and he included Arista boss Clive Davis, who had originally been encouraging about the project, among them. The album detailed Reed's crumbling relationship with Rachel. They were temporarily separated, and would part for good the following year, so he wasn't in a good emotional shape. Though the innovative title track showed Reed was still capable of breaking new ground both lyrically and musically, at this point his creative flow was very limited. Lou was as proud as usual, but had an unrealistic view of his position: "I'm right in step with the market. The album is enormously commercial." Actually it wasn't, and reviews and sales were both grim. Though it was definitely an improvement on the previous album, that wouldn't have been all that hard.

Reed bought time with a pretty dreadful live album, *Take No Prisoners*, and used it to produce something a little more interesting in the studio. 1979's *The Bells* showed more experimentation, but nothing that remarkable or melodic – but Reed was obviously enthusiastic, and pleased with his band. However, Arista hated *The Bells*, and Clive Davis thought it only half-finished. Once again, Reed dug his heels in and refused to alter the record at all – with the result that the label gave it minimal promotion. Reed later complained that *The Bells* had been "dropped into a dark well" by Arista. Hardly anybody else liked it either, with the exception of Lester Bangs, who called it "the only true jazz-rock fusion anybody's come up with since Miles Davis' *On The Corner* period." In 1996, asked which

of his albums was the most underrated, Lou replied: "*The Bells*. I really like that album. I think it sold two copies, and probably both to me."

Around the time Rachel disappeared from his life for good, Lou started playing the field. He was living in an apartment on Christopher Street, the hub of Greenwich Village's gay community, and was now outspoken about his homosexuality, and the fact that his love songs were homosexual ones: "I just wouldn't want listeners to be under a false impression".

In April 1979 Reed had a legendary fist-fight with David Bowie in a London restaurant, witnessed by journalists Allan Jones and Giovanni Dadomo. It started after Reed had supposedly asked Bowie to produce his next album, and had been turned down. Bowie had allegedly told Reed, "clean up your act", and had promptly been biffed by Lou.

In fact, Reed was all too aware that he had problems. A shortage of speed in New York had forced him to quit using it, and he'd become overweight as a result; he had also stepped up his already serious alcohol intake to compensate, and had simply replaced one addiction with another. In addition, he was also having financial problems. "I need money to live!" he'd yelled at Arista's Clive Davis during a gig at the Bottom Line in June 1979. In January 1980 Reed and his band flew to Monserrat, to record Lou's final album for the label. They were, according to Lou, thoroughly rehearsed and knew exactly what they were about. But Lou's new muse, alcohol, created a certain amount of mayhem in the studio, as he later admitted: "*Growing Up In Public* is one of *the* drinking records of all time... Me and Fonfara were ridiculous. We almost

THE VELVET UNDERGROUND

4

drowned in the pools that they've got there. It's not a good way to make a record. We were animals."

On a more positive note, Reed began seeing a psychotherapist and was delighted with the early results. He also acquired another stabilising influence in his life at this point, when he began dating Sylvia Morales. The couple began dividing their time between Manhattan and a house Lou had bought in Blairstown, New Jersey. They would marry the following year.

Regardless of Lou's drinking problem, *Growing Up In Public* was still the best album he'd made in nearly a decade, and – despite a lack of sales – a sign of real hope. As it turned out, that hope was not misplaced. Treated for anxiety and depression in 1980, Reed was diagnosed with bipolar disorder. And then, at the start of 1981 Reed joined both Alcoholics Anonymous and Narcotics Anonymous and generally cleaned up his act. He had badly needed to. Asked in the early Nineties how bad his addictions had got, he replied simply: "As bad as it gets." Both as a person and as an artist, Reed had painted himself into a corner; now he was "starting at square one again." Eventually Reed would give up cigarettes and caffeine as well, and he soon discovered health foods and Taoism, and new forms of physical release like Tai Chi, motorbikes, pinball, snorkelling and basketball. He also found time to play a cameo role (as a record executive) in Paul Simon's movie *One Trick Pony*, and to contribute some lyrics to *Music From The Elder*, a concept album by Kiss that was produced by Bob Ezrin.

Speaking of his drink and drug problems in 1990 Reed admitted: "It got very out of control. So, it was just obvious it had to stop. To really get a grip on my career and

be true to the talent and everything I have to have control." He had no problems in talking about the recovery process, or about drugs in general. The man who had been one of rock's most celebrated drug users evidently now held very different views: "I think drugs are the single most terrible thing, and if I thought there was anything I could do which I thought might be effective in stopping people dealing in drugs and taking them, I would do it." But although Lou had definitely given up hard drugs, it would seem he continued to struggle with his addiction to alcohol – and some believe he continued to drink even after doctors had warned him that he had liver damage. Cigarettes – and possibly marijuana as well – also remained a part of his life. He was also taking lithium for his bipolar disorder.

Regardless, his life changes resulted in Lou taking the next two years off from music. He ceased to tour, and said goodbye to his band of over five years' standing; though Reed had been happy to explore jazz and funk, he now felt he'd "carried this experiment far enough. It's not working." When he re-emerged, he'd switched record labels and had re-signed with – of all people – RCA, and his band was stripped down to a four piece with a completely different approach, which included former Richard Hell sideman Robert Quine (who Reed had admired for years) on guitar.

Lou's recording technique for *The Blue Mask* was also brand new, and largely improvised. Reed gave each of the musicians a cassette of his demos of the songs, and left them to come up with arrangements. When it came to recording, Quine later reported that they'd entered the studio "with no rehearsals. None of us had ever played together before, but it

4

All smiles: a cheery-looking Reed in 1984

just clicked immediately. What you hear on the record is totally live. There are no overdubs, except on one track... any mistakes that happen are on the record. If I take a solo, I stop playing rhythm. There is no rhythm guitar fill going underneath. It's the way they used to do things in the Fifties. I'm especially proud of that record." The two guitarists were especially sympatico. Quine was already a fan of Reed's, and had been since the days of the Velvets (his live recordings of the band would eventually be released as *The Bootleg Tapes Volume I*). The two became close friends (drummer Lenny Ferrari described them as being like "the Odd Couple"), though the relationship would eventually (and inevitably) sour.

Released just before Reed's fortieth birthday, the album's cover (designed by Sylvia Reed) was a clever pastiche of

that of *Transformer*. The album itself is variable – sometimes meandering and ragged, sometimes genuinely exciting – but mercifully the music was a lot more bluesy, accessible and exciting than anything Reed had done in years, and lyrically he'd obviously matured an enormous amount. His songs were far more confessional than anything he'd ever done, many of them seeming to fall under the general heading of therapy; the working title of the album was *Heaven & Hell*.

Reviews were largely ecstatic, which certainly helped restore Reed's artistic confidence. When critic Robert Palmer complimented Reed on the album, he was generous in sharing the credit: "It's mostly working with the right musicians." As Reed commented years later: "I was playing guitar with a *sympathetic* guitar player. A monumental bass player, Fernando

THE VELVET UNDERGROUND

4

Saunders. And Doane Perry on drums. Plus a good engineer. And I'd made some strides in the improvement of the production." This time around, his pride seemed genuine: "This is my best album to date. This one was pretty much perfect – it came out the way it was supposed to."

But if making the album had been a psychological release, it had also taken its toll as, for Reed, writing his lowlife characters was comparable creatively to method acting, and "doing those characters long enough – it gets to you. Some of those lyrics are very rough."

Sadly, with 1983's follow-up, *Legendary Hearts*, things ran a lot less smoothly: according to Robert Quine, the working title for the album was *The Argument*, reflecting the atmosphere inside the studio. Lou no longer wished to collaborate freely, but this time wanted things done his way. He took the sole production credit, and Robert Quine's guitar parts ended up being buried way down in the mix (and at times were missing altogether). Quine was angry when he heard the results, and though he remained with Reed for another two years, "things were never the same after that." *Legendary Hearts* didn't gain the attention of its predecessor, partly because this time there wasn't the same 'back from the grave' angle. Reviews ranged from indifferent to bad and sales were comparatively slim.

Next, Reed finally released his first decent live album, *Live In Italy*, recorded on the autumn 1983 tour, and quickly followed it with another studio album. Reed later stated that he'd "wanted to have fun" with

New Sensations, and had rediscovered the joys of guitar playing. Perhaps that was why he fired Robert Quine just two days before the recording sessions were due to start.

Thanks largely to the single 'I Love You, Suzanne' getting lots of airplay, *New Sensations* became Reed's most successful record in years, artistically as well as commercially. Typically, the next album, 1986's *Mistrial*, was another step backwards – a messy experiment with synthesizers and drum machines that just didn't work. Predictably, reviews were terrible, and Reed was touchy enough to dredge up his previous credentials: "It's very easy to see that the person who wrote the Velvet Underground stuff wrote *Mistrial*. It's not all that different, it's just a little older."

The previous year had seen Reed doing ads for American Express, and using 'Walk On The Wild Side' to advertise scooters for Honda, but now he was also displaying a more political side. In 1985 he'd taken part in Steve Van Zandt's anti-apartheid project *Sun City*, and in 1986 he toured the world on behalf of Amnesty International (in the company of U2 and Peter Gabriel, among others). That year he also delivered an anti-drug TV commercial on behalf of Rock Against Drugs; since the spot was aimed at 8-year-olds, Lou kept it simple: "I did drugs... Don't you." Regarding all this activity he said: "Just because I write about what I write about, doesn't mean I don't care about what's going on around me. The days of me being aloof about certain things are over." More proof would come with his very next album.

FOREVER CHANGED
The Reunion Years 1987–1993

5

"There were always conflicts, and presumably always will be"

JOHN CALE, 1974

FOREVER CHANGED 5
The Reunion Years 1987–1993

Although Lou Reed's friendship with Andy Warhol had continued long after the managerial split, relations between them worsened during the Eighties. Warhol was hurt that Reed had not invited him to his wedding, and the two had not even spoken for years. But Reed was still deeply saddened by Warhol's death, on 22 February 1987, and commented that the artist's way of looking at things still influenced him greatly. With almost poetic symmetry, it was Warhol's death that reunited Reed with John Cale once again.

Billy Name had brought them back together after Warhol's memorial service at St Patrick's Cathedral on 1 April. It was the first time the pair had met since Cale sobered up, Reed having conspicuously avoided Cale on several occasions during the latter years of his drinking. Cale had also been fairly scathing in his public comments about Reed's post-Velvets career (as had Sterling Morrison), but the two evidently managed to put that behind them, and discovered that the core of their friendship was still intact.

Later that year, Cale began working on a musical tribute to Warhol, an instrumental piece which Reed would later describe as "a mass, of sorts". Cale also toured Japan with Nico as his support act; they played together for the last time at the Palais des Beaux-Arts in Brussels. During this period Cale also became interested in the possibility of becoming an actor, taking acting lessons from F Murray Abraham and discussing a possible horror movie role with director George A Romero. Cale would eventually make cameo appearances in several low-budget independent films, and played a

villain in a 1989 episode of TV show *The Equalizer*. In May 1988 Cale contacted Reed, and asked him to listen to the work-in-progress that was his Warhol piece. The two started discussing Andy and his impact upon their own lives, and, as Reed would later put it, "the opportunity arose to do the bigger thing." After hours of discussion, the two both agreed that there was a need to correct the public perception of the artist, because of what Reed called "these evil books presenting Andy Warhol as just a piece of fluff. I wanted to show the Andy I knew."

It was also, as he later said, "a great chance to play together. Here was a subject that we both felt passionately and positively about." And so Cale's mass began to slowly metamorphose into what would become the *Songs For Drella* song-cycle, titled after Andy's nickname – a composite of Cinderella and Dracula. Reed later described the work as "a brief musical look at the life of Andy Warhol" and also "entirely fictitious." Interestingly, there's film footage of Warhol and Reed in conversation circa 1975, with Reed suggesting the possibility of a musical biography of Andy.

THE VELVET UNDERGROUND

5

Over Christmas 1988 Reed and Cale worked on the piece in a small rehearsal studio and at Reed's house. Both men had had remarkable solo careers since parting company 20 years earlier; both had also survived battles with drink and drugs and were now happily clean and sober. Cale admitted they were "bringing a lot of baggage to the project", but this time they were mature enough to work around any creative arguments that would inevitably rear up. While working on the project, added poignancy came with the news of another death in the 'family'; now Nico was gone as well.

Working on *Drella*, John Cale was "really excited by the amount of power just two people could generate without needing drums, because what we have there is such a strong core idea that the simpler the better ... Although I think Lou did most of the work, he has allowed me to keep a position of dignity in the process." The entire work is co-credited. Cale claims that both of them wrote lyrics, but Reed evidently had the final say, and described the album as being "an

NICO'S DEATH

After the death of Andy Warhol, Nico seemed to become conscious of her mortality and the need to take care of herself. She exchanged heroin for methadone, adopted a healthier diet and took up cycling. She talked of the future, and of writing her autobiography. In March 1988 she performed her last tour (Japan and Europe), as a support act for John Cale. Her final concert took place in Berlin.

Nico died while on holiday in Ibiza on 18 July 1988, having collapsed by the roadside a few hours after riding off on her bicycle. The song lyric she was working on that morning was titled 'The Last Days Of A Singer'. What caused Nico's fainting fit is unknown: possibly heatstroke, since she was wearing a heavy woollen scarf as a turban on an extremely hot day; possibly a heart attack. But what killed her was the fact that she'd hit her head on the ground. A taxi driver found her, but three hospitals refused to take her because she was a foreigner, and one with needle marks on her arms. At the fourth hospital she was diagnosed with sunstroke, and she died that night, from the after-effects of a cerebral haemorrhage (apparently not drug-related). She was 49 years old. Her body was flown to Berlin, where it was cremated; her ashes were then buried in the grave of her mother, in the Grünewald-Forst cemetery on the outskirts of Berlin. None of the Velvet Underground nor anyone from the Factory attended her funeral.

Christa Päffgen's grave in Berlin

5

excruciating son-of-a-bitch to write", at least partly because it involved dealing with his own feelings about Warhol. The results were, as John Cale observed, "an elegant piece of reporting, really. Reporting how misfits get together and create art." The instrumentation itself was kept sparse and tight: Reed on guitar, Cale on keyboards and viola, both sharing the vocals.

Drella remains one of Reed's most satisfying and mature works. Few people have ever received such a touching and intelligent eulogy as Warhol is given here, though in the course of it Reed spares neither Warhol nor himself. Throughout, Andy's own talent and humour shines through, as does Reed's evident affection for his mentor. Afterwards, Cale stated that he felt they had captured the man, but not his art.

Meanwhile, Reed was also recording his first solo album in nearly three years, for a new record label, Sire. In Sire's head, Seymour Stein, Reed found the most sympathetic executive he'd ever had to deal with. Reed had also acquired a new guitarist, Mike Rathke, who would become a long-term collaborator (he was also briefly married to Sylvia Reed's sister). The album was *New York*, a cycle of songs celebrating Reed's adopted city, warts and all. The year before, Reed had written an article for *New York* magazine that listed the things he liked (and disliked) about the city: "Freedom, endless opportunities in everything – films, Chinese culture, people, places, things – a city of wonderful, impossible mixtures and energies. The only city in the world deserving the name. What I don't like: crime, traffic, a criminal subway system, a city government that is oblivious to the plight and feelings of the poor, the minorities, the homeless... Antiquated criminal justice system, antiquated

civil service and union rules, regulations and membership, second-rate public school system." The city was a subject that he felt passionately about, and despite its shortcomings he loved the town passionately: "I can't do anything outside of New York. It's death."

Reed as protest singer was something new, but he seemed genuinely driven by anger at the city's – and the country's – decline, writing searing attacks on homelessness, pollution and racism. Reed rewrote and polished the songs on *New York* countless times, and the result is a (slightly flawed) masterpiece, an extremely mature work, and the album Reed's fans had been hoping he'd pull out of his sleeve for decades. It re-established him as a major player in the eyes of both the critics and the public, breaking into the *Billboard* Top 50. Reed's plans for a world tour to promote the album fell apart after a few dates, when he fell offstage and broke his leg, which meant that the rest of the dates had to be cancelled.

Cale, meanwhile, had been bringing to fruition a project he'd started many years before: *Words For The Dying*. Cale's original intention had been to write an opera about the life of Dylan Thomas, but this had metamorphosed into an adaptation of Thomas's poetry, although in the end, Cale found only nine poems suitable for musical interpretation. Four of these became known as the 'Falklands Suite', since they were completed during that conflict.

The work was premiered in 1987 at the Paradiso in Amsterdam and at St Ann's Church in Brooklyn, and might not have gone any further had not Brian Eno become involved. Eno signed the project up for his own record label, and offered to produce the album. However, the cost of a full orchestral backing

THE VELVET UNDERGROUND

proved a stumbling block until Eno's wife Anthea suggested they record in Russia, where orchestras and studios were much cheaper. In spring 1989 Cale and Eno duly decamped to Moscow, where the sober Cale felt somewhat isolated among all the vodka drinkers.

Lou Reed later stated that *Songs For Drella* had been "written for the stage", and that's where the work was honed. An incomplete version was first performed in January 1989 at St Ann's Church in Brooklyn; when the duo were reunited later in the year Reed had refined the lyrics, and also added the pivotal number 'A Dream', which echoed lines from Warhol's *Diaries*. In December 1989 the completed *Drella* premiered with a four-night run at the Brooklyn Academy of Music; on the last night Maureen Tucker joined her ex-cohorts onstage for an encore rendition of 'Pale Blue Eyes'.

In 1989 Tucker had quit her job as a computer operator in a Wal-Mart shipping warehouse in Tucson, Arizona, and moved to a small town in Georgia; she'd also released another album, the splendidly titled *Life In Exile After Abdication* (with Lou Reed guesting on a version of 'Pale Blue Eyes', which he considered to be the best recording of the song). That year she'd also supported Reed in concert for a few dates, and played on his *New York* album.

The day after the last Brooklyn concert, Cale and Reed performed the song cycle once again, this time in front of the video cameras, for a later commercial release. On film the duo are professional, confident and assured, with a rapport that verges on the telepathic, and where each nod speaks volumes. They would perform the entire piece only once more in front of an audience, in Japan in 1992. Meanwhile, recording the album version of *Drella* had become stressful. Having decided

not to use an outside producer, the duo argued about every little detail, and Reed – who had earlier described the project as a "hundred percent collaboration" – later implied to others that Cale had not pulled his weight, and even went so far as to try and remove Cale's name from the project.

Of Warhol, the inspiration of it all, Reed said simply and eloquently: "We miss him very much." Still, he insisted there would be no further collaborations. Cale said, shortly after the album's completion, that "working with Lou is never dull, but I wouldn't want to go through it again". But he remained optimistic: "I think we could do anything. I don't think there's a limit." Sadly, *Drella* never really received the attention it so clearly deserved. Reed stated that he'd hoped the album "would open up a whole new genre of musical biography on CD. There are so many people it would be interesting to learn about through music."

In spring 1990 Reed sang at a benefit concert at London's Wembley Stadium for the recently released Nelson Mandela; he then flew to Prague to interview Vaclav Havel for *Rolling Stone* magazine, discovering in the process that journalism was a lot harder than it looks (the finished article was rejected, but Reed included it in his first collection of lyrics).

Cale went straight from *Drella* into another difficult collaboration, this time with Brian Eno. He moved into Eno's house in Suffolk (where the pair had mixed *Words For The Dying*) and the two began work on a joint rock album – the first rock music Eno had produced on his own behalf for over a decade. There were fights and misunderstandings from the start, with Eno making arbitrary decisions to erase musical ingredients, evidently regarding himself as the sole producer. When it was done, Eno refused to tour with Cale to support its release; worse, he issued a press statement announcing that he'd never work with Cale again. That year Cale indulged his love of extraordinary clothing by becoming a fashion model for Yohji Yamamoto and Comme Des Garçons, making catwalk appearances in Paris and Tokyo.

Although *Drella* had certainly augured well for future collaborations, few (including any of the band) would have bet money that it might lead to a full-scale Velvet Underground reunion. Reed and Morrison hadn't even talked to each other in years: royalties and songwriting credits were the principal bones of contention, along with Morrison's anger at Reed for making him tell Cale he was out of the band back in 1968.

Then, in June 1990, Reed, Cale, Tucker and Morrison all agreed to attend the opening of the Cartier Foundation's Andy Warhol Exposition in the small town of Jouy-en-Josas, 20 miles outside Paris. Right up until the last minute Reed was still insistent that "you'll never get the four of us together on one stage again ... ever," and no one was sure how Sterling Morrison would react upon meeting Reed. Even so, Morrison stated that he wanted a reunion to happen, if at all possible.

On the opening day, Billy Name defused the tension with humour and Reed mellowed, inviting Morrison, Cale and Tucker to have lunch with him. Fences were mended, and that afternoon (15 June) Cale and Reed performed five songs from *Drella* in front of the audience of 300 invited guests – they were mainly journalists, "a nightmare come true", in Reed's words. And then Tucker and Morrison joined them on stage for a 15-minute version of 'Heroin'. No rehearsal,

no soundcheck, just straight in at the deep end: The Velvet Underground together again, against all expectations. Naturally, the crowd went nuts.

Afterwards, Reed was noticeably tearful. "That was extraordinary," he later said. "To have those drums behind me, that viola on one side, and that guitar on the other again – you have no idea how powerful that felt." An exhilarated Cale stated, "Three hours ago this was not possible. Now, I'm overcome with emotion." Maureen Tucker was similarly exultant, while Morrison commented simply: "Not bad. Was I in tune?"

Reviewing the event, Nick Kent wrote: "It was ample enough demonstration of a musical chemistry that still smoulders after 22 dank, mostly bitter years apart." Now the ice had been broken, and the four of them spent the next few days together and met again several times over the course of the following two years. But still no one suggested a more formal reunion, and meanwhile there were solo careers to concentrate on.

Reed's next project tackled subjects hitherto almost completely ignored in rock: death and mortality. Specifically, the *Magic And Loss* album was inspired by the passing of two people that Reed described as "two of the most important people in my life": a woman named Rita, and the songwriter 'Doc' Pomus, both of whom had died of cancer. Reed read a lesson at the memorial service for Pomus, who died in March 1991, calling him as "a wonderful writer, a wonderful man... I grew up listening to so many songs written by Doc Pomus. It was a pleasure to know him, he was a great spirit." 'Rita' was more mysterious. The album was dedicated "especially" to her, but her last name remained unknown, and Reed wasn't saying; some thought 'Rita' might even have been Rachel. Reed's former

5

lover was sighted several times around 1988 and 1989, and was said to be extremely thin, and living on the streets. Since that was the last anybody heard of her, she may well have died. Others think that 'Rita' could have been the Factory-era speed-dealer known as 'Rotten Rita' (real name Kenneth Rapp), but that seems somewhat unlikely in the context of the lyrics.

But death isn't exactly MTV-friendly and the album delivered no hits. Reed insisted that the record wasn't morbid or gloomy: "This isn't a bleak record. I'm not the only person in the world who's experienced loss – especially these days, with what AIDS and other diseases are doing. These are complex emotions... The record is like a friend talking to you. It's cleansing for the soul. That's why I think it's such a positive record, because it gives you something you can really grasp

onto. The record gives the listener something more than music. When loss enters your life, what do you do? Do you go out and get drunk? In the end you wake up, the person's still gone. You can't stay drunk forever – you've still got to deal with it."

On a more personal note, he stated simply: "I just wrote it – I didn't have any choice about it, that's why I wrote. That's all I could do at the time." He also railed against those critics who thought illness wasn't a fit subject for rock music: "You don't have anything of any depth in rock." As he pointed out, a writer has to deal with life in all its aspects: "What is there? Birth, life, death and the conflict in between." On its release, *Newsweek* called the album "the most grown-up rock record ever." Reed toured the world in support of the *Magic And Loss* album, requesting that audiences not eat, smoke, drink, talk or

DOC POMUS

'Doc' Pomus (real name Jerome Solon Felder) was born in 1925, and began his musical career as a blues singer. With his partner Mort Shuman, Pomus had an incredibly successful run of hits in the Sixties, working in New York's Brill Building; their success is comparable to Lieber and Stoller, with whom they collaborated at times. Their first major hit was 'A Teenager In Love' for Dion, and they also wrote songs for (amongst others) the Coasters, the Drifters, Fabian, Andy Williams and Elvis Presley (including 'Viva Las Vegas', 'His Latest Flame' and 'Suspicion'). In later life Pomus worked with Mink DeVille, and co-wrote BB King's *There Must Be A Better World Somewhere* with Dr John. As a result of childhood polio, Pomus spent the last 30 years of his life in a wheelchair.

The late blues and R&B singer Doc Pomus, a huge influence on Lou Reed

during his performances.

Although *Magic And Loss* was completed in April 1991, its release was delayed until January 1992, so as not to harm sales of a three-CD retrospective of Reed's solo career released that spring. Reed simultaneously celebrated his past by issuing his first published collection of lyrics, and both items bore the same title, *Between Thought And Expression* (a quote from 'Some Kinda Love'). That summer, Reed gave two public readings of his lyrics in New York.

In 1991 Cale released *Paris S'Eveille* on the Belgian label Crépuscule. Comprised mainly of instrumental music written for movies and ballet, the album also contained an unreleased Velvets track: a live instrumental of 'Booker T' from 1968. The following year, Cale's beloved mother died, which affected him greatly. His financial affairs were also still in disarray, and he soon found himself in trouble with the taxman, having moved into an expensive Greenwich Village house as well as renting a summer home in the Hamptons.

Cale buried himself in work, producing more music for ballet (including one called *Iphigenia In Taurus*), and also working on several multi-media pieces. One was *Life On Earth*, a collaboration with the musician and artist Bob Neuwirth, which would be released in album form several years later. The other (in 1993) was *Life Underwater*, a reworking of the Orpheus myth that featured a string quartet, a barbershop quartet and slides and films by independent director Zoe Beloff.

Moe Tucker made another album in 1991, *I Spent A Week There The Other Night*, which featured her playing with John Cale and Sterling Morrison on several tracks, with Lou Reed on another, and with all of them on one track, 'I'm Not'. Having managed to coax Morrison back into playing guitar again, she

persuaded him to join her band in 1992 for several tours of Europe, and one of the States. A live album, *Oh No, They're Recording This Show* came out in 1992.

When Lou Reed's *Magic And Loss* tour hit Paris, he crossed paths with Morrison and Tucker, who were also playing a gig in town – for which, Reed joined them onstage. Reed had been made a Knight of the French Ordre des Arts et des Lettres that year, and while in Paris he received his investiture from the French minister for culture, Jacques Lang.

Meanwhile, Lou and Sylvia Reed had begun to drift apart; though he'd publicly debated the issue of having children with her on 'Beginning Of A Great Adventure', he'd finally decided against it, and stopped sleeping with her. They continued to live together, and she continued to manage his affairs, but relations were severely strained as Reed tried to decide if he wanted a divorce or not. He also seemed to be in denial about his past, and allowed no one to make any references to his previous drug use or his past sexual relations with men. He had, however, begun to drink again, though this time he seemed to be able to keep it under control.

During 1992, all four members of the Velvet Underground got together on several occasions to discuss a couple of pending projects such as Sterling Morrison's proposed history of the band – provisionally titled *The Velvet Underground Diet* – and a retrospective boxed set intended to stem a tide of bootlegs. They also started informally rehearsing, to see if they could still play together with any degree of enjoyment and enthusiasm.

When Reed joked that they ought to play Madison Square Garden for a million dollars, it opened the door for discussions about the possibility of a proper, full-scale reunion. Since Lou Reed's schedule was clear for 1993,

5

THE VELVET UNDERGROUND

5

things began to roll, with Sylvia Reed setting up concert dates in Europe, including plans to make a live album and a video. Morrison and Reed joined Cale onstage during a solo gig at New York University, and afterwards Cale announced the Velvets' forthcoming reunion on *The Tonight Show*. As Sterling Morrison later told David Fricke: "It was pride that kept us apart. But it was also pride that made us do well. Nobody cares more about our legacy than we do." Within months the four of them were rehearsing for a European tour: since 80% of their record sales were in Europe, it made sense to begin their comeback there, rather than in the USA.

Three quarters of the Velvet Underground in 1992: Lou Reed, John Cale and Sterling Morrison

That the motive for the reunion may have been largely financial scarcely mattered to their expectant audience. And Morrison and Tucker both truly needed the money. Moe didn't even own a car, confessing to Max Bell: "The money aspect is like winning the lottery to me." At the tour's end, Moe was able to buy herself a house. Sterling Morrison had to take six weeks off work as a tugboat pilot in order to tour, but he didn't quit the day job. Morrison was laconically philosophical about the band's turbulent history: "It is odd the way the band just sort of dissolved, without any seeming reason. There were no big blow-

ups, no angry fights. People just ... fell off as it went along. *Lou* just dropped off. It was very strange ... and since there never was any great apocalyptic moment where we said, 'Screw it, enough is enough, no more of this', that's made it possible for us to come back, just as casually." Cale was "cautiously optimistic" that the tour would lead on to other things, hopefully including new studio recordings – but it was Lou Reed who had the best one-liner about the fact that they were reforming: "Does that mean 'reformed' as in: now we're good?"

So in the summer of 1993, thousands of Velvets aficionados of all ages (and this was a band who were *never* unfashionable) were finally able to see them live in concert. Needless to say, the gigs sold out in seconds, leaving thousands more out in the cold. After another brief rehearsal period in London, the June 1993 tour took in Edinburgh, London, Amsterdam, Rotterdam, Hamburg, Basle and Prague, where the group and their entourage (including Tucker's five kids and her mother, who'd flown in to see her play) were the honoured guests of Czech President Václav Havel.

As a student, Havel had bought a copy of the second Velvets album in New York, and then brought it back into Czechoslovakia, where taped copies of the album and hand-produced lyric books subsequently became symbols of free speech and artistic expression amongst those opposing the oppressive yoke of the USSR; even the possession of such a book could lead to arrest. Years later, when the Velvets-influenced Czech rock band Plastic People Of The Universe were later arrested for playing their music, this provided the impetus for the beginnings of the Charter 77 human rights movement. Whether this has any bearing on the fact that Czechoslovakia's

eventual peaceful transition from communism to democracy was nicknamed the 'Velvet Revolution' seems unlikely.

After Prague, the tour resumed in Paris, and moved on to Berlin and Strasbourg. The Velvets then played five stadium dates in Europe, supporting U2; they also played a brief and fairly shambolic set at Britain's Glastonbury Festival, another festival in Copenhagen and four dates in Italy.

And then it was all over. But at least the three Paris shows (at L'Olympia Theater) had been taped and filmed, resulting in a live double CD (produced by Mike Rathke) and a video. For fans who might not otherwise be tempted to buy yet another live Velvets album, incentive lay in the inclusion of the first new Velvets song for decades: 'Coyote'. The song had emerged out of their first week of rehearsals together; Cale hoped they'd create others, but Tucker and Morrison were content to simply rely on their back catalogue. As it was, they still argued with Reed about the music publishing – but Cale was still optimistic that the reunion would last and produce more work: "I hope we do. That was really the premise under which I really participated in this, and I hope it's borne out."

But behind the scenes, all was not well. Tucker and, even more so, Morrison were badly out of practice compared to the others, and playing to festival crowds was both daunting and unsatisfying. Also, throughout the tour, Lou Reed had distanced himself from the others, travelling alone and seeming to regard his colleagues as nothing more than just the latest in a long series of backing bands.

Unfortunately, tour manager Sylvia Reed was treating them the same way, considering them all second-rate compared to Lou and

THE VELVET UNDERGROUND

5

insulting them to their faces. Reed's guitar effects had caused innumerable sound problems live, and Lou's guitar technician had also treated the band badly. Morrison in particular was furious about their treatment and Morrison was a sick man, though nobody knew yet just how badly.

Hopes that there would be more concerts to satisfy the thousands who didn't get to see the European dates, perhaps even a new studio album, were dashed in November 1993 when plans for a proposed US tour fell apart in a flurry of "fax fights" between Reed and the others. Though Cale – who had learnt how to pacify Reed during their work on *Drella* – had played peacemaker during the tour, Reed's attitude to a proposed MTV *Unplugged* show (and album) had the duo clashing yet again, this time because Reed was adamant that he would only record with

the Velvets if he got to produce the resulting album. Cale pointed out the advantages of working with an outside producer, emphasizing the fact that all the top producers in the industry would be overjoyed to work with the Velvets, but Reed wouldn't budge. When Tucker tried to soothe the troubled waters, Reed sent her faxes that Cale thought were both patronising and insulting, and the Welshman finally lost the last of his patience. He sent Reed a nine-page fax telling him exactly what he thought of him.

And that was that, again. The official statement from Sylvia Reed stated that: "Lou feels he accomplished what he set out to do with the European shows ... That being done, he intends to return to his solo work." More sadly, Cale would later describe the state of play as "the end of a very fruitful relationship."

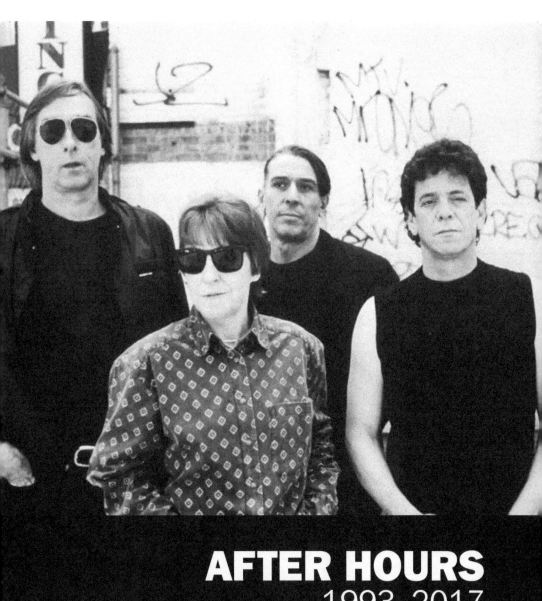

AFTER HOURS
1993–2017

6

"The Velvet Underground will never play again – not that Velvet Underground, which is the only Velvet Underground"

AFTER HOURS
1993–2005

As the Velvet Underground broke up once again, it seemed ironic that their public profile had never been higher. In December 1993 the UK's Channel 4 TV station screened an eight-hour-long tribute to the Velvets and Andy Warhol. Official viewing figures showed an audience of 400,000 – impressive, considering that the show was broadcast in the wee small hours of a Sunday morning.

Meanwhile, Lou Reed's personal life underwent a radical transformation as a result of his becoming romantically involved with the musician and performance artist Laurie Anderson (who some thought resembled the young Shelley Albin). The pair had first met at an arts festival in Munich in October 1992, and began properly dating a year later – after which point they were pretty much inseparable. Laurie was Lou's junior by five years, and the pair had much in common: both were New Yorkers, both loved art and the avant-garde and high-tech gadgetry.

Their relationship was seemingly much more romantic than any Reed had previously known. He would dedicate his next solo album, *Set The Twilight Reeling*, to Anderson, and spoke publicly about his joy at being involved with another artist, and of being with someone who understood his work and his world: "It's a great relief to have that kind of compassion and back-up available, to have someone who understands what's happening and can actually help you get through it." Reed also claimed to be working on a novel, but Anderson was obviously his main priority. She moved into Lou's new apartment on Christopher Street (though she hung onto her own apartment), and the pair duetted on 'In

Our Sleep', a track they had co-written for Anderson's album *Bright Red*. There was talk of them making a whole album in this vein, but it never materialized.

Lou adopted all the things that Laurie loved, including cycling and Buddhism, and most observers thought the relationship had mellowed and humanised him – though perhaps to a limited extent, since in his relationships with others he often remained so lacking in empathy as to appear borderline autistic.

Lou's new relationship did not go down well with Sylvia Reed, and in March 1994 she filed for divorce. Lou responded by firing Sylvia as his manager, cancelling her credit cards and other accounts, and changing the locks on his properties. Reed was also not on good terms with his record company, who were unhappy that he had blown the chance to create more Velvet Underground albums; when Lou approached them with the idea of recording an album of cover versions, they turned him down flat. Tellingly, around this time Lou's lawyer told him that he would no longer represent him.

In 1994 Lou appeared as himself in *Blue In The Face*, an independent film by the novelist Paul Auster and Wayne Wang, delivering

6

rambling philosophy while chain smoking in a cigar store. Reed told Auster that he was trying to write a crime novel; six months or so later he told Auster he'd been unable to finish it, and had been forced to abandon the project. "It was touching to see him admit failure," commented Auster.

In 1994 Moe Tucker released the album *Dogs Under Stress*, which featured Sterling Morrison playing on five tracks. Morrison also toured as part of her band for several months. The pair reunited with Cale that November, performing live as a trio at Pittsburgh's new Andy Warhol Museum, improvising soundtracks for Andy Warhol's films *Eat* and

Kiss. Reed had decided not to join them for the project. The trio had earlier recorded demos for a possible album project, plus a cover version of Jim Carroll's 'People Who Died' for Cale's *Antardida* album (with Chris Spedding on guitar). There was talk of the three of them taking the Warhol soundtrack show on a European tour in late 1995, but it wasn't to be.

The others had been shocked by Morrison's appearance when he arrived, and he was soon complaining about pain, thinking that he pulled a muscle. Over the course of the next week it became apparent that, as Moe put it, "something much more serious was

LAURIE ANDERSON

Laurie Anderson was born on 5 June 1947, and taught art history before launching herself as a performance artist in the late Seventies, at which point she was involved with the late comedian Andy Kaufman. Anderson's pieces incorporated music, poetry and the visual arts, but she might well have remained a figure known only to the avant garde had she not scored a crossover pop hit with 1981's 'O Superman (For Massenet)' single, taken from her lengthy *United States* piece. The record tipped its hat to Jules Massenet's 1885 aria 'O Souverain' while critiquing American foreign policy through a vocoder, and sold enormous quantities in Britain – with the result that Anderson was promptly signed up by Warner Brothers. The best introduction to her work is probably the two-CD anthology *Talk Normal*. Anderson became NASA's first artist-in-residence in 2003. She describes herself as "a storyteller."

6

wrong." After the show, Morrison attempted to resume work as a tugboat captain, but his condition deteriorated and he became wheelchair-bound before being diagnosed with cancer (non-Hodgkin's lymphoma).

A bone-marrow transplant failed to stop the progress of the disease, and on 30 August 1995, the day after his 53rd birthday, Sterling Morrison died, a few hours after Moe Tucker had left his side after an extended visit. How long he'd actually been ill is unknown. He does not appear to be very well in the *Velvet Redux* video, and in the sleeve notes to the live album Reed refers to Morrison's "courage". Morrison chose to spend his last weeks at home in Poughkeepsie, New York, with his family, and was also visited there by Cale and by Reed, who would later write a moving account of his visit for the *New York Times* magazine, titled 'Velvet Warrior'. Morrison told Reed that he had watched – and counted – as seven layers of skin had peeled from his body. He was survived by his wife Martha, and their children Thomas and Mary Anne.

Understandably, the others were devastated by Morrison's passing, perhaps none more so than Moe Tucker, who had known him since she was eleven. Lou Reed was also stunned, finding the loss very hard to accept: "Jesus, how is it possible? Guy worked out, never sick a day in his life. Literally. He fucking *jogged.*" He talked at length to the press about Morrison, describing his fellow guitarist's musicianship in glowing terms: "It was hard for other people to appreciate him because he wasn't flashy. But he was holding down our version of the groove. If Cale and I took off, we always had some place to come back to. Because Sterling was there." He also stated that: "No one will ever hear the four of us play again. That's really sunk in: the Velvet

Underground cannot exist."

But in a sense they still did. On 16 January 1996, the Velvet Underground were officially inducted into the Rock & Roll Hall of Fame. Reed, Cale and Tucker all attended the award ceremony at New York's Waldorf Astoria, along with Sterling's widow Martha, and performed a new song about Morrison written by Tucker only two days previously: 'Last Night I Said Goodbye To My Friend'. Introducing the song Reed says the three of them wrote it together, but Moe is given the writer's credit on her solo recording included in her solo anthology *I Feel So Far Away*. It proved to be the last performance of the Velvet Underground, and although it remains officially unreleased, it can easily be found on YouTube. Reed, Cale and Moe each sang one of the song's three verses, Reed's eyes were visibly moist, and the whole thing is incredibly moving. Even so, Reed hadn't attended Morrison's memorial service some months before, something Cale found hard to forgive.

Cale's acceptance speech at the Hall of Fame induction paid tribute to the contribution to the Velvet Underground of Nico, but no mention was made of Doug Yule. Yule had been told that if he wished to attend he'd have to pay his own air fare, and would be restricted to sitting in the audience, rather than joining his former bandmates on stage. He opted to stay at home instead.

The Velvets' retrospective boxed set *Peel Slowly And See* was finally released just weeks after Sterling Morrison's death. Reed's 1996 solo album *Set The Twilight Reeling* contained 'Finish Line', a song that was dedicated "for Sterl" containing intimations of mortality. The album had taken Reed two and a half years to complete, and many of the songs seemed to concern his relationship with

THE VELVET UNDERGROUND

6

Laurie Anderson. The album appeared on the Warner Brothers label, where Lou had been moved to from Warners' subsidiary Sire.

The previous year Reed had begun working on *Timerocker*, a stage musical with designer/director Robert Wilson, who had worked with Philip Glass on *Einstein On The Beach*. *Timerocker*, which Wilson called an opera, was performed in Germany, and then Amsterdam and New York in 1996. Reed wrote 16 songs for the project, and explained that the play was "more or less" based on HG Wells' novel *The Time Machine*. According to Mike Rathke, when Reed was writing these songs "he would go in and see a scene Robert Wilson was working on, and they'd talk about it a little bit, he'd watch it, and he'd sit down with his guitar and a pen, then he'd write the song." Plans for an album of the cast recording came to nothing, but clips of the play which surfaced in the *Rock And Roll Heart* video documentary looked truly imaginative in terms of sets, staging and costumes, and – although the New York reviews were bad – one can only hope the entire play will surface on DVD eventually.

Meanwhile, Cale had been commissioned by the city of Vienna in Austria to write an opera about the femme fatale and World War I spy Mata Hari. Twenty years earlier Cale had turned down a request from the reclusive Thomas Pynchon to write an opera based on Pynchon's novel *Gravity's Rainbow*; playwright Sam Shepherd had also unsuccessfully tried to get Cale to turn his story 'The Sad Lament Of Pecos Bill On The Eve Of Killing His Wife' into an operetta. Cale premiered an unfinished version of the Mata Hari work in Vienna in October 1995, and the performance was filmed. Cale's solo performances now increasingly featured a literary component, with readings from numerous writers including Oscar Wilde, Michael Ondaatje, Tennessee Williams, Edgar Allan Poe, T.S. Eliot and Ezra Pound. He also talked of setting some of Pound's *Cantos* to music.

Cale returned to rock in 1996 with his well-received solo album *Walking On Locusts*, which featured a song about Sterling Morrison titled 'Some Friends'. He also composed the music for a 90-minute ballet inspired by the life of Nico, for the Scapino Ballet of Rotterdam, which premiered in October 1997. Choreographer Ed Wubbe discussed the singer at length with Cale while preparing the piece.

In January 1997 Reed made a guest appearance at a Madison Square Garden concert to celebrate David Bowie's 50th birthday. The publicly reconciled duo performed four songs together, including 'I'm Waiting For The Man'. Bowie would be one of the numerous vocalists drafted in for the charity version of 'Perfect Day' later that year.

Laurie Anderson was the guest organiser for 1997's Meltdown arts/music festival in London. She invited Lou to participate, and the result was an acoustic concert, captured on the *Perfect Night: Live In London* album.

In late 1997 Cale and his wife Risé separated, though he remained close to his daughter Eden. Cale then moved into the same apartment building in Christopher Street in which Lou Reed lived; when their paths occasionally crossed, conversation was said to be strained. A year or so later Cale moved downtown, near the World Trade Center. He was now obsessed with electronic gadgets and would spend time online tracking the paths of diseases and exploring the intricacies of Chinese politics. He also found a new girlfriend, Claudia Gould of the Institute Of Contemporary Arts at the University of Pennsylvania.

6

Reed also moved home. After a lifetime of renting he invested a duplex apartment on the corner of West 11th Street and the West Side Highway. A home studio and a custom-built library were installed, along with original artwork and ceremonial swords Lou used in his Tai Chi practice. There was a view clear across the Hudson River to New Jersey, and on a strip of land by the river the couple would walk Laurie's dog Lolabelle; the apartment was also a short walk from Laurie's studio/apartment on Canal Street. But despite the domestic bliss, Lou was drinking again, though he made periodic attempts to quit.

In 1999, four CDs of recordings of John Cale's experimental music from the Sixties began to surface, the tapes having been compiled by Tony Conrad. One of these, *Day Of Niagara*, featured the entire La Monte Young ensemble; Young threatened legal action over the ownership of the copyright, with Cale and Conrad seeking credit for their co-authorship of the music. The situation seems unresolved, but the discs remained available.

That year Cale contributed soundtrack music to Mary Harron's film adaptation of *American Psycho*; he would also contribute an instrumental piece to her film about Valerie Solanas, *I Shot Andy Warhol*. In May 1999 Cale received an honorary doctorate from the University of Antwerp and in the autumn he also published his autobiography, *What's Welsh For Zen?*, to general critical acclaim. The following year Lou Reed joined him on the bookshelves with *Pass Through Fire*, an anthology of his collected lyrics.

In April 2000 saw the release of Lou Reed's *Ecstasy* album, his first new work in four years. Many of the songs described relationships in trouble, though it would seem that Reed was recalling his marriage to

Sylvia, rather than describing a rocky patch with Anderson. Though lyrically interesting, memorable tunes were largely absent – as they had been since *Magic And Loss*. Sales – and concert sales – were poor. At the Jubilee 2000 Concert in Italy, organised by Bono to focus attention on world debt, Reed performed before Pope John Paul II.

2000 also saw the return of Doug Yule to live performance – his first gigs since the mid-Seventies. He played a couple of sets for charity in his hometown of Seattle (a recording of which was released two years later as *Live In Seattle*), featuring three Velvets songs and eight new compositions from a 'song cycle' he'd been working on for several years about a couple's relationship, set circa 8000 BC. Three songs from this story had been recorded by Yule in Boston in 1999, and one – 'Beginning To Get It' – had appeared on a benefit album for adopted children, *A Place To Call Home*.

The second Yule gig also featured a set by Moe Tucker's band, and she and Yule duetted on an unrehearsed version of 'I'm Sticking With You', much to the delight of the crowd (the performance is included on Tucker's album *Moe Rocks Terrastock*). According to Lou Reed, the surviving Velvets had debated whether to invite Yule to join them for their Rock & Roll Hall Of Fame appearance, but had decided against it.

Meanwhile, Reed had been working for several years on another theatrical collaboration with Robert Wilson. *Poe-try* was based on the works of Edgar Allan Poe and opened first at the Thalia Theatre in Hamburg, Germany, in February 2001. Poe was a long-time hero of Reed's and the subject matter was something he obviously felt he could get his teeth into for a serious art project. By the end of 2002 the piece had

THE VELVET UNDERGROUND

developed into what would become a double-CD titled *The Raven*, featuring contributions from various actors including Willem Dafoe, Amanda Plummer and Steve Buscemi, and musical guests including David Bowie, Ornette Coleman, Laurie Anderson and the Blind Boys Of Alabama.

Reed called the work "the culmination of everything I've ever done," and admitted that artistically it would be hard for him to top. Critics thought otherwise, largely finding it worthy but dull. The work was once again dedicated to Laurie Anderson, "a constant source of inspiration". But Reprise – the final subsidiary label of Warners that would give him a home – hated the record, and didn't want to put it out. The release was delayed to 2003, and not given much promotion.

In September 2001 both Reed and Cale had a horrifying grandstand view of the terrible events of 9/11. Lou Reed could see the World Trade Center from his apartment, and John Cale was living even closer to it, just a few blocks away. Cale e-mailed friends a running commentary on the events outside and, when the area was evacuated, Cale moved in for a while with Claudia Gould, in a state of deep shock.

At the end of 2002 Cale mended fences with Brian Eno, when the two played together at the opening of a major Warhol retrospective at London's Tate Modern; Eno (and his daughters) subsequently made a guest appearance on Cale's 2003 rock album, *Hobo Sapiens*, which was generally well received. Cale also continued to record soundtracks for movies, including 2003's *Otherworld*, a cartoon adaptation of Welsh myths from *The Mabinogion*.

In 2004 Lou Reed released his last solo rock album, a live recording called *Animal Serenade* which marked the end of his contract with Reprise; he also had a surprise single

hit with Dab Hands' remixed version of 'Satellite Of Love', which charted in the UK. Interviewing Reed in his apartment in spring 2005, journalist Sylvie Simmons noted the presence of a well-thumbed copy of a book about Prozac and mood swings; whether or not Reed was using that medication, he was visibly smoking cigarettes again. He announced the news that the German classical ensemble Zeitkratzer planned to perform an orchestral version of *Metal Machine Music* at the Berlin Philharmonic Hall; they claimed to have actually transcribed the piece, which they later recorded. He also talked of his interest in meditation and Buddhism, and his love for macrobiotic food and Tibetan music, as well as promoting his range of specially designed eyewear, and a book of his photographs entitled *Emotion In Action*. He went on to follow it up with several other photographic books as well.

After Sterling Morrison's death, Lou had commented: "The Velvet Underground will never play again – not that Velvet Underground, which is the only Velvet Underground." These sentiments were echoed by Moe Tucker: "None of us would want to perform as the Velvets without Sterl". Even if that aspect could have been overcome, it seemed unlikely that Cale and Reed could ever repair their friendship. In 1995, when Cale was asked about Lou in an interview he'd pondered aloud: "I can't understand how somebody who wrote such intelligent and beautiful songs could be the exact opposite as a person."

Nevertheless, fans held out hope for some kind of reconciliation. Though it seemed extremely unlikely that the surviving Velvets would ever reunite again, far stranger things had already happened in the course of their story. But it wasn't to be.

6

Lou Reed at the Schnitzer Concert Hall in Portland, Oregon, in 2004

In January 2005 Lou's father Sid Reed died. Though the two had been seemingly reconciled in later years – as much as they were ever likely to be – Lou's feelings were almost certainly ambiguous, with many issues remaining unresolved. Though Lou would go on to write a touching song about his father, in September 2013 – a mere month before his own death – when Reed was asked by an interviewer whether his father had given him his first guitar, his reply was: "My father didn't give me shit."

Lou remained a walking contradiction, often acting cruelly towards his associates and employees, yet also capable of random acts of great kindness towards friends and relatives in need. Even so, he was also just as likely to completely turn his back on them.

By now he had been diagnosed as diabetic, but was still prone to food fads – on tour he was known to eat different coloured salads depending on what day it was. Though he drank alcohol only lightly by most people's standards – a glass of wine or a spritzer with meals – he was still really wrestling with his addiction, and regularly attended AA meetings. He had ongoing liver problems, and his health in general was not good.

Late in 2005 John Cale released *Black Acetate*, a new rock album heavily influenced by hip-hop, a genre Cale called "the new jazz" because it was constantly evolving (much like Cale himself); he followed it in early 2007 with a lengthy live album, *Circus*.

During 2006 Reed toured Europe and the USA, and in December of that year he launched a theatrical presentation of his *Berlin* album which ran for five nights at St Ann's Warehouse in Brooklyn. The show was visually designed and directed by artist Julian Schnabel (who also filmed it for eventual DVD release), with musical direction by Hal Willner and Bob Ezrin, producer of the original *Berlin* album (who also acted as conductor). In addition to a band, choir, strings and horns, featured personnel included Reed, Sharon Jones, Antony Hegarty (of Antony & The Johnsons), Rupert Christie, Steve Hunter, Fernando Saunders,

THE VELVET UNDERGROUND

Lou Reed performs his Berlin
album in Stockholm, 2008

Tony Smith and Rob Wasserman, among
others. The show played in Sydney, Australia,
in January 2007 and also toured the UK that
year to rave reviews from the British press.

In 2007 Reed also released *Hudson River
Wind Meditations*, a collection of instrumental
meditation music he'd created. He was also
occasionally producing *Lou Reed's New York
Shuffle*, a radio show for the Sirius network.
Presented by a double-act of Lou and Hal
Willner, the show delivered an eclectic mix
of jazz, electronica and doo-wop.

Laurie Anderson remained the core of
Lou's life. On 12 April 2008 the couple finally
married at a friend's house in Boulder,
Colorado. As Billy Name later commented,
"she made his life beautiful". The two
even made music together live, often
accompanied by saxophonist John Zorn.
The year after their wedding Lou and Laurie
bought a holiday home in fashionable East
Hampton on Long Island (which some found

ironic, since Lou had always hated Long
Island so much).

In October 2008 John Cale hosted *Life
Along The Borderline*, a music festival honouring
what would have been Nico's 70th birthday,
had she lived. The following year Cale
performed his classic *Paris 1919* album in its
entirety live in Cardiff, then took it on tour
across Europe and the USA. In an interview
with the BBC that year, in answer to a
question about his drug use, Cale said that
the "strongest drug" he was currently using
was tea.

In 2010 Cale received an OBE in the
Queen's Birthday Honours list. Then in 2011
he released a five-track EP titled *Extra Playful*.
His first studio work for six years, it was
as good as anything he'd ever done. The
following year came another album of new
songs, *Shifty Adventures In Nookie Wood*, which
was almost as good. In the photographs
included with the album's lyric book he

looked as maverick as ever, more like a Dickensian conman than a 21st century artiste. Reviews for both works were good.

Between 2008 and 2010 Lou toured with Ulrich Krieger and Sarth Calhorn as the Metal Machine Trio, playing electronica in the vein of *Metal Machine Music*, which they termed Deep Noise.

But there had been no new recordings from Moe Tucker since 2002's *Moe Rocks Terrastock*. When she resurfaced, it was in an uncharacteristically controversial manner. In April 2009 Moe was interviewed by NBC TV in the street at a Tea Party rally in Tifton, Georgia, declaring that she was "furious about the way we've been led towards socialism." The clip quickly went viral, and Moe subsequently gave an interview to

Riverfront Times to clarify her position, stating that anyone who thought she was aligning herself with Sarah Palin or Bush was making "quite the presumption".

"I'm not involved with the Tea Party," Moe stated, adding that she'd attended the meeting "because it was in striking distance and I wanted to be counted." A lifelong Democrat, Moe felt that current government spending seemed intended to create a "Utopian dream-land" that would inevitably create higher taxes for the poor. Genuinely upset that people thought badly of her for speaking her mind, Moe said: "Anyone who knows me knows that I'm not a fool, a racist, a Nazi. Anyone who knows me knows I'm afraid of flying, afraid of bugs, but not afraid to say what I think."

6

John Cale at the Urban Simple Life festival in 2010

THE VELVET UNDERGROUND

6

She also told *Riverfront Times* that she had effectively retired from music because she had "no time for it anymore. I take care of my eight-year-old grandson, and it's a full-time job." In 2012 she issued a double-CD solo retrospective, *I Feel So Far Away*.

Meanwhile, by 2011 Lou had also begun work on songs for another of Robert Wilson's theatrical projects – this time an updating of Frank Wedekind's 19th century *Lulu* plays: *Earth Spirit* and *Pandora's Box* (filmed in the silent era with Louise Brooks). Some of these songs Reed would play live with Laurie Anderson and John Zorn, and his recording of them in some manner seemed a certainty.

Then Lou teamed up with the heavy rock group Metallica to perform live at Madison Square Garden for the 25th anniversary of the Rock 'N' Roll Hall of Fame. Afterwards, there was talk of Lou recording an album with the band, which would basically be a reworking of his greatest hits. It all seemed somewhat strange, given that Lou had been extremely uncomplimentary about the group in the past.

A 'greatest hits' package, however odd that might have been, made a lot more sense than what actually happened: Lou teamed up with Metallica to make an album of the *Lulu* songs. Basic tracks were recorded in ten days flat, with Lou acting as complete dictator of the sessions. Lou was writing in the voice of a depraved woman, and the work seemed to celebrate violence and perversion, though Lou had always had a talent for finding beauty where few others did. The album's mix of thrash metal and electronica wasn't

John Cale performs live in Angers, 2011 (above) and Lou Reed at the Hop Farm musical festival in the same year (right)

6

everybody's cup of tea, and, going by his vocals, Lou sounded ill.

Reviews were mixed. David Quantick in *Uncut* magazine wrote: "Everything on this immense album is intense, exciting, loud and generally all three." Meanwhile, the *Quietus* website called it "a candidate for one of the worst albums ever made." Lou maintained his disdain for critics, stating "I have no interest in what they have to say about anything." But although the sales of *Lulu* were healthy by Lou's standards, they were poor by Metallica's, and both sets of fans disliked it. As a result, a proposed joint tour was cancelled.

Lou was indeed seriously ill. He and Laurie had already made their retirement plans – they wanted to create an 'art ranch' to share with other artists, including a club where musicians could play. But it wasn't to be. After Lou's 70th birthday he made his will, played a handful of small gigs, then cancelled all his plans for 2013. He checked into Cleveland Clinic in Ohio to try various liver treatments, hoping against hope that a suitable liver donor might appear. One did, and Lou underwent an operation to have the new liver transplanted.

The operation seemed to have been a success, and Laurie was cautiously optimistic. On a post-op high Lou was more confident, declaring, "I am a triumph of modern medicine, physics and chemistry. I am bigger and stronger than ever."

Undoubtedly, Lou's brush with his own mortality had a profound effect on him. The Velvet Underground's lawyer Chris Whent later said that after the operation Lou became "a changed person". He involved himself deeply in the proposed 'deluxe' reissues of the MGM Velvets albums and was, according to Whent, "much easier to

deal with, much mellower, more ready to share affection and prouder than I can tell you of what the Velvets did." Meanwhile, the Velvet Underground were also seeking an injunction against the Andy Warhol Foundation for the Visual Arts for trademark infringement over the 'banana' image from the first album, after the Foundation had announced plans to license the image to Apple Inc for use as covers for iPads and iPhones. The whole business all seemed very postmodern, and very Andy Warhol.

During this period Reed also mended fences with John Cale over the phone, discussing plans for a possible new arrangement of *Songs For Drella*. Nor had Lou forgotten Moe Tucker, who one day received a box of candy through the mail from Lou with a card that read, "To Moesy, with all love and respect." Tucker later said that she'd thought this "really unusual", but although the two of them then talked on the phone, Lou made no mention of his health problems. Speaking after his death, Moe said that she felt the candy had been part of Lou's process of "starting to say goodbye".

In September Lou travelled to London to help Mick Rock promote his book of *Transformer*-era photographs, and later also helped promote the book in New York – but he looked terribly ill, and his skin had turned yellow. It soon became clear that his new liver wasn't working, and that nothing more could be done.

Lou retreated to his home at East Hampton. On 27 October 2013, he sat with Laurie doing breathing exercises and chanting a Buddhist mantra. After a while he asked her to take him into the light, and then sat on the sun deck outside making Tai Chi gestures with his hands while Laurie held him. At 12.30pm, Lou Reed died when

THE VELVET UNDERGROUND

his heart stopped beating. He was cremated the next day.

"He wasn't afraid," Laurie later wrote in *Rolling Stone*. "I have never seen an expression as full of wonder as Lou's as he died." For the seven-week 'bardo' period following Lou's death, Laurie celebrated his life according to Buddhist tradition, meeting with friends to talk about Lou, in the belief that this would help him in his onward journey towards his next life.

On 14 November outside New York's Lincoln Center there was a three-hour-long public memorial playback of Reed's recordings, as chosen by his family and friends. And at the end of the seven-week 'bardo' period there was a memorial concert for Lou on 16 December at the Harlem Apollo; taking part were Paul Simon, Patti Smith, Antony Hegarty, John Zorn, Philip Glass and Debbie Harry. There, Laurie spoke of the love and companionship that they had shared, describing Lou as an emotional man who often cried, and of her belief that he had finally learned to conquer his own anger. Both John Cale and Moe Tucker were also supposed to appear at the concert, but as the time for it drew near both stood down, as neither felt emotionally capable of taking part.

Other tributes had flooded in, as everyone from Morrissey to Miley Cyrus acknowledged their debt to Reed. David Bowie called him "a master". Patti Smith called him "a very special poet" and "a New York writer". David Byrne pointed out that "lots of creative types retreat after they achieve a certain level of success or renown – Lou seemed to maintain his curiosity and willingness to take risks."

Within hours of Reed's passing a shocked John Cale wrote briefly on Facebook: "The world has lost a fine songwriter and poet... I've lost my 'school-yard buddy'." Within 24 hours he issued a longer statement, which seemed both gentlemanly and affectionate: "The news I feared the most pales in comparison to the lump in my throat and the hollow in my stomach. Two kids have a chance meeting and 47 years later we fight and love the same way – losing either one is incomprehensible. No replacement value, no digital or virtual fill... broken now, for all time. Unlike so many with similar stories – we have the best of our fury laid out on vinyl, for the world to catch a glimpse. The laughs we shared just a few weeks ago will remind me of all that was good between us."

Cale was then in the middle of recording his *M: FANS* album, a modern reworking of the songs from *Music For A New Society*. In response to Lou's death Cale recorded an extra version of 'If You Were Still Around'; even though the lyrics had been written by the playwright Sam Shepard, Cale thought them appropriate to a relationship he described as "really scattered and ill-defined".

In truth, as a reformed alcoholic Cale had been deeply shocked to witness Lou's return to drinking, stating "when he got sick it felt like a very public suicide", and his grief hit him hard. When a reporter from Channel 4 TV asked him a year later if he was over Reed's death yet he replied: "Not really. I don't think that will happen".

Moe Tucker was equally grief-stricken, and wrote a moving tribute for *The Guardian* which concluded: "Now Andy's gone, Sterling's gone, Nico's gone and Lou's gone. It feels strange. I miss them all, but I really miss Lou. He was a great songwriter who pushed the boundaries in terms of what he was writing about, but more importantly,

6

he was a good and loyal friend. It doesn't seem right that I won't be sending him a Christmas card."

In 2015 Lou Reed was posthumously inducted into the Rock & Roll Hall of Fame by Patti Smith, who publicly thanked him for "brutally and benevolently injecting your poetry into your music."

With Lou dead, some witnesses came forward to speak that might never have done so had he still been alive, including Lou's first wife Bettye Kronstad (who published a memoir in 2016), and also Lou's sister Merrill Reed Weiner (known as Bunny), who talked for the first time about the Reeds' home life, and Lou's electroshock treatment. In his will Lou had left her 25% of his $30million estate, with the proviso that she care for their 93-year-old mother (who passed away nine days after Lou).

The balance of the estate went to Laurie, who announced in March 2017 that Lou's archives were to be donated to the New York Public Library for the Performing Arts at Lincoln Center – a hoard which included 3,600 audio tapes and 1,300 video recordings, as well as original manuscripts, lyrics, fan mail, photographs and Lou's personal collection of books. Laurie explained that the manuscripts contain no rough lyrics or early drafts, as Lou would simply write a song in his head, and once he was satisfied he wrote it down or typed it. There were no rewrites.

Nor are there any writings that reflect Lou's spiritual side. Laurie later spoke of his dedication to meditation: "He made a very extensive study of the nature of mind, but there is no physical trace of it. He left no footprints."

Judging by Moe Tucker's appearance in 2006's *Velvet Underground Under Review* DVD,

it would seem that she may also have experienced a bout of ill health; if so, hopefully she has fully recovered. She is now a grandmother, and – despite the Tea Party affair – probably the sanest person in this entire story.

And John Cale soldiers on. With Moe seemingly retired he is now the last Velvet standing, a role he seems to have accepted with justifiable pride as he continues to write and record and tour and generally wave the flag for the Velvets' legacy. In July 2015 at the Albert Hall he stole the show at a David Bowie tribute concert with a stunning version of the Merseys' 'Sorrow' (which Bowie had also covered).

In January 2016 Cale re-released his album *Music For A New Society*, which included the brand-new recording *M: FANS*. "It was time to decimate the despair from 1981 and breathe new energy, rewrite the story." Cale would follow the project up later in the year with a reissue of his classic live album *Fragments Of A Rainy Season*, remastered and containing a whole CD of extra material.

In April 2016 the Philharmonie de Paris mounted an exhibition titled *The Velvet Underground New York Extravaganza*, featuring rare photographs and memorabilia, which John Cale called the best Velvets exhibition he'd ever seen. As part of the celebration, Cale played the first two Velvets albums live in concert, aided by guest stars Pete Doherty, Mark Lanegan and Animal Collective.

The following month Lou's guitar tech Stuart Hurwood took six of Lou's guitars and amps off to the Brighton Festival in England (curated by Laurie Anderson that year), and set them up to create a loop of feedback for live 'performances' in the style of *Metal Machine Music*, under the title 'Lou Reed

THE VELVET UNDERGROUND

Drones'. Also in 2016, Tony Conrad died. He'd spent the fifty years since his days with the proto-Velvets pursuing his love of avant-garde experimental music.

At the 59th Grammy Awards in February 2017 John Cale collected a Lifetime Achievement Award Grammy on behalf of the Velvet Underground. His date for the evening was Betsey Johnson, his wife of 50 years earlier. Asked how Lou Reed would have felt about the award, Cale replied, "He would have been very excited."

In May 2017 he repeated the format of his Paris concert in Liverpool, to celebrate the fiftieth anniversary of the Velvets' first album. Guest stars included Super Furry Animals frontman Gruff Rhys, The Kills, Clinic, Nadine Shah, Fat White Family and Wild Beasts. Reviews were poor, largely on account of a substandard sound system and other technical problems, but still hinted at what might have been had all gone more smoothly. A third concert will take place in New York in November 2017, at the Brooklyn Academy of Music – apparently with a vague promise from Moe Tucker that she might join him onstage, as long as she doesn't have to fly there.

In fact, Moe turned up earlier than expected, and on July 11 2017 she joined John Cale onstage at the Beacon Theater in New York to perform 'Sunday Morning' and 'I'm Waiting For The Man' together. The set was a part of the Grammy Awards' "Salute To Music Legends," about which Cale jokingly observed that "the establishment caught up with us at last." Whether or not he and Moe will share a stage again remains to be seen.

Some Velvet Underground material from the Sixties still remains unreleased, but whether it ever will be is another matter. Whether Morrison's history of the band was ever finished, and whether Reed ever completed the book of short stories that he'd been promising for years, are questions that only time will answer. Regardless, it's a safe bet that John Cale will keep making music until the day he drops dead – and whatever that work may be like, it will at the very least be extremely interesting.

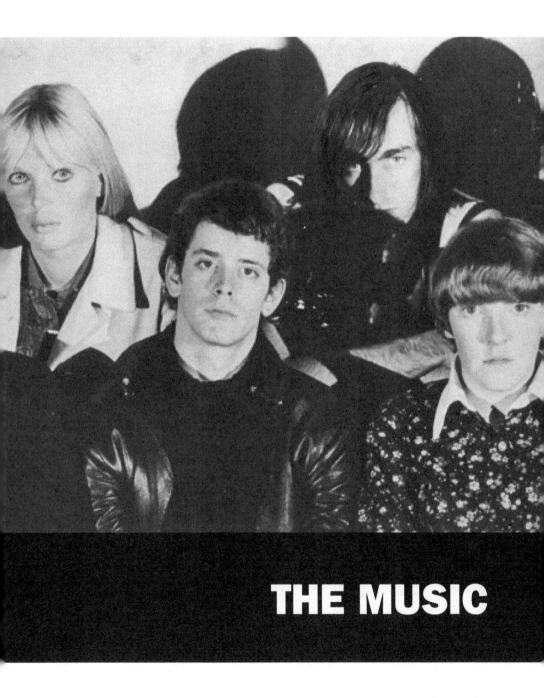

THE MUSIC

7 THE ALBUMS

Andy Warhol

THE VELVET UNDERGROUND & NICO

*Sunday Morning/I'm Waiting For The Man/
Femme Fatale/Venus In Furs/Run Run Run/
All Tomorrow's Parties/Heroin/There She
Goes Again/I'll Be Your Mirror/The Black
Angel's Death Song/European Son*

Verve; recorded April, May and November 1966;
released March 1967. Personnel: John Cale (electric
viola, bass, piano); Sterling Morrison (rhythm guitar,
bass); Lou Reed (lead guitar, ostrich guitar, vocals);
Maureen Tucker (drums); Nico (chanteuse). All songs
credited to Lou Reed, except 'Sunday Morning' and
'Black Angel's Death Song' to Reed and Cale, and
'European Son' to all four Velvets

In April 1966 the Velvet Underground recorded
the bulk of their debut album at Scepter
Records 4-track recording studio in New

York; the following month they re-recorded
'European Son', 'Heroin', 'Waiting For The
Man' and 'Venus In Furs' at T.T.G.'s Sunset-
Highland studio in Hollywood. Cale claims
these re-recordings were far superior to
those from the Scepter sessions ("we really
didn't do anything great in New York").
In November 1966 'Sunday Morning' was
recorded as a last-minute addition at New
York's Mayfair Sound studios.

Engineers at Scepter were Norman Dolph
and John Licata; in California the engineer
was Omi Haden. Tom Wilson produced the
'Sunday Morning' session, and also converted
the group's original mono mix of the earlier
tapes into reprocessed stereo (though Sterling
Morrison always insisted that the mono
version of the album is superior). None of
the above are credited on the album sleeve,
with the sole production credit going to Andy
Warhol – which seems somewhat churlish
considering that it was the others who did the
actual work.

For a debut album, *The Velvet Underground &
Nico* is absolutely stunning, as much so today as
in 1967. It sounded like nothing else that was
being produced at the time. Much as one may
love psychedelia, the genre was very much a
product of its era (and sounds it), whereas the
Velvets' first album could have been recorded
yesterday. It doesn't even matter that it
displays so many different musical styles, since
the songs themselves are all so good.

Its gently pretty opener 'Sunday Morning'
doesn't sound that revolutionary, seeming

recognizably akin to much of the electric folk-rock then being produced – but there's still the paranoia of the lyrics and Cale's droning viola to prove this is by no means run of the mill. The driving rock beat of 'I'm Waiting For The Man' shifts proceedings a gear, while its lyrics are clearly about buying drugs. The Harlem references make it obvious that it's hard drugs under discussion here, since the drugs that were deemed more socially acceptable at the time (marijuana and LSD) were a lot more easily available. 'Femme Fatale' introduces the world to Nico, with a sleepy ballad in which she uses both of her singing voices: the wispy, whispery one and the more strident one that Sterling Morrison called her "Götterdämmerung voice".

At first hearing, it's obvious that Nico is one of the most arresting female singers in rock; certainly there had been nothing like her before. One could say the same about 'Venus In Furs', which makes the listener sit up, from its opening chords onwards. Not only does Cale's viola cut like a razor, but the tambourine, bass and drums all make

THE BANANA COVER

The one area of the Velvets' debut where Andy Warhol did undeniably make an important contribution was the album's cover, which he designed. This wasn't his first venture into record sleeve design; in 1958 he'd produced a cover for jazz guitarist Kenny Burrell's Blue Note album *Blue Lights Volume I*, for which Warhol had done an illustration in the style of Jean Cocteau.

For the Velvets album Warhol had originally planned to use one of his 'plastic surgery' series of images of "nose jobs, breast jobs and ass jobs". Fortunately for posterity, Andy came up with something else instead. The famous yellow silkscreened banana sticker which – when peeled slowly – revealed a pink banana underneath made the cover into a memorable and elegant icon. As with his famous soup cans, the banana itself was a 'found' image, taken from a promotional campaign for the fruit that read simply 'Enjoy Banana'. Promotional ashtrays showing the original banana exist, but are incredibly rare.

Warhol had explored the banana as sexual metaphor several times prior to this, most notably in his film *Mario Montez Eating Banana*. In 1966 bananas also had a drug culture significance, since smoking banana skins was at that time rumoured to get you high (it doesn't). However, the cover also created problems, since printing difficulties with the sticker contributed to the album's delayed release. Also, nowhere on the front of the record was the Velvet Undergound's name even mentioned – just the legend 'Andy Warhol', which led many to assume that the artist had now made a rock album. As such, it probably didn't make the Velvet Underground any easier to market. Warhol designed many other rock album covers over the years: for John Cale's *The Academy In Peril*, the Rolling Stones' *Sticky Fingers* and *Love You Live*, and the posthumous John Lennon album *Menlove Ave* among them. The cover for *White Light/White Heat* was executed by Factory stalwart Billy Name, from a "concept" by Warhol.

THE VELVET UNDERGROUND

7

this sound like the soundtrack to some depraved ritual – which is of course all heightened by the lyrics.

To an era that found the Rolling Stones' 'Let's Spend The Night Together' controversial, glorifying sado-masochism was totally beyond the pale. The 'ostrich' guitar used by Reed on this track (and on 'All Tomorrow's Parties') was a semi-hollow-bodied Gretsch with its frets removed, and all its strings tuned to the same note. It made what Cale called "an horrendous noise", and was subsequently stolen from Reed's apartment.

For a throwaway song written in a hurry, 'Run Run Run' isn't at all bad, if obviously influenced by the Dylan of *Highway 61 Revisited*. Once again, it's about buying drugs on the street, compounding the Velvets' already-depraved image. 'All Tomorrow's Parties' is more accessible, though for all its folk-rock trimmings the drums alone make it sound more sinister – and the sadness of the lyric is turned into real tragedy by Nico's voice, which sounds like an angel heralding inevitable doom. 'Heroin' is awesome by any standards, and its tendency to speed up and slow down again is utterly compelling – as are the lyrics: once you've started listening to this, you have to hear how it ends. Since the song doesn't take an obvious stance against the drug, many listeners at the time assumed it must be advocating it.

'There She Goes Again' returns to fast-paced folk-rock territory, with jangly Byrds-style guitar, and high-pitched backing harmonies. The implicit misogyny might even pass the listener by on a first hearing. 'I'll Be Your Mirror' is back to the world of the gentle ballad, with an ethereal, moving love song that ignored sentiment entirely, describing real emotions instead. 'The Black Angel's Death Song' kicks off with Cale's screeching viola, with Reed spitting out a

Dylanesque stream of nonsense verse; it's musically interesting, but a little on the annoying and pretentious side. 'European Son' wraps up the album with driving urban blues (punctuated by noise), turning into a raucous extended guitar jam that rattles on for nearly eight minutes. At this time, rock songs of this length were still very rare and the ones that did exist usually made more of an effort to please the listener than this one, which sounds like a giant 'fuck you' to the world. The Velvet Underground had arrived, and they weren't messing around.

Had this album come out in 1966, it would surely have attracted more attention than it did. As it was, in the year of peace and love it was deemed both sick and unfashionable, and was generally lost in a deluge of other, more psychedelic, debut albums. But for those who heard it, it was instantly unforgettable – it was obvious from the off that Reed was one of the most talented songwriters in rock, and that he had a band that complemented that talent perfectly. For a glimmer of the album's eventual impact – which took decades to merge – one can't better the verdict of contemporary journalist John Wilcock, reviewing the Velvets live in the *East Village Other*: "Art has come to the discotheque, and it will never be the same again".

The standard CD release of the album replaces the original version of 'All Tomorrow's Parties' with a 'previously unreleased' one. Both feature the same backing track, but whereas the original featured Nico's vocals double-tracked, the CD has only one vocal track. It's not an improvement, but the situation was rectified with the restored version of the album included in the *Peel Slowly And See* boxed set. A deluxe double-CD version of the album also exists, which is recommended. This contains both mono and stereo mixes of the whole album, all of the edited singles released, plus the five Velvets-related tracks from Nico's *Chelsea Girl* album. It also restores the complete cover artwork.

In 2012 an expanded 45th anniversary 'super deluxe' edition was issued. This four-CD set contained the stereo and mono mixes, Nico's *Chelsea Girl* album in its entirety, plus rehearsal tapes from the Factory, some live performances with Nico from November 1966 and the Scepter Studio Sessions acetate (see separate entry for the *Scepter Sessions*). Is it worth the extra money for the extra material? Only if you're a completist.

WHITE LIGHT/WHITE HEAT

White Light–White Heat/The Gift/Lady Godiva's Operation/Here She Comes Now/I Heard Her Call My Name/Sister Ray

Verve; recorded September 1967; released January 1968. Available on CD. Personnel: John Cale (vocals, electric viola, organ, bass); Sterling Morrison (vocals, guitar, bass); Lou Reed (vocals, guitar, piano); Maureen Tucker (drums). *White Light/White Heat* was recorded at Mayfair Sound Studios in New York. Again produced by Tom Wilson, and engineered by Gary Kellgren

It's been claimed that the Velvet Underground recorded their second album in its entirety in under three days. According to Moe Tucker it took "approximately seven sessions over a period of two weeks"; even so, that was fast work even in those days. John Cale has implied that the time factor was a deliberate artistic choice, rather than a limitation imposed by poverty: "We decided to make that album as live as possible. We told Tom Wilson we were gonna do it as we do it on stage." In fact, how much Tom Wilson had to do with the record is debatable, and the bulk of the work was done by Kellgren, since Wilson was constantly making phone calls. Tucker complains to this day that Wilson didn't turn on one of her drum mics for 'Sister Ray' because he was "more interested in the blondes running through the studio."

The Velvets attempted to create a 'live' sound, resulting in an album that was murky in the mix, with a ridiculous amount of distortion and feedback – the Yardbirds and the Who being big influences upon the group at this point. Sterling Morrison later explained that: "There was fantastic leakage because everyone was playing so loud and we had so much electronic junk with us in the studio – all these fuzzers and compressors. Gary Kellgren the engineer, who is ultra-competent, told us repeatedly: 'You can't do it – all the needles are on red'". The group simply told Kellgren that they didn't care, and that he should just do the best he could. The distortion and white noise were the inevitable result.

"We wanted to do something electronic and energetic," explained Morrison. "We had the energy and the electronics, but we didn't know that it couldn't be recorded ... What we were trying to do was to really fry the tracks." Tucker is more candid: "We didn't know what we were doing." The record was a release of emotion

THE VELVET UNDERGROUND

7

and energy for the band, as all the anger and frustration and resentment they felt at their lack of commercial success boiled over onto the tape. "Our lives were chaos," Morrison has stated. "That's what's reflected in the record." Any listeners expecting more ballads in the vein of 'I'll Be Your Mirror' were going to be sorely disappointed – *White Light/White Heat* was all-out guitar-based mayhem, with lyrics that were as much of a full-frontal assault as the music.

The title track concerns the joys of amphetamine, but – apart from the distortion – is quite jaunty, dominated by Cale's pounding piano. 'The Gift' is truly macabre: a short story of Reed's, recited by Cale over backing music which was basically a piece they'd performed live, an R&B instrumental titled 'Booker T'. As well as reciting the narrative for 'The Gift', Cale also took lead vocals for 'Lady Godiva's Operation', which starts as a prettily psychedelic ballad before turning into something disturbing, with lyrics to match. 'Here She Comes Now' is the only song on the record that might have fitted on the previous album, and even that has lyrics that imply sexual problems. 'I Heard Her Call My Name' is bluesy garage thrash laced with feedback (and very bad guitar solos from Reed), with lyrics that concern love after death.

Tucker and Morrison were both disgusted when Reed remixed this track to bring his own part up in the mix, drowning all the others out; Morrison actually claims to have quit the band for several days over this incident. The album closes with 'Sister Ray', a distortion-heavy blues strut with lyrics that were blatantly about sexual activity and hard drug use (not to mention a murder), inspired by a black queen Reed and Cale had met on the street in uptown New York. For this one the entire band turned all their amps up to ten and just played variations on the riff until they ran out of

steam, seventeen minutes later, the two guitars dueling with Cale's organ throughout.

All in all, not exactly easy listening, then or now. As Lou put it in 2013: "No one listened to it. But there it is, forever – the quintessence of articulated punk, and no one goes near it."

The album was also unlike anything else coming out that year, and added greatly to the band's word-of-mouth reputation. Though largely ignored by the media, a review of the album by Wayne McGuire in *Crawdaddy* magazine called the Velvets "the most vital and significant group in the world today". Reed certainly felt that way too. Speaking of the album decades later he stated proudly: "That was monumental. I would match it with anything by anybody, anywhere, ever. No group in the world can touch what we did."

The album's original black-on-black cover included a photograph by Billy Name of a skull and crossbones tattoo; this was chosen by Reed from Name's portfolio, and was originally a small detail from a still taken from Warhol's movie *Bike Boy*, the tattoo in question belonging to 'actor' Joe Spencer. Name greatly enlarged the detail, which is why the image is so grainy. The album design is credited to Billy Name from a 'concept' by Andy Warhol. The album has also appeared with several other cover designs.

In 2013 a 'deluxe' two-CD version of the album was released, which included the complete stereo mix of the album, plus outtakes and alternate versions, with a second CD containing the group's entire show recorded at The Gymnasium in New York in April 1967, including five previously unreleased songs. Tracklisting is as follows:

Disc One

White Light–White Heat/The Gift/Lady Godiva's Operation/Here She Comes Now/I Heard Her Call My Name/Sister Ray/ I Heard Her Call My Name (Alternate Take)/Guess I'm Falling In

THE MUSIC: **THE ALBUMS**

Love (Instrumental Version)/Temptation Inside Your Heart (Original Mix)/Stephanie Says/Hey Mr Rain (Version One)/Hey Mr Rain (Version Two)/Beginning To See The Light (Early Version)
Disc Two
Booker T/I'm Not A Young Man Anymore/ Guess I'm Falling In Love/I'm Waiting For The Man/Run Run Run/ Sister Ray/ The Gift

A three-CD 'super deluxe' version was also released at the same time, which included both mono and stereo mixes of the album, the live album and a few more outtakes.

THE VELVET UNDERGROUND

Candy Says/What Goes On/Some Kinda Love/Pale Blue Eyes/Jesus/Beginning To See The Light/I'm Set Free/That's The Story Of My Life/The Murder Mystery//After Hours
MGM/Verve; recorded November-December 1968; released March 1969. Personnel: Sterling Morrison (guitar); Lou Reed (vocals, guitar); Maureen Tucker (drums); Doug Yule (vocals, bass, organ, piano)

The imaginatively titled *The Velvet Underground*

(sometimes known as 'the gray album', on account of the cover's colour) was recorded just over two months after the departure of John Cale at TTG Studios in Hollywood. Credits state that it was "arranged and conducted" by the Velvet Underground, assisted by engineer Louis Pastor 'Val' Valentin. The album cover photograph was taken by Billy Linich.

Confusingly, there are two different versions of this album: a mix by Lou Reed, which was used for the original vinyl release, and a mix by Valentin (used for the CD re-release). Valentin's mix was made first; after which Reed returned to the studio with the tapes and did his version, christened the 'closet mix' by Sterling Morrison, who thought it sounded like it had been recorded in a closet. Reed's 'closet mix' brought his vocals to the fore, while Valentin's approach was more orthodox (and reveals instrumentation inaudible on the closet mix, like the bass on 'Afterhours'). The Valentin mix remains available as the standard CD release, but at Reed's insistence the 'closet mix' – which is admittedly a lot cleaner and clearer – was the one chosen for inclusion in the *Peel Slowly And See* boxed set.

The album is another radical change of pace; there are no electronic effects, distortion or feedback this time around – just a collection of songs that were far more straightforward, lyrically as well as musically, than anything the Velvets had done before. Most concerned love, in one form or another, and the individual songs could be seen as comprising parts of a larger whole. Doug Yule takes lead vocal on several tracks, as Reed had strained his voice singing live – but since Yule's voice was quite similar in tone to Reed's, the change isn't too jarring. Reed's vocal problems may also be the reason why Maureen Tucker stepped into the vocal spotlight for 'After Hours', although Reed has since claimed this was a deliberate

THE VELVET UNDERGROUND

7

choice, because Moe's voice suited the lyric better than his own. The album kicks off with 'Candy Says', a ballad gentler even than 'I'll Be Your Mirror', with Yule's backing vocals making it evident from the start that this was a somewhat different band to the one that had made the previous album. 'What Goes On' is, for the Velvets, a comparatively straightforward rocker, while 'Some Kinda Love' is a more straightforward blues (the Valentin mix of the album features a completely different take of this song to the 'closet' mix).

'Pale Blue Eyes' is a gentle but incredibly powerful love song fairly obviously inspired by Reed's on/off relationship with Shelley Albin. Sterling Morrison – already upset about Cale's departure – was unhappy about the fact that Reed was now writing songs about his girlfriend, considering it a step backwards in terms of subject matter. However, he allowed Reed to have his way: "My position on the album was one of acquiescence."

'Jesus' comes as a real shock, coming from the band known for songs about hard drugs. The song is, very simply, a prayer and undoubtedly genuine, though it betokened no conversion. 'Beginning To See The Light' is a joyfully upbeat rocker, 'I'm Set Free' an epic ballad of loss and resignation, while 'That's The Story Of My Life' is practically vaudeville, with fairly nonsensical lyrics. 'The Murder Mystery' is the most experimental track here, with two sets of vocals performing two different sets of lyrics over a R&B instrumental dominated by Yule's organ. It doesn't really work, but at least provides proof that Reed hadn't totally given himself over to orthodox song structures. The album closes with 'After Hours', a fragile celebration of loneliness and alcohol as a refuge. After this, it was impossible to predict where the Velvets might head next.

In 2014 a 'deluxe' 2-CD version of the album

was released, which contained the remastered Valentin stereo mix, plus a whole disc recorded live at the Matrix in 1969, comprised of the following tracks: 'I'm Waiting For The Man', 'What Goes On', 'Some Kinda Love', 'Over You', 'Beginning To See The Light', 'Lisa Says', 'Rock And Roll', 'Pale Blue Eyes', 'I Can't Stand It Anymore', 'Heroin', 'White Light-White Heat' and 'Sweet Jane'. A six-CD 'super deluxe' version was also released at the same time, which was a completist's delight, including: the Valentin mix and the 'closet' mix, both in stereo; the mono version of the Valentin mix; the live Matrix disc; a whole disc of material from *VU* and *Another View*, plus outtakes. It's expensive, unsurprisingly.

LOADED

Who Loves The Sun/Sweet Jane/Rock & Roll/Cool It Down/New Age/Head Held High/Lonesome Cowboy Bill/I Found A Reason/Train Round The Bend/Oh ! Sweet Nuthin'

Cotillion/Atlantic; recorded April-July 1970; released September 1970. Personnel: Sterling Morrison (guitar); Lou Reed (guitar, piano, vocals); Billy Yule (drums); Doug Yule (organ, piano, bass, drums, guitar, vocals)

Given how beset with problems the band were while recording this album – lacking Moe Tucker, and with Lou Reed suffering from not only a strained voice but also a fragile mental state – it's amazing that it turned out as well as it did. Once again, Doug Yule had to take over lead vocals for several tracks – though Reed later attacked Yule's interpretations of the songs (he claimed Yule "didn't understand" the lyrics to 'New Age').

Recorded at Atlantic Studios, New York, the album's production would eventually be credited to Geoffrey Haslam, Shel Kagan and the Velvet Underground; Atlantic staff producer Adrian Barber acted as engineer and originally oversaw the proceedings,

until first Kagan and then Haslam were brought in to hurry things along. Reed would subsequently criticize all the work that was done after he quit the band: the mixing and production of the album, the running order the songs had been given and what he called the "severe" editing of several of the tracks.

His carping was understandable and inevitable, given his wounded pride. But the production is in fact excellent, while Yule's vocals sounded just fine to everyone but Lou, and the edits actually improved the songs in question, tightening them up. If this wasn't quite the album "loaded with hits" that Reed claimed it was, it *was* loaded with extremely commercial material that

MAX'S KANSAS CITY

"Everybody went to Max's, and everything got homogenised there," stated Andy Warhol. He described Max's Kansas City as "the exact place where Pop Art and Pop Life came together in the Sixties" From the start, Mickey Ruskin's two-storey bar/restaurant at Park Avenue South and 16th/17th Street attracted a large number of celebrities and artists among its clientele – partly because Ruskin happily gave many artists, Warhol included, credit in return for their paintings. Max's soon became the regular late-night hangout for the Factory crowd, with Warhol holding court (and picking up the tab) after midnight in the back room dining area. "At Max's the heavyweights of the art world hang around the long bar," wrote 'superstar' Ultra Violet, "and in the back room, kids, groupies, dropouts, beautiful little girls of fourteen who've already had

abortions, get noisy or stoned."

Not to mention drag queens, speedfreaks, the occasional celebrity and the whole Factory crowd. Doug Yule later recalled that "Walking into Max's the first time was like walking into the bar scene in *Star Wars*; a slow pan across alien beings engaged in unfathomable activity." This included people having sex in public, mainly under tables and in the phone booth. The back room was called 'Siberia' by Max's waitresses, since most of its inhabitants were so addled on drugs that they never tipped. Upstairs was originally a disco (the DJ was Wayne County, later Jayne County, of The Electric Chairs), which later became a small club where bands played, including the Velvets. Max's Kansas City closed its doors in 1974, opened again a year later and finally closed for good in 1981.

THE VELVET UNDERGROUND

7

not only echoed Reed's doo-wop roots, but also investigated the borders between rock and country (territory being simultaneously explored by many of the Velvets' contemporaries), and did so in an extremely fresh and interesting way.

Plus, it boasted a couple of bona fide classic guitar-based rockers in 'Sweet Jane' and 'Rock & Roll', both exultant celebrations of life and music that would become staples in the sets of indie guitar groups from then on, with innumerable cover versions being recorded.

The album opens with the countryish pop of 'Who Loves The Sun' before moving on to the double-whammy of 'Sweet Jane' and 'Rock & Roll'. 'Cool It Down' is almost bluesy, while 'New Age' is an epic romantic ballad that's literate, funny *and* moving. 'Head Held High' and 'Lonesome Cowboy Bill' are both throwaways, but enjoyable; 'I Found A Reason' is a gentle and sincere love song that's almost doo-wop, thanks to the multi-layered vocal arrangement; 'Train Round The Bend' is fairly conventionally bluesy; 'Oh! Sweet Nuthin'' is another epic ballad, closing the album with its almost gospel-style lament. All of which earned *Loaded* a rave review from *Rolling Stone*, but the irony was tragic; in a sense, the Velvet Underground's story was already over before this record even came out.

The album cover illustration was by Polish designer Stanislaw Zagorski, who had been doing covers for Atlantic's jazz artists for many years. Zagorski rendered a somewhat literal interpretation of the term 'underground', showing a subway entrance with pink smoke emanating from it. Some find the cover charming; others think it a bit of a plunge into tackiness, especially for a band who'd once had Andy Warhol.

LIVE AT MAX'S KANSAS CITY

I'm Waiting For The Man/Sweet Jane/ Lonesome Cowboy Bill/Beginning To See The Light/I'll Be Your Mirror/Pale Blue Eyes/ Sunday Morning/New Age/Femme Fatale/ After Hours

Cotillion/Atlantic; recorded August 1970; released May 1972. Personnel: Sterling Morrison (lead guitar);Lou Reed (vocals, rhythm guitar); Doug Yule (bass guitar, vocals); Billy Yule (drums)

During the summer of 1970 the Velvets played a ten-week residency at Max's Kansas City, towards the end of which run Lou Reed quit the band. Although an official Atlantic release, *Live At Max's* is effectively a bootleg. The Velvets knew nothing about it, and it was recorded on a very basic Sony TC120 cassette player belonging to Factory stalwart Brigid Polk on August 23 1970, Lou Reed's last night with the band.

The tape is in mono, and pretty poor in terms of technical quality, since Polk's tape recorder had just been lying on a table; the audience, particularly those seated at Polk's table, is frequently louder than the group. According to Jim Carroll, who was seated with Polk, the club was packed that night – although for much of the Velvets' run at Max's the place had been half-empty (hard as that may be to believe today).

Once Reed had left the group, Danny Fields persuaded Polk that the recording might be of value as the group's last recording; they sold the tape to Atlantic for $10,000 outright (which they split between them). Atlantic released an edited version of the concert despite the band's objections, claiming it as the second album the Velvets had contracted for. It was originally released at a budget price, probably because the label were self-conscious about the extremely poor sound quality.

But despite the sound, *Live At Max's* has several things going for it. On the downside, though the 17-year-old Billy Yule is a competent enough drummer, he's certainly no replacement for Moe Tucker. But although the group (especially Reed) are obviously fairly weary and ragged, what's amazing is how poppy and commercial they sound, especially on the *Loaded* material – as if they might be on the verge of great things. There's certainly no faulting their enthusiasm, backing up Morrison's assertion that "we were ten times better live than on our records." Even Reed seems to be enjoying himself; one can't help but wonder how successful they might have become if he'd only stuck around a while longer... although Reed claimed afterwards that his last night at Max's "was the only night I really enjoyed myself. I did all the songs I wanted – a lot of them were ballads." Even if you hate the rest of the album, it's worth the price

of admission to hear Lou Reed singing 'Afterhours' in a joyously cynical way (Tucker's comment was: "He sings better than I do").

Though the group objected to the album's release at the time, Reed would later acknowledge its worth: "The Max's live set, now that's another album I really love. If you want to know what Max's was really like – and now you can't – it's there, for real, because Brigid was just sitting there with her little Sony recorder. It's in mono, you can't hear us, but you can hear just enough. We're out of tune, per usual ... but it's Sunday night, and all the regulars are there, and Jim Carroll's trying to get Tuinols, and they're talking about the war ... We were the house band. There it is."

The original release contained only a part of Polk's tape. 'Some Kinda Love' was included on *Peel Slowly And See*, and the complete tape – consisting of both the Velvets' sets in their entirety across two CDs – was finally released in 2004 on Atlantic/Rhino. If you like the album at all, it's worthwhile getting the expanded version, which contains a nicely put together booklet about Max's and the concert. Track listing is as follows:

Disc One
I'm Waiting For The Man/White Light-White Heat/I'm Set Free/ Sweet Jane (Version #1)/ Lonesome Cowboy Bill (Version #1)/New Age/ Beginning To See The Light
Disc Two
Who Loves The Sun/ Sweet Jane (Version # 2)/ I'll Be Your Mirror/Pale Blue Eyes/Candy Says/Sunday Morning/After Hours/Femme Fatale/Some Kinda Love/Lonesome Cowboy Bill (Version #2)

THE VELVET UNDERGROUND

7

SQUEEZE

Little Jack/Crash/Caroline/Mean Old Man/
Dopey Joe/Wordless/She'll Make You Cry/
Friends/Send No Letter/Jack And Jane/Louise
Polydor/Loaded; recorded summer 1972; released
February 1973. Personnel: Doug Yule (lead vocals,
guitars, keyboards, bass guitar); Ian Paice (drums,
percussion)

All titles are credited to Doug Yule, who
is thought to play all the instruments here
except the drums (provided by Deep Purple's
Ian Paice, though he doesn't get a sleeve
credit); there are also some female backing
vocals (thought to be by Yule's girlfriend,
but again uncredited) and saxophone by
'Malcolm' (surname unknown). The sleeve
also states that the album was "arranged and
produced by the Velvets" i.e. Doug Yule,
since he was the only one left. Yule has
subsequently stated that the lyrics to both
'She'll Make you Cry' and 'Mean Old Man'
were actually written by Steve Sesnick, to
which Yule put music. Sesnick also came up
with the album title and oversaw its sleeve
design, both chosen to seem like a thematic
continuation from *Loaded*.

But compared to *Loaded*, this sounds
pretty poor. What you get on *Squeeze* are
so-so pop songs – by no means unpleasant,
but also a fairly unremarkable mixture
of ragtime, folk-rock, blues and country
influences. The best of the songs (such as
the Beates-ish 'She'll Make You Cry' and
the semi-psychedelic 'Louise') are actually
pretty good; but the worst of them ('Send
No Letter', which sounds like a very bad Lou
Reed pastiche) proves that whatever it may
say on the sleeve, this definitely *isn't* the
Velvet Underground.

The song 'Caroline' was inspired by the
legendary groupie Christine Frka, a.k.a. Miss
Christine of the GTOs (who appears on the
cover of Frank Zappa's *Hot Rats* album, and
who had also inspired The Flying Burrito
Brothers' 'Christine's Tune'). Yule had
evidently been one of her conquests; when
the Velvet Underground played Los Angeles
gig, Frka and another GTO girl had sent the
band "a dozen roses with our pictures on
the back. You can't be too subtle." She died
of a drug overdose in 1972. Coincidentally,
GTO member Cindy was at this time married
to John Cale.

For curiosity value alone, *Squeeze* deserves
a CD release, but Cale and Tucker would
presumably be opposed to the idea of the
album being reissued under the Velvet
Underground name. However, there's no
reason why it couldn't be marketed as a
Doug Yule solo album instead – after all,
that's exactly what this record is. Meanwhile,
original vinyl copies are quite hard to
find, since *Squeeze* was only pressed in
England, and the album was also deleted
quite quickly. Some copies were apparently
pressed in France during the Eighties, but it's
unknown whether these were legitimate or
pirate copies.

1969: THE VELVET UNDERGROUND LIVE

Waiting For My Man/Lisa Says/What Goes On/Sweet Jane/We're Gonna Have A Real Good Time Together/Femme Fatale/New Age/Rock And Roll/Beginning To See The Light/Heroin/Ocean/Pale Blue Eyes/Heroin/Some Kinda Love/Over You/Sweet Bonnie Brown/It's Just Too Much/White Light-White Heat/I Can't Stand It/I'll Be Your Mirror (The second version of 'Heroin' and 'I Can't Stand It' were added for the CD release.)

Mercury double LP; recorded 1969; released April 1974. Personnel: Sterling Morrison (guitar, vocals);Lou Reed (vocals, guitar); Maureen Tucker (percussion); Doug Yule (bass guitar, organ, vocals)

This is supposedly drawn from over eight hours of tapes, but no recording details are given on the sleeve. 'Rock And Roll' was recorded by Robert Quine at The Matrix in San Francisco on November 25 1969; most (if not all) of the rest of this album is supposedly drawn from a gig at the End Of Cole Avenue club in Dallas, Texas on October 28 1969. At least one other Texas show was taped during this period – at the

Vulcan Gas Company in Austin – but that tape is missing, presumed lost.

Despite Sterling Morrison's assertion that "other performances on that tour are ten times better," the record is actually fairly stunning (despite having one of the tackiest covers of all time). The sound quality is almost infinitely superior to the *Max's Kansas City* album, and the band seem in good shape and humour – Reed even chats with the audience, asking them what kind of gig they want. Listening to this alongside the *Quine Tapes* from the same era, it's hard to believe that this is a band on the verge of disintegration; yet by the time the *Max's* album was recorded (less than a year later), Reed was barely able to complete a sentence.

But here, they're playing well, and Reed in particular sounds relaxed and assured. For most listeners, this was the first chance to hear the Velvets really stretching out, and playing lengthier versions of their album tracks (most of which were quite long to start with). The general approach is slower and more laid back than on the studio albums – even 'White Light/White Heat' is slowed to a crawl. Doug Yule's extended organ forays (reminiscent of The Band's Garth Hudson) give songs like 'What Goes On' an added dimension, with the others laying down a solid groove as the organ soars above them, the twin guitars constantly jockeying for position. The results are bluesy and energetic, and often surprising. The other really striking component of the album is Sterling Morrison's guitar fills, which are delicately graceful throughout.

'Lisa Says' segues into another, more vaudevillian song (possibly titled 'Why Am I So Shy') before turning back into

THE VELVET UNDERGROUND

'Lisa Says' again. 'Sweet Jane' is a radically different version to that on *Loaded* – slower and bluesier, with completely different words, it sounds a lot like the Cowboy Junkies' later arrangement of the song.

According to Reed, the version here has "the original lyrics, even recorded the day I wrote it". 'New Age' also has very different lyrics, namedropping "Frank and Nancy" (Sinatra, presumably) and generally sounding a lot more cynical and world-weary.

As well as previewing tracks from *Loaded* and running through a smattering of their greatest hits – including an exquisite version of 'Pale Blue Eyes' – they also play several songs from the 'lost' album. In 1974 these songs were new to most listeners, though Reed had already re-recorded three of them as a solo artist: 'Lisa Says', 'Ocean' and 'I Can't Stand It' (though this track was only released in the late Eighties, when it was added as a bonus track for the CD release). Reed would also re-record 'We're Gonna Have A Real Good Time Together' a few years later.

The Velvets' studio versions of all these tracks would also surface in the Eighties, but two songs remain available only on this recording (though neither are that remarkable): 'Over You' is a gentle, double-edged love song that could have easily fitted on the third album; 'Sweet Bonnie Brown/It's Too Much' is fast-paced R&B, but goes nowhere interesting.

Critically, the album went down extremely well. For some reason, it took another five years before the record was released in the UK; when it finally appeared in 1979, British critical response was just as enthusiastic. Post-punk, the Velvets still looked pretty good.

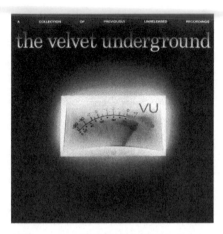

VU

I Can't Stand It/Stephanie Says/She's My Best Friend/Lisa Says/Ocean/Foggy Notion/Temptation Inside Your Heart/One Of These Days/Andy's Chest/I'm Sticking With You
Verve/Polygram; recorded 1968-69; released February 1985. Personnel: John Cale (viola, celesta, vocals; Sterling Morrison (guitar, vocals); Lou Reed (vocals, guitar); Maureen Tucker (percussion, vocals); Doug Yule (bass guitar, keyboards, vocals)

Subtitled "a collection of previously unreleased recordings", this album was compiled from tapes discovered in the Verve vaults during the process of re-issuing the first three Velvets albums on CD. Most of these were unmixed master tapes (only 'Ocean' had been properly mixed at the time of recording); utilising state-of-the art technology, the tapes were cleaned up and properly mixed in June 1984 by engineer Michael Barbiero at MediaSound in New York. The executive producer for the project was Bill Levenson.

'Stephanie Says' and 'Temptation Inside Your Heart' were both recorded in February 1968 at A&R Studios, New York, and feature

7

John Cale in the line-up; all of the other songs here are taken from the sessions for the 'lost' fourth Verve album, which was recorded at the Record Plant in New York between May and October 1969 and engineered by Gary Kellgren. All songs are presumably credited to Lou Reed (no songwriting credits are given on the sleeve) and were produced and arranged by the Velvet Underground. The version of 'Foggy Notion' which appears on the CD is slightly shorter than the one on the vinyl version – a situation that would be rectified when the track was included on *Peel Slowly And See*.

When this album was released, critical reaction was near-ecstatic – and not simply because ageing rock critics had been given a chance to indulge their nostalgia, but because the contents of *VU* were actually extremely good. Kicking off with the irresistible, riff-driven 'I Can't Stand It', the album gives way to the delicate ballad 'Stephanie Says', which features Cale and proves that he had much to offer Reed's new, softer direction, if the two could only have reconciled. 'She's My Best Friend' is poppier than anyone might have expected from the Velvets, and the bluesy 'Lisa Says' is infinitely superior to the version on Reed's debut solo album. The same can –but only just – be said of 'Ocean', which remains a

dull song in its every incarnation. 'Foggy Notion' is back-to-basics riff-driven rock, and utterly wonderful. 'Temptation Inside Your Heart' is a mess, but a really interesting one, with a great, Motown-inspired tune. 'One Of These Days' is slow country-blues, but not that remarkable. 'Andy's Chest' is Reed's tribute to Warhol after his near-assassination – and also a rarity, in that his solo version (on *Transformer*) is actually far superior to this, which sounds thrashy in comparison. The album closes with Moe Tucker's second vocal outing (accompanied by Lou), 'I'm Sticking With You' – which is either fey and embarrassing, or an utter delight, depending on your taste. Either way, it has one of those tunes that stick in the brain forever.

As a collection, *VU* was additional and totally unexpected proof of just how good this band really was. In some ways, the album is actually more accessible than *Loaded*, supposedly the Velvets' most openly commercial work; one can't help but wonder what impact the 'lost' album might have had, had it been released back in 1969. As Allan Jones noted in *Melody Maker*: "Twenty years on, listening to the Velvet Underground is still like dancing with lightning ... They remain, arguably, the most influential group in the history of rock."

THE 'LOST' ALBUM

14 of the tracks on *VU* and *Another View* comprise what would have been the Velvet Underground's 'lost' fourth album (which even had a catalogue number, MGM SE-4641). The songs are listed here in the order in which they were recorded (which is almost certainly not the running order the actual album

might have had): 'Foggy Notion'; 'Coney Island Steeplechase'; 'Andy's Chest'; 'I'm Sticking With You'; 'She's My Best Friend'; 'I Can't Stand It'; 'Ocean'; 'Ferryboat Bill'; 'Rock And Roll'; 'Ride Into The Sun'; 'One Of These Days'; 'I'm Gonna Move Right In'; 'Real Good Time Together'; and 'Lisa Says'.

THE VELVET UNDERGROUND

ANOTHER VIEW

We're Gonna Have A Real Good Time Together/I'm Gonna Move Right In/Hey Mr. Rain (Version I)/Ride Into The Sun/Coney Island Steeplechase/Guess I'm Falling In Love/ Hey Mr. Rain (Version Ii)/Ferryboat Bill/ Rock And Roll

Verve/Polygram; recorded 1967-69; released July 1986. Personnel: John Cale (viola, bass guitar); Sterling Morrison (guitar, backing vocals, bass guitar);Lou Reed (vocals, guitar, piano); Maureen Tucker (percussion); Doug Yule (bass guitar, keyboards, backing vocals)

Following the critical and commercial success of *VU*, the following year saw the release of a second batch of unreleased material from the Verve vaults. Again, most of the material was drawn from the 'lost' album – but inevitably the second scoop was not quite as impressive as the first, and there was the distinct impression of a barrel being scraped. Utterly minimal sleeve notes are provided, the only clues as to the personnel involved being the recording dates. 'Guess I'm Falling In Love' dates from December 1967, and is thus an outtake from *White Light/*

White Heat. The two versions of 'Hey Mr Rain' were recorded in May 1968 at TTG studios in Hollywood, while everything else here was recorded in May-September 1969 during sessions for the 'lost' album. All songs are credited to the Velvet Underground. 'I'm Gonna Move Right In', 'Ferryboat Bill' and 'Rock And Roll' were all mixed at the time of recording; all other tracks were mixed during March 1986 by J.C. Convertino at Sigma Sound. As with *VU*, Bill Levenson was executive producer of the project.

'We're Gonna Have A Real Good Time Together' is a straightforward rocker, minor but enjoyable, while 'I'm Gonna Move Right In' is a lengthy but unremarkable blues/ soul instrumental. The first version of 'Hey Mr Rain' is a folk/blues ballad, launched into another league by Cale's soaring viola; the second version is slightly more upbeat, but less successful in terms of effect. The version of 'Ride Into The Sun' here is an instrumental, but a lot more powerful and likeable than the version with words which appears on *Peel Slowly And See*; as it stands, it's probably the Velvets' finest instrumental.

'Coney Island Steeplechase' is a vaudevillian throwaway, 'Guess I'm Falling In Love' a thrashy instrumental version of a song that would also appear (in a live version) on the boxed set – it has some nice guitar work, but is otherwise unremarkable. 'Ferryboat Bill' is simply nonsensical novelty, and also utterly disposable. The album closes with the "original version" of 'Rock And Roll', which is both fascinating and likeable – and in some ways preferable to the finished article.

Though not as immediately impressive as the first collection, *Another View* still contains three absolute gems – more than enough to make the album an essential purchase.

Lou Reed & John Cale

SONGS FOR DRELLA – A FICTION

Smalltown/Open House/Style It Takes/Work/
Trouble With Classicists/Starlight/Faces
And Names/Images/Slip Away (A Warning)/
It Wasn't Me/I Believe/Nobody But You/A
Dream/Forever Changed/Hello It's Me
Sire/Warner Brothers; recorded winter 1989/90;
released April 1990. Personnel: Lou Reed, vocals
and guitars; John Cale, vocals, keyboards and viola.
Produced and written by Lou Reed and John Cale

Since this record is such a key part of
the Velvet Underground story, it's being
considered here rather than under solo
recordings. Reed and Cale's first collaboration
for over 20 years can arguably hold its head
up proudly alongside their early work, and
is certainly in the top rank of solo output
for both of them. Their inspiration here
comes from the passing of their mentor Andy
Warhol, and the album provides an overview
of the artist's life and work, beginning with
his childhood in a 'Smalltown' – except
that, although Warhol sometimes claimed to

come from the small town of McKeesport,
Pennsylvania, in reality he'd grown up in
Pittsburgh. Still, even Pittsburgh is small
compared to New York (and Reed is also
clearly drawing on his own upbringing in New
Jersey). As with most of the songs here, Reed
sings in the first person as if he *were* Warhol.

'Open House' explores Warhol's enduring
love of (and need for) company, as well
as his early career in New York. John Cale
takes over the vocals (and the role of Andy)
for 'Style It Takes', an exploration of some
of Warhol's most famous work, and a
depiction of how the artist could sweet-talk
and flatter whatever was required – money,
space, a performance – out of whoever was
being asked. 'Work' sees Reed abandoning
the Warhol persona and recounting some of
his own memories of Warhol – including his
firing of Andy as the Velvets' manager – and
exploring the workaholic nature of the man
who once asked, "Why do people think
artists are special? It's just another job."

Cale returns for 'Trouble With Classicists',
a comparative analysis of artistic methods and
their failings, before Reed returns to examine
Warhol's films (and his approach and attitudes
to the medium) in 'Starlight'. Back to Cale
for 'Faces And Names', which illustrates that
although Warhol was seemingly incessantly
drawn to fame and beauty, many claim he
treated *everybody* alike. The fact that Andy had
a terrible memory for names might explain
his view that life would be a lot simpler if
we were all interchangeable, though he also
pointed out that "if everybody's not a beauty,
then nobody is."

A viola-drone riff dominates in 'Images',
in which Reed (as Warhol) defends the
artist's most famous stylistic trademark:
multiple images of the same thing, each
subtly different from the others. In 'Slip

THE VELVET UNDERGROUND

7

Away (A Warning)', Reed-as-Warhol is warned that the Factory is getting out of hand, but refuses to listen. In 'It Wasn't Me', Reed-as-Warhol denies responsibility for the high mortality rate (via suicides and drug-related deaths) in the social world which revolved around him. Many accusations were hurled at Warhol, prompting several responses from him: "Now and then someone would accuse me of being evil – of letting people destroy themselves while I watched, just so I could film them and tape-record them. But I don't think of myself as evil – just realistic. I learned when I was little that whenever I got aggressive and tried to tell someone what to do, nothing happened – I just couldn't carry it off." More philosophically, he once stated: "When people are ready to, they change. They never do it before then, and sometimes they die before they get round to it. You can't make them change if they don't want to, just like when they do want to, you can't stop them."

Reed abandons the Warhol persona for 'I Believe', personally entering the fray to describe Valerie Solanas' assassination attempt, Warhol's injuries and recuperation, and his own feelings of a need for retribution – that Solanas got off way too lightly – and personal guilt that he never visited Warhol in hospital. He also states outright that it was "the hospital" that eventually killed Warhol.

"There is nothing like getting shot to kill a party," Factory photographer Nat Finkelstein once bitchily observed, and 'Nobody But You' examines the aftermath of the Solanas incident. Most observers agree that the artist was a completely different person afterwards: Andy II, who went to parties and nightclubs and dinners but produced (for him) very little worthwhile

work. Reed's lyric explores the artist's own reactions to his new life and the mood is one of utter, crippling, isolation. 'A Dream' resulted from Cale's suggestion that Lou write a short story about Warhol, and that they set it to music the way they had with 'The Gift'. Reed decided to make it like a dream, rather than something event-based. "That way we can have Andy do anything we want," he explained. The result is an imagined reverie inisde Warhol's mind shortly before his death.

When the lyrics were published in his *Between Thought And Expression* collection, Reed wrote: "This is not an excerpt from Andy's diaries." Reed had in fact been appalled by the shallow inanity and bitchiness of Warhol's published *Diaries* – something he'd emphasize further on 'Hello, It's Me' – and he wove verbatim quotes from the book, including Warhol's remarks about himself and Cale, into a monologue that reveals much about what Warhol was actually like as a person. Though Reed has performed this live in concert, here it's Cale who takes the vocal, his Welsh lilt heightening the dreamlike atmosphere. Added in its later stages, this became the album's centrepiece and undisputed gem.

In 'Forever Changed', Cale-as-Warhol muses on the different changes his life passed through – including, presumably, the final one. There is, of course, also an album by Love entitled *Forever Changes* – but the use of the past tense here underlines the sense of finality. The album closes with its most personal (and moving) song in 'Hello It's Me', in which Lou Reed bids Warhol a final farewell. Few people have ever received a tribute on a par with this album; it's far more important than most critics gave it credit for, and was clearly made with both care and love.

LIVE MCMXCIII

Disc One

We're Gonna Have A Real Good Time Together/Venus In Furs/Guess I'm Falling In Love/Afterhours/All Tomorrow's Parties/Some Kinda Love/I'll Be Your Mirror/Beginning To See The Light/The Gift/I Heard Her Call My Name/Femme Fatale

Disc Two

Hey Mr Rain/Sweet Jane/Velvet Nursery Rhyme/White Light-White Heat/I'm Sticking With You/Black Angel's Death Song/Rock 'N' Roll/I Can't Stand It/I'm Waiting For The Man/Heroin/Pale Blue Eyes/Coyote

Sire/Warner Bros; recorded June 1993; released October 1993. Recorded at the three Paris shows (at L'Olympia Theater) and produced by Reed's guitarist Mike Rathke. Personnel: John Cale (viola, keyboards, bass guitar, vocals); Sterling Morrison (guitar, bass guitar, vocals); Lou Reed (vocals, guitar); Maureen Tucker (percussion, vocals)

Reviews of the reunited Velvet Underground's live shows were mixed and reviews of the album and video would be equally divided. Once the emotional impact of seeing the four of them together on stage again, against

all expectations, had subsided, many critics leveled accusations that the whole thing was just too 'showbiz' for comfort. The fault doesn't really lie with the music – which veers from the amateurish ('We're Gonna Have A Real Good Time Together') to the epic ('Hey Mr Rain') – but which has enough truly stunning moments to make it worth hearing. The main problem lies with Reed, whose vocals aren't invested with any real feeling much of the time, to the point that they approach self-parody.

On much of the record he sounds like a lounge singer in a cheesy rock cabaret act, and everything suffers accordingly. Cale and Reed had divided Nico's vocal role between them, Reed taking 'I'll Be Your Mirror' while Cale took the rest (to much better effect, as it happens). Another low point is the 'Velvet Nursery Rhyme', Reed's introduction to the band in verse, which only *just* avoids making the listener wince with embarassment.

There are many plus points, however: Morrison's tasteful guitar fills; Tucker's drumming and show-stealing solo spots; Cale's searing viola; and great versions of 'All Tomorrow's Parties', 'I Can't Stand It' and 'I'm Waiting For The Man'. You also finally get to hear the words to 'Guess I'm Falling In Love', which features the line "I've got the fever in my pocket", a quote from Bob Dylan's 'Absolutely Sweet Marie'. And 'Pale Blue Eyes' sounds as if it was always *meant* to feature Cale's mesmeric viola-playing. And, for once, Reed's world-weary vocal approach fits perfectly; this 'Pale Blue Eyes' is the definitive version, and worth the price of admission on its own.

Though the band are sometimes ragged, most of the time they're in great form, their rapport often uncanny and their playing occasionally approaching the sublime. The

7

THE VELVET UNDERGROUND

7

real stars of the show are John Cale and Moe Tucker. The sheer *solidity* of her drumming is astonishing; it's also a stunning visual spectacle, as the video proves. And, of course, state-of-the-art recording technology makes this a lot more accessible than their previous live albums – though it does make you wish someone had made a professional live recording of them back in 1966. As for the one new song, 'Coyote', Reed's laconic tale of desert dogs could be an allegory for the Velvets' own troubled history; it could also easily have fitted on *Loaded*. With thunderous bass/drum combination, Morrison's delicate guitarwork and the dry observations of Reed's lyric it proved to be a more than adequate swan song.

An abbreviated, single-CD version was also released at the same time (and with the same title, confusingly). The track listing is: 'Venus In Furs', 'Sweet Jane', 'Afterhours', 'All Tomorrow's Parties', 'Some Kinda Love', 'The Gift', 'Rock 'N' Roll', 'I'm Waiting For The Man', 'Heroin' and 'Pale Blue Eyes'.

the velvet underground
what goes on

WHAT GOES ON

Disc One

"Andy Warhol Presents"/Melody Laughter/ Heroin/I'm Waiting For The Man/Sunday Morning/I'll Be Your Mirror/Run Run Run/ All Tomorrow's Parties/Venus In Furs/Femme Fatale/It Was A Pleasure Then/From The Music Factory/White Light-White Heat/Lady Godiva's Operation/I Heard Her Call My Name/Untitled

Disc Two

Sister Ray/Here She Comes Now/Guess I'm Falling In Love/Stephanie Says/Hey Mr Rain # 2/ Candy Says/Some Kinda Love/Pale Blue Eyes/ Beginning To See The Light/I'm Set Free/The Murder Mystery/Foggy Notion/I Can't Stand It

Disc Three

Ocean/One Of These Days/Introductions/Too Much/Sweet Jane/New Age/Over You/What Goes On/Afterhours/I'm Sticking With You/ Train Round The Bend/Head Held High/Who Loves The Sun/Rock And Roll/Ride Into The Sun/Afterhours/"No More Reunions"/Thanks Andy Warhol

Raven; recorded 1966–1970; released 1993

An Australian compilation, which was of note at the time for containing several then-unreleased tracks (and the then-unavailable 'closet mix' of six tracks from the third album), all of which have since been collected on either *Peel Slowly And See* or *Fully Loaded*.

The only material left on this set which is still unavailable elsewhere (or at any rate, very hard to find) are the spoken-word tracks: a brief interview with Warhol promoting the Dom gigs; a conversation between Reed and Tom Wilson circa *White Light/White Heat*, with Reed trotting out some great fine art ideas; a 1966 conversation between Nico, Cale, Reed and others (from *Andy Warhol's Index Book*,

THE MUSIC: **THE ALBUMS**

discussing the book); a snatched quote from Reed on the street in 1985, denying the possibility of any reunion; and eight minutes' worth of fascinating interviews with all four Velvets and MC Kostek at the opening of the Cartier Warhol retrospective at Jouy-en-Josas in June 1990. The live version of 'Heroin' performed that day can be heard running underneath the interviews. This track first appeared on a free flexidisc inserted into issue four of the Velvets fanzine *What Goes On*.

Leaving aside the spoken material, this is also an excellent compilation, and one which takes in a slightly broader sweep of the Velvets' career than *Peel Slowly And See*. Its appearance also doubtlessly galvanised the Velvets into putting together their own official retrospective boxed set.

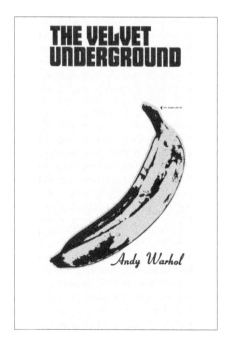

PEEL SLOWLY AND SEE

Five CDs including the albums *The Velvet Underground & Nico*, *White Light/White Heat*, *VU* and *Loaded*, alongside "closet mixes", demos and A-sides (from singles), with some *Chelsea Girl* tracks
Previously unreleased tracks include:
Venus in Furs (demo)/Prominent Men (demo)/Heroin (demo)/I'm Waiting for the Man (demo)/Wrap Your Troubles in Dreams (demo)/All Tomorrow's Parties (demo)/Melody Laughter (live edit)/There is No Reason (demo)/Sheltered Life (demo)/It's All Right (The Way That You Live) (demo)/I'm Not Too Sorry (Now That You're Gone) (demo)/Here She Comes Now (demo)/Guess I'm Falling in Love (live)/Booker T. (live)/
What Goes On (live)/ It's Just Too Much (live)/ Countess from Hong Kong (demo)/Satellite of Love/Walk and Talk/Oh Gin/ Sad Song/Ocean/Ride into the Sun/Some Kinda Love (live)/I Love You
Polydor; recorded 1965-1970; released September 1995

The Velvets' official boxed retrospective is a lavish affair, containing five CDs. On these could be found the band's first four albums (re-edited and remixed where necessary), plus a wealth of unreleased material – including a whole disc full of early demos. The set's packaging echoed that of the Velvets' first album, complete with (peelable) banana, and the box also contained a well-designed booklet containing an excellent career overview by David Fricke. Released shortly after Sterling Morrison's death, the set amply fulfilled its purposes – to set a seal on the band's history, and to stem the tide of bootlegs. Much of the unreleased material had been supplied by Morrison from his archives, and *Peel Slowly And See* stands as a worthy epitaph for him.

THE VELVET UNDERGROUND

7

Disc One consists of previously unreleased demo material from John Cale's archives, recorded at his Ludlow Street apartment in New York during July 1965. Reed and Morrison play guitars, while Cale plays viola and *sarinda* (an Afghani stringed instrument). There is no drummer, since Angus MacLise had forgotten to turn up for the session. "Angus was really living on the Angus calendar," explained John Cale. "If you told Angus that there was a rehearsal at two o'clock on Friday, he wouldn't understand what you were talking about. He would just come and go, whenever and wherever he pleased." Though the material here is definitely interesting, one listening is sufficient for most people. For one thing, there are multiple takes of most of the songs; for another, most are delivered in an acoustic, folky style that gives little hint of where they'd end up eventually. According to Cale, their months of experimentation during rehearsal were what paid off in the long term: "We started detuning instruments, playing with gadgets, puttering about in general until we landed with something."

'Venus In Furs' is sung by Cale as a folky ballad, almost in medieval minstrel mode, and sounding somewhere between 'Scarborough Fair' and 'Greensleeves'. It's very surprising, considering how much Cale hated folk music; it sounds almost like parody. Several takes of the song pretty much all run together without a break (lasting over fifteen minutes). 'Prominent Men' (written by Cale/Reed and sung by Reed) is a Dylanesque protest song, complete with harmonica, that rails against the high and mighty. It's fairly unremarkable, and doesn't really fit with the other material, which probably explains why the Velvets dropped it from their repertoire. 'Heroin' gets five different takes, not all of which make it all the way through (over thirteen minutes'

worth). The lyrics are slightly different, but otherwise the bones of the finished version are all present here, from the arrangement to the pacing – though Reed's wavering vocals sound ultra-nasal and Dylanish.

'I'm Waiting For The Man' rates three takes (just under ten minutes' worth), which feature some painfully messy harmonica and viola. The song is done as a ragtime country-blues, complete with slide guitar and a bizarre vocal interjection from Cale. Reed's 'Wrap Your Troubles In Dreams' is sung by Cale as a mournful folk dirge. The metronomic percussion here is provided by Sterling Morrison rapping his knuckles against the back of Cale's sarinda. The song would later be recorded by Nico on her *Chelsea Girl* album (a version that is infinitely better than this). There are several takes of this (nearly sixteen minutes' worth), and one features a brief argument which is a lot more interesting than the music. 'All Tomorrow's Parties' is also given the folky ballad treatment, with Cale and Reed harmonizing (but still sounding like Dylan). The first version is really fast, but collapses in a shower of Anglo-Saxon. Eight more (mainly incomplete) takes follow, with varying degrees of success (over eighteen minutes' worth). The most interesting aspect here is that this was recorded nearly six months before they met Warhol, which gives the lie to the theory that Reed had written it to please Andy's sensibilities.

Disc Two consists of *The Velvet Underground & Nico* in its entirety, plus four extra tracks. These include a mono single version of 'All Tomorrow's Parties', originally released in July 1966. It's a drastically edited version of the album track (cut from almost six seconds down to just under three). The second, 'Melody Laughter', was a previously unreleased drone-like improvisation piece

7

that, when played live, could last anywhere from two minutes to 42, and which would feature almost any combination of their instruments. This version was recorded live at the Valleydale Ballroom, Columbus, Ohio on 4 November 1966 and edited down to just under 11 minutes (from 30). The writing is credited to all four Velvets plus Nico, who sings wordlessly – or as Tucker put it, "just warbles". It veers between being interesting to just plain self-indulgent; at times it's pretty painful.

The third track is 'It Was A Pleasure Then', first released on Nico's 1969 solo album *Chelsea Girl*, and written by Nico, Cale and Reed – though it sounds like it almost certainly developed out of 'Melody Laughter'. Dirge-like and gothic, it was the first hint of the template that Nico would mine for most her future career. Recorded at Mayfair Sound Studios in New York, April/May 1967. Produced by Tom Wilson, engineered by Gary Kellgren.

The fourth, 'Chelsea Girls', was written by Reed/Morrison, and was also included on Nico's *Chelsea Girl* album. Commissioned for the Warhol movie of the same name, but completed too late for inclusion in the film, the song is a very folky ballad that lists various characters that haunted the Factory and the Chelsea Hotel. Recorded at Mayfair Sound Studios in New York, between April and May 1967, it was produced by Tom Wilson and engineered by Gary Kellgren. Nico hated Larry Fallon's orchestral arrangement for the song, as did Reed. "Everything on it, those strings, that flute, should have defeated it," he said. "But the lyrics, Nico's voice ... It managed somehow to survive."

Disc Three consists of: *White Light/ White Heat* in its entirety; 'Stephanie Says' and 'Temptation Inside Your Heart' (from

VU); and 'Hey Mr. Rain (Version I)' (from *Another View*). There are also five previously unreleased tracks from a demo acetate recorded early in 1967 at John Cale's Ludlow Street apartment.

The first, 'There Is No Reason' is an acoustic folky ballad and a lover's complaint – fairly unremarkable, and also fairly amateurish. Written by Reed/Cale, sung by Reed. 'Sheltered Life' is written (and sung) by Reed. It's really enjoyable psychedelic ragtime-folk, with downright funny nonsense lyrics and a kazoo solo, sounding like something The Purple Gang (of 'Granny Takes A Trip' fame) might have come up with. Reed would later re-record the song for his 1976 album *Rock And Roll Heart*. 'It's All Right (The Way That You Live)' is again fairly ordinary, a mixture of folk and R&B, with a great booming bassline. Written by Reed/Cale, sung by Reed. 'I'm Not Too Sorry (Now That You're Gone)' is Beatles-ish folk/pop, overlaid with a lot of psychedelic guitar work. Another minor work, but enjoyable. Written by Reed/Cale, sung by Reed.

'Here She Comes Now' has different lyrics to the version later recorded for *White Light/ White Heat*, and some very weird echoing viola that makes it sound much more psychedelic. Written by Reed/Cale/Morrison, and sung by Reed in Dylan mode.

Additionally, there are two good quality live tracks recorded live at the Gymnasium in New York, April 1967, both of which are credited to all four Velvets. 'Guess I'm Falling In Love' is a high energy performance of the song, which pisses all over the version on the 1993 live album *and* the instrumental one on *Another View*. 'Booker T' is an R&B instrumental, inspired by Booker T & The MGs' 'Green Onions'. The track would later evolve into the backing music for 'The Gift'.

THE VELVET UNDERGROUND

7

A three-minute extract from this (fairly sloppy) six-and-a-half-minute performance had previously been released in 1992, on John Cale's solo album *Paris S'Eveille*.

Disc Four features the 'closet mix' of *The Velvet Underground* album in its entirety, plus 'Foggy Notion', 'I Can't Stand It', 'I'm Sticking With You', 'One Of These Days' and 'Lisa Says' (from *VU*) and three previously unreleased tracks. 'What Goes On' was recorded live on 2 October 1968 at La Cave, Cleveland, Ohio: it's a fairly undistinguished live version, with pretty rough sound quality. The point of interest here lies in the fact that this gig was supposedly Doug Yule's concert debut with the band.

'It's Just Too Much' comes from the same era as the version on *1969: Velvet Underground Live*, but this one was recorded live on 28 October 1969 at The End of Cole Ave, Dallas, Texas. It's country blues, and pretty dull. 'Countess From Hong Kong' is a demo version of a song co-written by Cale and Reed, but not recorded until late 1969 (i.e. long after Cale's departure). No other recording details are given. Reed plays harmonica, which sounds incongruous given that the general treatment here is more like bossa nova than folk. The song takes its title from Charlie Chaplin's last film as a director: a romantic comedy that starred Sophia Loren and Marlon Brando, it was released in 1967. Lou Reed is evidently a big Chaplin fan – check out 'City Lights' on his solo album *The Bells*.

Disc Five gives us *Loaded* in its entirety, but with full-length versions of 'Sweet Jane' and 'New Age' replacing the edited ones from the original release. 'Sweet Jane' gains Reed's intended ending; 'New Age' has an extended closing refrain. It has to be said that neither of these restored versions is actually an improvement on the edited ones.

Also included here are a live version of 'I'll Be Your Mirror' (from *Live At Max's Kansas City*) and a laconically bluesy live version of 'Some Kinda Love' (an outtake from the same album). There are also seven previously unreleased outtakes from *Loaded*.

'Satellite Of Love', the first of these, would be revived by Reed (with slightly different lyrics) for his *Transformer* solo album. Here it's still overtly a pop song, but nowhere near as hummable and commercial as it would become with the Bowie/Ronson arrangement. The subject matter is the painfully promiscuous infidelity of one's partner, and the resultant jealousy of the singer.

'Walk And Talk' is an undistinguished folk/blues sung by Reed (with harmonies by Yule), who would re-record it for his first solo album. Some think the song was influenced by Hubert Selby's novel *Last Exit To Brooklyn*, but it's hard to see how.

'Oh Gin' is another minor blues, which Reed would re-work (to even lesser effect) as 'Oh Jim' for his solo album *Berlin*. 'Sad Song' is an achingly beautiful ballad about a rocky relationship. By the time Reed re-recorded it for *Berlin*, three years later, it had become a fairly bitter song about divorce.

The version of 'Ocean' here was originally thought to be one that featured John Cale. When *Peel Slowly And See* was released, no one was aware of the fact that Cale had briefly returned to the Velvets fold in 1970. "I was brought in by Steve Sesnick in a half-hearted attempt at re-uniting old comrades," he explained to David Fricke. However, it subsequently turned out that this wasn't the version with Cale after all, which would eventually surface on *Fully Loaded*. The version here actually features

Doug Yule on an organ part that swells like a tide, includes some great guitar work and is more moodily melodramatic and vocally atmospheric than the version on *VU*. Reed would re-record the song yet again for his eponymous debut album in 1972.

'Ride Into The Sun' had already appeared on *Another View* as an instrumental; this time it has words about wishing for an escape from the city (and it *still* sounds very Beatle-influenced). Also re-recorded by Reed for his first solo album. 'I Love You' is, as its title implies, a straightforward love song from Reed; sadly, it isn't a very good one. All seven songs are credited solely to Reed except 'Ride Into The Sun', which is credited to Reed/Cale/Tucker/Morrison.

FULLY LOADED

Disc One

Who Loves The Sun/Sweet Jane/Rock & Roll/Cool It Down/New Age/Head Held High/ Lonesome Cowboy Bill/ I Found A Reason/ Train Round The Bend/Oh ! Sweet Nuthin'/ Ride Into The Sun/Ocean/I'm Sticking With You/I Love You/Rock & Roll/Head Held High

Disc Two

Who Loves The Sun/Sweet Jane/Rock & Roll/Coolit Down/New Age/Head Held High/ Lonesome Cowboy Bill/ I Found A Reason/ Train Round The Bend/Oh ! Sweet Nuthin'/ Ocean/I Love You/Satellite Of Love/Oh Gin/ Walk And Talk/Sad Song/Love Makes You Feel Ten Feet Tall

Rhino; recorded 1970; released February 1997

After *Peel Slowly And See*, most people assumed that the well of unreleased Velvets studio material was now exhausted. Then several boxes of tapes were discovered in Atlantic's vaults, some of them apparently labelled "garbage", and these formed the core of this double-CD set. 17 of the 33 tracks had never been available before, and though a few are simply alternate mixes, the rest are a revelation. Remastered by engineer Bob Ludwig, *Fully Loaded* was thoughtfully packaged, with a lenticular sleeve that echoed the original *Loaded* album cover. The booklet liner notes were once again by David Fricke.

Disc One contains a 'restored' version of the original *Loaded* album, including "full-length" versions of 'Sweet Jane' and 'Rock & Roll', and a "long version" of 'New Age'. Of the remaining six tracks on the disc, three had already appeared on *Peel Slowly And See*, while the remainder included previously unreleased alternate mixes of 'Rock & Roll' (with grotesque backing vocals) and 'Head Held High', plus an outtake of 'I'm Sticking With You' that simply isn't as good as the one on *VU*.

Disc Two contains an *alternate* version of *Loaded* that's comprised of demos, early versions and alternate mixes (of 'Who Loves The Sun' and 'Train Round The Bend', neither being an improvement).

THE VELVET UNDERGROUND

There's an incredibly slow early version of 'Sweet Jane' with slightly different lyrics and highly erratic percussion, which is fascinating without actually being much good; a wonderful demo of 'Rock & Roll' which features some incredibly delicate guitar work; an equally fine piano-driven early version of 'Cool It Down'; the "full-length" version of 'New Age' (which fades on a very nice guitar solo); early (and unimpressive) versions of 'Head Held High' and 'Lonesome Cowboy Bill'; a great, country-folk demo of 'I Found A Reason' (with Dylanesque harmonica); and a bluesy early version of 'Oh ! Sweet Nuthin'' that features a very wheezy organ, but isn't that marvellous.

In addition to this, Disc Two also contains seven more tracks. Three of these had already been included on *Peel Slowly And See*, while the other four were new. There's an early (and rather tentative) demo of 'Ocean', featuring John Cale on organ; an outtake of 'I Love You' which has a much more interesting arrangement than the version on the boxed set (though it's still not impressive as a song); and a very stripped-down demo of 'Satellite Of Love' to the one included on the boxed set (still nowhere near as good as the *Transformer* version). There's also the demo for a hitherto unknown song called 'Love Makes You Feel Ten Feet Tall', which is Reed in pure Dylan mode – but the backing is a lot better than the song.

All in all, a very interesting compilation. Is it worth the price of admission if you already own a copy of *Loaded*? Definitely. It's also a much better deal than *Reloaded*, the 45th anniversary edition of *Loaded* that came out in 2015. For rich completists only, this comprised five CDs and one (audio-only)

DVD containing: stereo and mono mixes of the original album; *Live At Max's Kansas City*; another live CD recorded at Second Fret in Philadelphia in May 1970, with truly terrible sound quality and inaudible vocals; a CD of outtakes, early versions and demos; and even more different mixes of the original album.

BOOTLEG SERIES VOLUME I: THE QUINE TAPES

Disc One
I'm Waiting For The Man/It's Just Too Much/ What Goes On/I Can't Stand It/Some Kinda Love/Foggy Notion/Femme Fatale/ After Hours/I'm Sticking With You/Sunday Morning/Sister Ray

Disc Two
Follow The Leader/White Light-White Heat/ Venus In Furs/Heroin/Sister Ray

Disc Three
Rock And Roll/New Age/Over You/Black Angel's Death Song/I'm Waiting For The Man/ Ride Into The Sun/Sister Ray/Foggy Notion

Polydor; recorded 1969; released 2001. Recorded at: The Family Dog, San Francisco (7–9 November 1969); The Matrix, San Francisco (23–25 November,

7

27 November, 1 December, 3 December 1969);
Washington University, St Louis (11 May 1969).
Personnel: Lou Reed, Sterling Morrison, Doug
Yule, Maureen Tucker. All tracks were recorded by
Robert Quine on a portable Sony cassette recorder
with a hand-held microphone. 'Rock And Roll' had
appeared on the 1969 live album, but everything
else was previously unreleased

Robert Quine (born 30 December 1942)
was a law student from Akron, Ohio, who
moved to San Francisco in the Fall of 1969
after passing his bar exams in Missouri.
Quine was already a devoted Velvet
Underground fan, and when the group came
to California Quine attended – and taped –
every gig. Noticing his presence, the Velvets
invited him backstage for a conversation,
and also to soundchecks and rehearsals.
Fortunately, Quine had the foresight to
transfer four hours' worth of the best
of the material onto reel-to-reel tapes,
from which these CDs were mastered; his
original cassettes subsequently suffered
damage and were eventually lost.

The sound quality is pretty good on the
Family Dog tapes, less so on the ones from
the Matrix, and the material is generally
comparable to that on the 1969 Live album.
If anything, the band are tighter and more
energetic, delivering driving versions of
'I Can't Stand It', 'Some Kinda Love' and
'Foggy Notion', and wonderfully ragged
versions of 'I'm Sticking With You' and
'Ride Into The Sun'. On the downside, Yule
is really no substitute for Cale on tracks
like 'Venus In Furs' or 'The Black Angel's
Death Song'. Worse, there's a general
tendency towards extended improvisation,
including a 17-minute meandering mess
entitled 'Follow The Leader' and no less
than three extremely long versions of
'Sister Ray', which feature as much lyrical
improvisation as they do musical. The
longest of these lasts for 38 minutes, and
they're either fascinating or self-indulgent,
depending on your point of view; such
lengthy jamming was de rigeur for the
times, but didn't really last beyond them –
punk rock happened for a reason.

ROBERT QUINE

Robert Quine never practiced law. After
two years in San Francisco, he moved to
New York, where he wrote textbooks on
tax law for three years and became friends
with Tom Verlaine and Richard Hell. Quine
had played guitar in various amateur bands
since his teens, and in 1975 decided to
finally abandon his textbooks and form a
serious band, The Voidoids, with Hell.

Lou Reed became a fan early on,
eventually hiring Quine for his new post-
rehab band in the early Eighties, beginning
with The Blue Mask. Quine remained

in Reed's band for nearly four years,
subsequently playing with numerous other
artists including Tom Waits, Brian Eno,
Lloyd Cole, Marianne Faithfull, Matthew
Sweet and John Zorn. After Quine's wife
Alice died of heart failure in August 2003,
he became severely depressed, and is
believed to have made at least one suicide
attempt during that winter. He died of
a heroin overdose – which was almost
certainly a deliberate suicidal act – on
or about May 31 2004; his body was
discovered approximately five days later.

THE VELVET UNDERGROUND

7

Nothing in this collection is truly essential, but there's more than enough good material included to make it well worth checking out. And the 'Volume I' part of the title at least holds out some vague hope for future releases in the series.

FINAL V.U. 1971–1973

Disc One
Chapel Of Love/ I'm Waiting For The Man/ Spare Change/Some Kinda Love/Turn On Your Love Light/White Light White Heat/ Pretty Tree Climber/Rock And Roll/Back On The Farm/Dopey Joe/Sister Ray/Never Going Back To Georgia/After Hours
Disc Two
I'm Waiting For The Man/Spare Change/ Some Kinda Love/White Light White Heat/ Hold On/What Goes On/Cool It Down/Back On The Farm/Oh Sweet Nuthin'/Sister Ray/ After Hours/Dopey Joe/Rock And Roll
Disc Three
I'm Waiting For The Man/White Light White

Heat/Some Kinda Love/Little Jack/Sweet Jane/ Mean Old Man/Run Run Run/Caroline/Dopey Joe/What Goes On/Sister Ray/Train Round The Bend/Rock And Roll/ I'm Waiting For The Man
Disc Four
I'm Waiting For The Man/Little Jack/ White Light White Heat/Caroline/Sweet Jane/Mean Old Man/Who's That Man/Let It Shine/ Mama's Little Girl/Train Round The Bend
Captain Trip Records; recorded 1971–1973; released 2002. Disc One recorded at School Of Oriental And African Studies, London, England, November 5 1971. Disc Two recorded at Concertgebouw, Amsterdam, Netherlands, November 19 1971. Personnel: Doug Yule (guitar and vocals); Walter Powers (bass); Willie Alexander (piano and vocals); Maureen Tucker (drums and vocals). Disc Three recorded at St David's University, Lampeter, Wales, December 6 1972. Personnel: Doug Yule, guitar and vocals; Rob Norris, guitar; George Kay, bass; Mark Nauseef, drums. Disc Four recorded at Oliver's, Boston, Massachusetts, May 27 1973. Personnel: Doug Yule (guitar and vocals); Billy Yule (drums); George Kay (bass); Don Silverman (guitar). The bonus tracks on Disc Four are radio broadcast versions of four tracks from Disc Two

These bootleg-quality recordings were licensed from Doug Yule, who also provided an essay in the illustrated booklet. The set is lavishly packaged in a box, which makes it seem far more important than it actually is, since what's included here is neither representative of any of the other Velvet Underground records, or very good. The recording quality veers from poor to atrocious, and the musical content is proof positive that anyone who paid money to see the 'Velveteens' live would have been sorely disappointed. They're simply a ramshackle bar band trotting out a lot of blues clichés (though the bass and guitar solos are actually of slightly more interest than the songs that surround them), albeit a bar band that happens to know a lot of Velvet Underground songs. Hearing Moe Tucker sing 'Afterhours' with this group sounds bizarrely out of place, and more than a little sad. Save your money.

LE BATACLAN '72

Lou Reed, John Cale & Nico

Waiting For The Man/Berlin/Black Angels Death Song/Iwld Child/Heroin/Ghost Story/ The Biggest, Loudest, Hairiest Group Of All/Empty Bottles/Femme Fatale/No One Is There/Frozen Warnings/Janitor Of Lunacy/I'll Be Your Mirror/All Tomorrow's Parties/ Bonus Rehearsal Tracks: Pale Blue Eyes/ Candy Says

Alchemy Entertainment; recorded 29 January 1972; released 2003. Personnel: Lou Reed (vocals, acoustic guitar); John Cale (vocals, guitar, viola and piano); Nico (vocals and harmonium)

Since this CD captures another key moment in the Velvet Underground story, it's being considered here rather than under solo recordings. After over thirty years, anyone

who was unable to attend the actual concert was now able to hear the results of the unexpected reunion of three of the Velvets' core personnel in January 1972. Paris's Bataclan Theatre was filled to its capacity of 1,000 people for the event (with an estimated 2,000 more disappointed fans turned away at the door).

What it actually sounds like is 'The Velvet Underground Unplugged': acoustic, often bluesy treatments of a half dozen Velvets' classics, plus a small selection from the trio's solo songbooks. 'Waiting For The Man' and 'Heroin' might well have sounded like this back when Reed and Cale were performing it as buskers. 'The Black Angel's Death Song' here resembles something Leonard Cohen might have come up with, while 'Wild Child' sounds like Bob Dylan on a bad day (though it's far better than the studio version). Cale contributes a lacklustre 'Ghost Story', plus 'The Biggest, Loudest, Hairiest Group Of All', a throwaway ballad about a rock band on the road – if it's intended to be about the Velvets, it doesn't do them justice. Cale is on firmer ground with 'Empty Bottles', but it's not as strong as many of the songs on *Vintage Violence* that he could have picked in its stead.

Nico weighs in with 'Femme Fatale' (with great harmonies from Cale and Reed), before heading for the harmonium and a selection of her solo material – all of which is great, but of a completely different mood to what's gone before. It's as if the audience has been suddenly transported to a gothic cathedral, then transported back again for the finale of 'I'll Be Your Mirror', followed by a somewhat ragged encore of 'All Tomorrow's Parties'. The rehearsal tape of 'Pale Blue Eyes' and 'Candy Says' consists of Reed actually teaching Cale the songs, and is thus very tentative and generally a bit of a mess – which is obviously

THE VELVET UNDERGROUND

why these songs didn't get included in the actual concert.

Given that Reed's solo career was in sorry shape at the time of this recording, he sounds both confident and in good voice – while Cale, who was then very inexperienced at singing before an audience, sounds pretty shaky. One can't help but wonder what might have happened at this point if the other two had agreed to Reed's suggestion of making this a more permanent reunion – which would have resulted in a Velvet Underground with three songwriters instead of just one. Sadly, we'll never know.

When an interviewer asked Reed about this album in 2003, Lou expressed surprise at the news that it had been released, and talked of getting an injunction to stop it being distributed. However, the sleeve clearly states that the record has been licensed from Sister Ray Enterprises and is thus legitimate (and definitely had the approval of Cale), so perhaps Reed was just living up to his public persona. The album sleeve states that the project was coordinated by one Carlton P Sandercock, which certainly sounds like a pseudonym for somebody. Regardless of its flaws, a great live album.

SCEPTER STUDIO SESSIONS

European Son/The Black Angel's Death Song/All Tomorrow's Parties/I'll Be Your Mirror/Heroin/Femme Fatale/Venus In Furs/ I'm Waiting For The Man/Run Run Run

Polydor; recorded 1966; released April 2013 (limited edition vinyl only). Personnel: Lou Reed, John Cale, Sterling Morrison, Maureen Tucker

In 2002, a Canadian record collector named Warren Hill bought a copy of what is probably the rarest Velvet Underground record in a yard sale in Manhattan for 75 cents. The record had no sleeve, and only the words "The Velvet Underground" and "Mr N. Dolph" scrawled on the label gave any clue to what was on it. It turned out to be a mono acetate copy of the first Velvet Underground album – or rather of the recordings made at Scepter Studios, before later re-recording of some of the songs at TTG in Los Angeles. After the sessions, Norman Dolph had had the acetate cut through his contacts at Columbia Records, and had then given it to either Andy Warhol or Paul Morrissey. He has no idea how it ended up for sale.

The mixes of all tracks on it differ from the released version, as does the running order. In addition, there are completely different takes of 'European Son', 'Heroin', 'Venus In Furs' and 'I'm Waiting For The Man'. Another acetate copy is owned by Maureen Tucker, and in 1966 or 1967 a third copy was given by Warhol to Ken Pitt, then David Bowie's manager (though this may well have been a later version of the album). Pitt gave his copy to Bowie, and it may still exist in Bowie's archives.

In late 2006 the 'Dolph' acetate was sold at auction for $155.401, though the bid was subsequently found to be fraudulent. In a second attempt at auction through eBay, it sold for $25,500. Norman Dolph then commented that it was possible that the original tape from which the acetate was made may still be lurking in long-term storage vaults. Universal immediately began negotiations with the owners for the recording rights; this must have been the case, since the recordings were included on the 2012 "super deluxe" reissue of the Velvets' first album.

The following year a limited edition of 5,000 copies were issued on vinyl. Outside of collectors interested in owning a facsimile artefact, it's hard to imagine anyone else buying a copy.

RARITIES

There are numerous pressings of all the Velvet Underground albums, and the singles taken from those albums. The rarer the pressing, the more its financial worth – and copies of the first album with its cover banana unpeeled tend to be very scarce (though pirate versions abound). However, there is actually very little material that was released on vinyl that has not been released on CD.

'Noise' featured on *The East Village Other Electric Newspaper* LP, released August 1966. It is a fragment (about a minute) of the Velvets playing live, but they're almost inaudible, since the radio broadcast of President Johnson's daughter Lucy's wedding, which runs through the whole record, virtually drowns out the band. 'Loop' is a feedback-based improvisational piece, given away as a flexidisc with *Aspen* magazine in December 1966. Moe Tucker doesn't play on this.

Both of these items usually fetch an asking price of around £100/$200 each (or a great deal more – probably a minimum of £600/$1,200 – if you want the *Aspen* magazine as well). Before parting with your cash, it's worth noting that the Velvets themselves chose not to include either of these items in the *Peel Slowly And See* boxed set.

'Conversation' was featured on a flexidisc (printed with a photograph of Reed) given away free with *Andy Warhol's Index* book (published February 1967). It consists of Reed, Cale Nico and various other people discussing Warhol's book while their first album plays in the background. The book usually sells for at least £700/$1,200 (hardback) or £500/$1,000 (paperback). The track itself can also be found on the *What Goes On* boxed set.

There are also a couple of MGM radio promo items from 1968 and 1969 (featuring an interview with Cale and Reed) which sell for around £500/$1,200 apiece.

THE VELVET UNDERGROUND

THE COMPLETE MATRIX TAPES

Set One

*I'm Waiting For The Man (Version One)/
What Goes On (Version One)/Some Kinda
Love (Version One)/Heroin (Version One)/
The Black Angel's Death Song/Venus
In Furs (Version One)/There She Goes
Again (Version One)/We're Gonna Have
A Real Good Time Together (Version
One)/Over You (Version One)/Sweet Jane
(Version One)/Pale Blue Eyes/After Hours
(Version One)*

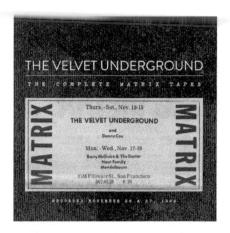

STILL-UNRELEASED TRACKS

'Get It On Time'
Rehearsal tape, recorded at the Factory, 1966.

'If I Tell You'
Details unknown.

'I'm Not A Young Man Any More'
Performed live, 1967.

'Kill Your Sons'
Reed re-recorded this for *Sally Can't Dance*. A version by the Velvets is thought to exist.

'Lonely Saturday Night'
A live performance from 1969.

'Lonesome Cowboys'
Recorded for the 'lost' album, according to Moe Tucker, and apparently a different song to 'Lonesome Cowboy Bill'. This was written for Andy Warhol's movie of the same name; since the movie opened in May 1969, the song may have been recorded even earlier; then again, Reed may have been as behind schedule as he was for Warhol's *Chelsea Girls*.

'Men Of Good Fortune'
A rehearsal tape, recorded at the Factory in 1966. Reed would re-record this for his solo album *Berlin*.

'Miss Joanie Lee'
Rehearsal tape recorded at the Factory, 1966. This 11-minute long extravaganza was due to be released on the 'deluxe' double-CD version of *The Velvet Underground & Nico*, but was pulled at the last minute when band members demanded a renegotiation of their record contract.

'Never Get Emotionally Involved With Man, Woman, Beast Or Child'
A demo tape from 1965 is thought to exist.

'The Nothing Song'
A lengthy instrumental, performed live with the E.P.I. in 1966.

'Passing By'
A song written by Doug Yule in 1969. The Velvets are thought to have recorded a demo.

THE MUSIC: **THE ALBUMS**

7

Set Two
I'm Waiting For The Man (Version Two)/Venus In Furs (Version Two)/ Some Kinda Love (Version Two)/ Over You (Version Two)/I Can't Stand It (Version One)/There She Goes Again Version Two)/After Hours (Version Two)/We're Gonna Have A Real Good Time Together (Version Two)/Sweet Bonnie Brown-Too Much/Heroin (Version Two)/White Light-White Heat (Version One)/I'm Set Free
Set Three
We're Gonna Have A Real Good Time Together (Version Three)/Some Kinda Love

(Version Three)/There She Goes Again (Version Three)/Heroin (Version Three)/Ocean/Sister Ray
Set Four
I'm Waiting For The Man (Version Three)/ What Goes On (Version Two)/Some Kinda Love (Version Four)/ We're Gonna Have A Real Good Time Together (Version Four)/ Beginning To See The Light/Lisa Says/ New Age/Rock & Roll/I Can't Stand It (Version Two)/White Light-White Heat (Version Two)/Sweet Jane (Version Two)
Universal; recorded 1969; released 2015. Personnel: Lou Reed, Sterling Morrison, Maureen Tucker, Doug Yule

---

'Sister Ray Part III'
Improvisational extension of 'Sister Ray', performed as an encore from 1967 to 1968.

'Sweet And Twenty'
Reed's adaptation of verses by Shakespeare (from *Twelfth Night*). Dates from 1969.

'Sweet Rock And Roll (Sister Ray Part II)'
Preamble to 'Sister Ray', performed live in 1968 (with John Cale). According to Sterling Morrison, a version was taped at a post-gig party in California.

'Sweet Sister Ray'
Preamble to 'Sister Ray', which may have

been an earlier version of 'Sweet Rock And Roll (Sister Ray Part II)'.

'A Symphony Of Sound'
Rehearsal jam session recorded at the Factory, 1966. Warhol also filmed it (without sound).

'Walk Alone'
Rehearsal tape recorded at the Factory, 1966. The song was co-written by Reed (with Jerry Pellegrino, Terry Phillips and James Smith) while working for Pickwick.

'Wild Child'
A demo from 1970.

Some of the these have been bootlegged; others are merely believed to exist, their whereabouts unknown; some may even be alternate titles for songs already released. There is also a vast amount of live material, including lengthy jam sessions. While none of the dozens, if not hundreds, of bootlegs that have circulated over the years are known to contain any unreleased studio material, many live recordings – of extremely variable quality – are only available this way. Additionally, there are the Morrison, Cale and Tucker demos from the *Eat/ Kiss* period, and the final Rock & Roll Hall Of Fame Velvet Underground performance of 'Last Night I Said Goodbye To My Friend'.

THE VELVET UNDERGROUND

7

What's the big deal? These concerts at San Francisco's Matrix Club, recorded in November 1969, had already provided a chunk of the material on the *1969: Velvet Underground Live* album, and further tracks had surfaced on both *The Quine Tapes* and as bonus material on a deluxe reissue of *The Velvet Underground*. So, with this four-CD set, are we hearing the sound of a barrel being scraped? Perhaps. But the whole thing has been remixed, and there are nine tracks making their first ever appearance here. Plus, this collection isn't exorbitantly expensive, and probably gives the best impression available of a Velvets gig to date, with four distinctly different and varied sets being included.

In fact, it catches the band at the peak of their powers, and the sound quality throughout is excellent. Plus, you get the occasional rambling song intro from Lou. True, the song versions here are incredibly long, with extended solos that often verge on the self-indulgent, but that was the fashion of the day – everybody did it. Sometimes the different song arrangements really work, even the incredibly slow and bluesy take of 'I'm Waiting For The Man', and there's something compelling about 'Sister Ray' even at thirty minutes long. But one can't help but feel that 'I Can't Stand It' was never meant to go on for as long as eight minutes, and the song simply crumbles beneath the weight of all the improvisation.

'Sweet Jane' and 'New Age' were evidently far from completed at this stage, with Lou still trying alternative lyrics out for size; Doug Yule's organ playing really makes a big impression, and is mostly great; Moe Tucker's epic drumming, especially on the versions of 'Heroin', is simply awesome; and the version here of 'Beginning To See The Light' is worth the price of admission on its own. For all its flaws, it's great.

COMPILATIONS

There have been numerous 'best of' the Velvet Underground compilations released over the decades, usually drawing their material mainly from the first and fourth albums. There seems little point in listing any of them here, since anyone buying this book will presumably already own much of the Velvets' output – failing which, the reader is advised to invest in a copy of the *Peel Slowly And See* boxed set as a starting point.

However, completists may care to note that the two-CD compilation *The Velvet Underground Gold* includes previously unreleased mixes of both 'Temptation Inside Your Heart' and 'Stephanie Says'.

LOU REED

7

LOU REED

*I Can't Stand It/Going Down/Walk And Talk
It/Lisa Says/Berlin/I Love You/Wild Child/Love
Makes You Feel/Ride Into The Sun/Ocean*
RCA; recorded January 1972; released May 1972

Recorded at London's Morgan Studios with a curious collection of British musicians, including Elton John's sideman Caleb Quaye, Rick Wakeman and Steve Howe from Yes and drummer Clem Cattini (who had played with Johnny Kidd And The Pirates, and on the Tornados' classic instrumental 'Telstar'). They were all capable musicians, but hardly sympatico to Reed's style or subject matter. Strangely, Lou himself did not play any guitar on the record.

The results are disappointing. For one thing, Reed didn't have a strong enough collection of material. Although he seemingly demoed a great many new songs, most of these he eventually rejected, opting instead to fill most of the album with re-recordings of songs he'd previously recorded with the Velvet Underground (although the Velvets' versions remained unreleased until the Eighties). Reed would continue to occasionally plunder the Velvets' unreleased back catalogue for many years to come – and even if his solo versions impressed at the time, in almost every instance the Velvets' versions would eventually be discovered to be far superior. Only four songs here are completely 'new': 'Going Down', 'Berlin', 'Wild Child' and 'I Love You' (the latter two both seemingly about his wife Bettye).

The whole album sounds limp and bland, largely because of the arrangements and playing – though the production was also tinny and sterile, something about which Reed later complained to his co-producer Richard Robinson. This was at least partially due to a major technical glitch which remained a mystery until certain tracks were remastered for the *Between Thought And Expression* boxed set. The entire album was remastered in 1999.

In hindsight, the record is of interest mainly for the song 'Berlin', an epic romantic ballad, set in Berlin "by the wall", but the orthodox rock arrangement the song receives here lets it down; Reed would briefly reprise it when he returned to the divided city as the territory for his third solo album song-cycle (in reality, he didn't actually visit the place until 1979). The cover painting by Tom Adams was commissioned by Reed. Adams had done covers for paperback editions of Raymond Chandler novels, which Lou had liked.

Sterling Morrison later called the album

THE VELVET UNDERGROUND

7

"derivative and not very good", but most reviews at the time weren't that bad (except for that of the *NME*'s Nick Kent, who hated it). Sales were another matter: they were appallingly low (about 7,000 worldwide). If not for David Bowie, the Lou Reed story might very well have ended right here.

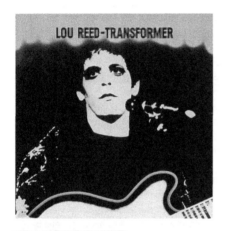

TRANSFORMER

*Vicious/Andy's Chest/Perfect Day/Hangin'
Round/Walk On The Wild Side/Make Up/
Satellite Of Love/Wagon Wheel/New York
Telephone Conversation/I'm So Free/
Goodnight Ladies*
RCA; recorded August 1972; released November 1972

Transformer remains one of the real highlights of Reed's long career, and a large part of the credit has to go to David Bowie and his regular guitarist Mick Ronson, who co-produced the album – although Ronson may well have actually done the lion's share of the work in the studio, dealing with all the string and brass arrangements. Bowie and Ronson got a further credit – alongside Lou – for "song arrangements".

The album was recorded at London's

Trident Studios, using a choice selection of session musicians. Ronson and Lou played guitars; on electric and string bass was Herbie Flowers (with Klaus Voormann also playing on some tracks), who also played tuba; drummers were John Halzey, Barry Desouza and Ritchie Dharma; Ronnie Ross played baritone sax; and piano and recorder were played by the incredibly versatile Ronson (who probably had more to do with the production than Bowie did). Backing vocals were by Bowie, Ronson, and some girl singers credited simply as "the Thunder Thighs". They were all white: Casey Synge was Irish, and her three friends – Karen Friedman, Jackie Hardin and Dari Lallou – were all American. Flowers' most notable contribution was the double bass tracking (upright and electric) that was the making of 'Walk On The Wild Side' (for which he received double the session fee).

This time around Reed had a much better selection of material, including at least three absolute classic songs: 'Perfect Day', 'Walk On The Wild Side' and 'Satellite Of Love'. True, the latter was another Velvets leftover (as was 'Andy's Chest'), but nobody knew that at the time – and for once these were actually better than the Velvets' versions, thanks to Ronson's arrangements. In addition, Reed had a clutch of songs he'd written in 1971 for a musical based (very loosely) on Nelson Algren's novel *A Walk On The Wild Side*, which was to have been produced by Andy Warhol and fashion designer Yves St Laurent but which never got off the ground. These definitely included 'Vicious', 'Walk On The Wild Side', 'Make Up' and 'New York Telephone Conversation', and possibly some of the others. The line about being hit with a flower in 'Vicious' is supposedly a direct quote from Warhol, made to Reed as they were strolling around New York discussing the show.

The whole album could be seen as a tribute to the Factory world. When the Algren project failed to get off the ground, Reed altered the lyrics to 'Walk On The Wild Side', changing the song's protagonists from Algren's characters into real people from Warhol's Factory: Holly (Woodlawn), Candy (Darling), 'Little' Joe (Dallesandro) and the Sugar Plum Fairy (possibly Joseph Campbell, who was a drug-dealer and "hustler out of San Francisco," according to Reed). Candy Darling, whose real name was James Slattery, had earlier been the protagonist of the song 'Candy Says' on the third Velvet Underground album. Speaking of Holly and Candy, Patti Smith commented: "They were the rag-tag queens of Max's Kansas City, and they've got very little in return for all of the groundbreaking things that they did, and to be heralded by someone like Lou was lovingly compassionate without being syrupy." As Nick Kent noted in the NME, "Any song that mentions oral sex, male prostitution, methedrine, valium... and still gets Radio 1 airplay, must be truly cool."

The album's second standout track is 'Satellite Of Love', which, with slightly different lyrics, was first recorded by the Velvet Underground during the sessions for *Loaded* (and eventually released on *Peel Slowly And See*). The song is partly about obsessional jealousy brought about by the painfully promiscuous infidelity of the singer's partner, and it's ironic that such a beautiful song (especially as arranged by Mick Ronson) is – if you listen to the words – actually pretty depressing. This sense of irony between lyrics and musical irony is almost a Lou Reed trademark. "I'm just glad the melody was pretty," commented Reed. The song got a new lease of life in 2004, when a remixed version became a minor hit.

The album's third masterpiece is 'Perfect Day', a gentle love song beautifully enhanced by Mick Ronson's piano and string arrangement. The relationship here would seem to be that of an illicit affair – almost certainly Shelley Albin – since all the lovers can have are stolen moments, like one "perfect day". On the other hand, Bettye Kronstad claims it's about her. As a measure of its timelessness, the song acquired a new lease of life in the Nineties, firstly through its appearance on the soundtrack of the hit movie *Trainspotting*, and then again in 1997 when an all-star cover version was produced to raise money for the BBC's Children In Need charity.

The subject matter of most of the album – drugs, bisexuality and homosexuality, bitchiness and transvestism – was very much in tune with the glam-rock 'divinely decadent' times, and with Bowie's audience – a lot of whom undoubtedly picked up on the album and helped make it a hit. The fact that there were several songs that celebrated homosexuality undoubtedly resonated with the gay community as well; Reed said of 'Make Up' that he'd wanted to write a song which made being gay sound "terrific, something that you'd enjoy". The album's back cover photograph featured Lou's tour manager Ernie Thormahlen in 'straight' guise, with a banana stuck down his trousers, gazing at a model that we're supposed to believe is Thormahlen in drag; in reality, it was fashion model Gala Mitchell.

Despite the fact that Ernie looked nothing like Reed, rumours persisted that this was Reed himself, which were probably started by Lou as a joke. The front cover featured Reed wearing eyeliner and ultra-white make-up, to accentuate his 'pale New Yorker' image.

Amazingly, the album both won radio

THE VELVET UNDERGROUND

7

airplay and spawned hit singles. In the US, the Candy Darling verse was cut from the single version of 'Walk On The Wild Side'; in the UK it went out uncensored, since British DJs apparently had no idea what "giving head" meant. Some US stations also bleeped out the references to "coloured girls" and "valium".

Extraordinarily, though sales for *Transformer* would be staggeringly good, the record received quite a few bad reviews when it was released – possibly on account of the controversial subject matter. It remains an extremely impressive pop record, and one which has stood the test of time far better than, say, *Ziggy Stardust*. Later CD versions also include acoustic demos of 'Hangin' Round' and 'Perfect Day', both of which are pretty unremarkable.

BERLIN

Berlin/Lady Day/Men Of Good Fortune/ Caroline Says I/How Do You Think It Feels/ Oh Jim/Caroline Says Ii/The Kids/The Bed/ Sad Song

RCA; recorded June 1973; released July 1973

A Brechtian operetta about two junkies that includes scenes of domestic violence,

Berlin features a woman losing custody of her children because of her promiscuity and activities as a prostitute, and ends with a suicide. It was never going to qualify as easy listening. In the wake of an album as determinedly commercial as *Transformer*, it came as a hell of a shock; Reed's most ambitious project to date inevitably alienated many of his listeners and critics. The late Lester Bangs dismissed it as "a gargantuan slab of maggotty rancour that may well be the most depressed album ever made." Reed himself called it "an album for adults".

Berlin was recorded at London's Morgan Studios (with later sessions taking place at New York's Record Plant). Orchestral arrangements were by producer Bob Ezrin (aided by Allan Macmillan), and the session musicians were a fairly stellar cast: Steve Winwood on organ and harmonium, Jack Bruce on bass, Aynsley Dunbar on drums (except for 'Lady Day' and 'The Kids', on which BJ Wilson – of Procul Harum – was the drummer), plus session guitarists Richard Wagner and Steve Hunter (both of whom had worked with Ezrin on Alice Cooper sessions).

Reed later said that Jack Bruce wasn't supposed to play on the whole thing, but stayed on because he was enjoying himself so much. He also noted that Bruce was the only musician he worked with in the early years of his solo career who actually bothered to read the lyrics, in order to play more empathically. Bruce had replaced an unnamed bass player who hadn't worked out, some of whose parts were later overdubbed in New York by Tony Levin (on 'The Kids') and Eugene Martynec (on 'Lady Day').

Lou's vocals were also later overdubbed in New York (at the Record Plant). Michael Brecker played tenor sax; Randy Brecker played trumpet; Jon Pierson played bass trombone; Bob Ezrin played mellotron and piano (Allan Macmillan played piano on 'Berlin'; Blue Weaver played piano on 'Men Of Good Fortune'). Backing vocals were by Reed, Ezrin, Dennis Ferrante, Steve Flyden, Elizabeth March and Richard Wagner.

Once again, several songs here were re-recordings of Velvets material: 'Oh Jim' (originally 'Oh Gin'), 'Caroline Says II' (albeit in a drastically different form, as 'Stephanie Says'), 'Men Of Good Fortune' and 'Sad Song' (supposedly recorded as a Velvets demo). The title track is a fragmentary reprise – dramatically reworked – of the song from Reed's first solo album (it's unknown whether the brevity is intentional, or just one of the edits Ezrin was forced to make). Apparently Reed had hated the way the song was arranged first time around.

Towards the end of the song 'The Kids', one can clearly hear – for over a minute - the sound of children crying in the background. Unsatisfied by tapes available from sound archives, Ezrin supposedly went home and kidnapped his own young children. Informing them their mother had left them, he then locked the by-now hysterical children in a cupboard (where a tape recorder had been set up) leaving them to howl their eyes out in the dark. "Even I thought that was going too far," said Reed. "But that's how fucked-up we got on that record." Ezrin later maintained that the anecdote was exaggerated. He'd told his seven-year-old son David that he was doing a play and needed voices of children who sounded scared because their mother was being taken away. The first two takes didn't really work, but on the third Ezrin's two-year-old joined in by screaming; both children screamed so loud that they distorted the tape. Ezrin compressed the recording in the studio, and "the more compressed it got,

the more anguished it seemed. Most people can't listen to it." Ezrin claims that the crying heard underneath was simply a pre-bedtime tantrum he'd recorded at home one night, but the compression on it "makes it so unbelievably emotional people accused me of beating my kids."

Berlin is an extremely odd mixture. Some songs (like 'The Kids') sound ponderous and Germanic, while others (like 'Caroline Says I') were so poppy that they could almost have fitted on *Transformer*, despite the unorthodox instrumentation – and 'Sad Song' sounds like something from a Disney movie (lyrics aside).

Lyrically, it's impossible not to see echoes of the lives of both Nico and Daryl (whose kids were taken into care) here, as well as of Reed's own collapsing marriage to Bettye and his own drug experiences. Bettye also saw elements of her own family history in some of the songs, and felt betrayed by their exposure.

As a whole, the record is undeniably depressing, but that doesn't make it bad. It's certainly ambitious, and a large chunk of it is very good indeed, but it's not something you'd want to play that often. Still, the fact that it *is* so powerful is surely a sign of its worth, and it's strange that a restoration of the work at its complete length has yet to appear – if the master tapes still exist, they should surely be worthy of release. At any rate, a recording of the 2006 theatrical version is fairly inevitable.

On a purely musical level, *Berlin* is largely superb; while still recognisably rock music, it draws on every other musical strand, from folk to musicals, and blends them into something very interesting indeed. And its influence on popular music has been huge. Four years after *Berlin* was released, David Bowie would set his epic romance 'Heroes' in the shadow of the Berlin wall.

7

may well have been unaware of his prior incarnation, and he admitted he wanted them "to know exactly what preceded 'Walk On The Wild Side'." Sadly, the music is... pretty pedestrian to modern ears. It's not that it's bad, it's just that these versions of the songs are nowhere near as good as the Velvets' originals (or even the Velvets' live versions). Reed himself would later dismiss the album as crass and commercial: "It was like a walking time-warp to me... but I had to get popular." Legend has it that the audience applause was overdubbed, having been lifted from live tapes of John Denver.

ROCK N ROLL ANIMAL
Sweet Jane/Heroin/White Light, White Heat/ Lady Day/Rock 'N' Roll
RCA; recorded 1973; released February 1974

Reed's touring band in the autumn of 1973 had been put together by Bob Ezrin, and consisted of guitarists Steve Hunter and Dick Wagner from the *Berlin* sessions, plus Ray Colcord on keyboards, Prakash John on bass and drummer Pentti Glan (from the Black Stone Rangers, a group that included Reed's future sideman Michael Fonfara).

Both sets from the last night of the tour – December 21 1973, at New York's Academy of Music – were recorded using a Record Plant mobile studio, and this live album was released six weeks later. It was co-produced by Reed and Steve Katz (brother of Dennis and once the guitarist for Blood Sweat & Tears).

As can be seen from the tracklisting, Reed's solo work barely got a nod here – this was a celebration of his years with the Velvet Underground, re-worked as heavy rock. Or "heresy of sorts", in the words of critic Nick Kent. Many of Reed's audience

SALLY CAN'T DANCE
Ride Sally Ride/Animal Language/Baby Face/N.y.stars/Kill Your Sons/Ennui/Sally Can't Dance/Billy
RCA; recorded June 1974; released September 1974

Ironically, this record – since disowned by both Reed and producer Steve Katz (who called it "a rotten album") – was incredibly successful. Personnel included Danny Weiss on guitar, Prakash John on bass, Michael Fonfara on keyboards, Richard Dharma and Pentti Glan on drums, Michael Wendroff and Joanna Vent on backing vocals, and an uncredited brass section. Weiss and Fonfara had both previously been in the Black Stone Rangers with Glan. Additionally – amazingly, given the bad blood that had existed between them – Reed had also dragged his former Velvet Underground colleague Doug Yule out of retirement to play bass on the song 'Billy'. Yule would also join Reed's band for the 1975 European tour.

The results are pretty awful. Steve Katz stated that he'd "take all the blame for this album," and the ball does seem to be in his court. The arrangements are overblown, making it sound like an attempt to recreate *Transformer*, but without the songs, the taste or the commitment from Reed. And without a producer/ arranger with the talent of David Bowie or Mick Ronson, for that matter.

As to the songs: 'Animal Language' was originally titled 'Mrs O'Riley's Dog', and was possibly influenced by Hubert Selby Jr's novel *The Room*, known to be one of Reed's favourites (though once again, it's hard to see how). Lyrically at least, 'Kill Your Sons' supposedly dates back to the days of the Velvets (some think it even predates them). Reed has stated that it's about the electroshock therapy he'd been subjected to at age 17, for which he blamed his father. The title track would seem to be about Edie Sedgewick, who did indeed "ball folksingers" (Bob Dylan, to be specific), though Reed has subsequently said that it was inspired by a murder on the Lower East Side – the reason Sally can't dance is because she's been raped and murdered, and her dead body is now in the trunk of her killers' car.

'Billy' is supposedly the story of one of Reed's contemporaries at college, who'd been a star student while Reed had been a drop-out. 'Billy' had gone to serve in Vietnam, while Reed had been exempted from the draft, and had returned as a shadow of his former self. Probably the best thing on this album, it's still not that great. The overall result veers from the saccharine to the raucous, to no real purpose, and Reed often sounds mannered to a point beyond self-parody. For completists only.

LOU REED LIVE

Vicious/Satellite Of Love/Walk On The Wild Side/I'm Waiting For The Man/Oh Jim/Sad Song
RCA; recorded December 1973; released March 1975

Released to capitalise on the success of *Sally*, this is the *second* live album to be taken from the tapes recorded at New York's Academy of Music in December 1973. Only two songs from the concert remain unreleased – Reed was unhappy with his vocals on 'Caroline Says' and 'How Do You Think It Feels'. This time the material is drawn more from Reed's

7

solo work than the Velvets' back pages, but otherwise it's of the same standard as *Rock 'N' Roll Animal*, displaying a heavy-handed heavy-rock approach to the material... and the fact that it's the second-best scoop from these tapes speaks for itself. Uncharacteristically, Reed left the production duties for *Lou Reed Live* entirely to Steve Katz.

METAL MACHINE MUSIC

Metal Machine Music, Part 1/Metal Machine Music, Part 2/ Metal Machine Music, Part 3/ Metal Machine Music, Part 4

RCA; recorded spring 1975; released July 1975

Lou Reed once claimed that this album was not only his revenge on his record company, but also his revenge on his audience – or at any rate, the ones who yelled out requests at concerts. Subtitled "An Electronic Instrumental Composition", *Metal Machine Music* was originally released as a double album, comprised of 'Metal Machine Music Parts 1–4': one part per vinyl side, with each side exactly 16:01 minutes in length. Reed bounced tapes of guitar feedback between two recorders, treating them electronically and varying the tape

speeds en route. It sounded like all his rage against the music industry unleashed at full volume, but he described it as "Combinations and Permutations built upon constant harmonic Density Increase and Melodic Distractions."

The novelist Neil Gaiman once stated that when he was writing a sequence for his fantasy comic *Sandman* that was set in Hell, he'd listened to *Metal Machine Music* to conjure up the necessary atmosphere. It's easy to understand why. The record is a strange mixture of cacophany and harmony, in which you seem to hear echoes of a thousand other things: birdsong and whalesong and traffic noise, and what sound like familiar tunes going by so fast that you can never pin them down.

It's an assault on the senses on a par with spending hours under a dentist's drill, yet buried deep within it are a few moments of absolutely dazzling beauty. Anyone who's sat all the way through it feels a real sense of achievement... and also never wants to hear the damn thing ever again. Reed claims that the balance on the CD version is off, and that it is not an accurate reproduction: "it's like the Mona Lisa missing a nose or something."

CONEY ISLAND BABY

Crazy Feeling/Charley's Girl/She's My Best Friend/Kicks/A Gift/Ooohhh Baby/Nobody's Business/Coney Island Baby

RCA; recorded October 1975; released December 1975

Reed had closed the sleeve notes to *Metal Machine Music* with the boast: "My week beats your year." But he'd had a particularly bad year himself, and this album was put together in the middle of extreme legal and financial problems. It was recorded at New York's Mediasound Studios with the Down-Trodden Three: Bob Kulick on guitar, Bruce Yaw on bass and Michael Suchorsky on drums. Steve Katz returned (briefly) as Reed's co-producer, before being replaced by engineer Godfrey Diamond. Backing vocals were by Reed, Diamond, Michael Wendroff and Joanne Vent.

Throughout, the band's playing is intelligent and sympathetic, unlike *Sally Can't Dance*'s parade of rock clichés – and Lou's vocals sound a lot more sincere. For all of the talk about Reed's drug intake at the time, it doesn't seem to be affecting his game in terms of performance. As for the material, while some of it is lacklustre and pointless ('Ooohhh Baby'), some of it is just enjoyably dumb pop ('Charley's Girl' and 'Crazy Feeling'), and some of it ('A Gift') is genuinely funny. As a collection it's competent rather than inspired, but at least Lou sounds like he's having fun. The album's worst fault – that of songs that aimlessly meander on forever – is simply par for the course in the pre-punk Seventies. 'Kicks' is a prime example of that – a jazzy rap that aims to take you inside the mind of a switchblade-wielding killer. "At the time I was hanging around the criminally inclined, put it that way," Reed commented in 1990, which explains but doesn't excuse the brutal misogyny.

But most of the songs here seem inspired by Reed's relationship with his new transsexual lover Rachel. 'She's My Best Friend' was an old Velvets number, but this is one of the few occasions when Reed's re-make almost lives up to the original: the Velvets' version was dumb beat-pop, while this is slower, bluesier, and more self-consciously epic. While in the Velvets Reed had written a song titled 'Coney Island Steeplechase,' so he was obviously fond of New York's old amusement park (which was well past its prime by the time of Reed's childhood). Victor Bockris claims that an early draft of 'Coney Island Baby' even pre-dates the Velvets, and was originally about Reed's college girlfriend Shelley Albin... but Rachel seems a much more believable inspiration, especially given the song's closing declaration of love. A smoky blues with jazz overtones, the song also bears witness to Reed's long-time love of close-harmony doo-wop. 'Coney Island Baby' was also the title of an obscure 1962 doo-wop song by the Excellents, while the "glory of love" chorus is a tip of the hat to the 1951 song of that name by the Five Keys (or the Harptones, depending which source you believe). Sadly, the song is nowhere near as good as most classic doo-wop.

Even so, the album as a whole is a revelation; at this point in his career, hardly anybody expected Lou Reed to come up with anything this good. Though the actual material is nowhere near as commercial, this is still easily his most accessible album since *Transformer*. A remastered 2006 reissue of the CD,

7

overseen by Reed, contained six extra tracks from 1975: 'Nowhere At All', 'Downtown Dirt' and 'Leave Me Alone' (all of which had previously appeared on the *Between Thought And Expression* boxed set), plus demos of 'Crazy Feeling', 'She's My Best Friend' and 'Coney Island Baby'. The demos all feature Doug Yule on guitar, but are really of interest only as sketches of work-in-progress.

ROCK AND ROLL HEART

I Believe In Love/Banging On My Drum/ Follow The Leader/You Wear It So Well/ Ladies Pay/Rock And Roll Heart/Chooser And The Chosen One/Senselessly Cruel/ Claim To Fame/Vicious Circle/A Sheltered Life/Temporary Thing

Arista; recorded summer 1976; released October 1976

Recorded in New York. Musicians included Michael Fonfara on keyboards, Bruce Yaw on bass, Michael Suchorsky on drums and Marty Fogel on saxophone.

The majority of the songs were written in the studio, and it shows. *Rock And Roll Heart* was a giant leap backwards. Lou sounds mannered throughout, the lyrics are minimal and substandard and the music is a mixture of blandly jazzy lounge music and nonsensical rock thrash.

'A Sheltered Life' dates back to the Velvets (a demo exists, from 1967). Here it's given a jazzy arrangement that makes it sound like Tom Waits on a very bad day. 'Temporary Thing', a mock-epic rock dirge about the end of a relationship, is bleak and pompous, taking over five minutes to go precisely nowhere. By the time it's over, you want to kill the drummer. The title track is a bouncy, joyously dumb celebration of rock 'n' roll – but it's way *too* dumb, and thus a real let-down. Clive Davis of Arista wanted to add strings to it, in the belief that with a little more work the song could be a hit single, but Reed refused.

'Ladies Pay' isn't bad – an atmospheric rock ballad about women generally not having an easy time of it in this world. The Velvets-style guitar-part aside, it sounds a bit like the Dylan or Springsteen of this era. Still, it's so depressing that it could have fitted comfortably onto *Berlin*.

'Vicious Circle' is also almost OK – a lyrically minimal and bitter ode to paranoia, with a folky approach. Supposedly Reed had been sent a poem with this title by a British fan, who was subsequently amazed to discover his hero using both the title and the theme for a new song. Originally titled *Nomad*, the album was supposed to have a cover by Andy Warhol, but that fell through. When released, reviewers largely thought it dull and lacklustre (which it is), and sales weren't that great; not surprisingly, since it's one of Reed's most inarticulate records, perhaps indicating that drugs were once again taking their toll.

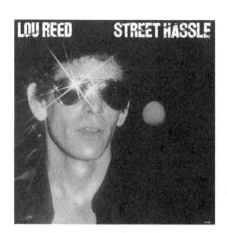

STREET HASSLE

Gimmie Some Good Times/Dirt/Street Hassle (A) Waltzing Matilda (B) Street Hassle (C) Slipaway/I Wanna Be Black/Real Good Time Together/Shooting Star/Leave Me Alone/Wait

Arista; recorded summer/autumn 1977; released February 1978

Some of *Street Hassle* was recorded live, during dates on Lou's 1977 European tour (at Munich, Wiesbaden and Ludwigshafen in Germany). The rest was recorded that autumn at New York's Record Plant Studios. Co-produced by Reed and Richard Robinson (though Robinson left before the album was completed). Musicians included Stuart Heinrich on guitar, Marty Fogel on saxophone and Michael Suchorsky on drums. Michael Fonfara played keyboards on 'I Wanna Be Black'. The album was mixed in the new binaural system that had claimed Lou as a disciple.

Street Hassle is a real mixture, and although a vast improvement on *Rock And Roll Heart*, still contains a heavy proportion of turkeys. Several of the songs dated back to *Coney Island Baby*, when they'd been rejected as

substandard – and they hadn't improved with time. But 'Gimmie Some Good Times' is strangely likeable, and quite funny. 'Dirt' is an incredibly slow and vitriolic blues – there's real *hate* here, and a rambling reference to Bobby Fuller's 'I Fought The Law' seems to imply a legal battle being part of the background to all this venom. Reed later confirmed that the song was aimed at his former manager, described here as "a pig of a person" and "uptown dirt". This was probably valuable as therapy, but the rest of us really didn't need to hear it.

The title track is divided into three sections: 'Waltzing Matilda,' 'Street Hassle' and 'Slipaway'. The middle section at least is several years old – Reed had wanted to record it for *Coney Island Baby*. Reed later claimed that after Arista boss Clive Davis heard the original two-minute version of the song, he told Reed to make it longer. The hypnotic cello riff – echoed on the bass – conjures up memories of Reed's partnership with John Cale. Reed plays the piano, with a guest vocal from Genya Ravan. The first section is about sex with a male prostitute (and not even remotely connected to the Australian song of the same name); the second section is about a drug-related death. According to Reed, he'd loosely based this on the drug overdose death of Factory associate Eric Emerson, changing only his gender. For the track's last section, Reed drafted a 'neighbour' in for a cameo vocal: Bruce Springsteen, who'd been mixing tracks in the studio below Reed. Reed said Springsteen was "really fabulous. He did the part so well that I had to bury him in the mix." Two years earlier, Reed had publicly described Springsteen to *Punk* magazine as "a shit" and "a has-been". Lyrically, Springsteen's cameo tips its hat to his own

THE VELVET UNDERGROUND

7

song 'Born To Run'. Although the track is way too long, and definitely flawed, it's still interesting and mesmeric. It's also head and shoulders above everything else here.

"He wants to be black," Nico had once said of Lou, and now he turned it into a boast, but claimed: "Nobody could possibly take 'I Wanna Be Black' seriously." At one point this was going to be the album title as well. It's a mediocre R&B shuffle with girlie backing singers, as Lou extols all the reasons he wishes he was black. It's in seriously bad taste, and would be downright racist if you didn't suspect Reed was doing it just to upset people. 'Real Good Time Together' is a limply mannered version of the Velvets song (from the 'lost' album).

The last track, 'Wait', is a tribute to early Sixties pop harmony groups and quotes both The Shirelles' 'Met Him On A Sunday' and Jan and Dean's 'New Kid In School', while singing the praises of virginity. It's not that great (and gets messy in the middle), but at least it has a sense of fun.

The album still maintains Reed's tendency to sink into a quagmire of messy jazz, but at least he seemed to be trying to improve.

LIVE: TAKE NO PRISONERS

Sweet Jane/I Wanna Be Black/Satellite Of Love/Pale Blue Eyes/Berlin/I'm Waiting For My Man (Sic)/Coney Island Baby/Street Hassle/Walk On The Wild Side/Leave Me Alone
RCA; recorded spring 1978; released November 1978

A live double-album, recorded at New York's Bottom Line in the spring of 1978 on the Record Plant's mobile, and mixed at Manfred Schunke's Delta studio in Wilster, Germany, for binaural sound. Reed took the sole production credit.

A contractual dispute with Reed's old label RCA resulted in them being given this album to release instead of Arista. Lou had heard the title as a phrase shouted from the audience, and fell in love with it: "It couldn't have been more appropriate. Don't take us prisoners, beat us to death, shoot us, maim us, kill us, but don't settle for less, go all the way. That's what I took it to mean."

And he took the maxim to heart. The set comprises jazzy extended versions that veer from the great ('Satellite Of Love' and 'Coney Island Baby') to the lacklustre ('Street Hassle') to the bombastic ('Berlin' and 'Leave Me Alone') to stuff so ramshackle that it makes you want to hurl bricks at the stage ('I'm Waiting For My Man').

But the music itself is almost irrelevant here – what lingers in the memory afterwards are Reed's improvised and extended 'lyrics', which are virtually a stand-up comedy routine that takes swipes at a wide variety of targets: Barbra Streisand, Patti Smith, Candy Darling, Joe Dallesandro, rock 'n' roll audiences, black people, Jews, Catholics, lesbians, rock critics John Rockwell and Robert

Christgau, Jane Fonda, Norman Mailer, politics in general, and – of course – the audience themselves. Amusing as some of it is, you don't want to hear it more than once. Reed himself later admitted that as a songwriter he'd "run out of inspiration" at this point. It should also be pointed out that this album also has one of the worst sleeves in history.

THE BELLS

Stupid Man/Disco Mystic/I Want To Boogie With You/ With You/Looking For Love/City Lights/All Through The Night/Families/The Bells
Arista; released April 1979

Recorded at Manfred Schunke's Delta studio in Wilster, Germany, it was produced by Reed, who also played electric guitar and guitar synthesizer (one of the first times this instrument had been used on a record).

This record was the first time in a decade that Reed had co-written with others: three songs here were written with Nils Lofgren (another three would surface on Lofgren's album *Nils*),

five more were written with various members of the band. Michael Fonfara played keyboards; Marty Fogel played saxophones, ocarina and Fender Rhodes (on the title track); Ellard Boles played bass (and electric 12-string on 'Families', which had Reed playing bass synthesizer); and Michael Suchorsky played drums. Don Cherry (a former Ornette Coleman sideman, and the father of Neneh) guested on trumpet and African hunter's lute.

The album continues Reed's dalliance with jazz – much of it ponderously meandering and instantly forgettable. Several songs actually sound like incidental music for a bad Seventies TV show. 'I Want To Boogie With You', co-written with Michael Fonfara, isn't bad – a slow, simple R&B love song. Reed had supposedly been enormously impressed by *Born To Be With You*, the album Phil Spector had produced for Dion in 1977, and had deliberately set out to recreate that sound here. 'City Lights', a Lofgren co-write, is also OK: a strong, romantic little ballad about Charlie Chaplin's banishment from America, which takes its title from one of his most famous movies. (Lou is evidently a big Chaplin fan – the Velvets had named one of their songs after another Chaplin film, 'Countess From Hong Kong'). It would have been better without the trumpet part, which sounds messy and bizarre.

'All Through The Night', co-written with Don Cherry, is a tuneful ode to nothing much at all, overlaid with studio chatter. A minor work, but quite enjoyable. 'Families', co-written with Ellard Boles, is an uncharacteristically rosy and nostalgic view of family life from Lou; there are certainly autobiographical elements, but

THE VELVET UNDERGROUND

7

Reed describes the family dynamics with sadness, instead of his usual venom. Lou later wrote that he'd never use words like "papa" in real life, so perhaps this should just be regarded as fiction. The title track is an atmospheric and jazzy performance piece, co-written with Marty Fogel. Supposedly inspired by the Edgar Allan Poe poem of the same name (though, apart from the title, they would seem to have nothing in common), and by Ornette Coleman's 'Lonely Woman', it clocks in at over nine minutes in length and ends with the sound of a fifteen-foot gong Lou had rented for the occasion. Reed had no lyrics prepared; undaunted, he just stepped up to the microphone and improvised the entire thing. Most of it is recited (and inaudible), until he starts singing.

"The vocal came to me as I sang, and each year since I wonder at its meaning," Reed once confided. According to him, the song is about a suicide. A man is "on the edge of the building, and he looks out and thinks that he sees a brook, and he says, 'There are the bells'. And as he points, he tumbles over a drum roll. It's beautiful." Reed loved the song so much, he chose it to conclude *Between Thought And Expression*, his first published collection of lyrics. As he wrote in 1991: "We had a beautiful instrumental track with no lyric. On microphone I found myself singing this lyric. Unchanged it remains my favourite to this day."

The album stays true to Reed's career path during the drug years: a step forward, a step back again. The good tracks aren't all that great, and saying that it manages to stay in the same place as *Street Hassle* would be a mite too generous.

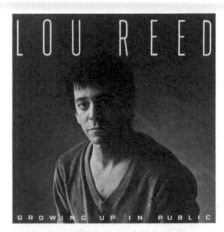

GROWING UP IN PUBLIC

How Do You Speak To An Angel/My Old Man/ Keep Away/Growing Up In Public/Standing On Ceremony/So Alone/Love Is Here To Stay/ The Power Of Positive Drinking/Smiles/Think It Over/Teach The Gifted Children

Arista; recorded January 1980; released April 1980

Recorded at George Martin's Air Studios on the island of Montserrat, the sessions were completed in three weeks flat and all Reed's vocals were done in one take – this was an economic decision, rather than an artistic one. The musicians involved included Stuart Heinrich and Chuck Hammer on guitar, Michael Fonfara on keyboards and guitar, Ellard Boles on bass and Michael Suchorsky on drums. Reed played no guitar at all.

Technical difficulties caused Reed to reluctantly and finally give up on binaural sound with this record. Fonfara co-produced the album with Reed, and also co-wrote all the songs with him. Several songs dealt with family, though Lou declared that they weren't autobiographical. However, on another occasion he admitted that 'My Old Man' actually was written for his father and he claimed that his parents "both like the album." Other songs here have a confessional feel to them, some concerning new girlfriend Sylvia Morales, soon to become his second wife and later also his manager. Reed's love songs to her are among the most naked he'd ever written, and 'Think It Over' is virtually a marriage proposal. 'So Alone' is a really good song about an awkward courtship. Driven by bass and piano, it touches on the confusion that arose when sex roles began to change, post-feminism, and is easily the best thing Reed had done in years.

'The Power Of Positive Drinking' is a joyous, reggae-tinged ode to the pleasures of booze, "written by two people who enjoy drinking" (i.e. Reed and Fonfara). Reed not only enjoyed it, he was almost evangelical about it. In 1978 there'd also been a country song with the same title by Mickey Gilley, but it's entirely possible that Reed was totally unaware of this, and that both writers were simply making the same pun on the title of Norman Vincent Peale's self-help bestseller *The Power Of Positive Thinking*.

'Teach The Gifted Children' is a slow gospel-blues reminiscent of Al Green's 'Take Me To The River' (a song which it actually quotes), about what education *ought* to be like. Reed's note in his selected lyrics dwells on how much he hated his own schooling. The song came about late at night in a hotel room, when Fonfara was tinkering around with the tune on an acoustic guitar, and Reed improvised the lyric in its entirety.

The album showed strong signs that Lou was slowly making his way out of the creative grave. His vocals were less mannered, his lyrics more articulate than they'd been in years – often downright funny (as in the title track), and often also

genuinely touching. Though the music itself remained at times messily jazzy, it was less so than on the previous three albums and had stronger tunes. There were clear signs that Lou's life was not only changing but improving. But no one could guess at this point just how far-reaching and radical those changes would be.

THE BLUE MASK

My House/Women/Underneath The Bottle/ The Gun/The Blue Mask/Average Guy/ The Heroine/Waves Of Fear/The Day John Kennedy Died/Heavenly Arms
RCA; recorded October/November 1981; released February 1982

With Robert Quine on guitar, Fernando Saunders on bass and backing vocals and Doane Perry on drums, Lou Reed decamped to RCA's New York studio, with Sean Fullan as engineer. Fullan was given a credit as Reed's co-producer; according to Reed, he gained the credit simply "to try to get him not to fuck around with the shit." Lou later proudly announced that there were no overdubs on *The Blue Mask*. Robert Quine

THE VELVET UNDERGROUND

insists that even the vocals were live (though these may only have been guide vocals): "That's what's really cool about that record. People are really intensely listening to each other, trying to cross barriers; they did that magical jazz thing. Something special is happening and you can hear it on the record. It still amazes me."

Lyrically, Reed was more thoughtful and intelligent than he'd been in a decade – doubtless, this was connected to the fact that he was now clean and sober. The bluesy ballad 'My House' was dedicated to Delmore Schwartz, and concerns Reed's belief that the ghost of Schwartz was haunting his New Jersey house, after the poet had seemingly contacted Lou and Sylvia via a ouija board. Regardless, there's beauty, humour and a real sense of contentment here. In 'Underneath The Bottle' Lou recalls his (mis)adventures with booze. Powerful lyrics, but sadly, the tune lets them down. 'The Gun' is a painful, slow tale of gun law in the hands of a psycho. Though it seems to detail an armed mugging, Reed disavowed any autobiographical ingredients; he also described the song's armed protagonist as "none of me" – as well he might, for his performance as the character sends a chill to the spine. An even more extreme version of the song was recorded but abandoned.

The title track is a tortuous, frenetic tale of sex, incest, pain and punishment and S&M; Lou has since described the song as a "self-portrait". Howling guitar and a driving bass make it very powerful, but not particularly easy listening. 'The Heroine' is a song of yearning for an idealised love. It's slow and turgid, and generally doesn't work. The recording is Reed's original solo demo (deemed to be better than the version the full band recorded). 'Waves Of Fear' is great –

really strident despite its oppressive subject, which would appear to be the mental and physical pain of drug withdrawal. 'The Day John Kennedy Died' is a mixture of reportage and idealism: Reed recalls hearing the news of the assassination when he was a college student, and juxtaposes this with an idyllic reverie about just how many other things were lost that day. It's slow, evocative and compelling. 'Heavenly Arms' is a touching song of love for Sylvia, which echoes 'Satellite Of Love.' It's slight, dumb and could easily have been mawkish. But it works.

Hailed at the time as showing a real return to form, *The Blue Mask* now seems more like a transitional work; nevertheless, not since John Lennon's first solo album had psychotherapy provided the spur for such interesting rock music, and listening to Reed claw his way back from oblivion is utterly fascinating. The band is also truly great: Saunders' booming bass style is often reminiscent of the late Jaco Pastorius, and Robert Quine's guitar is delicate and tasteful throughout. The guitar on the left-hand channel is Robert Quine, the one on the right is Reed.

LEGENDARY HEARTS

Legendary Hearts/Don't Talk To Me About Work/Make Up My Mind/Martial Law/The Last Shot/Turn Out The Light/Pow Wow/ Betrayed/Bottoming Out/Home Of The Brave/Rooftop Garden
RCA; recorded late 1982; released May 1983

The album was dedicated "to Sylvia". It's a patchy work, though it certainly has its moments. The title track is a wonderful pop-rocker about "legendary love," contrasting romantic ideals with human frailty. The band – Robert Quine on guitar and Fernando Saunders on bass once again, but this time with Fred Maher on drums – are on top form here, Saunders in particular.

'The Last Shot' is a powerful and honest song about quitting alcohol and drugs, admitting just how hard it is. 'Turn Out The Light' is an enjoyably gentle blues-folk stomp about the joys of soft lighting and a nocturnal lifestyle. 'Pow Wow' is dumb but fun: a potted history of the centuries-long plight of the Native American, performed as a lightweight pop song; Lou says he wants to dance with them! 'Home Of The Brave' is a slow and brooding ballad about loneliness and alienation in the modern world; despite its intensity, it's really quite beautiful. One of the characters in the song is clearly Reed's old college room-mate Lincoln Swados. The song concludes by quoting from Arthur Alexander's Sixties soul hit 'Everyday I Have To Cry'. 'Rooftop Garden' is acoustic folk-rock (with wonderful bass), about having your own romantic private world upstairs. Lyrically, it tips a hat to The Drifter's 'Up On The Roof' (which was co-written by Doc Pomus, whom Reed would later befriend).

Otherwise, the proceedings meander a lot, but at least do so prettily; however, in some

cases, like 'Bottoming Out', the tunes just don't live up to the lyrics. As a whole, *Legendary Hearts* is simply average, and that's being kind.

7

LIVE IN ITALY

Sweet Jane/I'm Waiting For My Man/Martial Law/Satellite Of Love/Kill Your Sons/Betrayed/ Sally Can't Dance/Waves Of Fear/Average Guy/White Light White Heat/Some Kinda Love/Sister Ray/Walk On The Wild Side/ Heroin/Rock 'N' Roll
RCA; recorded September 1983; released January 1984

Reed's fourth live album was – finally – a good one, due to the presence of a tight and sympatico band. He sounds confident and assured, and the playing throughout is first-rate. Though the set is heavily slanted towards the Velvets-era, there are two tracks apiece from Reed's previous two studio albums and, strangely, two tracks from the dire *Sally Can't Dance*, including the dreadful title track. But here 'Kill Your Sons' has an air of real sadness that transforms it into something far more touching (the same is true of 'Betrayed' here), and even 'Sally Can't Dance' is halfway bearable. Highlights include 'Satellite Of

7

Love' (despite a sparse arrangement, it's truly beautiful), 'White Light' (performed with real joy) and 'Walk On The Wild Side' (with some wonderful basslines). Most of the tracks are too long, but the band is so good you don't really mind. It was recorded at gigs at the Verona Arena and Rome's Circus Maximus, with the Quine/Maher/Saunders line-up. At the Rome performance, the band had been teargassed, as Robert Quine explained: "We were playing Circus Maximus – an outdoor place. Apparently a crowd had gathered outside the fence before the concert, and the police dispersed them using teargas the moment before we came out. When we came onstage, the wind blew the teargas directly on us. So during the first forty-five minutes of the show I could not see a thing. I could not even see the little dots on the neck of my guitar. And there was snot running down my face and they were throwing wine bottles full of piss on the stage. People said we were really brave to stay onstage, but we had to. There would have been a riot. There were God knows how many of them. And it was a pretty emotional performance."

NEW SENSATIONS

I Love You, Suzanne/Endlessly Jealous/My Red Joystick/Turn To Me/New Sensations/ Doin' The Things That We Want To/What Becomes A Legend Most/Fly Into The Sun/ My Friend George/High In The City/Down At The Arcade

RCA; recorded between December 1983 and February 1984; released April 1984

At the time, the two months Reed took to record *New Sensations*, was the longest he'd ever spent on an album. It was co-produced by Reed and engineer John Jansen, about whom Reed was uncharacteristically complimentary: "I think Jansen did an incredible job. His stereo spread is really awe-inspiring." Typically, Reed also stated the contrary, claiming that he'd had "a relationship with the engineer that was more involved than I would normally like to have."

Reed himself played all the guitars (having just fired Robert Quine), with a little assistance from Fernando Saunders, who played rhythm guitar on two tracks (in addition to also playing both string and electric bass); Fred Maher played drums; L. Shankar played electric violin; Peter Wood played piano, synthesizers and accordion. Backing vocalists were Jocelyn Brown, Fernando Saunders, Connie Harvey, Eric Troyer and Rory Dodd. Also featured was a horn section that was comprised of Michael and Randy Brecker, Jon Faddis and Tom Malone (who also did the arrangements).

Throughout, Lou certainly seems to have rediscovered a joy in the guitar. The album kicks off with 'I Love You, Suzanne' – a great single, and deservedly a hit. It kicks off with a quote from 'Do You

7

Love Me (Now That I Can Dance)' before launching into a bouncy and brilliantly dumb love song. The drums now sound a bit dated, but otherwise it's wonderful. 'My Red Joystick' would seem to be an ode to compulsive masturbation – the protagonist would rather deal with his "red joystick" than with women. As if to undermine all this double-entendre, the cover photograph proves Lou is actually referring to his home videogame controls. The tune is very reminiscent of Talking Heads, but marred by irritating backing vocals. 'Turn To Me' sees Reed turning in a passable Keith Richards impression on a bluesy – and very funny – statement of commitment.

The title track kicks off with an insistent soul beat, before turning to Lou's laconic list of things he'd like to do, be and have – which then turns into an account of an idyllic motorbike ride. The arrest Reed refers to is indeed autobiographical – he spent one Christmas in jail for trying to cash someone else's illegal drug prescription (and was subsequently defended by one of Richard Nixon's Watergate lawyers).

'Doin' The Things That We Want To' is more irresistible intelligent pop. "Sam's play" refers to Sam Shepard's 'Fool For Love', and this describes the impact the play had upon Reed. Supposedly, the song prompted Shepard to enter the rock arena himself with 'Brownsville Girl,' a song he co-wrote with Bob Dylan (for the *Knocked Out Loaded* album), which proved to be one of the few high spots of Dylan's career during the Eighties. By a neat piece of coincidence that closes the circle, Dylan saw Lou performing 'Doin' The Things That We Want To' live, and supposedly

told Sylvia Reed afterwards that he wished he'd written it himself. Reed compares Shepard's play with the movies of Martin Scorcese, going on to namecheck Travis Bickle (from *Taxi Driver*) and Johnny Boy (from *Mean Streets*), and ending with the assertion that he considers Shepard and Scorcese to be his peers. An oddity, but curiously compelling.

'What Becomes A Legend Most' features an electric violin that conjures up a Velvets atmosphere. It's a mock-epic ode to an ageing Nico-esque singer who's living an empty and loveless existence on the road. Totally over-the-top arrangement (including Beatles-style harmonies), but it works and is utterly wonderful – sort of a successor to the Velvets' 'New Age'. The title phrase was a highly successful advertising slogan for the furriers Blackglama during the 1950s. 'Fly Into The Sun' of course echoes the Velvets' 'Ride Into The Sun', and is so unusual – for Reed – that it makes you really sit up and pay attention. It's a joyously optimistic slab of pure mysticism, a hymn to life and love and God, delivered to an upbeat blues that's almost gospel.

'My Friend George' is an odd little number. Insistent and likeable, it's about a friendship gone awry. thinks it's about Lincoln Swados ... but though Swados was certainly (from all accounts) odd, there's no evidence to suggest that he was a murderer! 'High In The City' is a joyfully cynical song about survival in New York. Gently catchy pop with a tinge of reggae (and a steel drum), all of which contrasts sharply with the lyrics. 'Down At The Arcade' is a heavy-rock strut about being the reigning champion of the video-game arcade. Dumb but fun, with

THE VELVET UNDERGROUND

7

some genuinely amusing lyrics. In all, *New Sensations* is a *vast* improvement – easily Lou's most tuneful album since *Transformer*. Even the filler is way above average.

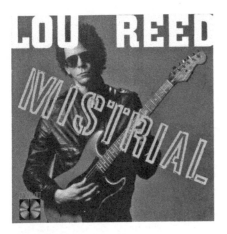

MISTRIAL

Mistrial/No Money Down/Outside/Don't Hurt A Woman/Video Violence/Spit It Out/The Original Wrapper/Mama's Got A Lover/I Remember You/Tell It To Your Heart

RCA; released April 1986

Reed's final album for RCA marked the end of another era. For one thing, it would conclude his long-standing collaboration with bassist Fernando Saunders, who co-produced this – though Saunders would eventually return ten years later for *Set The Twilight Reeling*. Unusually, this album was recorded in reverse of the conventional pattern: vocals and guitars were recorded first, drums and bass last. One reason for this may have been that no other musicians were used, and Reed was relying on computerised percussion and synthesizers, although Reed's old friend

Rubén Blades – whose solo album Lou would later co-produce – sings backing vocals on two tracks. Unfortunately, the era ended badly. The album is a weak one, both in terms of the songs and their execution. The drum machines and synthesizers sounded bad enough at the time; now they sound incredibly dated. Worse, much of the material here is downright dreadful, and sounds as contrived and empty as anything on *Sally Can't Dance*. 'The Original Wrapper' is the one really interesting track, which sees Lou experimenting with rap and commenting on the contemporary moral vacuum and all manner of social concerns: herpes, the middle East, abortion and much more. En route he points an accusing finger at (amongst others) Ronald Reagan, Jerry Falwell and Louis Farrakhan. It's effective stuff (and a precursor of things to come with *New York*), but the percussion gets very annoying towards the end. Otherwise, although there's some nice guitar playing throughout the album, only 'Don't Hurt A Woman', 'Mama's Got A Lover' and 'Tell It To Your Heart' are even worth a listen as songs – and then only just.

NEW YORK

*Romeo Had Juliette/Halloween Parade/
Dirty Blvd./Endless Cycle/There Is No
Time/Last Great American Whale/Beginning
Of A Great Adventure/Busload Of Faith/
Sick Of You/Hold On/Good Evening, Mr
Waldheim/Xmas In February/Straw Man/
Dime Store Mystery*
Sire; recorded autumn 1988; released January 1989

Nearly three years after *Mistrial*, Reed
returned with one of the finest albums
of his career. *New York* was recorded in
the city itself (naturally), at Mediasound
studios. The album came as a revelation:
at this point, virtually nobody thought
Reed was still capable of work of this
quality. There's scarcely a bad number on
it, and it's both melodic and intelligent,
with a theme of social comment that
was more acutely observed than the
work of any other lyricist in rock apart
from Bob Dylan. Subject matter included
homelessness, AIDS, ecology, racism and
more. Reed's sleevenote stated that *New
York* was intended to be listened to in a
single sitting, "as though it were a book or
a movie". He was insistent that there was
a definite sequence to the songs, that they
built as you went along.

Reed co-produced the album with Fred
Maher, who also played drums on most
of the tracks. On 'Last Great American
Whale' and 'Dime Store Mystery' the
drummer was Moe Tucker. Reed's guitar
is on the left-hand channel, with the
other guitarist, Mike Rathke (Sylvia
Reed's brother-in-law), on the right-
hand channel; and the bassist was Rob
Wasserman, apart from 'Romeo Had
Juliette' and 'Busload Of Faith', where bass
was played by Fred Maher.

The album kicks off with 'Romeo Had
Juliette', a rocking, guitar-driven, literate
love story set against a backdrop of
streetcrime and drugs (though the idea of
updating Shakespeare's teenage romance
into a fable of cross-cultural love between
New Yorkers had first been done several
decades earlier, by Stephen Sondheim and
Leonard Bernstein, with *West Side Story*).
The Latin inscription Reed refers to which
translates as "It's hard to give a shit these
days" is (according to Reed): 'Asperum
Aestimare Fimi Alquid Hodie'. 'Halloween
Parade' is a bouncy, theatrical singalong
celebrating the annual (and predominantly
gay) Hallowe'en costume parade in
Greenwich Village, and mourning the
losses of a community that had been
decimated by AIDS. It's genuinely moving.

'Dirty Blvd.' is an irresistibly compelling
rocker that details a hellish childhood
of beatings and poverty, contrasting it
with the affluence others enjoy, and also
celebrating the magic of the New York
streets, and the power of hope. 'Endless
Cycle' is a gentle but pessimistic folk-rock
about cycles of abuse, and the genetic
factor in addiction. 'There Is No Time'
sees Reed ranting and railing at just about
everybody, urging the need for immediate
and drastic action on social issues. The
tune sounds like 'Bottoming Out' revisited.

'Last Great American Whale' is almost a
talking blues, dominated by booming, whale-
like bass. It's the mythic account of a totemic
whale freeing a Native American chief who'd
killed a racist; the whale is then killed by a
bazooka-wielding NRA member (this from a
man who'd given up drugs, remember); the
rest of the song is an diatribe about selfish
Americans thoughtlessly polluting the planet.
'Beginning Of A Great Adventure' is a jazzy

7

7

rap, with Lou deliberating the pros and cons of possible fatherhood. Reed's eventual decision that he didn't want children is thought to have been a major factor in the eventual disintegration of his marriage to Sylvia.

'Busload Of Faith' is a driving, bluesy slow rocker. Lyrically, it's a gloomy catalogue of woes, insisting that we're all on our own; though Reed insists we all need a "busload of faith to get by", he spends the rest of the song pessimistically dismembering the concept of faith in anything. 'Sick Of You' is bouncy, countryish rock – a grimly funny rant that Reed described as a "fantasy newscast", a long list of environmental disasters and political corruption. 'Hold On' is social protest set to driving rock, listing incidents of New York street-crime and political unrest. On May 10 1989 the song's lyric was reprinted in the pages of the *New York Times* under the headline "Anarchy In The Streets."

'Good Evening Mr Waldheim' is more electric protest, about racism and hypocrisy (Kurt Waldheim was the Austrian politician who had denied his Nazi past). The song also targets Jesse Jackson, Louis Farrakhan and the Pope. 'Xmas In February' is an elegant and extremely moving, gently electric talking blues, about the plight of the Vets who returned home from the Vietnam war crippled and scarred (and not just physically). 'Strawman' is a searing electric rant against consumerism and greed, with an epic guitar solo. 'Dime Store Mystery' is a moody, brooding talking blues dedicated to Andy Warhol. Reed contemplates Warhol's death, the mysteries of existence, and the memorial Mass for Warhol to be held at St Patrick's church the following day. Realizing he'd never see his mentor again hit Lou

Reed very hard indeed, as *Songs For Drella* would prove.

"You can't beat guitars, bass, drum," stated Lou's sleeve note. When they're played at this standard, he's absolutely right.

LOU REED & JOHN CALE: SONGS FOR DRELLA – A FICTION

See under Velvet Underground: Albums

MAGIC AND LOSS

Dorita/What's Good/Power And Glory/ Magician/Sword Of Damocles/Goodby Mass/Cremation/Dreamin'/No Chance/ Warrior King/Harry's Circumcision/Gassed And Stoked/Power And Glory Part Ii/Magic And Loss

Sire/Warner Bros; recorded April 1991; released January 1992

"Between two Aprils I lost two friends," reads Lou's cover note, these friends being 'Doc' Pomus and the mysterious 'Rita'. Most of the album is about watching these friends suffer through terminal illness. Each of the songs here is given a subtitle as well as a title, the overall effect seemingly that of a journey from grief and loss through to acceptance and growth. The territory explored is not pretty: cancer, radiotherapy and chemotherapy (with Reed musing on his own experiences with dexedrine and morphine), funerals and cremation and pain and absence. You thought *Berlin* was hard? This is harder. But Reed maintained that it was "inspiring to see real people facing death."

There's a strange shift of pace with 'Harry's Circumcision', a bizarre little fable about self-mutilation, recited over an exquisitely delicate guitar instrumental. Vaguely reminiscent of 'The Gift' on the second Velvet Underground album (Reed even sounds a little like John Cale here), the song was another inspired by Reed's college roommate Lincoln Swados: "He was a very talented guy. He was just insane. I always thought he made the people at the Factory pale by comparison. Nothing I saw there was anything compared to what I saw him do."

Elsewhere, Reed touches on alchemy, shamans, philosophy and mysticism, seeking some kind of answers. The title track closes the album, a powerful and wonderful song about rebirth, be it psychological or literal (the symbolism here is almost Buddhist). After travelling through some of the bleaker passages on this record, it makes the journey worthwhile.

Recorded at the Magic Shop in New York, the album's band was once again Mike Rathke on second guitar and Rob Wasserman on bass, with Michael Blair on drums. Backing vocals were by Reed, Michael Blair, Roger Moutenot (on 'What's Good') and "the legendary Little Jimmy Scott" (on 'Power And Glory'). The album was co-produced by Reed

and Mike Rathke (who also co-wrote four of the songs). Musically, *Magic And Loss* veers from monotone dirges to sweeping rock epics to folk-blues ballads of farewell; but the tunefulness (when it occurs) doesn't make it any easier to listen to.

For marketing reasons the album's release was delayed until January 1992 – four months before Lou Reed's fiftieth birthday. It's a difficult record – at just under an hour long, quite an ordeal. Although it's undeniably extremely good, it's not something you'd play for fun, or even that often. Nonetheless, it's courageous.

BETWEEN THOUGHT AND EXPRESSION

Disc One

I Can't Stand It/Lisa Says/Ocean/Walk On The Wild Side/Satellite Of Love/Vicious/ Caroline Says/How Do You Think It Feels/ Oh Jim/Caroline Says Ii/The Kids/Sad Song/Sweet Jane (Live, From Rock 'N' Roll Animal) /Kill Your Sons/Coney Island Baby.

Disc Two

Nowhere At All/Kicks/Downtown Dirt/Rock

THE VELVET UNDERGROUND

*And Roll Heart/Vicious Circle/Temporary
Thing/Real Good Time Together/Leave Me
Alone/Heroin/Here Comes The Bride/Street
Hassle/Metal Machine Music/The Bells*
Disc Three
*America/Think It Over/Teach The Gifted
Children/The Gun/The Blue Mask/
My House/Waves Of Fear/Little Sister/
Legendary Hearts/The Last Shot/New
Sensations/My Friend George/Doin' The
Things That We Want To/The Original
Wrapper/Video Violence/Tell It To Your
Heart/Voices Of Freedom*
RCA; recorded 1972–1991; released April 1992

A three-CD retrospective of Reed's solo
career prior to *New York*. He'd used the
same title for his first collection of lyrics,
which had been published several months
previously. This is the only compilation
album in which Reed had been personally
involved, selecting tracks and remastering
them with the aid of engineer Bob Ludwig.
Reed stated: "Short of a manufacturing
glitch which I can't control this should
stand, for now, as a definitive post-Velvet
Underground collection and the only one
in which I have had the luxury of technical
involvement."

'Nowhere At All' was first released
as the B-side of the single release of
'Charley's Girl'. Recorded during the
sessions for *Coney Island Baby*, but left off
the album – not that surprising, since it
doesn't sound anything like the rest of
that record. It's more like glammed-up
heavy rock, with Reed in Dylannish world-
weary mode. Great stuff.

'Downtown Dirt' was previously
unreleased. Line-up: Lou Reed, guitar;
Michael Fonfara, keyboards; Doug Yule,
bass; Bob Meday, drums. Recorded in

January 1975. A slow and bluesy ode to the
lowlife and its denizens. The song was later
rewritten, and re-recorded for *Street Hassle*.

'Leave Me Alone' was also previously
unreleased. Line-up: Lou Reed, guitar and
vocals; Bob Kulick, guitar; Bruce Yaw,
bass; Michael Suchorsky, drums; Michael
Wendroff and Joanne Vent, background
vocals. Recorded during sessions for *Coney
Island Baby*. A choppy Dylannish rocker that
sounds like it grew out of a jam session,
it's nothing special. The song was later
re-recorded for *Street Hassle*.

'Heroin' is a previously unreleased
live version, recorded December 1 1976
at The Roxy in Los Angeles. Engineered
by Ray Thompson for radio broadcast by
station KMET. Line-up: Lou Reed, guitar
and vocals; Michael Fonfara, keyboards;
Bruce Yaw, bass; Michael Suchorsky,
drums; Marty Fogel, saxophone; Don
Cherry, trumpet. Clocking in at over
twelve minutes, this has a distinctly jazzy
feel, with Cherry's gently atmospheric
trumpet adding a sense of real melancholy.
Sadly, Reed's voice sounds ragged and raw,
and the jazz aspect gets very messy and
annoying before the end.

'Here Comes The Bride' is a previously
unreleased outtake from *Take No Prisoners*,
recorded live at the Bottom Line in New
York City on May 21 1978 (the late show).
Line-up: Lou Reed, guitar and vocals;
Michael Fonfara, keyboards; Ellard 'Moose'
Boles, bass; Michael Suchorsky, drums;
Marty Fogel, saxophone; Stuart Heinrich,
guitar; Angela Howard and Chrissie Faith,
background vocals. Reed described it in 1990
as "A fun song." Actually, it sounds like a
slowed-down 'Sweet Jane', and though the
song itself isn't that bad – a Springsteenish
tale of an interrupted wedding – the band

turn it into something truly dull.

'Metal Machine Music' is a one-and-a-half-minute extract from the album of the same name. For the version of 'The Bells' on this disc, Reed had problems, since the master tapes no longer existed as a result of record company neglect. In the end, a vinyl copy of the record was taped, then 'cleaned' by a special computer program.

'America' (aka 'Star Spangled Banner' is an outtake from *Growing Up In Public*, with the same line-up as for that record (it was left off the album simply for reasons of length). Reed's version of Francis Scott Key's anthem owes practically nothing to Jimi Hendrix's famous Woodstock instrumental; this is a vocal version, with Reed making it sound like the rousing climax to a Broadway musical. Interesting (if bizarre), but Fonfara's synthesizer is really annoying. In 1990 Reed pondered: "I don't know why we did it. It would be interesting to know what was going on in the world that would have caused that. It had to be something that set that off. Maybe they were kidnapping Americans, I don't know".

'Little Sister' comes from the soundtrack of the movie *Get Crazy*, was recorded during the sessions for *New Sensations* and written especially for the movie. Reed made a cameo appearance in the film (a black comedy that starred Malcolm McDowell), performing the song at the end of the movie, backed by the *Legendary Hearts* band. The song itself is a gently touching ballad with a lengthy guitar solo; Reed said his little sister loved it.

'Voices Of Freedom' was recorded live in London, March 1987, at a benefit concert for Amnesty International, for which the song was especially written. Line-up: Lou Reed,

guitar and vocals; Rick Bell, saxophone; Youssou N'Dour and Peter Gabriel, backing vocals. First released on *The Secret Policeman's Third Ball (The Music)*. A gloriously dumb rocker with gospel overtones and the audience clapping time. Also recorded at this concert (but still unreleased) is a version of 'Tell It To Your Heart'.

SET THE TWILIGHT REELING

Egg Cream/NYC Man/Finish Line/Trade In/Hang Onto Your Emotions/Sex With Your Parents Part II/Hookywooky/The Proposition/Adventurer Riptide/Set The Twilight Reeling
Warner Brothers; released March 1996

Despite the inclusion of a song about Sterling Morrison's passing, death took a back seat this time around, and *Set The Twilight Reeling* was as different from its predecessor as it could possibly be. There were lots of love songs, for one thing and Reed's new muse, Laurie Anderson, contributes electronically treated backing

THE VELVET UNDERGROUND

7

vocals to 'Hang Onto Your Emotions'. Lou Reed played virtually all the guitars; Fernando Saunders returned on bass; and Tony 'Thunder' Smith played drums. Produced by Reed, it was recorded live at The Roof (Reed's own studio in downtown Manhattan) and at The Magic Shop.

The results are patchy and disappointing, since most of the songs are below par (musically, if not lyrically) and often way too long. 'Egg Cream' is named after the sweet soda drink that was one of Lou's childhood treats back in Brooklyn. 'NYC Man' is a slow and bluesy love song which makes reference to no less than five Shakespearean tragedies (*Julius Caesar*, *Hamlet*, *Macbeth*, *King Lear* and *Othello*). Mature and soulful, it's gorgeously enhanced by a gently swelling horn section (comprising Oliver Lake, JD Parran and Russell Gunn Jr.) and Fernando Saunders' acoustic guitar.

'Finish Line', dedicated "for Sterl", is Lou's farewell to Sterling Morrison, and comprises gentle musings on mortality, set to a slow rock rhythm, and ending with a quote from 'The Bells'. It's touching, but not that great musically. 'Hang Onto Your Emotions' is a bizarre-but-pretty love song, with some great bass from Saunders.

'Sex With Your Parents' is a bluesy rap, with Reed scathing in his targeting of a wide range of "right wing Republican shit", including Republican Presidential candidate Robert Dole. Republicans have all committed incest with their parents, Reed insists — that's why they're so messed up. It's funny, but it doesn't bear repeated listening.

'Hookywooky' is a gentle, humorous rocker about sex and jealousy, with a great guitar solo. Released as a single, to zero airplay and terrible reviews (which it didn't deserve). Mildly infectious, it definitely grows on you. The title track is a gentle, subtle song about the rebirth that love can bring. Great bass from Saunders, a blistering guitar conclusion from Reed, and another grower.

But even the good stuff is nowhere near as good as one had come to expect from Reed in the Nineties, and overall this is his least satisfying album since *Mistrial*.

PERFECT NIGHT: LIVE IN LONDON

I'll Be Your Mirror/Perfect Day/The Kids/ Vicious/Busload Of Faith/Kicks/Talking Book/Into The Divine/Coney Island Baby/ New Sensations/Why Do You Talk/Riptide/ Original Wrapper/Sex With Your Parents/ Dirty Blvd

Reprise; recorded July 1997; released 1998

The annual arts festival Meltdown, at the Royal Festival Hall in London, was curated by Laurie Anderson in 1997, and this concert was part of it, recorded on July 3. Produced by Lou Reed and Mike Rathke. The band line-up is the same as for *Set The Twilight Reeling*, but this time Reed was playing a new acoustic guitar that he'd fallen in love with – one "with the sound of diamonds." This made him revise his standard live set, to see what would work with the new instrument, the result being that the evening kicks off with four acoustic numbers before the band kicks in.

Reed sounds relaxed, mellow and assured throughout (even gently humorous at times), even if his vocals are a tad laconic; the acoustic treatment gives new delicacy and grace to familiar material, and the band is superb. The three new songs from *Timerocker* were at least interesting, if not particularly memorable: 'Talking Book' seems to be about the pros and cons of computers, and is folky, but also tuneful and profound; 'Into The Divine' is a moving rocker about love and conflicting worldviews; 'Why Do You Talk' is a bluesy complaint about a lover's quest for spiritual answers. In fact, the whole album tends towards the bluesy, with 'Perfect Day' sounding positively doomy and depressed. But there are really nice versions of 'Coney Island Baby' and 'New Sensations'. His best live album to date.

ECSTASY

Paranoia Key Of E/Mystic Child/Mad/ Ecstasy/Modern Dance/Tatters/Future Farmers Of America/Turning Time Around/ White Prism/Rock Minuet/Baton Rouge/ Like A Possum/Rouge/Big Sky

Reprise; recorded 1999; released April 2000

Ecstasy is a thoughtful album, though not exactly a cheerful one. Many of the songs were written in the wee small hours, because Reed was suffering from insomnia, and deal with collapsing relationships. "It's not a life, being a wife," he sings on 'Modern Dance'. Since Laurie Anderson actually plays on the album it seems unlikely that Reed was writing about her (though with Reed, you never know). It seems more likely that his tales of infidelity and sleeping apart hark back to the last days of his marriage to Sylvia Morales, possibly to exorcize ghosts and guilt.

In addition to Anderson, Reed was joined by Mike Rathke on guitar, Fernando Saunders on bass, Tony 'Thunder' Smith on drums, alongside various strings and brass players. Unfortunately, most of the songs are over-long and lack a decent tune. The title track is good, as is 'Modern Dance' and 'Rock Minuet'. The latter was described by Reed as a "light-hearted" look at Oedipal problems. But 'Like A Possum' almost sums up the album's problems – it runs for over 18 minutes, without much of a tune, and doesn't really repay the journey. Both 'Possum' and 'Minuet' concerned sex and violence, abuse and murder, and it felt like Reed was being deliberately edgy to prove his artistry; then again, he may have just been following his muse... but if so he wasn't cutting his audience much slack.

THE VELVET UNDERGROUND

7

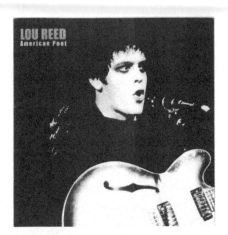

AMERICAN POET

*White Light White Heat/Vicious/I'm Waiting
For My Man/Walk It Talk It/Sweet Jane/
Interview/Heroin/Satellite Of Love/Walk On
The Wild Side/I'm So Free/Berlin/Rock 'N' Roll*
Superior; recorded December 1972; released 2002

Another Lou Reed live album, this one
was recorded in Hempstead, New York, on
Boxing Day 1972 – or to put it another way,
one month after the release of *Transformer*.
The concert was evidently recorded in
front of an audience in a radio recording
studio, for broadcast (probably live, since
they plug Reed's gig the following night)
on station WLIR FM.

The set is interrupted halfway through
for a five-minute interview, in which
Reed is amenable and funny – although
extremely prickly on the subjects of
Doug Yule and *Loaded*. He also credits his
backing band – The Tots, who were Bobby
Riscinio, Vinnie LaPorta, Eddie Reynolds
and Scott Clark – though with no clues
given as to who plays what. The recording
quality is pretty good, and as Reed's live
albums go, this is excellent.

The set list alternates between Velvets
songs and Reed's solo work, and although
the proceedings are a mite ramshackle,
Reed sounds relaxed and confident
throughout (though occasionally singing
flat). The band are no more than adequate,
with one of those drummers who think
cymbals should be virtually continuous,
and the lack of decent backing vocals is
noticeable; even so, the whole thing has a
fair amount of vital energy.

Quite how this album came to be
released at all is something of a mystery
– perhaps Reed simply had no objections,
since the quality is so good. Grab it
while you can, just in case. The booklet
contains a few really good photos by Mick
Rock, from the same photo session as the
Transformer cover.

THE RAVEN

Disc One
*The Conqueror Worm/Overture/Old Poe/
Prologue (Ligeia)/Edgar Allan Poe/The
Valley Of Unrest/Call On Me/The City In
The Sea/Shadow/A Thousand Departed
Friends/Change/The Fall Of The House Of*

*Usher/The Bed/Perfect Day/The Raven/
Balloon*
Disc Two
*Broadway Song/The Tell-Tale Heart Part
I/Blind Rage/ The Tell-Tale Heart Part II/
Burning Embers/Imp Of The Perverse/
Vanishing Act/The Cask/Guilty (Spoken)/
Guilty (Song)/A Wild Being From Birth/I
Wanna Know (The Pit & The Pendulum)/
Science Of The Mind/Annabel Lee/The
Bells/Hop Frog/Every Frog Has His Day/
Tripitena's Speech/Who Am I? (Tripitena's
Song)/Courtly Orangutans/Fire Music/
Guardian Angel*
Single CD version
*Overture/Edgar Allan Poe/Call On Me/The
Valley Of Unrest/A Thousand Departed
Friends/Change/The Bed/Perfect Day/
The Raven/Balloon/Broadway Song/Blind
Rage/Burning Embers/Vanishing Act/The
Cask/Guilty/I Wanna Know (The Pit & The
Pendulum)/Science Of The Mind/Hop Frog/
Tripitena's Speech/Who Am I? (Tripitena's
Song)*
Reprise; recorded and released 2003

"He likes Edgar Allan Poe," Reed had written of himself in 'Love Is Here To Stay' back in 1980, and this album is ample proof of a love that's practically obsession. *The Raven* was released in both a double CD and a single CD version. The shorter of the two, Reed explained, was "for those who don't want to listen to two hours of it, or who want to try it out before committing to the two hours. So there's the *grand mal* version or the exquisite but smaller version." The project began life as a theatrical piece (in collaboration with Robert Wilson) that was performed in Germany in February 2001, which evolved into this two-hour long conceptual work.

Reed's regular band of Mike Rathke, Fernando Saunders and Tony Smith are augmented by a horn and string section (the latter largely under the supervision of cellist Jane Scarpantoni, who would later tour with Reed) and half a dozen other session musicians. The album was co-produced by Reed and Hal Wilner (who was well used to working on complicated musical projects involving numerous artists). The work features extracts from Poe's verse and prose performed by actors Willem Dafoe, Elizabeth Ashley, Amanda Plummer, Fisher Stevens and Steve Buscemi, with musical contributions from David Bowie, Antony, Kate and Anna McGarrigle, Ornette Coleman, Laurie Anderson and the Blind Boys Of Alabama (the album was once again dedicated to Anderson, "a constant source of inspiration").

Unfortunately, it's a muddle – the recitals of Poe's work well enough (especially the title track), although it should be pointed out that many of the pieces are Poe rewritten by Reed (and rather well, too). But although it contains some gorgeous instrumental passages, Reed's actual song contributions are almost all both substandard and hackneyed. Possibly this is why he chose to include new (and extremely good) versions of a couple of his 'classics': 'The Bed' (from *Berlin*) and 'Perfect Day' (the latter performed by Antony, a truly extraordinary singer). Both songs are head and shoulders above anything else on the album, and almost worth the price of admission on their own.

Of the guest spots, three get the best new tunes: the MacGarrigles on 'Balloon', Bowie on 'Hop Frog' and the Blind

Boys Of Alabama on 'I Wanna Know'. Steve Buscemi sings on 'Broadway Song' – a pastiche of a show number that's completely unremarkable.

There's even some *Metal Machine*-style electronics in 'Fire Music,' which was recorded two days after 9/11, in a studio close to Ground Zero (but it's still unforgiveable noise, frankly). Since Poe's endings tend to be dark and Reed wanted something lighter to finish, the album closes with the more personal 'Guardian Angel'. Both that and 'Vanishing Act' are quite touching and enjoyable, yet without being at all memorable.

As per usual, Reed thought his new album was great, and called it "the culmination of everything I've ever done," saying he thought it would be hard for him to top artistically. Sadly, he may be the only person who feels that way. The whole thing's overly self-conscious, and sorely in need of a few more actual tunes.

As it stands, it's the kind of record you play once and then file away forever. Do you really need the longer version? Not really.

ANIMAL SERENADE

Disc One
Advice/Smalltown/Tell It To Your Heart/ Men Of Good Fortune/How Do You Think It Feels/Vanishing Act/Ecstasy/The Day John Kennedy Died/Street Hassle/The Bed/ Revien Cherie/Venus In Furs
Disc Two
Dirty Blvd/Sunday Morning/All Tomorrow's Parties/Call On Me/The Raven/Set The Twilight Reeling/Candy Says/Heroin
Sire/Reprise; recorded 24 June 2003; released 2004

Yet another live album, this one was recorded at LA's Wiltern Theater during a 60-date tour. As well as the regular band of Rathke and Saunders, the line-up includes two of the contributors to *The Raven*: cellist Jane Scarpantoni, and Antony Hegarty on backing vocals. Curiously, there are no drums (except for a couple of tracks where percussion is provided by Saunders).

Reed is in good humour and is very laid-back throughout; his vocals are less throwaway than on previous live recordings, and largely stick to the tune in question. The backing vocals and Scarpantoni's cello add a new dimension to the more minor material, but the rest is very variable – 'Sunday Morning' is great, 'All Tomorrow's Parties' is awful. 'Revien Cherie' is a solo spot for Fernando Saunders (who wrote the song).

At its best the album's pleasant, at its worst it's self-indulgent – the world didn't really need a ten-minute version of 'Venus In Furs'. There's very little here other than 'Set The Twilight Reeling' (with a great vocal from Antony) that isn't better in its studio incarnation.

HUDSON RIVER WIND MEDITATIONS

Move Your Heart/Find Your Note/Hudson River Wind (Blend The Ambiance)/Wind Coda
In his sleeve notes (dated October 2006)
Sounds True; released 2007

Reed states: "I first composed this music for myself as an adjunct to meditation, Tai Chi, and bodywork, and as music to play in the background of life – to replace the everyday cacophony with new and ordered sounds of an unpredictable nature. New sounds freed from preconception. This was two years ago, and over time, friends who heard the music asked if I could make them copies. I then wrote two more pieces with the same intent: to relax the body, mind, and spirit and facilitate meditation. I hope you find as much use for this music as I have in both writing and listening to it and exploring inner spaces." It consists of four pieces (two long and two short). Lou played all the instruments and co-produced the album with Hal Willner (for whose compilation of Brecht-Weill songs Lou had contributed 'September Song'). The album was recorded at Animal Lab in New York. 'Move Your Heart' is a mesmerizing ambient piece that's soothingly wavelike. It's utterly beautiful, and the last thing you'd ever have expected from Lou Reed – or even thought him capable of. 'Find Your Note' is the exact opposite. Where 'Move Your Heart' is restful, this is discordant and distracting and sombre. It sounds alien – in some ways similar to the *Forbidden Planet* soundtrack, only less tuneful. Here there's moaning and high-pitched whines and what sounds like traffic noise. Perhaps all this works in the context of physical exercise, but for the casual listener it's hard work – comparable to *Metal Machine Music* slowed down to a funereal pace. 'Hudson River Wind' seems like a continuation of the previous piece, and does indeed sound like rushing wind, coupled with an airplane taking off. It's irritating, but at least also mercifully brief. 'Wind Coda' attempts to blend the ambience of the first piece with the approach of the second, but it's more mess than success.

What few reviews the album received weren't good, but it's still worth the price of admission for 'Move Your Heart' alone – a fascinating glimpse into Lou's gentler, more spiritual side.

THE VELVET UNDERGROUND

THE CREATION OF THE UNIVERSE (LOU REED'S METAL MACHINE TRIO)

Disc One
Night 1
Disc Two
Night 2
Sister Ray; 2008

As the band name implies, this is Lou Reed exploring his experimental side again (on guitars and electronics). His collaborators here include Ulrich Krieger (tenor saxophone and live-electronics) and Sarth Calhoun (live processing and 'continuum fingerboard').

The two-CD set divides the piece into two halves, each of which is also divided into two halves: the whole thing lasts for about 110 minutes. At times it's drone-like and ambient and quite pleasant, and very much of a mood with *Hudson River Meditations*; but most of it is discordant, and more likely to fray your nerves than soothe them. Those who think *Metal Machine Music* was a work of genius will probably love it.

LULU (LOU REED & METALLICA)

Disc One
Brandenburg Gate/The View/Pumping Blood/Mistress Dread/Iced Honey/Cheat On Me
Disc Two
Frustration/Little Dog/Dragon/Junior Dad
Vertigo; released 2011 Personnel: Lou Reed (guitars, continuum, vocals); James Hetfield (guitars, vocals); Lars Ulrich (drums); Kirk Hammett (guitars); Robert Trujillo (bass). Sarth Calhoun (electronics); Jenny Scheinman (violin, viola and string arrangements); Megan Gould (violin); Ron Lawrence (viola); Marika Hughes (cello); Ulrich Maas (cello on 'Little Dog' and 'Frustration'); Rob Wasserman (stand-up electric bass on 'Junior Dad'); Jessica Troy (viola on 'Junior Dad'). Produced by Lou Reed, Metallica, Hal Willner and Greg Fidelman.

It seems odd that Lou Reed's last album should not only be a joint-billing collaboration, but one that almost seems designed to alienate many of his listeners. For one thing, how you feel about this album will largely depend on how you feel about heavy metal. It is, after all, a collaboration with Metallica. For another, the subject matter of the *Lulu* plays – by definition – makes for deliberately uneasy listening. "I want to see your suicide," Lou sings on 'The View', where he also notes that "pain and evil have their place". 'Pumping Blood' is basically a graphic ode to Jack The Ripper. Of course, Reed is only echoing the territory and themes of Frank Wedekind's plays, but in an impressionistic rather than a narrative way. Even so, he does seem to be revelling in the squalor.

Additionally, some of the songs seem to be shoehorned in, and one can't help that feel that 'Little Dog' and 'Junior Dad' are here simply to help Reed exorcize the ghosts of his recently deceased dog Lolabelle and his father Sid. Since 'Lulu' had been Reed's Factory-era nickname, we can definitely mark that one down to simple coincidence, albeit one that Reed was obviously aware of and which may well have amused him.

Then there's the music itself. There are those close to Reed who questioned the sanity of this project, feeling that Metallica just didn't possess the subtlety to do these songs justice. One can't help thinking that in this choice Lou was just being cantankerous – that he wanted his last project to be not only blatantly 'arty', but also as noisy as possible. The result is that at its worst, the material here is musically doom-laden, heavy-handed, ponderously bombastic and a complete bloody racket; but at its best, as on 'Brandenburg Gate' and 'Iced Honey', it's delicate and compelling, with strong and definite tunes and melody (even if Lou's voice is too weak to deliver them properly). And bizarrely, it all ends well. 'Junior Dad' is nothing less than a triumph – a tender and touching song of loss and love and forgiveness. Though it runs for over 19 minutes, after about 12 it transforms into a wave-like drone performed by the string section, similar to one of Reed's better meditation pieces while also echoing the early collaborations with John Cale. It's as if the personal demons that had driven Reed's entire career are dissolving into the ocean, and it's the perfect coda to all his previous work.

THE VELVET UNDERGROUND

7

LOU REED RARITIES & ODDITIES

Much of the Velvets' solo output is rare by definition, since many albums are quite hard to track down. There are also a few items that aren't actually very good musically, like Lou Reed's 1998 Live At The White House, an eight-track CD recorded during the Clinton administration. This was never commercially released, but distributed to Reprise staff members; copies currently fetch about £275/$550. There are also numerous uncollected Lou Reed B-sides and guest appearances, none of which are really essential except for:

1) Reed's version of Kurt Weill and Maxwell Anderson's 'September Song', from the 1985 tribute album compiled by Hal Willner, Lost In The Stars: The Music Of Kurt Weill. He makes the song his own; it was also released as a single.

2) Reed's sublime take on a song made famous by Frank Sinatra, Arlen and Mercer's 'One For My Baby (And One More For The Road)', can be found on Rob Wasserman's 1988 album Duets.

3) 'Leave Her Johnny', on the 2006 Hal Willner-produced compilation Rogues Gallery. The theme for the album was pirate songs and sea shanties, and Reed's contribution is superb – weird folk-rock storytelling at its best.

4) Reed covered Buddy Holly's 'Peggy Sue' for the Holly tribute album Rave On.

5) Lou Reed collaborated with The Killers on 'Tranquilize', a track from their 2009 album Sawdust. Written by Brandon Flowers, the song sounds like a glam- rock refugee that's just arrived here from the mid-Seventies – it's that good.

6) Reed's 'The Power Of The Heart' was a tender and powerful love song to Laurie Andersen, released only as a free download from the Cartier Foundation in 2008 as part of a fundraising exercise for the charity Action Against Hunger. Now sadly unavailable; hopefully it'll get some kind of posthumous release.

7) 'The Power Of The Heart' was also covered by Peter Gabriel on his 2010 album Scratch My Back. For the 'answer' album And I'll Scratch Yours the following year, Lou delivered an enjoyable cover of Gabriel's 'Solsbury Hill'.

8) The 1997 all-star cover version of 'Perfect Day', which was available only as a single and is now hard to find. This featured vocals (and instrumental contributions) by a host of stars, including Laurie Anderson and Reed himself. All profits were donated to the BBC-sponsored charity Children In Need. The record is an utter delight (as was the video) and thoroughly deserved its hit status (it reached No 1 in the UK). Reed had approval over all the participants, but one of his choices – Curtis Mayfield – was unable to take part because of illness. Still, Reed declared himself pleased with the final result: "It flowed, it sounded like one breathing unit."

JOHN CALE

7

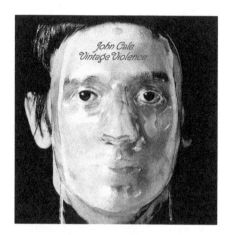

VINTAGE VIOLENCE

*Hello, There/Gideon's Bible/Adelaide/Big
White Cloud/Cleo/Please/Charlemagne/
Bring It On Up/Amsterdam/Ghost Story/
Fairweather Friend*

Columbia; recorded 1969; released July 1970

"I was trying to see if I could write songs,"
John Cale later said of his solo debut – and
the result leaves no doubt that he could. As
he'd do throughout his career, Cale peopled
his songs with characters – and performing
them became akin to method acting for
him. *Vintage Violence* was also the public's first
proper introduction to Cale's singing voice,
which critic Allan Jones memorably termed
an "unforgettably moving Eisteddfod tenor, a
voice of blasted Welsh beauty". The album was
supposedly recorded in ten days, though Cale
claims to have taken only three, one of which
was spent teaching the band the songs. He

also claims this was recorded the week after
recording the *Church Of Anthrax* album (which
was released some months later).

The musicians on the album (sometimes
referred to as 'Penguin'), were actually
Grinderswitch, Garland Jeffreys' backing band:
Harbey Brooks (bass); Ernire Coralla (guitar);
Garland Jeffreys (guitar and backing vocals);
Sanford Konikoff (drums); and Stan Szelist
(piano). Konikoff was, at the time, dating
Debbie Harry, who was then working as a
waitress at Max's Kansas City. Jeffreys had been
a contemporary of Lou Reed's at Syracuse, and
he and Cale had become friends; he wrote one
song on the album ('Fairweather Friend') and
also a poem about Cale for the sleeve notes.

As to the music, it runs the gamut of
everything from driving rockers ('Hello,
There') to gentle country/soul ballads ('Please')
to epic, Spectoresque pop ('Big White Cloud').
Cale's lyrics were literate and memorable
without being obvious, often evocative of
a mood (or a place, or a person) without
necessarily following a linear narrative –
"stretching out the verbs and nouns", as he
put it on 'Gideon's Bible'. Certainly he was
obviously well read, and had a gift for word
games and a vocabulary to match.

Often he'd name a song after a person or
a place, yet it would be impossible for the
listener to find a lyrical connection to the
title, or even to analyse the lyrics closely
at all; yet the songs would still succeed on
some level. *Vintage Violence* was a stunningly
capable and impressive debut – even its
throwaway fluff, like 'Adelaide' and 'Cleo',
is enjoyable – and proved beyond a doubt

THE VELVET UNDERGROUND

7

that Cale was a major talent in his own right. Ed Ward's review in *Rolling Stone* compared the album to Van Morrison's *Astral Weeks* and Dylan's *Highway 61 Revisited*; decades later, this still seems a fair assessment.

An early CD pressing of the album on Edsel has poor quality reproduction; the later release (on Columbia) contains two extra tracks: an alternate version of 'Fairweather Friend' and an unreleased instrumental called 'Wall', which is six minutes of viola drone.

John Cale & Terry Riley

CHURCH OF ANTHRAX

Church Of Anthrax/The Hall Of Mirrors In The Palace Of Versailles/The Soul Of Patrick Lee/ Ides Of March/The Protégé

Columbia; recorded 1969; released February 1971

Recorded before *Vintage Violence*, this collaboration between Cale and minimalist composer Riley was mainly improvised on the spot, and recorded in four days at CBS Studios in New York. John McClure of CBS nominally produced it, but Cale did the actual studio

work; Cale also mixed the album, though Riley disapproved of the results. Cale played bass, harpsichord, piano, guitar and viola; Riley played piano, organ and soprano saxophone; session players Bobby Columby (of Blood, Sweat & Tears) and Bobby Gregg both played drums. Cale had also asked both Sterling Morrison and Angus MacLise to play on the session, but both were out of town at the time.

The album consists of four instrumental pieces (two lengthy, two short), which marry Riley's repetitive minimalist keyboard parts with a rock/blues backing, with varying degrees of success. At their worst (as on the title track), the results resemble the more annoying kind of jazz-rock fusion that was then fashionable, with flute parts soaring above the proceedings to no real effect. At its best, as on 'The Hall Of Mirrors In The Palace Of Versailles', despite some awkward changes of pace it approaches the ambient, and is rather pleasant. The title refers to the location of the signing of the Versailles Peace Treaty in 1919, which divided up the spoils of Europe after World War I (thus sowing the seeds for World War II).

The album also includes one Cale song, 'The Soul Of Patrick Lee'. This is sung by Adam Miller, a songwriter friend of Cale's who mainly worked on commercials, and whose voice is vaguely reminiscent of the Zombies' Colin Blunstone. Cale almost certainly took a back seat here because he lacked confidence in his own vocals – and this was also the first of his own songs ever to be recorded. The fairly impenetrable lyrics sound somewhat like those for a traditional folk ballad – but the choir of harmony vocals launch it into territory somewhere between epic pop and the theme for a spaghetti Western. Definitely worth tracking down to hear, it could easily have fitted on *Vintage Violence*.

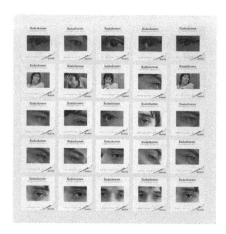

THE ACADEMY IN PERIL

The Philosopher/Brahms/Legs Larry At
Television Centre/The Academy In Peril/
Intro/Days Of Steam/3 Orchestral Pieces: (A)
Faust (B) The Balance (C) Captain Morgan's
Lament/King Harry/John Milton
Reprise; recorded early 1972; released July 1972

This record grew out of Cale's desire to
do a "straight classical music thing," and
was arranged and recorded (at the Manor,
Oxfordshire) in just three weeks, aided by
mixing engineer 'Jean Bois' (John Wood).
For the orchestral pieces he used the Royal
Philharmonic Orchestra. Cale later realised
three weeks had not been long enough. The
album is an odd mixture, kicking off with

7

TERRY RILEY

Minimalist composer Terry Riley came to
prominence with his piece *In C*, which was
premiered in 1964 and recorded in 1968,
and proved influential on other composers
working in this field, such as Philip Glass and
Steve Reich.

Riley played with La Monte Young circa
1966–68, and recorded a more accessible
work, *A Rainbow In Curved Air* in 1969 (in
fact, he was recording it at the same time
as working on *Church Of Anthrax*). This
album would be a major influence on the
Soft Machine and Tangerine Dream, as well
as on the Who's Pete Townshend, who
acknowledged the debt with 'Baba O'Riley' on
Who's Next (named after Riley and the spiritual
master Meher Baba, who was Townshend's
guru). Riley went on to record approximately
40 more albums, including one with the
Kronos Quartet. Also recommended: 1972's
Persian Surgery Dervishes.

7

the instrumental 'The Philosopher' (with Ron Wood on slide guitar), which starts sounding basic and bluesy, then gets complicated and interesting. 'Brahms' is a very dull piano piece – as is the title track – while 'Legs Larry At Television Centre' features the Bonzo Dog Doo Dah Band's 'Legs' Larry Smith doing a 'comedy' TV producer's voiceover while Cale plays an otherwise dull string piece. Short though it is, 'Days Of Steam' is a wonderfully involving tune, and one can see exactly why Andy Warhol wanted to use it for film music the second he heard it. Cale would later dismiss the three orchestral pieces as "wishy-washy Vaughan Williams stuff", and they are pretty unremarkable; but at the time Cale was simply happy to have finally gotten around to working with an orchestra at all, and it revived his ambition to write a proper symphony one day (which he still hasn't done – though the instrumental music he's produced from the Nineties onwards is much better than most of the tracks here). 'King Harry' is interesting (though one wishes that Cale would burst into actual song, rather than the whispered vocal he delivers), and the closing 'John Milton' is another unimpressive instrumental. In all, the album is disappointing – but it's still worth getting for 'Days Of Steam' alone.

PARIS 1919

Child's Christmas In Wales/Hanky Panky Nohow/The Endless Plain Of Fortune/ Andalucia/Macbeth/Paris 1919/Graham Greene/Half Past France/Antarctica Starts Here
Reprise; recorded late 1972; released March 1973

Paris 1919 was a return to the melodic and memorable pop of *Vintage Violence*, only this time augmented by a full orchestra. Cale has asserted that this was the first album of his where the songs had been properly written and arranged in advance, and Chris Thomas

ANDY WARHOL'S ACADEMY COVER

The Academy In Peril's cover was designed by Andy Warhol, and featured 25 colour photos of Cale (mainly of his eyes) framed by Kodakchrome colour slide mounts.

Always one to barter where possible, Warhol's fee for the work was the right to use 'Days Of Steam' as the theme for his film *Heat*. A copy of the album signed by Warhol was recently seen for sale at £500. Warhol was originally supposed to have provided a cover for *Vintage Violence*, with a similar idea – laying strips of black and white film against a plain white background – which looked "fantastic", according to Cale. The idea wasn't used simply because Cale had cut off his long hair just after the photographs were taken.

had been recommended to Cale as a producer because of his work on Procol Harum's *Live With The Edmonton Symphony Orchestra*. But, curiously, Cale had apparently not originally intended to use any orchestration for this album – it was added as an afterthought, with Thomas providing the arrangements for the UCLA Symphony Orchestra.

The engineer was Phil Sheer, once tour manager for the Velvet Underground. Backing musicians this time included Wilton Felder from the Crusaders on bass, and three members of Little Feat (though guitarist Lowell George left early, having apparently fallen out with a drunken Cale).

Although musically it was possible to see the influence of songwriters that Cale admired (such as Brian Wilson and the brothers Gibb), lyrically the songs were as evocative – and obscure – as on Cale's debut. There was certainly a literary theme, though: the opening 'A Child's Christmas In Wales' was not only autobiographical, but had the same title as a Dylan Thomas prose piece (a writer to whose work Cale would return much later in his career). There were also songs about *Macbeth* and the author Graham Greene (in probably the only rock song ever to make reference to both Chipping Sodbury and the incendiary British MP Enoch Powell).

The amazingly catchy and baroque title track again concerned the location of the peace treaty that concluded World War I (see *Church Of Anthrax*), and thus had contemporary resonance with the closing days of the Vietnam War. Paris in 1919 was also the setting for the early days of both Dada and Surrealism, both loves of Cale's (he was very influenced at this time by Guy De Maupassant and various surrealist writers).

The album has the occasional weak track ('Macbeth') but is otherwise remarkably tuneful and tasteful throughout, wrapping up with the slow ballad 'Antarctica Starts Here', which – like the Velvets' 'New Age' – concerned an ageing film star. It was supposedly influenced by Billy Wilder's *Sunset Boulevard*, and was a song that Cale would return to several times in the decades to come.

Despite receiving critical acclaim and being a solidly commercial work, *Paris 1919* was deleted after only a year. A 2006 reissue of the album on Reprise/Rhino contains an extra eleven tracks, ten of which are rehearsal tapes, alternate takes and different mixes, plus one unused song from the sessions, 'Burned Out Affair' (a fairly weak song about childhood). While none of these extra tracks are indispensable, as works-in-progress they do all provide interesting glimpses into the creative process.

FEAR

Fear Is A Man's Best Friend/Buffalo Ballet/ Barracuda/Emily/Ship Of Fools/Gun/The Man Who Couldn't Afford To Orgy/You Know More Than I Know/Momamma Scuba

Island; recorded spring 1974; released September 1974

THE VELVET UNDERGROUND

Producer Phil Manzanera, who also played guitar, drafted in his former Roxy Music cohort Brian Eno to contribute electronic treatments, plus the rhythm section of Kevin Ayers' band alongside a couple of members of Eno's band and Bryn Haworth on slide guitar. Richard Thompson (who Cale knew through Joe Boyd) also makes a guest appearance. The album was recorded at Sound Techniques and Olympic studios in London; the engineer was John Wood. Darker and rockier than *Paris 1919*, the album kicks off with the title track, an insistent rocker about paranoia that eventually dissolves into vocal and instrumental histrionics.

'Buffalo Ballet' is a cinematic piano ballad that could easily have fitted on the previous album; 'Barracuda' was like mutant reggae, odd but irresistible, and

BRIAN ENO

Brian Peter George St John le Baptiste de la Salle Eno was born in Woodbridge, Suffolk, on May 15 1948. In 1969 he moved to London, and as a result of accidentally bumping into old friend Andy MacKay on a train joined him as one of the founder members of Roxy Music, despite the fact that he didn't play any orthodox musical instruments. Instead, Eno applied his electronic synthesizer 'treatments' to the others' instruments – which, coupled with his flamboyant stage appearance, made him seem more of a novelty figure than he actually was. Leaving Roxy Music after their second album, Eno went on to carve an extraordinary musical career despite having famously described himself as a "non-musician". In 1974 he collaborated with ex-King Crimson guitarist Robert Fripp on the instrumental *No Pussyfootin'*, and also issued his first album of original songs, *Here Come The Warm Jets*. After *Fear* Cale recruited Eno to play on Nico's *The End* album, and the pair also collaborated on the *June 1, 1974* concert. Cale played on Eno's 1975 album *Another Green World*, and Eno would also be involved in several further solo projects of Cale's in the decades to come. Eno would attain his greatest commercial successes as a record producer working with numerous first division artists, including David Bowie and U2.

the first of several songs here about drowning (which in terms of his personal life Cale was, in a sense). The epic piano ballad 'Emily' continues the marine motif, while the rockily Dylanesque 'Ship Of Fools' concerns life on the road, namechecking both Tombstone and Swansea. 'Gun' is a eight-minute-long hard-edged, guitar-driven rocker about police detectives that eventually turns into an extended guitar thrash.

Backing vocals on the album were supplied by Irene and Doreen Chanter and Liza Strike. On 'The Man Who Couldn't Afford To Orgy' the spoken word backing was by Judy Nylon, a friend of Eno's (who would later form the duo Snatch with Patti Paladin, going on to tour with Cale as a backing vocalist in the late Seventies and early Eighties). 'The Man Who Couldn't Afford To Orgy' (in which "orgy" is deliberately mispronounced with a hard 'g') is a wonderfully swingalong ode to compassion, punctuated by Judy breathy verbal improvisation; it's infectious without being the least bit commercial – as is the folky 'You Know More Than I Know'. The album wraps up with 'Momamma Scuba', a song about a man who wants his girlfriend to drown him, delivered in the rock style of 'Gun'.

Throughout, the songs conjured an atmosphere of sex and death, love and dread – and did so to a backing of memorable tunes. Lester Bangs' review of *Fear* compared the album to the kind of music Lou Reed that could have been making "if his imagination had not short-circuited", noting that it "does the Velvet Underground tradition proud". The public, to some extent, agreed, and the record initially sold over 30,000 copies.

JUNE 1, 1974: KEVIN AYERS/JOHN CALE/ENO/NICO

Driving Me Backwards/Baby's On Fire (Brian Eno)
Heartbreak Hotel (John Cale)
The End (Nico)
May I ?/Shouting In A Bucket Blues/Stranger In Blue Suede Shoes/Everybody's Sometime And Some People's All The Time Blues/Two Goes Into Four (Kevin Ayers)
Island; recorded 1 June 1974; released summer 1974.

A recording of the one-off concert at London's Rainbow Theatre, featuring ACNE (Kevin Ayers/John Cale/Eno/Nico). It was basically Ayers' gig, with the others as guest stars; backing was provided by Ayers's regular band The Soporifics (Ollie Halsall on guitar and piano, John 'Rabbit' Bundrick on organ, Archie Leggatt on bass and Eddie Sparrow on drums). Also on board are Ayers' former bandmates Robert Wyatt (on percussion) and guitarist Mike Oldfield (then beginning to enjoy phenomenal success with his *Tubular Bells* album). Backing vocals are provided by Liza Strike, Doreen Chanter and Irene Chanter. Cale's contribution is a cover of something that would become a staple of his live act: a version of Elvis Presley's 'Heartbreak Hotel' that attempts to properly explore the dread and loneliness of the subject matter.

The version here is nowhere near as dark as later ones. Nico (aided by Eno on synthesizer) contributes a doom-laden version of 'The End' (the title track of the album she was then in the process of recording with Cale and Eno). Cale also plays on both Eno tracks, and contributes some viola to Ayers' 'Two Goes Into Four.'

It was probably fun on the night, but there's nothing that remarkable here – for completists (and Kevin Ayers fans) only.

SLOW DAZZLE

Mr Wilson/Taking It All Away/Dirty-Ass Rock 'N' Roll/Darling I Need You/Rollaroll/ Heartbreak Hotel/Ski Patrol/I'm Not The Loving Kind/Guts/The Jeweller

Island; recorded winter 1974; released April 1975

Cale's follow-up to *Fear* was the most commercially successful of his Island albums, although his conscious decision to "write singles" for the album doesn't really pay off. Several of the songs on *Slow Dazzle* are very substandard (while several of the tunes on *Fear* are a lot memorable than anything here). Most of the material was written in the studio.

This time Cale produced himself, since Manzanera was busy elsewhere (though both he and Eno made guest appearances). The album was recorded at Sound Techniques, and the backing musicians would go on to become Cale's touring band. Personnel included Chris Spedding (guitar), Pat Donaldson (bass), Timmy Donald and Gerry Conway on drums and Chris Thomas (violin, electric piano). Maria Muldaur's husband Geoff provided harmony vocals on two tracks.

The overall sound is rock that is musically less edgy – still good, but a lot more predictable. The bouncy opener 'Mr Wilson' was apparently about both Prime Minister Harold Wilson and Brian Wilson (and fades on music comparable to *Smile*-era Beach Boys), but most of the songs here concerned Cale's "misery and pain" (as he sang on 'Taking It All Away') and his collapsing personal life. At times this is almost tuneful, as on the bluesy 'Darling I Need You'; elsewhere it was a scream of sheer agony, as on Cale's dark and ominous studio reworking of 'Heartbreak Hotel'.

Several songs concern infidelity and betrayal, with the opening line of the impassioned and memorable 'Guts' ("the bugger in the short sleeves fucked my wife") referring to Kevin Ayers' seduction of Cindy Cale. The song was originally titled simply: 'Bugger'. The album closes with the mirror-imagery of 'The Jeweller', a successor to 'The Gift' in that it's 'lyrics' are a short prose piece recited over moody organ music, and one which reveals beyond doubt that Cale had some major emotional problems at this point. But although Cale's personal pain is audibly mirrored in *Slow Dazzle*'s music, it sadly doesn't make for great listening – and the album sounds a lot less impressive now than it did then.

Two extra tracks were recorded during these sessions, which would surface on the anthology *The Island Years*: 'All I Want Is You' and 'Bamboo Floor'.

JOHN CALE
HELEN OF TROY

HELEN OF TROY

*My Maria/Helen Of Troy/China Sea/Engine/
Save Us/Cable Hogue/I Keep A Close
Watch/Pablo Picasso/Coral Moon/Baby
What You Want Me To Do/Sudden Death/
Leaving It Up To You*
Island; recorded summer 1975; released
November 1975

For reasons unknown, Cale decided to produce this album himself. It was recorded and mixed (at Sound Techniques again) amid traumatic and shambolic circumstances – namely Cale's final split with Cindy, after which he went to New York to produce Patti Smith's debut album, returning to London to mix *Helen Of Troy* afterwards. It wasn't an ideal way to work.

All songs were Cale originals except for a Dylanesque cover of Jonathan Richman's 'Pablo Picasso' and a slow and dirty treatment of Jimmy Reed's bluesy 'Baby What You Want Me To Do'. Many of Cale's own songs here are about lust, and/or the rarity of trust – but only 'I Keep A Close Watch', 'Coral Moon' and 'Leaving It Up To You' are strong enough to stay in the memory. Cale "got the title" for 'Cable Hogue' from the 1970 Sam Peckinpah western *The Ballad Of Cable Hogue* (Cale was a big Peckinpah fan), but the song itself isn't as good as the movie.

The chorus of 'I Keep A Close Watch' quotes lyrically from Johnny Cash's 'I Walk The Line' and is a song Cale would return to several times during his career; here it's performed as an epic and stately ballad, with a lavish orchestral arrangement. Cale once stated that he had hoped Frank Sinatra might record a cover version.

Cale was ably supported once again by Chris Spedding (guitar) and Pat Donaldson (bass), with Brian Eno on synthesizer and Timmy Donald and Phil Collins on drums. The American release of the album omitted 'Leaving It Up To You' (apparently because the song mentioned Manson victim Sharon Tate), and replaced it with 'Coral Moon' (which was not included on the UK vinyl release). Both tracks are included on the CD. Also recorded during these sessions were versions of 'Willow Weep For Me' and 'God Only Knows', which remain unreleased. Another outtake, 'Mary Lou' was included on the *Island Years* compilation.

THE VELVET UNDERGROUND

SABOTAGE/LIVE

*Mercenaries (Ready For War)/Baby You Know/
Evidence/Dr Mudd/Walkin' The Dog/Captain
Hook/Only Time Will Tell/Sabotage/Chorale*

Spy; recorded June 1979; released December 1979

A live album, *Sabotage* was recorded over three
summer nights at CBGBs in New York and
produced by Cale, who later admitted that
taping the gigs had "killed the atmosphere".
Despite being a live album, there are no old
favourites here, all the material being new
(though a studio version of 'Mercenaries'
had been released as a single). Apart from a
brooding cover of Rufus Thomas's 'Walking
The Dog', these songs had been written on
the road, most of them growing out of live
improvisation; the sound was hard-edged
in-your-face guitar rock.

Lyrically, the album – particularly the
opening 'Mercenaries (Ready For War)',
which opened with a quote from Machiavelli
– reflected the rise of Reagan and Thatcher,
the Russian invasion of Afghanistan and
the numerous conflicts in Africa and South
America; the more personal songs concerned
paranoia and drunkenness ("I can't keep

living like this", Cale sings on 'Captain
Hook'). The album's title track was both
experimental and extreme, and practically a
rant. Only the gently pretty ballad 'Only Time
Will Tell' (sung by Deerfrance, and featuring
some delicate viola work) and the moving,
hymnlike 'Chorale' offered relief from the
onslaught; as a gig it was probably very
impressive, but – apart from the two gentler
tracks – the album is not one that one tends
to return to.

As well as John Cale's piano, guitar,
fretless bass, viola and vocals, the gigs
featured Marc Aaron (lead guitar), Joe Bidwell
(keyboards, vocals), George Scott (bass,
vocals), Doug Bowne (drums, vocals) and
Deerfrance (backing vocals). The CD release
also contains the lethargically menacing
'Rosegarden Funeral Of Sores' (the B-side to
the 'Mercenaries' single; the master tape for
the studio version of 'Mercenaries' itself is
lost, which is why it is not included here),
plus the three tracks from Cale's *Animal Justice*
EP (recorded in 1976, released in August
1977): 'Chickenshit', 'Memphis' and 'Hedda
Gabler'. 'Chickenshit' refers to the incident
in Croydon where Cale beheaded a chicken

7

onstage, causing his band to quit; 'Memphis' is a cover of the Chuck Berry song, with added paedophile overtones; the gothic, doomy 'Hedda Gabler' is "inspired by" Norwegian dramatist Henrik Ibsen's 1891 play – except that Cale seems to be setting his version in the 1930s, judging by the reference to Hitler.

HONI SOIT

Dead Or Alive/Strange Times In Casablanca/ Fighter Pilot/Wilson Joliet/Streets Of Laredo/ Honi Soit/Riverbank/Russian Roulette/Magic & Lies

A&M; recorded late 1980; released March 1981

This was the last album to be recorded at the historic CBS Studios in New York, where Cale had recorded *Church Of Anthrax*, as it was demolished soon afterwards. It was produced by Mike Thorne, whose work with Wire and Soft Cell Cale had admired.

Though more accessible musically than *Sabotage*, many of the songs here were improvised in the studio, with Cale free associating the stream-of-consciousness lyrics. The subject matter included war, global politics, the fate of Vietnam vets and cruelty on both

a personal and global scale – or "death, decay, corruption", as critic Allan Jones put it. The one cover – the traditional 'Streets Of Laredo' – slotted perfectly into this mix, played more as an angry complaint than a sad lament (Cale had wanted Nico to cover the song on *The End*, but she refused).

Even though Cale was now far happier emotionally, he evidently still had a lot of pain and anger to express; the trouble was that the material was again substandard, the worst of it (the title track) approaching the downright dumb. The only moments of real beauty on the album come with the trumpet part (by John Gatchell) on 'Dead Or Alive' (which is utterly joyous, though the song itself is pretty bleak), the haunting ballad 'Riverbank' (which is still fairly tragic territory) and the impressively epic ode to damaged romanticism, 'Magic And Lies' which is insistently hummable (the title for this presumably inspired Lou Reed's *Magic And Loss* many years later).

The album's title refers to the phrase 'Honi Soit Qui Mal Y Pense', which translates as 'shamed be he who thinks evil of it'. The words appear upon the crest shown on British passports, and it is also the motto of the Order of the Garter. Subtitled "La Premiere Leçon De Francais", the album's name was originally to be titled *Russian Roulette*.

The cover's concept – featuring Cale's passport – was suggested by Andy Warhol, who also thought that it should appear in black and white. Cale opted for blue and pink instead, and subsequently realized that he should have listened to Warhol. During cover discussions, Warhol's business manager Fred Hughes came up with a suggestion that both Cale and Warhol liked: that Cale should be photographed with Yoko Ono, so that the album could then be titled *John And Yoko*.

THE VELVET UNDERGROUND

MUSIC FOR A NEW SOCIETY

MUSIC FOR A NEW SOCIETY

Taking Your Life In Your Hands/Thoughtless Kind/Sanities/If You Were Still Around/Close Watch/Mama's Song/Broken Bird/Chinese Envoy/Changes Made/Damn Life/Risé, Sam And Rimsky Korsakov

Ze-Passport; recorded spring 1982; released July 1982

An optimistic title for a dark and pessimistic record: the result of a five-day writing session in New York, during which Cale wrote and recorded 30 songs which he then edited, adding snippets of compositions by Beethoven, Debussy and Rimsky-Korsakov en route. Cale claimed the record explored what he termed "the terror of the moment"; he had wanted to record simply, improvising with just a piano, but the record company insisted that at least one track feature a band (the mediocre 'Changes Made'). Engineer David Lichtenstein (son of the Pop Art artist Roy) ended up playing drums, while assistant engineer David Young played guitar. Both would later tour with Cale, and play on his next album; Young would co-write and

generally collaborate for years to come. In addition, there were half a dozen guest musicians, including Chris Spedding and the Blue Oyster Cult's guitarist Alan Lanier.

The record is decidedly experimental, with random percussion and bizarre interjections (such as laughter and bagpipes) revealing Cale's avant-garde roots for the first time in years. Musically and lyrically, it's pretty bleak territory – though Cale's anger had now seemingly been replaced by melancholy; even though he was happily married at this point, there's genuine heartache in 'If You Were Still Around'.

Perhaps he was exorcising old ghosts, or simply dealing with his ongoing substance problems. Other songs concerned self-pity and familial problems, or the general angst of existence; there is hope for the future here, but it's pretty faint. "It was kind of rabid," he said of the album in 2007, admitting that he "wasn't in the most stable frame of mind." The ethereally beautiful 'Taking Your Life In Your Hands' concerned a murderess (who had possibly killed her own children). 'Thoughtless Kind' was supposedly about the Velvet Underground; if true, Cale hadn't forgotten or forgiven.

The title of 'Sanities' was the result of someone's accidental misreading of the word "Sanctus", which Cale preferred (though he'd later use 'Sanctus' for a title as well). 'Risé, Sam and Rimsky-Korsakov' adapted a poem about the radio written by Sam Shepard, recited by Risé Cale. Risé also co-wrote 'Damn Life' with Cale (and Beethoven, come to that). While there's no denying that *New Society* was a bold and adventurous step forward, sadly most of its songs were mournful ballads that meandered along without much of a tune – an absence that was thrown into sharp

7

relief by the inclusion of a new version of 'I Keep A Close Watch'. Here given a statelier and simpler arrangement than on *Helen Of Troy*, it's easily the best thing on the album.

Cale's ex-wife Betsey Johnson provided the cover photo. The CD release adds an extra track, an outtake from the sessions titled 'In The Library Of Force'

CARIBBEAN SUNSET

Hungry For Love/Experiment Number 1/
Model Beirut Recital/Caribbean Sunset/
Praetorian Underground/Magazines/Where
There's A Will/The Hunt/Villa Albani
Ze-Island; recorded 1983; released January 1984

This time Cale avoided improvising material in the studio: many of the songs here had already been honed on the road; most of them Cale had co-written with David Young, with a couple more being co-written with maverick journalist Larry Sloman. The exception is 'Experiment Number 1', which is obviously improvised – with Cale shouting out chord changes to the band as it goes along. Joining Cale

were Dave Young (guitar, vocals), Andy Heermanns (bass, vocals), Dave Lichtenstein (drums) and Brian Eno (on 'AMS pitch changer'). There were some love songs, with other material once again concerning matters military and/or political.

'Model Beirut Recital' obviously focussed on the Middle East ("something must be done about it"), while 'Villa Albani' (which translates as 'White House') was about corruption, and arms-for-oil deals; both are pretty dull, the latter being enlivened somewhat by the presence of Eno. On a more personal level of politics, 'Praetorian Underground' concerned the reassessment (and imitators) of the Velvet Underground.

Cale compared *Caribbean Sunset* to *Fear*, but he was being over-optimistic and his other comment is far more accurate: it's an album that "lurches along with good intentions." The title track's pleasantly moody with interesting instrumentation (strings, kettle drums, a fairground organ), but no more; several other songs sound like they're going to go somewhere interesting but don't (though wishing for an end to 'Magazines' is a laudable sentiment). Distinctly below average.

7

JOHN CALE COMES ALIVE

Ooh La La/Evidence/Dead Or Alive/Chinese Envoy/Leaving It Up To You/Dr Mudd/ Waiting For The Man/Heartbreak Hotel/Fear/ Never Give Up On You

Ze-Island; recorded February 1984; released September 1984

An unremarkable live set recorded at the Lyceum in London and bookended with two new studio tracks. Of the live material, the only aspect of note is that both 'Dead Or Alive' and 'Chinese Envoy' are revealed as being stronger songs than had previously been apparent.

The studio tracks are both mediocre and unimpressive. Though 'Ooh La La' (an ode to lechery co-written with Larry Sloman) has vaguely amusing lyrics, it also has mannered vocals and not much of a tune.

The same is true of 'Never Give Up On You', co-written by the entire band (Dave Young, Andy Heermanns and Dave Lichtenstein on guitar, bass and drums respectively), which also has some truly awful female backing vocals. Even the album's production (by Cale) was weedy; he reportedly seemed disinterested in the project.

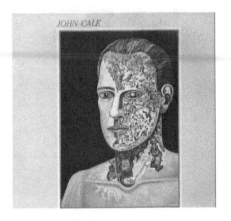

ARTIFICIAL INTELLIGENCE

Everytime The Dogs Bark/Dying On The Vine/The Sleeper/Vigilante Lover/Chinese Takeaway (Hong Kong 1997)/Song Of The Valley/Fadeaway Tomorrow/Black Rose/ Satellite Walk

Beggar's Banquet; recorded September 1985; released October 1985

Produced by Cale, *Artificial Intelligence* was recorded at Strongroom Studios in London, where Cale had just finished producing Nico's *Camera Obscura* album. James Young (keyboards) and Graham Dowdall (percussion) were both members of Nico's band, while David Young (guitars) and Suzie O'List and Gill O'Donovan (backing vocals) made up the rest of Cale's group. Unfortunately, the drum sound and tinny synthesizers mark this album as a product of its era, and it sounds very dated now.

All the songs here were co-written with Larry 'Ratso' Sloman, sometime editor of *High Times* magazine and author of a very good book about Bob Dylan's Rolling Thunder tour. The two used Brion Gysin's cut-up technique on the lyrics (which David Bowie has also always been fond of using); 'Everytime The Dogs Bark' and 'Vigilante Lover' were both co-written by Cale, Sloman and David Young. 'Chinese Takeaway (Hong Kong 1997)' is an improvised instrumental incorporating snatches of (amongst other things) Bach, Ennio Morricone and the *Archers* theme!

The songs told of damaged romance, reflecting Cale's increasing desperation as he stuggled with cocaine and booze problems. Unfortunately, once again they're distinctly average, with only one real standout track: 'Dying On The Vine' is a superb song about self-destruction, though the arrangement here lets it down.

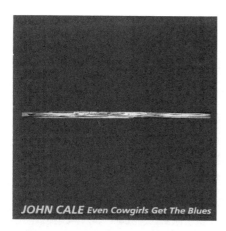

JOHN CALE *Even Cowgirls Get The Blues*

EVEN COWGIRLS GET THE BLUES

*Dance Of The Seven Veils/Helen Of Troy/
Casey At The Bat/Even Cowgirls Get The
Blues/Jack & The Moulin Rouge/Dead Or
Alive/Somebody Should Have Told Her/
Instrumental For New Year's 1980/Magic
And Lies (Guts)/Memphis*
Special Stock; recorded 1978 and 1979;
released 1986

Another live album, originally available
only from a gig at CBGBs in December
1978; the second half is taken from a gig a
year later at the same venue, recorded on
New Years Eve 1979/1980. Between these
two recordings the *Sabotage/Live* album had
been recorded at the same club.

The sound quality is pretty poor, and the
main point of interest with this album is
that several of the songs had not appeared
before; unfortunately, most of them aren't
that remarkable. 'Dance Of The Seven
Veils' features Judy Nylon improvising a
version of the tale of Salome, which is
interesting but not that great; the title
track (named after Tom Robbins' novel) is

good but sounds far from finished, and is
dominated by Nylon's fairly tuneless scat
backing vocal.

The one real gem is 'Jack & The Moulin
Rouge', a macabre little pop song about
Jack the Ripper's adventures in Paris, it's
reminiscent of songs by the Who's John
Entwistle, and Cale really should have
released the studio version at the time.

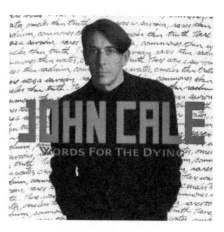

WORDS FOR THE DYING

The Falkland Suite
*Introduction/There Was A Saviour/Interlude
I/On A Wedding Anniversary/Interlude II/Lie
Still, Sleep Becalmed/Do Not Go Gentle Into
That Good Night*
Songs Without Words
*Songs Without Words I/Songs Without
Words II/The Soul Of Carmen Miranda*
Opal/Land; recorded spring 1989; released
October 1989

Produced by Brian Eno for his Land label,
the core of this album is 'The Falklands
Suite', Cale's symphonic adaptation of the
poetry of Dylan Thomas, so titled because

THE VELVET UNDERGROUND

he'd worked on it during the Falklands/ Malvinas war. The orchestra was recorded in Moscow with Gostelradio's Orchestra Of Symphonic & Popular Music, conducted by Alexander G Mikhailov. Choral parts featuring the Llandaff Cathedral Choir School were recorded in Cardiff.

The two 'Songs Without Words' were recorded in New York; 'The Soul Of Carmen Miranda' was a Cale/Eno collaboration, recorded at Wilderness, Eno's studio in Woodbridge.

The work is easily Cale's strongest and most tuneful in over a decade. It had been premiered live in Amsterdam in November 1987; by the time he got around to recording it Cale's drug and alcohol problems were behind him – as was his initial work on the stunning *Songs For Drella* – and the whole project exudes his confidence in the material and his own talent.

'The Falklands Suite' is a moving and epic pastorale; having Dylan Thomas for a lyricist had evidently brought out the best in Cale. The most successful of the adaptations is 'Do Not Go Gentle Into That Good Night', the arrangement for which is irresistible... though some may find the childrens' voices cloying and prefer Cale's solo versions of the material on *Fragments Of A Rainy Season*.

The two 'Songs Without Words' pieces are graceful piano instrumentals, but neither are as good or as memorable as some of the piano pieces Cale would later write for film soundtracks. 'The Soul Of Carmen Miranda' is a likeable, haunting and evocative ballad, enhanced by Nell Catchpole's violin and viola. Cale had been lost for a long time; now he had found himself again.

John Cale & Brian Eno

WRONG WAY UP

Lay My Love/One Word/In The Backroom/ Empty Frame/Cordoba/Spinning Away/ Footsteps/Been There Done That/Crime In The Desert/The River

Opal/Land; recorded summer 1990; released November 1990

Seemingly a true collaboration on equal footing, with Cale and Eno sharing the credit for all the songwriting and playing most of the instruments (augmented by half a dozen session players). Cale is credited as co-producer, but the final say was Eno's as the main producer; in fact, this project seems more weighted in Eno's favour, and the two argued frequently about production issues (presumably other bands that Eno has produced were content to leave him to his own devices).

Halfway through the sessions Cale went off to play at the first Velvet Underground reunion at the Cartier Foundation, and was presumably under a lot of stress; for whatever reason, the two fell out badly and the album cover reflects this, showing the two men separated by a row of naked daggers.

The songs also seem to be predominantly Eno's, with Cale not even appearing on the closing 'The River' at all. This was Eno's first demonstration of his songwriting abilities since *Before And After Science* over ten years earlier, and his last until 2005. In fact, it's a remarkably strong collection, much of the music here incorporating folk and world music influences, as well as approaching the ambient.

Cale wrote the lyrics for three songs, and co-wrote lyrics with Eno for three more. The gently seductive 'One Word' is a return to the pop sensibilities of *Vintage Violence* and *Paris 1919*; 'In The Backroom' is a likeable blend of Latin beat and ambient background, but goes on too long. The menacing 'Cordoba', described by Cale as being a "portrait of a terrorist", had lyrics Eno had found from phrase book entitled *Spanish In Three Months*; it's reminiscent of 'Dying On The Vine', but not as good. 'Footsteps' is fairly substandard, as is the singalong 'Been There, Done That' and the country rocker 'Crime In The Desert'. By contrast, all the Eno songs are good.

PARIS S'EVEILLE

Paris S'eveille/ Sanctus/Animals At Night/The Cowboy Laughs At The Round-Up/Primary Motive/Booker T/Antarctica Starts Here

Crepescule; released 1991

A mixed bag, containing Cale's soundtrack for Olivier Assayas' *Paris S'Eveille* ('Paris Wakes Up') performed by the Soldier String Quartet, plus five other instrumentals and one song. Two were music for ballet: 'Sanctus' or 'Four Etudes For Electronic Orchestra' was written for the Randy Warshaw dance company; 'Animals At Night' for the Ralph Lemon dance company. 'The Cowboy Laughs At The Round-Up' may have been music abandoned from the soundtrack to Julian Schnabel's film *Basquiat*, while 'Primary Motive' was for a film by Dan Adams. The album closes with a fairly unremarkable reworking of 'Antarctica Starts Here' from *Paris 1919*. The instrumentals are all enjoyable enough (some of them verging on the ambient), but for most people the real reason to buy this at the time was the inclusion of 'Booker T', a live Velvet Underground performance from 1968 which would subsequently be included on *Peel Slowly And See*.

THE VELVET UNDERGROUND

7

FRAGMENTS OF A RAINY SEASON

A Child's Christmas In Wales/Dying On The Vine/Cordoba/Darling I Need You/Paris 1919/Guts/Fear (Is A Man's Best Friend)/ Ship Of Fools/Leaving It Up To You/The Ballad Of Cable Hogue/Thoughtless Kind/ On A Wedding Anniversary/Lie Still, Sleep Becalmed/Do Not Go Gentle Into That Good Night/Buffalo Ballet/Chinese Envoy/ Style It Takes/Heartbreak Hotel/(I Keep A) Close Watch/Hallelujah

Hannibal; recorded spring 1992; released 1992

This solo live album acts as an extremely good career retrospective, with Cale accompanying himself on piano and acoustic guitar – an approach then in vogue because of MTV's 'Unplugged' format. In fact, the album is not only a reminder of how many great songs Cale had written, but also a measure of how strong those songs are that they still work with such sparse arrangements; in some cases (as with the Dylan Thomas pieces and 'Dying On The Vine'), these stripped-down versions are far better than the earlier studio outings.

Leonard Cohen's epic 'Hallelujah' was usually the closing number on this tour. Cale had opted to cover this song – a fairly obscure choice until then, from Cohen's album Various Positions – as his contribution to the I'm Your Fan Leonard Cohen tribute album. Noting that the song often had different lyrics when performed live, Cale had asked Cohen if there were any alternative lyrics. Cohen duly faxed him 15 pages of lyrics for dozens of unrecorded verses, which Cale edited down to the version familiar today, changing the wording slightly en route. Cale's final selection of lyrics included all the Biblical imagery and all the "cheeky" sexual verses.

Cale's arrangement of the song was swiftly covered by Jeff Buckley for his debut album, which subsequently became the best known recording. Cale's own version appeared on the soundtrack of the animated movie Shrek (though not on the soundtrack album, where a version by Rufus Wainwright was substituted). All of this laid the foundation for the song's massive popularity and current position as a modern standard.

In 2016 Cale re-released the 'Fragments' album on the Domino label, and instead of a simple reissue he and his co-producer Nita Scott took the opportunity to issue what amounts to a 'director's cut' of the album, not only enhancing the sound but also altering the running order. In addition, a second disc of live outtakes from the same era was included, many of them featuring a string section and providing a dramatic contrast to the solo recordings. You're not missing anything that essential here if you already have the original recording, but it's still nice to see it 'restored'.

Disc One

On A Wedding Anniversary/Lie Still, Sleep Becalmed/Do Not Go Gentle Into That Good Night/ Cordoba/ Buffalo Ballet/A Child's Christmas In Wales/ Darling I Need You/ Guts/ Ship Of Fools/Leaving It Up To You/ The Ballad Of Cable Hogue/Chinese Envoy/Dying On The Vine/Fear (Is A Man's Best Friend)/Heartbreak Hotel/ Style It Takes/ Paris 1919/(I Keep A) Close Watch/Thoughtless Kind/ Hallelujah

Disc Two

Fear (Is A Man's Best Friend) – Outtake/ Amsterdam – Outtake/Broken Hearts – Outtake/ I'm Waiting For The Man – Outtake/Heartbreak Hotel – Outtake (Strings)/Fear (Is A Man's Best Friend) – Outtake (Strings)/Paris 1919 – Outtake (Strings)/Antarctica Starts Here – Outtake (Strings)

7

23 SOLO PIECES FOR *LA NAISSANCE DE L'AMOUR*

La Naissance De L'amour I/If You Love Me No More/And If I Love You Still/Judith/Converging Themes/Opposites Attract/I Will Do It, I Will Do It/Keep It To Yourself/Walk Towards The Sea/ Unquiet Heart/Waking Up To Love/Mysterious Relief/Never Been So Happy (In Lonely Streets)/ Beyond Expectations/In The Garden/ La Naissance De L'amour Ii/Secret Dialogue/Roma/ On The Dark Side/ La Naissance De L'amour Iii/ Eye To Eye/Marie's Car Crash & Hotel Rooms/ La Naissance De L'amour IV
Crepescule; recorded and released 1993

Cale's soundtrack for the French/Swiss feature film *La Naissance de l'Amour (The Birth Of Love)*, directed by Philippe Garrel, who Cale had first met through Nico in the late Sixties. The 23 short piano instrumentals are uniformly pleasantly melodic; though not as memorable as his best rock work, it's still well worth a listen, the tunes lying somewhere between Erik Satie and Joni Mitchell. All of this was improvised by Cale – at Garrel's insistence – while he watched the film being screened. Cale's motto for the project was "letting the piano breathe."

John Cale & Bob Neuwirth
LAST DAY ON EARTH

Overture/Café Shabu/Pastoral Angst/Who's In Charge?/Short Of Time/Angel Of Death/ Paradise Nevada/Old China/Ocean Life/ Instrumental/Modern World/Streets Come Alive/Secrets/Maps Of The World/Broken Hearts/The High And Mighty Road
MCA; recorded 1994; released 1994

John Cale and Bob Neuwirth first played together live – and began working on this project – in September 1982. *Last Days On Earth* was performed as an "evolving multi-media piece" at St Ann's Church in Brooklyn in March 1990, and again in Germany in March 1991. The album version was recorded at Skyline Studios in New York and produced by Cale and Neuwirth; all songs were co-written by the duo, who were augmented by half a dozen session players and the Soldier String Quartet. The ad for the original concert read in part: "The meek, if they so want, can inherit the Earth, and it's time the road maps were re-written." The 'plot' of the piece concerns

7

travellers meeting at the mysterious Café Shabu and exploring time, culture and themselves, and contains spoken passages and instrumentals as well as songs. Undoubtedly ambitious, the work as a whole skirts the edges of pretentiousness, but the music is largely both adventurous and interesting, and the actual song content isn't bad either. Even so, only the countryish 'Old China' is really impressive, and this is probably not an album you'd return to that often.

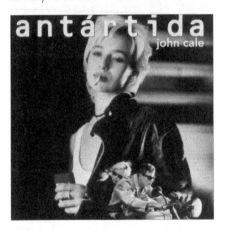

ANTARDIDA

Flashback 1 # 1/Antartida/Velasco's Theme/Maria's Apartment/ Flashback 1 # 2/On The Waterfront/Pasodoble Mortal/ Maria's Dream/Bath/ Flashback 1 # 3/Antarctica Starts Here/Flashback 3/Sunset/Get Away/ Flashback 1 # 4/ Antartida Starts Here/Frame Up/Barn/ People Who Died/Flashback

Crépuscule; recorded 1994-1995; released in 1995

Another soundtrack, for the film by director Manuel Herga. It's a real mixture: there are atmospheric, ambient electronics, orchestral passages that sound like variations on folk airs, doomy organ pieces, some tunelessly chaotic meandering and two more versions of 'Antarctica Starts Here'(Cale must really like the song), one of them a classical guitar instrumental by Chris Spedding. There's also a rocking cover version of Jim Carroll's 'People Who Died', featuring Spedding, Moe Tucker and Sterling Morrison. About half the album is tuneful and memorable, the other half discordant and dull.

BOB NEUWIRTH

Bob Neuwirth has been producing music as a singer-songwriter since the days of the early Sixties folk scene in Boston and Cambridge, though according to Andy Warhol Neuwirth initially only turned to music to subsidise his painting. A friend of Bob Dylan, Neuwirth became the singer's road manager and confidant (he can be seen in DA Pennebaker's documentary *Don't Look Back*). He probably first encountered John Cale

during the Factory era; both men had dated Edie Sedgwick (as had Dylan). Neuwirth also co-wrote the song 'Mercedes Benz' with Janis Joplin for her *Pearl* album, and assembled the backing band for Dylan's 1975 Rolling Thunder Revue. In more recent years, Neuwirth was also active as a visual artist and as a documentary film and record producer. Now in his eighties, Neuwirth stopped recording some years ago.

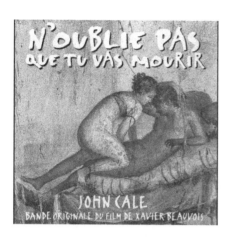

7

N'OUBLIE PAS QUE TU VAS MOURIR

Welcome To Europe/Everybody's Cold Sometimes/A Snake In China/Fast Train To Heaven/Martyrs& Madmen/Take A Deep Breath/ Never Seen Anything So Beautiful/Angels In The Clouds/Madonna's Blues/Sunflowers Fields/Al Dente/Hadrian Was Here/Kiss Me Once More My Love/Alive At Dawn/Skin In The Mirror/Who Said Love's Safe?/100% Pure/Do Not Forget/Last Train To Bosnia/Cold And Crimson/So Far So Good
Crépuscule; released 1995

The soundtrack to a film by Xavier Beauvois, consisting of mock-baroque instrumentals for both solo piano and a string quartet. The tunes aren't as instantly accessible as on some of Cale's other instrumental work, but there are still some gorgeous passages.

WALKING ON LOCUSTS

Dancing Undercover/Set Me Free/So What/Crazy Egypt/So Much For Love/Tell Me Why/Indistinct Notion Of Cool/Secret Corrida/Circus/Gatorville & Points East/ Some Friends/Entre Nous
Rykodisc; recorded 1996; released 1996

Sadly, Cale's first 'proper' solo outing since *Artificial Intelligence* isn't much of an improvement; in fact, apart from the gorgeously orchestral 'Circus' and 'Gatorville & Points East' what's on offer here is distinctly average. The gentle 'Set Me Free' started life as another song about the circus, but in the writing process turned into a song about the Velvet Underground, something from which Cale "never wanted to be set free". 'Some Friends' is a slow intimations-of-mortality ballad about the passing of Sterling Morrison. The album features BJ Cole, Maureen Tucker and David Byrne, who plays guitar on 'Crazy Egypt', a song he co-wrote with Cale.

EAT/KISS: MUSIC FOR THE FILMS OF ANDY WARHOL

Kiss Movements 1-11/Eat Movements 1-4
Rykodisc; released 1997

The soundtrack for Warhol's films which Cale had put together with Sterling Morrison and Moe Tucker for Pittsburgh's Warhol Museum in 1994 was never actually recorded. This album is a live recording of part of a subsequent

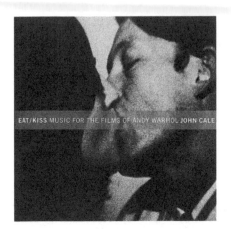

performance at the Theatre Sebastopol in Lille, France. Prior to the concert, sections of the original music were expanded upon during a week's rehearsal. Apart from Cale (who played keyboards) and Tucker, personnel here include a four-piece string section, vocalists Tiyé Giraud and Jimmy Justice, and pedal steel guitarist B.J. Cole. The piece contains a so-so version of Nico's 'Frozen Warnings' and a reading/recital by Cale of Emmanuel Swedenborg's mystical essay 'Melanathon'. For the rest, there's a certain amount of tuneless meandering, but much of the music is highly atmospheric and enjoyable – and the sound of Tucker's drums playing against Cale's viola can't help but evoke the ghost of something Velvet.

DANCE MUSIC

Intro/New York Underground/Night Club Theme/Modelling/Out Of China/Death Camp/Ari Sleepy Too/Iceberg I/Jim/Iceberg Ii/Espana/Nibelungen
Detour; recorded 1997; released 1998

This contains Cale's music for *Nico, The Ballet*, which was commissioned by the Scapino company of Rotterdam and choreographed by Ed Wubbe. The album was recorded live during the ballet performances, the ballet itself being an interpretation of Nico's life. "Biography is best left to historians, ballet to visionaries," Cale observed in his sleevenotes, a touching account of why he attempted to create what amounts to a musical biography of Nico anyway. The music is mainly performed by the nine-piece orchestral group Ice Nine. 'Ari Sleepy Too' features Nico's spoken words (from the floppy disc in the *Andy Warhol Index* book); 'Espana' is a solo piano piece performed by Cale (recorded in New York); the album closes with 'Nibelungen' by Nico (from the *Marble Index* CD). It's hard to judge the music outside of its context, but all of the pieces are evocative and fairly intense, with elements that sound Middle Eastern or oriental. Not as immediately accessible as *Eat/Kiss*.

LA VENT DE LA NUIT

On The Road To Portofino/At The Boats/ Naples/On The Road To Turin/Turin At Night/ The Seine At Night/Suicide I/Truck Parking Lot At Night/On The Road To Germany/ Waiting/Thinking And Acting/Suicide Ii/ President Y Is Still Stable/B. Calls/Darkness

On The Delta/What Mrs Ives Said To Mr Ives/
My Piano Thanks You For Visiting
Crépuscule; released 1999

The soundtrack for the film of the same name, by director Philippe Garrel (and starring Catherine Deneuve), was recorded at Dubbing Brothers and Acousti studios in Paris. It consists of piano pieces (occasionally with harpsichord) by Cale, accompanied by slide guitar from Mark Deffenbaugh, and punctuated by the sound of a thunderstorm. It's all pleasant, but none of it is that remarkable or memorable. Once they'd finished the soundtrack the duo kept recording more music in a similar vein, and the final five tracks on the album are bracketed together under the subtitle 'Memories Of Paris'.

THE UNKNOWN
The Unknown Parts 1–8
Crépuscule; released 1999

In late 1993 John Cale was commissioned by the Italian Pordenone Silent Film Festival to write a new electronic score for the 1927 silent film *The Unknown*. Directed by Tod Browning (of *Freaks* fame) and starring Lon

Chaney Sr, the film is a melodramatic and bizarrely horrific tale of love, mutilation and revenge. Cale's new score premiered at a screening of the film in Pordenone in October 1994, and the soundtrack album was recorded at another screening in Paris two months later. It's a succession of moody keyboard-based instrumentals, most of which sound as doom-laden as the plot, though without seeing the accompanying film it's hard to know how well they work in context. For completists only.

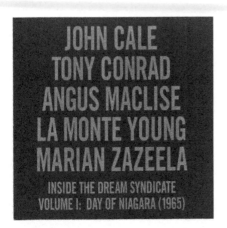

SAINT CYR

*Opening Theme/Ironic Trumpet/Stately/
Esther/Opening Theme No. 2/Pillar Theme/
Pillar Theme No. 2/2Nd Theme/2Nd Theme
No.2/War Time/War Time No.2*

Virgin France; released 2000

Another soundtrack, this time to a period film set in the 18th century by Patricia Mazuy, and starring Isabelle Huppert. The music is fully orchestral (featuring brass and harpsichord), with a few choral passages and a suitably period feel. More accessible than many of Cale's instrumental soundtracks. If you like baroque classical music, this is recommended.

INSIDE THE DREAM SYNDICATE VOLUME I: DAY OF NIAGARA

Table Of The Elements; recorded 1965; released 2000

Recorded in New York on 15 April 1965, this is exactly what you would expect if you knew anything about the group, which consisted on Cale on viola, Tony Conrad (violin), Angus MacLise (percussion), La Monte Young and Marian Zazeela (vocals). It's a single piece of music lasting just over 30 minutes, which is basically a drone (and nothing but), varying only slightly in pitch and intensity throughout. While this may have once been revolutionary – and we can be thankful for its influence on the Velvets and others – it's not exactly easy listening, being only fractionally more bearable than Reed's *Metal Machine Music*.

SUN BLINDNESS MUSIC

Sun Blindness Music/summer Heat/The Second Fortress

Table Of The Elements; recorded 1965–1968; released 2000

Produced by Tony Conrad, these are three pieces recorded by Cale during his time with the Velvet Underground (in 1967, 1965 and 1968) at his apartment in LaGuardia Place and elsewhere. The first piece lasts for nearly 43 minutes, for which Cale produces a sequence of sustained chords on a Vox Continental organ. The results are minimalist music reminiscent of Terry Riley, though somewhat more demanding.

Even so, it has tuneful passages as well as jarring sequences, and some moments of extreme beauty.

The second piece is just over 11 minutes long, and features Cale strumming away with great precision on a distorting rhythm guitar, barely varying the pace or the key. It's pretty monotonous. Finally, Cale delivers a ten minute drone piece created with "electronic sounds". For fans of avant garde music only.

INSIDE THE DREAM SYNDICATE VOLUME II: DREAM INTERPRETATION

Dream Interpretation/Ex-Cathedra/Untitled, For Piano/Carousel/A Midnight Rai Of Green Wrens At The World's Tallest Building/Hot Scoria
Table Of The Elements; recorded 1965–1969; released 2000

More of Cale's experimental music from the Sixties, some of it produced in tandem with Tony Conrad or Angus MacLise. Much of it is drone-based or experimenting with sustained notes, or else completely random and, frankly, cacophonous. For diehards only.

INSIDE THE DREAM SYNDICATE VOLUME III: STAINLESS GAMELAN

Stainless Steel Gamelan/At About This Time Mozart Was Dead And Joseph Conrad Was Sailing The Seven Seas Learning English/Terry's Cha-Cha/After The Locust/Big Apple Express
Table Of The Elements; recorded 1965–1968; released 2000

More of the same, though this time Sterling Morrison joins in for a couple of tracks, along with Conrad, MacLise and saxophonist Terry Jennings. It's mildly more listenable than the previous volume. But only mildly – though 'Terry's Cha-Cha' is quite likeable, and actually has a tune (even if it does get a bit monotonous after eight minutes).

5 TRACKS

Verses/Waiting For Blonde/Chorus Of Dumpty/ E Is Missing/Wilderness Approaching
EMI; recorded 2003; released 2003

As its title suggests, this is a slender volume, lasting for just over 19 minutes. These are slow and moody songs composed on the computer,

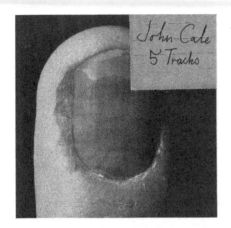

and more interesting and likeable than most of the material on *Walking On Locusts*. In 2007 Cale indicated that of all his output this record had come closest to satisfying his original ambitions for it. 'Verses' veers from pretty (with wordless female backing vocals, supposedly by Cale's daughter Eden) to ugly (shouting and feedback); the female vocal makes it sound almost like the soundtrack to a romantic French movie. The subtle 'E Is Missing' is a real grower, with gothic strings, Duane Eddy-style guitar and a snatch of the Christmas carol 'Noel'. The stately and likeable piano ballad 'Wilderness Approaching' is from the soundtrack to the film *Paris*, and boasts a terrific performance by a (sadly uncredited) female backing singer.

collection, though still far stronger than *Walking On Locusts*. 'Reading My Mind' is infectiously bouncing, as is 'Things' (which lyrically references Brian Eno's *Taking Tiger Mountain By Strategy*, Warren Zevon's 'Things To Do In Denver When You're Dead' and Charles Schultz's *Peanuts* cartoon). 'Bicycle' features a drum part by Brian Eno (and giggling by his two daughters). The delicate 'Archimides', 'Caravan' and 'Over Her Head' are slower, but gently impressive; 'Bicycle' could easily be a Lemon Jelly track. Despite its dull moments and some annoyingly contrived experimentation, still a very likeable album. The record also contains a 'hidden' track, 'Set Me Free'. The album title was originally Cale's jocular nickname for Bob Dylan.

HOBO SAPIENS

Zen/Reading My Mind/Things/Look Horizon/Magritte/Archimedes/Caravan/ Bicycle/Twilight Zone/Letter From Abroad/ Things X/Over Her Head

EMI; recorded 2003; released 2003

Co-produced by Cale and Lemon Jelly's Nick Franglen, and featuring numerous session musicians and backing singers, it's a patchy

PROCESS

Theme Intro/Theatre/Post-Sex/Museum/ Radiology/Candles/ Bedroom/Car Blue/Packing Books/Reading Poem/Burning-Painting/La Defense-Metro/Suicide Theme/Ascenscion

Syntax; released August 2005

Cale's soundtrack for CS Leigh's independent French film consists of 14 instrumental pieces – mainly solo piano,

7

sometimes organ, and for the most part fairly tuneless. For completists only.

BLACK ACETATE

*Outta The Bag/For A Ride/Brotherman/
Satisfied/In A Flood/Hush/Gravel Drive/
Perfect/Sold-Motel/Woman/Wasteland/Turn
The Lights On/Mailman (The Lying Song)*
EMI; recorded 2005; released October 2005

This album is far harder-edged than *Hobo Sapiens*, and right from the start the listener is thrown off balance by the musical approach (basically a mixture of hip-hop and funk influences) and also by Cale's bizarre falsetto vocal on the likeable 'Outta The Bag', which he claims was done "just for the humour and the charm of it". The personnel are basically a trio of Cale, Herb Graham Jr (on drums and bass) and Dave Levita (guitars), augmented by other session musicians, although 'Sold-Motel' features a different band and is a rather dull rocker). Herb Graham Jr co-produced the album except for 'Sold-Motel', which was co-produced by Mickey Petralia. Some of what's on offer here is dull or irritating (or both), but the record still definitely has

its share of good moments: 'Satisfied' is a seductive and charming love song; 'In A Flood' is a good Dylanesque blues; 'Gravel Drive' (with wonderfully atmospheric backing vocals by Jaspr Baj) is a sweetly gentle song about leaving home to tour, and was written for Cale's daughter; 'Perfect' is infectiously dumb beatpop; and 'Mailman (The Lying Song)' is wonderfully atmospheric, experimental but accessible. With *Black Acetate* Cale demonstrated that he was still travelling; at least half the time he still arrives somewhere interesting.

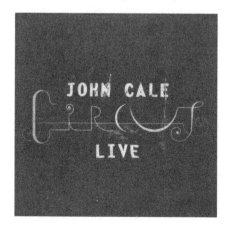

THE VELVET UNDERGROUND

CIRCUS

Disc 1
*Venus In Furs/Save Us/Helen Of Troy/Woman/
Buffalo Ballet/Femme Fatale-Rosegarden
Funeral Of Sores/Hush/ Outta The Bag/Set Me
Free/The Ballad Of Cable Hogue/Look Horizon/
Magritte/Dirty Ass Rock And Roll*
Disc 2
*Walking The Dog/Gun/Hanky Panky Nohow/
Pablo Picasso-Mary Lou/Drone Intro/Zen/Style It
Takes/Heartbreak Hotel/Mercenaries/Outro Drone*
EMI; recorded 2006; released February 2007.
Personnel: John Cale (lead vocals, guitars, keyboards,
electric viola, samples), Dustin Boyer (lead guitar,
toys, backing vocals), Joseph Karnes (bass, Nord 3,
samples, backing vocals), Michael Jerome (drums,
samples, backing vocals). Personnel on Disc 2, tracks
6–9: John Cale (lead vocals, keyboards, samples),
Mark Deffenbaugh (guitars, banjo, harmonica),
Deantoni Parks (drums, samples). Personnel on Disc
2, tracks 5 and 10: John Cale (samples), Charlie
Campagna (samples).

A boxed set of live material, packaged with
a lavish colour booklet, this a truly career-
spanning selection – with large chunks
deriving from *Helen Of Troy* and *Hobo Sapiens* –
but also a real mixture quality-wise. Overall,
the rockier tracks are the least rewarding
– often verging on gothic thrash – while
the more delicate material comes off best,
with really good versions of 'Woman',
'Buffalo Ballet', 'Set Me Free', 'Cable Hogue',
'Hanky Panky Nohow' and 'Style It Takes'.
'Femme Fatale' gets a genuinely innovative
treatment, as a growling Cale segues into
'Rosegarden Funeral Of Sores', while both
'Gun' and 'Heartbreak Hotel' are slowed to
a crawl (which considerably increases the
atmosphere of menace). The proceedings
close with a brooding, world-weary reading
of 'Mercenaries', its anti-war message even

more relevant than when the song was
written.

The set also contains a third disc, this being
a DVD that includes black and white footage
of tour rehearsals in Los Angeles, both electric
and acoustic sets. These include fragments
of 'Model Beirut Recital', 'SoldMotel', 'Gun',
'Reading My Mind', 'Heartbreak Hotel',
'Dancing Undercover', 'You Know More Than
I Know', 'GravelDrive', 'Chorale' and 'Ghost
Story'. As with the live album, the acoustic
material is far more interesting than the electric
(with great versions of all those songs), but the
footage itself is visually very straightforward.
Perhaps that's why Cale chooses to don
his old hockey mask for the closing 'Ghost
Story',which seems more than a little excessive!
The disc also contains an animated video for
'Jumbo In Tha Modernworld' (sadly, a fairly dull
song) and two audio tracks: a 'Blathamix' remix
of 'GravelDrive' (depressing and doom-laden)
and 'Big White Cloud 2007' (a good version of
the *Vintage Violence* track – but not as good as
the original). Possibly not the best of career
retrospectives, but there's still more than
enough good material here to reward the
faithful and to intrigue the newcomer.

JOHN CALE & BAND **LIVE**

JOHN CALE & BAND LIVE AT ROCKPALAST

Disc 1

Autobiography/Oh La La/Evidence/Magazines/ Model Beirut Recital/Streets Of Laredo/ Dr Mudd/Leaving It Up To You/Caribbean Sunset/The Hunt/Fear Is A Man's Best Friend/ Heartbreak Hotel/Paris 1919/Waiting For The Man/Mercenaries (Ready For War)/Pablo Picasso/Love Me Two Times/Close Watch

Disc 2

Ghost Story/Ship Of Fools/Leaving It Up To You/Amsterdam/A Child's Christmas In Wales/ Buffalo Ballet/Antarctica Starts Here/Taking It All Away/Riverbank/Paris 1919/Guts/Chinese Envoy/Thoughtless Kind/Only Time Will Tell/ Cable Hogue/Dead Or Alive/Waiting For The Man/Heartbreak Hotel/Chorale/Fear Is A Man's Best Friend/Close Watch/Streets Of Laredo

Mig; recorded 1983 and 1984; released 2010.

Two concerts originally recorded in 1983 and 1984 for the German TV show Rockpalast. The first features a band (David Lichtenstein on drums, Andy Heermans on bass, and David Young on guitar), and includes several tracks from *Caribbean Sunset*, the album that Cale was then promoting. Of note is the song 'Autobiography', on the grounds that it's never appeared anywhere else; unfortunately, it's pretty unremarkable (apart from Cale shouting out the chord changes to the band en route). In fact, the whole concert is pretty awful – rocking and energetic, but extremely ramshackle, with Cale himself obviously the worse for alcohol.

The second set is a solo performance by Cale, on piano and guitar, and is far, far better. Cale's sober, for one thing – and there are some great performances, including an absolutely straightforward reading of 'Streets Of Laredo', which is lovely. But this set's in the same general territory as the Fragments Of A Rainy Season, and that's a far superior option. A DVD version of these concerts also exists.

7

EP: Extra Playful

EP: EXTRA PLAYFUL

Catastrofuk/Whaddya Mean By That/Hey Ray/Pile A L'heure/Perfection

Domino/Double Six), released 2011. Produced by John Cale. Personnel: John Cale (vocals, guitar, bass, keyboards, viola and synthesizers), Dustin Boyer (guitar, synthesizers and backing vocals), Erik Sanko (bass and backing vocals), Michael Jerome (drums, percussion and backing vocals), Deantoni Parks (drums on 'Whaddya Mean By That'), Noelle Scaggs and Destani Wolf (backing vocals on 'Hey Ray').

Cale's first studio outing for six years doesn't disappoint, even if it is only five tracks long. "Say hello to the future and goodbye to the past," he announces on the opening track, going on to skilfully blend elements of electrofunk, trip-hop and intelligent pop. 'Catastrofuk' seems to concern the ups and downs of relationships ("she doesn't live here any more"), as does 'Whaddya Mean By That' ("take me to the bedroom and lay me on the floor/before we get started, better lock the

THE VELVET UNDERGROUND

7

door"); 'Hey Ray' includes a dissection of the 1960s and may be nothing more nor less than a succession of jokes, which is fine since they're laugh-out-loud funny the first time you hear it (but only then); 'Pile A L'Heure' is sung in French through a vocoder, like something deeply moody from the 1980s; 'Perfection' is a slab of regret, though whether it's optimistic or pessimistic about the future is deliberately unclear.

Overall, *Extra Playful* is a fab little collection of songs that augured well for the future. There's also a special 'Black Edition' of this, with two extra tracks: 'Bluetooth Swings' and 'The Hanging'. This was a limited edition of 2,000 copies, available only through indie record shops on Black Friday (November 25) 2011.

SHIFTY ADVENTURES IN NOOKIE WOOD

I Wanna Talk 2 U/Scotland Yard/Hemingway/ Face To The Sky/Nookie Wood/December Rains/Mary/Vampire Café/Mothra/Living With You/Midnight Feast/Sandman (Flying Dutchman)

Domino/Double Six; released 2012. Produced by John Cale and recorded in Los Angeles at ARM Studio and Mondo Studio.

Most of this features Cale playing a multitude of instruments. No other musicians are credited, but are thought to include : Dustin Boyer (synths, guitars and backing vocals), Joey Maramba (bass), Eden Cale (backing vocals on 'Hemingway'), Erik Sank (bass on 'Scotland Yard') and Danger Mouse (synths and co-production on 'I Wanna Talk 2U').

On first hearing this album seems nothing special – just a collection of solid but very unremarkable rock songs. Then, about halfway through the record it shifts gear and suddenly takes off. As is usual with Cale, the song titles here bear little or no relation to the lyrical subject matter. 'Hemingway' is a notable exception to that rule, since it actually seems to be about the writer – a somewhat bleak mood-portrait that's both compelling and sinister. Otherwise Cale's lyrics throughout are more in the realm of abstract poetry, with a somewhat science-fiction feel to them that's heightened by his use of a vocoder on several tracks, and complemented by a ton of studio gimmickry. It's fun.

Highlights include 'Mary', a haunting, poignant look at identity and gender; 'Mothra' is an intriguing and memorable exploration of the balance of freedom and control in a relationship; 'Living With You' is fantastic, a soaring celebration of domesticity and everyday love; 'Midnight Feast' another interesting look at a collapsing relationship; 'Sandman' is beautiful and irresistible, somewhere between a waltz and a hymn. Overall, *Shifty* is definitely a grower, and most of the reviews were good. "It's an album that combines the 70-year-old's experience with the glee of a small child," said The Guardian, and I can't argue with that.

There were also three different vinyl versions of this album, each one featuring a different bonus track : 'Bluetooth Swing Redux', 'Hatred' or 'Cry'.

M:FANS

Prelude/If You Were Still Around/ Taking Your Life In Your Hands/Thoughtless Kind/Sanctus (Sanities Mix)/ Broken Bird/Chinese Envoy/ Changes Made/Library Of Force (Feat. Man In The Book Excerpt)/Close Watch/If You Were Still Around (Choir Reprise)/Back To The End Domino; released 2016. Produced by John Cale; recorded 2013–2015; studio details unknown. Musicians are largely the same band as on *Shifty Adventures in Nookie Wood.*

Packaged as a double CD with the reissue of *Music For A New Society*, this album is mostly a radical reworking of the *New Society* material, using 'modern' instrumentation and studio technology (the exception being 'Back To The End', which is a "previously lost" track from the original New Society sessions). Some of the New Society songs are omitted here, while several others are added.

The results are remarkable. Though the overall mood remains sombre, it's far less bleak than in its previous incarnation; also more tuneful and user-friendly, occasionally approaching the joyous.

'Prelude' features a snatch of Cale's long-dead mother singing in Welsh; 'Broken Bird' is now a majestic ballad; 'Chinese Envoy' is now downright poppy; 'Close Watch' is unrecognisable from earlier versions, and features background vocals from Amber Coffman (of the band The Dirty Projectors) that echo those of Cale, and make it sound like 1980s synth-pop; 'Back To The End' is epic and elegiac. Most notably, there are two different versions of 'If You Were Still Around'. The second was added as a response to the death of Lou Reed, which occurred as Cale was in the early stages of work on this album. It features a female choir, and is a deeply touching farewell to a complicated relationship that ran deeply through Cale's life for nearly 50 years. Worth searching out this track, even if you skip the rest.

THE VELVET UNDERGROUND

7 JOHN CALE'S PRODUCTION WORK

John Cale has also worked as a record producer and/or arranger. His production and arrangement credits include:

Lester Bangs	Les Nouvelles Polyphonies	Nico
Art Bergman	Corses	Sham 69
Big Vern	Lio	Siouxsie And The
Chunky, Novie and Ernie	Los Ronaldos	Banshees
Julie Covington	Made For TV	Patti Smith
Cristina	Anne Magnuson	Snatch
Element Of Crime	Maids Of Gravity	Squeeze
Louise Feron	Marie Et Les Garcons	Alan Stivell
Garageland	The Mediaeval Babes	The Stooges
Goya Dress	Menace	Harry Toledo And The
Happy Mondays	Model Citizens	Rockets
Jesus Lizard	Modern Guy	Jennifer Warnes
David Kubinec	The Modern Lovers	
Larry and Tommy	Necessaries	

Cale once stated that the one artist he'd really like to produce is Captain Beefheart. Since Beefheart died in 2010, this now seems somewhat unlikely. But there is a compilation CD of Cale's productions, entitled *Conflicts & Catalysts: Productions & Arrangements 1966–2006* (Big Beat, 2012). It's a curious selection of tracks produced by John Cale for other artists. While it's strange and random to listen to in one sitting, it is also an excellent way to plug some interesting holes in one's collection.

1. 'Venus In Furs' The Velvet Underground
2. 'I Wanna Be Your Dog' The Stooges
3. 'In Excelsis Deo'/'Gloria' Patti Smith
4. 'Afraid' Nico
5. 'Pablo Picasso' The Modern Lovers
6. 'Who Is That Saving Me' Harry Toledo & The Rockets
7. 'Re-Bop' Marie Et Les Garcons
8. 'Disco Clone' Cristina
9. 'Italian Sea' Chunky, Novi & Ernie
10. 'No King' Ventilator
11. 'Sex Master' Squeeze
12. 'Take Your Place' Alejandro Escovedo
13. 'Kuff Dam' Happy Mondays
14. 'Runaway Child (Minors Beware)' The Necessaries
15. 'Omnes Gentes Plaudite' Mediaeval Baebes
16. 'Needles For Teeth' The Jesus Lizard
17. 'Scorch' Goya Dress
18. 'Dallas' Lio
19. 'Tearing Apart' Siouxsie & The Banshees
20. 'Spinning Away' Brian Eno & John Cale

NICO

7

CHELSEA GIRL

The Fairest Of The Seasons/These Days/Little Sister/winter Song/It Was A Pleasure Then/ Chelsea Girls/I'll Keep It With Mine/Somewhere There's A Feather/Wrap Your Trouble In Dreams/Eulogy To Lenny Bruce

Verve; recorded April/May 1967; released October 1967. Recorded at Mayfair Sound Studios, New York. Produced by Tom Wilson; arranged and conducted by Larry Fallon. Musicians are uncredited.

Five tracks here have Velvets connections and feature the playing of Reed, Cale and Morrison. 'Wrap Your Troubles In Dreams' (written by Reed) and 'Little Sister' (written by Reed and Cale) had both been recorded during sessions for the first Velvets album (with the orchestration added later by Wilson). Three other tracks were recorded specifically for this album: 'Little Sister' (written by Cale), 'Chelsea Girls' (written by Reed and Morrison) and 'It Was A Pleasure Then' (written by Nico, Reed and Cale), the last of which had evolved out

of the Velvets' live piece 'Melody Laughter'. Three tracks were written or co-written by the 18-year-old Jackson Browne: 'The Fairest Of The Seasons', 'These Days' and 'Somewhere There's A Feather', the first two of which are the real highlights of the album (over 20 years later, both songs would appear on the soundtrack of Wes Anderson's quirky comedy *The Royal Tennenbaums*). Bob Dylan's touching 'I'll Keep It With Mine' was a song he'd written for Nico long before she gained any fame outside of modelling circles, and one of his best (it would be covered by Fairport Convention the following year). Tim Hardin's sombre 'Eulogy For Lenny Bruce' celebrates the dead comedian, and is as doom-laden as anything Nico would record later. Nico hated the orchestration the songs were given ("I asked for drums, they said no"), and claims to have cried with frustration and anger when she heard it. In truth, the arrangement of 'Wrap Your Troubles In Dreams' is a heavy-handed mess, but in the main the results are gorgeous – baroque folk-pop with soaring strings and a psychedelic tinge, which was perfectly suited to the times (though 'It Was A Pleasure Then' sounds like it belongs on a different record). *Chelsea Girl* is easily Nico's most commercial album, though it didn't fare well at the time. Had she recorded an album like this a few years earlier, she might have carved out a career in this style. As it was, she faced stiff competition from a new wave of female singers like Judy Collins and Joni Mitchell, whose voices were a lot less idiosyncratic and more radio-friendly – but Nico would choose a different path for her next album, and rather than covering the work of others she would mine her own unsuspected talents instead.

THE VELVET UNDERGROUND

7

THE MARBLE INDEX

Prelude/Lawns Of Dawns/No One Is There/Ari's Song/Facing The Wind/Julius Caesar (Memento Hodie)/Frozen Warnings/Evening Of Light

Elektra; recorded October 1968; released January 1969

The Marble Index couldn't be more different to its predecessor. Nico's voice had become even more otherworldly, her meandering tunes owing a debt to the traditions of German lieder and at times becoming almost chantlike. Cale's arrangements for the songs veer from the tunelessly avant-garde to the neo-classical, while Nico's harmonium evokes an atmosphere of medieval religious doom, somewhere

THE CHELSEA HOTEL

The Chelsea in question is New York's Chelsea Hotel on West 23rd Street, which has been home to many literary and artistic types down through the decades (usually when they were young and struggling). Tennessee Williams, Dylan Thomas, Arthur Miller, Jackson Pollock, Allen Ginsberg, Edith Piaf, Gore Vidal, Bob Dylan, Leonard Cohen and Janis Joplin have all lived there; Sid Vicious and Nancy Spungen played out the final act of their tawdry tragedy there. Lou Reed's almost-Dylanesque lyric for 'Chelsea Girls' reads like a rollcall of Warhol's Factory crowd (and their sexual and narcotic proclivities); among those mentioned are Ondine, Bridget (Berlin, aka Polk), Ingrid (Superstar), Mary (Woronov) and Susan (Bottomley, aka International Velvet). Nico herself briefly lived at the Chelsea, as did Edie Sedgwick (who nearly burned the place down when a fire started in her room) and John Cale.

between the monastery and the madhouse (small wonder she'd be repeatedly described as 'gothic'). It's not exactly easy listening, though it is remarkable – and at this point there'd certainly been nothing like it in rock before. The album title comes from a passage in Wordworth's *The Prelude* concerning Louis-Francois Roubilliac's statue of Sir Isaac Newton: "The marble index of a mind forever voyaging through strange seas of thought alone". Some of Nico's lyrics show a marked debt to Sylvia Plath and to William Blake, and there is no doubt that she wanted to be taken seriously as an artist herself. As John Cale once remarked: "She was quite clear about it; she wanted to be the female Jim Morrison."

Nico once said that 'No One Is There' is about Richard Nixon; 'Ari's Song' is a lullabye of farewell to her son; 'Frozen Warnings' concerned a hermit (Nico has intimated that the song is about Jim Morrison) and is the album's strongest track, with a comparatively strong tune and a minimal arrangement reminiscent of Terry Riley. Nico played a toy piano on the album's closing track, 'Evening Of Light', which fittingly concerned "the end of time".

As John Cale would point out, the album was an artistic endeavour, "not a commercial commodity. You can't sell suicide." One reason for the album's short running time is thought to be the fact that neither Mohawk nor engineer John Haeny could stand to listen to much more of it. The CD release contains two extra tracks: 'Roses In The Snow' (which is comparable to 'Frozen Warnings', but not as good) and the *a capella* 'Nibelungen' (which is certainly striking, but not exactly merry).

DESERTSHORE

Janitor Of Lunacy/The Falconer/My Only Child/Le Petit Chevalier/Abschied/Afraid/Mütterlein/All That Is My Own

Reprise; recorded spring/summer 1970; released December 1970

Recorded at Vanguard Studios, New York, with further sessions at Sound Techniques in London, and produced by John Cale and Joe Boyd. Nico made some changes after Cale had flown back to New York; what they were is not known, but Cale was not pleased. Much more tuneful than its predecessor, *Desertshore* is an album that not only convinces the listener that Nico had real talent as a writer and performer, but shows huge promise for her future.

The songs it contained were originally written as a soundtrack for Philippe Garrel's film *La Cicatrice Interieure*, and Cale gives them a hugely sympathetic arrangement, mainly consisting of delicately tuneful piano fills. He also provided backing vocals, along with Adam Miller (of *Church Of Anthrax* fame). Occasionally Cale allows Nico's harmonium to hold sway, as on the gothic 'Janitor Of Lunacy' (supposedly written about Brian Jones). 'The Falconer' was about Andy

THE VELVET UNDERGROUND

Warhol, while two songs were about Nico's son: 'My Only Son' (which has gorgeous, multi-tracked *a capella* vocals) and 'Le Petit Chevalier' (sung by young Ari); two more were about her mother: 'Mütterlein' and 'Abschied' ('Farewell Song'), both of which are sung in German and are fairly doomy – the former has some deeply ominous viola from Cale. The album's remaining tracks are perhaps its best: the deeply moving ballad 'Afraid', and the closing 'All That Is My Own', which sounds as if Brecht and Weill had decided to write a song with *Arabian Nights* overtones (the lyric contains the titular "desert shore" reference). Throughout the album, Nico's voice (and talent) rings clear as a bell, and (with a few exceptions) sounds far more modern than medieval. A truly impressive album.

THE END

It Has Not Taken Long/Secret Side/You Forgot To Answer/Innocent And Vain/Valley Of The Kings/We've Got The Gold/The End/Das Lied Der Deutschen

Island; recorded summer and released November 1974

The follow-up to *Desertshore* was a giant leap backwards. John Cale again produced, drafting in Brian Eno (on synthesizer) and Phil Manzanera (on guitar), with whom he had just worked on his solo album, *Fear*. Cale himself played 12 different instruments, with backing vocals from Vicki Woo and Annagh Wood. But despite such a distinguished cast, Eno delivers little irritating noises, Nico's harmonium positively warbles and there's no relief from any other quarter. The songs themselves are plodding, tuneless and exude nothing but doom and angst. The word that springs immediately to mind is 'goth' and there are passages that sound exactly like soundtrack music Danny Elfman might have come up with for a particularly gloomy Tim Burton picture. None of Nico's original songs sticks with the listener and the album ends with two cover versions that are only mildly better.

The first is the title track, the Freudian melodrama by Jim Morrison that was first heard on the Doors' eponymous 1967 debut. Nico's version is not an improvement, and sounds even more pompous and po-faced than the original (though Nico apparently didn't like Cale's arrangement). Nico had also wanted to record another Doors' song, 'You're Lost, Little Girl' but Cale vetoed it; Cale wanted her to record the traditional cowboy ballad 'Streets Of Laredo' instead, but she refused (he'd later record it himself, on the *Honi Soit* album). Either would have been a welcome addition. As it is, the only truly memorable song on this record is its closer, a controversial cover version of 'Das Lied Der Deutschen' (or 'The Song Of The German People'), written by August Heinrich Hoffman Von Fallersleben. The song is better known as 'Deutschland Uber Alles' which, though written long before the Nazi era, immediately evokes the ghost of Hitler. God only knows what point Nico was trying to make by covering it (her politics were at best an addled form of nihilism), but at least it has a tune, and a clarion-voiced Nico gives it her all.

DRAMA OF EXILE

*Genghis Khan/Purple Lips/One More
Chance/Henry Hudson/Waiting For The Man/
Sixty Forty/The Sphinx/Orly Flight/Heroes*

Recorded 1981. German version: Aura/Line; released
July 1981. French version: Paris; released 1982; may
be available on Czech CD

As stated elsewhere, there are two versions
of this album. Having sold the tapes to Aura
for German release, Nico subsequently
re-recorded the same material for the French
release, using the same musicians. These
included Corsican guitarist Muhammad Hadi,
drummer Steve Cordona, bassist Philippe
Quilichini (who also produced the record),
keyboard player Andy Clarke (who had
played on David Bowie's 'Ashes To Ashes')
and Davey Payne (of the Blockheads) on sax.
Although the raucous rock arrangements
framing Nico's voice here initially come
as a bit of shock, they also make this a far
more accessible album than *The End*. The
songs are also slightly more tuneful this
time around, though only slightly. 'Genghis
Khan' and 'Henry Hudson' were inspired by
the historical personalities (the barbarian

and the explorer), while Nico dedicated
'The Sphinx' to terrorist Andreas Baader,
"because he had that hypnotic look" and
it's given a vaguely Arabic arrangement, as
is 'Orly Flight'. None of the above songs are
particularly memorable in any way, but the
album does boast one absolutely standout
track: the atmospheric 'Sixty Forty', about
a doomed relationship in New York, which
is worthy to sit alongside the very best of
Nico's output (including her work with
the Velvets). As to the two cover versions
included: 'Waiting For The Man' simply
proves that Lou Reed had been right not to
let Nico sing it in the first place. It's not
only pedestrian, it sounds like self-parody.
Her version of David Bowie's 'Heroes' is
only mildly better. Nico was convinced that
the song had been written about her; she'd
supposedly been in Berlin when Bowie had
been recording there, and she also claimed
he'd long been infatuated with her. The
truth was that when she tried to contact
him, he refused to see her (probably because
he was in the process of giving up drugs, and
she was a junkie). Regardless, her cover of
the song is second-rate and unnecessary.

7

CAMERA OBSCURA

*Camera Obscura/Tananore/Win A Few/
My Funny Valentine/Das Lied Von Einsanen
Madchens/Fearfully In Danger/My Heart Is
Empty/Into The Arena/Konig*

Beggars Banquet; recorded 1985; released August 1985

Nico's final studio album was recorded at Strongroom Studios in London, and is credited to 'Nico + the faction', who consisted of two members of her regular touring band, James Young on keyboards and Graham Dids (aka Dowdall) on percussion, plus Ian Carr on trumpet. She was also reunited with John Cale in the producer's chair, and Cale apparently thought Nico was in better shape than when he had seen her last, and had deepened personally, musically and lyrically in that time. Unfortunately, Nico had been suffering from writer's block for some time, and had come up with only six new (and fairly unremarkable) songs for the album – and one of these, the title track (credited to Nico, Young, Dowdall and Cale), sounds very much like it was improvised on the spot.

Since actual tunes are thin on the ground, much of the record only works – or rather, half-works – because of Young's arrangements, some of which conjure echoes of John Barry's jazzier theme music. The album also boasts a memorable and genuinely moving cover of the Rodgers and Hart standard 'My Funny Valentine' – a song Nico had sung in cabaret long before she ever heard of Lou Reed – with a great trumpet part from Carr and some lovely piano from Young. The other cover version here is 'Das Lied Von Einsanen Madchens' ('The Song Of The Lonely Girls'), a traditional German ballad given an atmospheric, lilting treatment. As an epitaph, the album could have been far worse – and for all its faults is still Nico's most interesting record for quite some time.

FEMME FATALE

Castle/Aura; recorded 1980-1985; released 2003.

This two-CD anthology includes the entire *Drama Of Exile* album (the first version). Also collected here are six *Drama Of Exile* outtakes, the so-so *Live At Chelsea Town Hall* album and two singles recorded in 1980, 'Saeta' and 'Vegas'. The former is doomy, sub-standard indie-rock; the latter boasts a drum machine and synthesizer backing that sounds vaguely like Duran Duran, against which Nico's vocal sounds somewhat incongruous. That said, it's actually not at all bad.

THE FROZEN BORDERLINE 1968-70

Rhino; recorded 1968-1970; released 2007

A two-CD set that includes remastered versions of *The Marble Index* and *Desertshore*, plus a wealth of unreleased material. This includes alternate versions of all the *Marble Index* tracks, demo versions of all the songs from *Desertshore* and four *Marble Index* outtakes. In addition to 'Roses In The Snow' and 'Nibelungen' (included

on the previous CD release) there are the previously unheard 'Sagen Die Gelehrten' and 'Rêve Réveiller', the first of which would have greatly improved the original release, had it been included. Clearly the definitive version of these albums.

Nico's live albums and guest appearances

The Nico story effectively ends with *Camera Obscura*. But there are at least nine more live albums (including one Peel Sessions album), recorded in every country imaginable and of varying quality (some very poor). *Live Behind The Iron Curtain* was actually recorded in Rotterdam! Most feature versions of the songs Lou Reed had written for her back in 1966 ("Those songs were Lou's gift to me. I sing them because I treasure that gift"). None of these records are particularly worth investing money in. For the completists: Nico also made guest appearances on Kevin Ayers' *The Confessions Of Doctor Dream*, Marc Almond's *The Stars We Are* and Bauhaus' version of 'I'm Waitin For The Man'.

7 MAUREEN 'MOE' TUCKER

awful one of Dylan's 'I'll Be Your Baby Tonight', with the best of the R&B material being her cover of Chuck Berry's 'Around And Around'. Easily the strongest track here is a multi-tracked guitar instrumental of Vivaldi's 'Concerto In D Major', which is an utter delight. Tucker also contributes another guitar instrumental of her own, 'Ellas', which goes on for too long but is still quite interesting – there are echoes of surf music, of Link Wray and Bo Diddley.

PLAYIN' POSSUM

Bo Diddley/Heroin/Slippin' And Slidin'/I'll Be Your Baby Tonight/Louie Louie/Slippin' And Slidin'/Concerto In D Major/Around And Around/Ellas
Rough Trade; released 1982
Basically a collection of cover versions, with one new track from Tucker. Moe plays all the instruments here, and proves herself an extremely competent guitarist; that said, the approach is basically punk-rock: garage music that's enthusiastic but fairly primitive (with times when it verges on the inept). Tucker's voice is also not the strongest in the world, though it does possess a certain ragged charm and sounds better when multi-tracked. There's a creditable version of 'Heroin', and a truly

LIFE IN EXILE AFTER ABDICATION

Hey Mersh/Spam Again/Goodnight Irene/ Chase/Andy/Work/Pale Blue Eyes/Bo Diddley/Talk So Mean/Do It Right
50 Skadillion Watts; released March 1989. The

Revola CD adds four tracks from Tucker's
MoeJadKateBarry EP:
Guess I'm Falling In Love/Baby What You
Want Me To Do/Why Don't You Smile Now/
Hey Mr Rain

Somewhat more professional and much
more impressive than her debut, and
recorded with a full band and some high-
profile guest stars, including Steve Shelley,
Thurston Moore and Lou Reed (who
contributes guitar to 'Hey Mersh' and 'Pale
Blue Eyes'). This was the first time Reed
and Tucker had played together since 1970.
John Cale was set to produce the album
at one point, but other commitments
prevented it. Tucker sings and mainly
plays guitar (and drums on two tracks),
also writing much of the material. The
infectious 'Spam Again' and the punk
protest 'Work' are both scathingly about
Tucker's previous employer, Wal-Mart,
while 'Andy' is a touching farewell to
Warhol. 'Mersh' was Tucker's nickname for
her old friend Martha Morrison, Sterling's
wife. 'Talk So Mean' is bluesy but on the
dull side, while 'Chase' is tuneless thrash;
'Goodnight Irene' a very conventional
reading of the Leadbelly song, and 'Pale
Blue Eyes' quite possibly the best version
of the song (Reed thought so). 'Do It
Right' is both charming and compelling,
and proof that Tucker can write a truly
interesting song. The whole album is
definitely worth checking out.

The *MoeJadKateBarry* material is more
mundane, very thrashy and basic: so-so
covers of two Velvets songs and one
by Jimmy Reed, plus 'Why Don't You
Smile Now', which is interesting – it's
a throwaway pop song written by Reed
and Cale (with Vance and Phillips) while
Reed was still at Pickwick.

I SPENT A WEEK THERE THE OTHER NIGHT

Fired Up/That's B.a.d./Lazy/S.o.s./Blue,
All The Way To Canada/(And) Then He
Kissed Me/Too Shy/Stayin' Put/Baby,
Honey, Sweetie/I'm Not/I'm Waiting For
The Man

New Rose; recorded 1991; released October 1991

More in the same vein, with a full band
and Tucker sticking mainly to guitar, and
sounding much more confident vocally.
Sterling Morrison appears on several
tracks, and on a somewhat bizarre cover
of Phil Spector's 'And Then He Kissed Me'
he and Tucker are joined by John Cale on
viola; Lou Reed plays guitar on 'Fired Up',
and all of the Velvets appear on the eerily
compelling 'I'm Not' (which is worth the
price of admission on its own).

Keeping it in the family, Martha
Morrison also appears as one of the
backing singers, and Syvia Reed was art
director for the cover. The material is
still largely fairly thrashy/garage: 'That's
B.A.D' is another diatribe against poorly
paid work, 'Lazy' a gripe against domestic

THE VELVET UNDERGROUND

chores; 'Blue, All The Way To Canada' is folkier, concerns Native Americans and Chrysler automobiles and is vaguely reminiscent of R.E.M.'s 'Belong'; 'Baby, Honey, Sweetie' is irresistible punkabilly, and 'I'm Waiting For The Man' is actually better than one could have imagined, with a tragically sad vocal from Moe. Worth tracking down.

DOGS UNDER STRESS

Crackin' Up/Me, Myself And I/I've Seen Into Your Soul/I Don't Understand/Crazy Hannah's Ridin' The Train/Danny Boy/Little Girl/Saturday Night/Train/Poor Little Fool/I Wanna
New Rose; recorded 1993; released 1994

Moe went back to the studio in 1993 and recorded a much more professional-sounding album: it was recorded at Reeltime in Savannah, Georgia, which was decidedly a step up on the kind of studios Tucker had used to date.

Sterling Morrison plays on five tracks. There are great covers of Bo Diddley's 'Crackin' Up' and Ricky Nelson's 'Poor Little Fool', plus a touching reading of 'Danny Boy'. All the rest are Tucker originals, though the standard isn't as high as on her previous two studio albums, and none of them are particularly remarkable or memorable. The original title for this album was to be *Inexplicably Spanked While Leading A Conga Line*. Probably a wise decision to change that one.

OH NO, THEY'RE RECORDING THIS SHOW

Spam Again/Hey, Mersh/Stayin' Put/ That's B.a.d./Goodnight Irene/Too Shy/Talk So Mean/Lazy/ Baby, Honey, Sweetie/S.o.s./ Fired Up/Too Shy/Bo Diddley
New Rose; recorded February 23 1992; released September 1992

A pretty good live album, recorded live at L'Ubu, Rennes, France. Featuring a five-piece band that includes Sterling Morrison. Good sound quality, and Moe's even more confident vocally; even though the studio versions are usually better, still well worth a listen.

THE MUSIC: **MAUREEN 'MOE' TUCKER**

WAITING FOR MY MEN

Fired Up/I'm Waiting For The Man/ Blue, All The Way To Canada/Too Shy//(And) Then He Kissed Me/I'm Not/ Me, Myself And I/ I Don't Understand/Danny Boy/Little Girl/I Wanna/Crackin' Up/ I've Seen Into Your Soul/ Saturday Night/Train

Rokarola; recorded 1991 & 1994; released 1998

Belgian compilation album comprising six tracks apiece from *I Spent A Week There The Other Night* and *Dogs Under Stress*, which is probably easier to track down than those two albums.

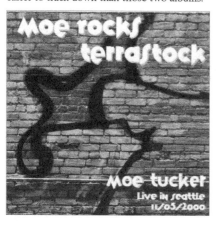

MOE ROCKS TERRASTOCK

Spam Again/I Wanna/I'm Sticking With You/Crackin' Up/B.a.d./Hey Mersh/Fired Up/Bo Diddley

Captain Trip; recorded November 5 2000; released 2002

Another live album, recorded in Seattle in 2000. It's not bad, though Moe's voice is a shade hoarse. The most notable aspect of this is the appearance of Doug Yule, who plays piano and sings on 'I'm Sticking With You' – though both he and Tucker occasionally lose their way vocally, it only adds to the charm of hearing the two of them reunited again. Yule also plays guitar on 'Crackin' Up'.

GRL-GRUP

Then He Kissed Me/Be My Baby/To Know Him Is To Love Him/Da Doo Ron Ron

Lakeshore Drive; released 1997

An EP celebrating the talents of girl group supremo Phil Spector. It's good fun and sounds pretty much how you'd expect. 'To Know Him Is To Love Him' was included as a tribute to Sterling Morrison, who'd always loved the song and had nagged Moe to record it.

7 I FEEL SO FAR AWAY: ANTHOLOGY 1974–1998

Disc One

*Bo Diddley/Heroin/Slippin' And Slidin'/
Around And Around/Will You Love Me
Tomorrow?/Ellas/I'm Sticking With You/
Guess I'm Falling In Love/Andy/Hey Mersh!/
Pale Blue Eyes/Chase/Talk So Mean
(Alternate Mix)/Do It Right*

Disc Two

*Fired Up (Single Version)/Too Shy (Single
Version)/That's B.a.d./Lazy/Blue All The Way To
Canada/Then He Kissed Me/ Fired Up/I'm Not/
I'm Waiting For The Man/Spam Again (Live)/
Crackin' Up/I've Seen Into Your Soul/Danny
Boy/Poor Little Fool/I Wanna/To Know Him Is
To Love Him/Last Night I Said Goodbye To My
Friend (Previously Unissued)/After Hours*

Sundazed; released 2012

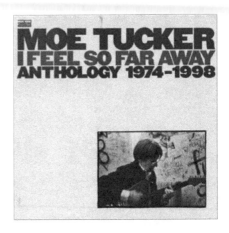

A great retrospective which offers a comprehensive view of Moe's solo career, which rounds up her singles as well as album tracks. It also includes Moe's previously unreleased version of her farewell to Sterling Morrison, 'Last Night I Said Goodbye To My Friend.' Worth buying this anthology for, even if you already own all the others. To be honest, if you have this anthology you probably don't need anything else.

STERLING MORRISON

There are no solo albums by Sterling Morrison. He does, however, play on two tracks on Luna's album *Bewitched* – 'Friendly Advice' and 'Great Jones Street' – as well as on some of Moe Tucker's solo albums.

DOUG YULE

AMERICAN FLYER

*Light Of Your Love/Such A Beautiful Feeling/
Back In '57/Lady Blue Eyes/Let Me Down
Easy/M/The Woman In Your Heart/Love Has No
Pride/Queen Of All My Days/Drive Away/Call Me,
Tell Me/End Of A Love Song*
United Artists; released 1976

SPIRIT OF A WOMAN

*Spirit of a Woman/Gamblin' Man/My Love
Comes Alive/Victoria/Dear Carmen/I'm Blowin'
Away/Flyer/The Good Years/Keep On Tryin'*
United Artists; released 1977

American Flyer produced extremely bland
Countryish AOR – somewhat like The Eagles,
except minus the tunes. Yule only takes a
songwriting credit for three tracks on the two
albums: 'Lady Blue Eyes' and 'Queen Of All My
Days' on the first and 'Flyer' on the second.
'Queen Of All My Days' isn't bad – a pleasant
enough gentle rocker with a reggae/calypso feel

– but the other two Yule compositions are both
fairly dull. For one half-way decent track, it's
scarcely worth the bother of tracking this down.

LIVE IN SEATTLE

*Candy Says/Beginning To Get It/What Goes
On/Sweet Jane/After The Fall/Love Song/White
Devils/Two More Hands/Rules/Purple Mountain
Glory/Beginning To Get It/What Goes On*
Captain Trip Records; recorded May 25 2000 and
November 4 2000; released 2002

Yule's first proper outing for 30 years was a
ramshackle but enjoyable live album, recorded
at the Crocodile Café, and the Terrastock 4
Festival, both of them in Seattle. Produced
by *VU* fanzine editor Sal Mercuri, it includes
creditable versions of three Velvets songs.
The remaining tracks are all Yule originals,
taken from his unreleased album *Song Cycle One*
(an "original, evolving, work in progress").
It veers between country, rock and folk, and

7

there are several songs (like 'Beginning To Get It' and 'Purple Mountain Glory') that could have fitted comfortably onto *Loaded* – though they're not *quite* in the same league. It's actually hard to judge, since Yule's vocals sound less comfortable on his own songs than on the crowd-pleasing Velvets material, and once or twice he falters. Still, it'd be nice to hear a studio version of *Song Cycle One*, but to date there's no sign of it.

ANGUS MACLISE 7

BRAIN DAMAGE IN OKLAHOMA CITY

Another Druid's Nest/Haight Riot Mime/ Epiphany/Loft Collage/Drum Solo/ Dreamweapon Benefit For The Oklahoma City Police Dept. Part I/ Dreamweapon Benefit... Part Ii/Cembalum

Quakebasket; recorded 1967–1970; released 2000

As could have been predicted, MacLise's solo output is not exactly tuneful; indeed, there are passages that rival Reed's *Metal Machine Music* for testing the endurance of the listener. There's a great deal of bongo-playing, vocals that are halfway between moaning and chanting, some minimalist organ pieces spiced up with percussion, a taped conversation that could match a Warhol movie for dullness, a mildly impressive drum solo, some obvious (but unmelodic) oriental influences

and a great deal of tuneless noodling. Experimentation is a good thing, but it doesn't always bear fruit.

ASTRAL COLLAPSE

Smothered Under Astral Collapse/6Th Face Of The Angel/Beelzebub/Cloud Watching/ Dracula/Dawn Chorus

Quakebasket; recording details unknown; released 2003

More of the same: MacLise recites poetry over a tape of Tibetan-inspired music, there's a lengthy repetitive ambient electronic piece (like Terry Riley, but not as much fun), a MacLise bongo solo (over tapes that sound like insects buzzing) and lots more tuneless meandering, some of it on an arp synthesizer. The album closes with more poetry, recited over tapes of local noise and music recorded by MacLise in India.

THE VELVET UNDERGROUND

SOLO COMPILATIONS AND STARTING POINTS

Lou Reed

There have been numerous Lou Reed compilations over the decades. The best currently available are the three-CD *Between Thought And Expression* (reviewed in the Lou Reed solo section) and the two-CD *NYC Man: The Ultimate Collection* (confusingly, there's also a single-CD version with the same title). Otherwise, good starting points would be *Transformer* or *New York*.

John Cale

Three compilations are available. The best is the two-CD Rhino anthology *Seducing Down The Door: A Collection*, which covers the years 1970-1990 and includes three rare tracks: the single 'Dixieland & Dixie', the *Academy In Peril* outtake 'Temper' and the unreleased single 'Jack The Ripper'. However, this may be hard to track down. Also good is the 16-track *Close Watch: An Introduction To John Cale*. The two-CD *The Island Years* contains *Fear*, *Slow Dazzle* and *Helen Of Troy* in their entirety, plus five rare tracks from that era: 'Mary Lou', 'All I Want Is You', 'Bamboo Floor', 'Sylvia Said' and 'You & Me'. The live *Fragments Of A Rainy Season* also provides a good career overview. Other good starting points would be *Paris 1919* or *Fear*.

Nico

Avoid *Innocent & Vain : An Introduction To Nico* (poor track selection). The best compilation is the US release *Classic Years*. Both compilations draw material from the first Velvets album, which seems unnecessary: a wiser investment might be the best two solo albums, *Chelsea Girl* and *Desertshore*.

Moe Tucker

The 2012 compilation *I Feel So Far Away* is what you need (see Moe's solo section entry).

50 ESSENTIAL VELVETS TRACKS

THE INSIDE STORY

What follows are reviews of an unapologetically subjective selection of Velvets songs, in roughly chronological order. Though it's mainly drawn from the first four studio albums, it also takes account of all the material released decades later.

1. SUNDAY MORNING

from *The Velvet Underground & Nico*

Added after the initial sessions at the request of Verve producer Tom Wilson, who'd wanted another Nico ballad for the album. When the time came, Reed refused to allow her to sing, and insisted on doing the vocals himself; Nico did occasionally sing the song with the band in concert. Supposedly written by Reed and Cale in a friend's apartment at 6 a.m. one Sunday morning after being up all night, it's a gentle, folky ballad of paranoia and reassurance. Sterling Morrison described it as capturing the feeling, "when you've been up all Saturday night and you're crawling home while people are going to church. The sun is up and you're like Dracula, hiding your eyes."

2. I'M WAITING FOR THE MAN

from *The Velvet Underground & Nico*

A driving urban blues with music that sounds as desperate as its subject matter – the travails

of attempting to score heroin in Harlem – but also a well-detailed and evocative account. Reed wrote the song while still in college, and its maturity and brutal realism shows exactly what made him different to every other songwriter of his generation.

Reed later observed that, while 26 dollars won't get you much of anything these days, everything about the song apart from the price still holds true. "PR shoes" refers to Puerto Rican Fence Climbers, an imaginative (if racist) nickname for the pointy-toed shoes known in Britain as winklepickers. To some extent the song is autobiographical, as Reed was known to acquire at least some of his drugs from Harlem.

3. FEMME FATALE

from *The Velvet Underground & Nico*

Lou Reed has occasionally claimed that this song is about Nico, but more often he's admitted that he wrote it at the request of Andy Warhol (who came up with the title)

7

and that it's about Edie Sedgwick. An etheric ballad sung by Nico, it's also a cautionary tale, as indeed was Edie's life story. Cale claims the song was "informed" by the making of Warhol's film *Chelsea Girls*, which he described as "harrowing. You'd see the girls disintegrating and sliding down walls with tears in their eyes."

4. VENUS IN FURS

from *The Velvet Underground & Nico*

A celebration of sado-masochism (and fetishist clothing), on which Cale's viola really comes into its own. Written by Reed after reading the novel of the same title by Leopold von Sacher-Masoch, the song basically recounts the story of the book (Sterling Morrison called it "a musical synopsis"), whose protagonist Severin is whipped by his cruel mistress Wanda while she's dressed in furs. The novel was supposedly at least semi-autobiographical; Sacher-Masoch considered himself the 'slave' of his mistress, Baroness Bogdanoff. Reed later said, "I just thought it would be a great idea for a song. Now everybody thinks I invented masochism." Sterling Morrison said that musically 'Venus In Furs' was "the closest we ever came in my mind to being exactly what I thought we could be".

5. RUN RUN RUN

from *The Velvet Underground & Nico*

More urban drug-related blues, this time about the perils of New York's Union Square, then infamous as a hangout for dealers and junkies. Keening guitar feedback heightens the mood of manic paranoia. Written just prior to the group's residency at the Café Bizarre in December 1965, when they realized that they were desperately short of original material. As Morrison later recalled, "I

remember we had the Christmas tree up, but no decorations on it. We were sitting around busy writing songs, because we had to, we needed them that night!"

6. ALL TOMORROW'S PARTIES

from *The Velvet Underground & Nico*

Cale's insistent piano drives this plaintive social lament. Despite rumours that the song was about Edie Sedgwick or Andy Warhol, or that it was written specifically for Nico to sing, it was actually written sometime early in 1965, long before the Velvets encountered the artist and his retinue. Straight-out psychedelic folk-rock, but even so it was still "Andy's favourite song," according to Reed. Which makes perfect sense – its Cinderella imagery would certainly appeal to a man nicknamed Drella – and as Reed has since pointed out, this is a Cinderella story with no Prince Charming in sight. He also claimed it was "a very apt description of certain people at the Factory at the time," although Cale claims that it was actually written about Daryl, who was also one of the inspirations for Reed's *Berlin* album. The song title has since been

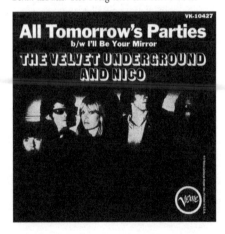

used for a 1999 novel by William Gibson (a Velvets fan), and for an annual alternative British music and arts festival.

7. HEROIN

from The Velvet Underground & Nico

Written by Reed while he was still in college, and experimenting with the drug himself. It was a period in which he would later categorize himself as a "rather negative, strung-out, violent, aggressive person. I meant those songs to sort of exorcise the darkness, or the self-destructive element in me." He'd spend a sizeable chunk of his career having to justify this song, since many assumed that he was actually extolling heroin use. As Reed later explained, the song "was about what it's like to take heroin. It wasn't pro or con. It was just about taking heroin, from the point of view of someone taking it." He also pointed out that if the song had been a novel, no one would have considered it shocking; years later he commented, "I'm still not sure what was such a big deal. So there's a song called 'Heroin'. So *what?*"

Musically, throughout the song Moe Tucker's persistent drumming keeps pace with the increasing tempo of Reed's strumming; coupled with Cale's seesawing viola, they vividly conjure up the desperation implicit in the lyric. The first time you hear it, it's awesome – though as Lou Reed has pointed out: "It's just two chords. And when you play it, at a certain point there is a tendency to lean in and play it faster. It's automatic. And when I first played it for John, he picked up on that. Also, if you check out the lyrics, there are more words as you go along. The feeling naturally is to speed up." When the song was re-recorded in California (the version included on the first album) Reed changed the opening line

from "I know just where I'm going" to "I don't know where I'm going", thus changing the entire meaning of the song. Cale for one thought it was a cop-out.

Tucker was also unhappy with the version on the record, but for a different reason; the band recorded it live, but since the others had plugged their instruments directly into the mixing desk, Tucker couldn't properly hear what they were playing "and it just became this mountain of drum noise in front of me. I couldn't hear shit ... So I stopped, and being a little whacky, they just kept going, and that's the one we took." Regardless, she considered 'Heroin' to be the band's "greatest triumph. Lou's greatest triumph too, maybe, songwriting-wise." The term "Jim-Jims" was a concoction of Reed's, who apparently thought that invented slang was the best kind.

8. THERE SHE GOES AGAIN

from The Velvet Underground & Nico

A re-working of Marvin Gaye's 'Hitchhike', and a pretty straightforward Buddy Hollyish pop song... except that it again messes around with tempo, with the guitar solo intentionally slowing down and speeding up again – and also advocates misogynist violence as a solution to relationship problems. Cale thinks it might be about either Electra or Daryl, who were both no strangers to domestic violence.

9. I'LL BE YOUR MIRROR

from The Velvet Underground & Nico

A folky love song, supposedly written for (and about) Nico – Reed claims the title was something she'd said to him, but according to Victor Bockris he'd started writing the song two years earlier for Shelley Albin. The lyric could just as easily be about deep friendship as about romantic love, although Cale has described it as "a song of infinite desire,

THE VELVET UNDERGROUND

strangely tender for us." Reed later described it as "very compassionate, very loving, very nice." According to Sterling Morrison, the band had to badger Nico to stop singing it stridently, until she finally burst into tears; the next take was perfect. Morrison also claimed that the "haunting" quality in Nico's voice was simply because she "was just really depressed."

10. THE BLACK ANGEL'S DEATH SONG

from *The Velvet Underground & Nico*
The song that supposedly got the group fired from their residency at Café Bizarre sounds more like a collision between avant garde classical music and modern jazz than rock. Reed later commented that "the idea here was to string words together for the sheer fun of their sound, not any particular meaning." Over Cale's swooping viola, Reed rapidly intones lyrics rich in imagery; comparisons with Dylan would be inevitable, though today it sounds rather pretentious. In fact, the song's lyrics began life as a poem written by Lou during his college days.

11. EUROPEAN SON

from *The Velvet Underground & Nico*
Driving psychedelia, dedicated to Reed's creative writing lecturer and college mentor Delmore Schwarz – probably because of its lyrical sparsity, since the poet hated rock music and all songs with lyrics. The vocal part sounds like a boogie version of one of Dylan's 'put down' songs; but most of the musical focus is on feedback, guitar solo and general experimentation (which just keeps going until it runs out of steam, after about eight minutes). Just after the vocal part you can hear John Cale scraping a chair across the floor, and then dropping a glass on the floor – in perfect time to the music. According

to Tucker, the song turned out differently every time they played it. As Cale put it, "we wanted to break the rules, so we broke every fucking rule we could."

12. WHITE LIGHT/ WHITE HEAT

from *White Light/White Heat*
Written by Lou Reed. A hymn to amphetamine, the drug of choice of the Factory crowd, and one that captures both the drug-enhanced energy and the paranoia that follows it. An insistently pounding rock/folk thrash that would end up influencing everybody from the Rolling Stones to Ziggy-era Bowie and on to the Ramones and Motorhead.

13. THE GIFT

from *White Light/White Heat*
The 'lyrics' to this were originally a short story written by Reed for his creative writing class at Syracuse University, and inspired by his first summer-long separation from girlfriend Shelley Albin. The tale of the unfortunate Waldo Jeffers and his love for his girlfriend Marsha plays like a cross between Roald Dahl and Stephen King; it was set to music at the suggestion of John Cale, who also narrates the piece in a deadpan manner, his lilting Welsh accent heightening the sense of the bizarre. Cale read the whole thing through in one take. To simulate the sound effect of Waldo being stabbed in the head, Reed recorded the noise of a cantaloupe being hit with a wrench, and was later disappointed that this noise wasn't clearer and louder on the finished track. The backing music (credited to all four Velvets) grew out of a live instrumental piece called 'Booker T' (see *Peel Slowly And See*) so called because it was inspired by Booker T and the MGs' 'Green

7

The Velvet Underground, shortly before the release of the White Light/White Heat album

Onions'. The track was mixed so that Cale's voice comes out of one speaker, and the music comes out of the other.

14. LADY GODIVA'S OPERATION

from *White Light/White Heat*

A baroque gothic horror piece that prefigures some of John Cale's later solo work but was actually written by Lou Reed. Referring to the use of sound effects, John Cale described the piece as "a BBC Radiophonic Workshop idea". Some think this is about a sex-change operation, but the lyrics actually sound like they're describing something even grislier – an operation for a brain tumour, perhaps. As with 'The Gift', it's not one for the squeamish. Reed subsequently blamed the 24 shock treatments he'd had when he was 17 for causing him to write songs like this one. He also said the

song was about "fear of sleep. The perfect thing for the people we were running around with, staying up 15 days at a time."

15. HERE SHE COMES NOW

from *White Light/White Heat*

Words by Reed, music by all four Velvets. Probably written with Nico in mind (she sung it with them in concert, but by the time they came to record it she was long gone), but sung here by Reed in folky/blues mode. Given the (extremely sparse) lyrics, it would seem to be about a male-female couple with sexual problems.

16. I HEARD HER CALL MY NAME

from *White Light/White Heat*

Written by Reed. A rocker so fast-paced it's practically manic, with Reed going truly

THE VELVET UNDERGROUND

7

berserk on the guitar. It seems to be about love beyond the grave – though whether it's actually describing necrophilia, the delusions of someone truly mentally disturbed or just the singer's sorrow for a dead love is left for the listener to decide.

17. SISTER RAY

from *White Light/White Heat*

Words by Reed, music by all four Velvets. Even to the most casual listener, the lyrics of this (possibly influenced by Hubert Selby's novel *Last Exit To Brooklyn*) are clearly depicting both hard drug use and homosexual activities. Musically, the track is structured mayhem, with Cale's R&B organ vying with the two guitars for your attention while everybody meanders towards and away from the tune; somehow, Tucker's drumming holds it all together. Reed claims to have written the lyrics while driving to a gig, and that it "was built around this story that I wrote about this scene of total debauchery and decay. I like to think of Sister Ray as a transvestite smack dealer. The situation is a bunch of drag queens taking some sailors home with them and shooting up on smack and having this orgy when the police appear."

Admitting that this was "a graphic song," Reed recalls Warhol telling him, "'Oh, Lou, make sure that you make them do the sucking-on-my-ding-dong song'. So we did it. Seventeen minutes of violence ... everyone was surprised." The music itself is just as uncompromising, with Reed later claiming that musically he was trying to create the rock 'n' roll equivalent of Ornette Coleman; he's also compared it to heavy metal. Unable to agree on an arrangement for the song, the band decided to record it in one take – during which engineer Gary

Kellgren actually left the studio. "He just said, 'Let me know when it's over'," Reed later recalled.

18. CANDY SAYS

from *The Velvet Underground*

A gently sad ballad of self-despair, which Reed described at the time as being "probably the best song I've written." Sung on the album by Doug Yule, who was teased unmercifully about his performance by Reed, since Yule had no idea what the song was actually about. The "Candy" of the title was Candy Darling, a drag queen and Factory 'superstar' from Long Island (real name James Slattery), who later died from cancer, apparently caused by either silicone breast implants or hormone injections (accounts differ). Apart from a few Warhol movies, Candy Darling also appeared in her own stage revue show, *Glamour, Glory and Gold*, in which she played multiple roles, while the ten corresponding male roles were played by the then-unknown actor Robert De Niro. Reed – who was very fond of drag queens – would later refer to Candy again, making her one of the characters in his solo hit 'Walk On The Wild Side'. The song's dissatisfaction with self-image is something universal, as Reed later observed: "I don't know a person alive who doesn't feel that way."

19. WHAT GOES ON

from *The Velvet Underground*

A rocking pop song with multiple guitar overdubs about being messed about and messed up by love. The first line echoes the Beatles song of the same title; 'Lady Be Good' is the title of a song by George and Ira Gershwin.

20. SOME KINDA LOVE

from *The Velvet Underground*

A bluesy (and darkly comic) exhortation to

sexual experimentation. The lyric echoes a line from T.S. Eliot's 'The Hollow Men': "Between the idea/And the reality/Between the motion/And the act/Falls the Shadow." Reed would later use *Between Thought And Expression* as the title for both his 1992 CD retrospective and his first book collection of selected lyrics. Reed considered Sterling Morrison's guitar part on this track to be one of the finest things he ever did.

21. PALE BLUE EYES

from *The Velvet Underground*

Perhaps Reed's most haunting ballad, this is a delicately arranged song of yearning loss; the relationship here (with Shelley Albin) is known to be doomed. Reed said simply that he'd written it "for someone I missed very much. Her eyes were hazel. It's been recorded by a lot of people, but my favourite version is by Maureen Tucker." Tucker's version (on which Reed plays guitar) can be found on her 1989 solo album *Life In Exile After Abdication*. The lyric echoes both 'I'll Be Your Mirror' and the title of a book – Richard Farina's 1966 cult novel *Been Down So Long It Looks Like Up To Me*.

22. JESUS

from *The Velvet Underground*

Lou Reed's gently beautiful plea for redemption surprised even him: "When I wrote 'Jesus', I said, 'My God, a hymn!'" It hovers somewhere between folk, country-blues and gospel.

23. BEGINNING TO SEE THE LIGHT

from *The Velvet Underground*

A bouncy rocker about the possibilities of hope and optimism. It sounds almost like a variation on 'I'm Waiting For The Man', but is a lot more joyous.

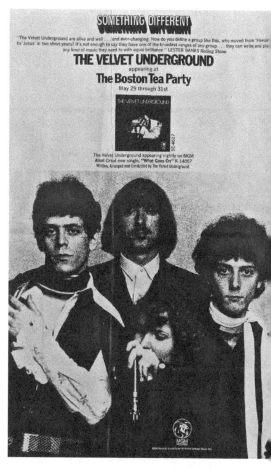

24. I'M SET FREE

from *The Velvet Underground*

Another driving rocker, but the exultant title is misleading – this is about heartbreak and pain, as the mournfully bluesy guitar solo attests. The relationship is now over; the best that can be hoped for is eventually to find another one, but even that will turn out to just be another

Advert for the group's residency at the Boston Tea Party and for their single 'What Goes On'

THE VELVET UNDERGROUND

"illusion." Covered by Brian Eno in 2016 on his album *The Ship*.

25. THAT'S THE STORY OF MY LIFE

from *The Velvet Underground*

Sheer bounce-along honky-tonk vaudeville, with lyrics that quote from (and refer to) Factory photographer, resident and unofficial caretaker Billy Linich aka Billy Name. At this point Reed and Linich were quite close, and used to visit gay bars together. As to Linich's opinions on good and evil, one should bear in mind something that Reed later pointed out: "He also told me I was a lesbian, so you have to take things with a grain of salt."

26. THE MURDER MYSTERY

from *The Velvet Underground*

An experimental track, with two sets of "lyrics" – recorded and mixed so that one set would emanate from each speaker, with the music in the middle. Sung by the entire band. Reed later explained that he'd been playing around with words "and wondering if you could cause two opposing emotions to occur at the same time." His stream-of-consciousness lyrics were subsequently published as a poem – or rather, two parallel poems – in the winter 1972 issue of *The Paris Review* (#53). What it's about, one wonders if even Reed knows, though he later admitted it was an experiment that had failed: "The idea was simple – have two lyrics running at the same time, so you get hit with one monologue in one ear and the other monologue in the other ear, like two guitar parts. Just as two guitar parts are supposed to interweave, so are these two poems. But it didn't work because you couldn't hear either one well enough to hear what was being said."

27. AFTER HOURS

from *The Velvet Underground*

A song of loneliness, and in praise of the solace found in alcohol; a song for those whose local bar has become the only bright and friendly place in the world. Sung by Moe Tucker, making her vocal debut here. "It's a terribly sad song, and I didn't sing it because I figured people wouldn't believe me if I sang it. But I knew Maureen for instance had a very innocent voice," Reed explained later. Tucker was so nervous about her vocals that she made everyone but Reed and the engineer leave the studio while she sang. The version on the Valentin mix sounds like more honky-tonk vaudeville, while Reed's mix sounds like folk/blues. "I loved after-hours bars," Reed comments in his *Between Thought And Expression* book, going on to relate a telling anecdote about Nico causing a bar fight to break out.

28. WHO LOVES THE SUN

from *Loaded*

A deceptively cheerful and poppy ode to nature, sung by Doug Yule. Despite the sting in the lyric, the fact that the Velvets were singing about something as good-time as sunshine in the first place was fairly astonishing. As with several other *Loaded* songs, this has a vaguely countryish feel, reminiscent of some of the music the Grateful Dead were making that same year.

29. SWEET JANE

from *Loaded*

Based around a rhythm riff that's practically a Reed trademark, this verges on the anthemic. The song's 'outsider' protagonist (a rock musician) is looking 'inwards', scrutinising the lives of his more orthodox

seem to be a hooker (he waits for her "on the corner", and she loves him "by the hour"). Honky-tonk piano by Yule; the vocal sounds like Reed double-tracked. There's an interesting (and radically different) early version of this on *Fully Loaded*.

32. NEW AGE

from *Loaded*

A song that's practically the screenplay for a movie, this tale of a movie star past her prime and her younger lover is evocative in mood of Billy Wilder's 1950 film *Sunset Boulevard*. The tone is appropriately mock-epic, approaching gospel territory towards the end. Vocal by Doug Yule. The "full-length" version (on *Fully Loaded*) fades with a guitar solo.

33. HEAD HELD HIGH

from *Loaded*

Enjoyably nonsensical R&B about self-respect (not to mention posture awareness). The Velvets almost sound like the Rolling Stones here.

34. LONESOME COWBOY BILL

from *Loaded*

Supposedly inspired by William Burroughs, author of *The Naked Lunch* and elder statesman of beat culture – but it's hard to see any connection to Burroughs in this country-rock number (complete with Reed yodelling) about a rodeo rider.

35. I FOUND A REASON

from *Loaded*

A graceful torch song with doo-wop harmonies, which could easily have fitted onto the third album. It sounds so personal (despite the self-mocking spoken middle section by Reed) that Lou must have winced

friends (a banker and a clerk), perhaps with envy, perhaps not. An instant classic.

30. ROCK & ROLL

from *Loaded*

Like most of his generation, Lou Reed discovered rock 'n' roll via the radio, and this nostalgic celebration of the medium is practically autobiography (both Reed and Morrison have gone on record to the effect that the music they heard on the radio in their teens gave them a lifeline to hang on to). First recorded for the 'lost' album (a version that would eventually surface on *Another View*), the song has an epic, joyous feel to it - plus some extremely tasteful guitar work. The version on *Another View* features Moe Tucker's great drum fills, and is more delicate than the *Loaded* version; there's also a great demo version on *Fully Loaded*.

31. COOL IT DOWN

from *Loaded*

An exhortation to relaxation, though whether it's about drugs or sex is anybody's guess ... though "Miss Lindy Lee" would

THE VELVET UNDERGROUND

7

at Yule's vocal interpretation (however good it was, it could never have been good enough). The version on *Fully Loaded* gets a completely different arrangement, and sounds like a completely different song.

36. TRAIN AROUND THE BEND

from *Loaded*

According to Moe Tucker, this is about the Long Island railroad, and is a song about going home to New York after too long on the road. The guitar screech at the start of this track sounds disconcertingly like John Cale's viola.

37. OH ! SWEET NUTHIN'

from *Loaded*

Bittersweet countryish blues about poverty (something the Velvets knew a lot about). Vocal by Doug Yule.

38. I CAN'T STAND IT

from *VU*

An irresistibly rocking Dylanesque lament for lost love, containing Reed's heartfelt plea for Shelley (Albin) to return. It's also infinitely preferable to the version Reed would later record for his first solo album in 1972.

39. STEPHANIE SAYS

from *VU*

John Cale's haunting viola announces his presence at the start of this gentle lament of regret. According to Cale, 'Stephanie' was Reed's nickname for Steve Sesnick ("To Lou, everybody's homosexual"). The song would receive its first official outing (in drastically rewritten form) on Reed's 1973 solo album *Berlin*, though by that time Reed had changed the protagonist's name to Caroline.

40. SHE'S MY BEST FRIEND

from *VU*

Unashamedly dumb beatgroup pop, and wonderful with it. As the vocal fades, Reed can be heard screeching gibberish in the background – much to Maureen Tucker's annoyance (she thought it was "childish"). The song was re-recorded by Reed for his *Coney Island Baby* album in 1975.

41. LISA SAYS

from *VU*

A moody complaint of dissatisfaction in the quest for love and/or sex. Once again, Reed would rework this song for his first solo album in 1972.

42. OCEAN

from *VU*

Originally titled 'Here Come The Waves', this concerns the ocean as an analogy for madness, the protagonist eventually being engulfed by the waves (and/or his own mental processes – perhaps why the lyrics reference Shakespeare's *Macbeth*.. The gentleness of mood here – and the sweetness of the backing vocals – just makes it sound all the more ominous. There are also earlier and later versions of the song, which would surface on *Peel Slowly And See* and *Fully Loaded* (and Reed would also re-record the song for his first solo album in 1972.

43. FOGGY NOTION

from *VU*

Peel Slowly And See credits this to Morrison, Tucker, Doug Yule and Hy Weiss. It's more dumb beatpop, this time positively dripping with lustful anticipation. According to Morrison, recorded totally live in the studio.

THE MUSIC: **50 ESSENTIAL TRACKS**

44. TEMPTATION INSIDE OF YOUR HEART
from *VU*

Spoof Motown, and irresistibly catchy; it also contains Reed's unforgettable physics theory: "electricity comes from other planets". According to Sterling Morrison, the idle chatter and asides from the participants (himself, Reed and Cale) was recorded unintentionally while they were crammed into a tiny vocal booth waiting to record their backing vocals; somehow, it accidentally ended up on the finished track. If true, then Reed's lead vocal is presumably only a guide track for finished vocals that were never recorded. It doesn't really matter – it's still great, exactly the way it is.

45. ONE OF THESE DAYS
from *VU*

A countryish blues, about being treated badly in love and drunkenly planning an exit, with slide guitar by Yule and Hank Williams-style yodelling by Reed.

46. ANDY'S CHEST
from *VU*

Reed stated that this song was about the shooting of Andy Warhol by Valerie Solanas, "even though the lyrics don't sound anything like that." In fact, the song is a poetic reverie (its title probably inspired by the famous Richard Avedon portrait of Warhol displaying his scars) that makes no direct mention of the shooting or Warhol's injuries – it's just a deeply affectionate get-well-note from Reed to his one-time mentor. The Velvets' version is minimalist folk/beat; when the song got its first official release on Reed's 1972 solo album *Transformer* it acquired a much more lavish treatment, courtesy of its arrangement by Mick Ronson and David Bowie.

47. I'M STICKING WITH YOU
from *VU*

Vocals by Moe Tucker (aided by Reed and the others) on a childlike and gently melodic affirmation of friendship/love, that's utterly irresistible. This is one of the few times that a Velvets song has dated due to a contemporary reference (to the Viet Cong), since Reed seldom commented on current affairs. In the Nineties it underwent a bizarre resurrection as the soundtrack for a Hyundai commercial.

48. HEY MR. RAIN
from *Another View*

There are two versions of this ethereal folk/blues ballad on the album, both dominated by John Cale's droning viola part. The first version is essential; the second somewhat more shambolic.

49. RIDE INTO THE SUN
from *Another View*

An exquisite guitar instrumental that starts off sounding like surf music and ends up sounding like the Beatles (just listen to the piano and the drum fill). Versions with vocals can be found on *Peel Slowly And See* and the *Quine Tapes*, where it's revealed as a song of longing for escape from the city. It works better as an instrumental.

50. SAD SONG
from *Peel Slowly And See*

How can you possibly resist a love song that's dedicated to Mary Queen of Scots ? Reed would re-record this song for his solo album *Berlin*, but this version is better.

7

20 ESSENTIAL SOLO TRACKS

LOU REED

1. SATELLITE OF LOVE
from *Transformer*

The Velvets recorded this first (see *Peel Slowly & See*), but for once Reed's solo attempt is infinitely better. Despite the fact that it's actually about helplessness in the face of a loved one's serial promiscuity, Mick Ronson's piano arrangement and David Bowie's backing vocals transform it into achingly beautiful pop.

2. WALK ON THE WILD SIDE
from *Transformer*

It's still extraordinary that Reed managed to take these ingredients (transvestites, rent boys, drugs, oral sex) and cook up a runaway hit record with them. Credit should go to the sweeping strings, the soulful sax solo, Herbie Flowers' double-tracked basses and the female chorus – and also to the radio DJs who didn't know what "giving head" meant.

3. PERFECT DAY
from *Transformer*

This account of an ideal date was supposedly sparked by Reed's adulterous relationship with Shelly Albin (hence his awareness that there'll be a price to pay), though Bettye Kronstad believes the song is about her. It became a surprise hit decades later as a result of its inclusion on the soundtrack of *Trainspotting*; the subsequent multi-vocal charity version helped dispel the druggy associations the film had given it.

4. VICIOUS
from *Transformer*

Reed's hilariously mannered strut – not so much vicious as fey and stroppy – was inspired by a comment made to him by Andy Warhol (the opening line), and rescued from slightness by Mick Ronson's spitting guitar fills.

5. ROMEO HAD JULIET
6. DIRTY BLVD
from *New York*

In these two songs, Reed manages to capture and convey the excitement and energy of the city he loves best, without airbrushing its downside in the slightest. Street gangs, crack dealers, drive-by shootings, prostitution, pollution, hopeless poverty, child abuse, homelessness... it's all here, but it still practically makes you feel homesick for the place, even if you've never even been there. Plus, both of these songs are set to irresistible rock riffs.

7. SWORD OF DAMOCLES
from *Magic And Loss*

Very few rock songs have been written about cancer, and it would be hard to better this one. Having watched two friends undergoing radiation therapy en route to painful deaths, Reed tackles the subject of mortality head on. It's an immensely mature work lyrically, the epic orchestration propelling Reed's frustration and sadness.

JOHN CALE

8. PARIS 1919
from *Paris 1919*

The highlight of what is perhaps Cale's most essential album. Even if you have no idea what this song is about (Europe between the wars), it really doesn't matter. The lyrics are intriguingly surreal, and the melody and singalong chorus confirm Cale's ability to produce some of pop's most compelling tunes.

9. FEAR IS A MAN'S BEST FRIEND
from *Fear*

A melodic celebration of paranoia and despair, the product of Cale's serious drug problems and his disastrous marriage. The tune slowly degenerates into hysteria, as does Cale's vocal; his adrenalin-driven rage at his own frustration was for real, and it shows.

10. GUTS
from *Slow Dazzle*

Fuelled by booze, drugs and the anger Cale felt at his wife's adultery with Kevin Ayers, this starts off as gentle rock but grows increasingly disturbing as it progresses. There's real hatred here, much of it directed at himself, and the whole thing eventually collapses into almost incoherent snarling.

11. HEARTBREAK HOTEL
from *Slow Dazzle*

Cale took Presley's hit off down a dark alleyway, then mugged it. Instead of a refuge for the lovelorn, the 'hotel' is now an abode of existential despair, if not actually a terror-infested tomb for the damned. Cale's anguished performance is amplified by the gospel-style wailing of the (uncredited) female backing vocalists.

12. DO NOT GO GENTLE
from *Words For The Dying*

Flexing his classical muscles on this orchestral adaptation of one of Dylan Thomas's best known poems, Cale produced a work that's both pastoral and challenging, the memorable string motif being truly irresistible. True, the children's chorus is a mite intrusive, but it's still a stunning piece of work.

13. DYING ON THE VINE
from *Fragments Of A Rainy Season*

Cale was still struggling with his own drink and drug demons when he and co-writer Larry Sloman came up with this superb tale of a man's realisation that his life has come to a dead end; change of some kind is now inevitable. This version is far better and more powerful than the song's original appearance on *Artificial Intelligence*.

14. HALLELUJAH
from *Fragments Of A Rainy Season*

When Cale told Leonard Cohen he planned to cover the latter's biblical epic of sex and salvation, the poet faxed him literally dozens

7

of verses. Cale culled these down to the ones he preferred and created what is probably the definitive version of the song, made familiar to millions through its inclusion on the soundtrack of *Shrek*.

LOU REED & JOHN CALE

15. A DREAM

from *Songs For Drella*

The jewel in *Drella's* crown, this meandering meditation in the mind of the dying Andy Warhol is one of Reed's finest lyrical achievements, conjuring up the ghost of the artist better than a dozen biographies. Appropriately, Cale's performance delivers an atmosphere that is downright dreamlike.

NICO

16. THE FAIREST OF THE SEASONS

from *Chelsea Girl*

An ethereally gorgeous slice of baroque folk-rock, co-written by Nico's then-teenage lover Jackson Browne. The delicately sweeping string arrangement and otherworldly vocals turn this fairly straightforward song about whether to end a relationship or not into a masterpiece, and a worthy successor to Nico's ballad work with the Velvets.

17. FROZEN WARNINGS

from *The Marble Index*

More chanted than sung, this tale of a hermit sounds positively medieval, Nico's

voice practically *a capella* at the start until Cale's atmospheric (and almost ambient) music rises from the background to embrace her. Supposedly inspired by her lover and mentor Jim Morrison, though it's hard to see exactly how.

18. JANITOR OF LUNACY

from *Desertshore*

Archetypal Nico, her clarion voice ringing out above her pumping harmonium like a demented nun wailing for her lost demon lover. In this case, reportedly Brian Jones of the Rolling Stones, who had died the year before. It's impossible to talk about this song without using the term 'gothic'; one imagines her performing it in a crumbling turret.

MOE TUCKER

19. SPAM AGAIN

from *Life In Exile After Abdication*

A Bo Diddley riff drives this song about the joys of doing low-paid, mindlessly mundane work for a rich but tight boss, inspired by Moe's days as an employee of Wal-Mart. It's practically a socialist calypso protest song. 'Spam' refers to the canned meat, which was presumably all she could afford to feed her family with on her salary.

20. DO IT RIGHT

from *Life In Exile After Abdication*

Insistent honky tonk piano tune with a singalong refrain of good advice ("Don't act dumb, don't play smart") about personal responsibility and generally getting your act together, presumably intended for Moe's children. It's just as charming as either of her solo spots with the Velvets.

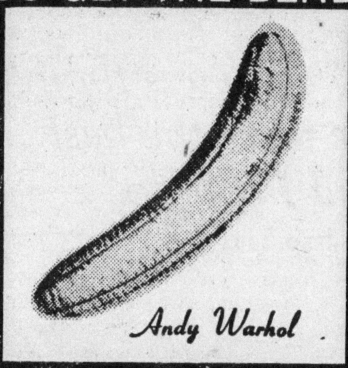

SO FAR UNDERGROUND, YOU GET THE BENDS!

Andy Warhol

V/V6-5008

VELVETOLOGY
FURTHER EXPLORATIONS

8

> ## "We always thought we were the best... and I still do"
>
> **LOU REED, 2001**

VELVETOLOGY
FURTHER EXPLORATIONS

Despite their relatively brief existence, the Velvet Underground's influence has been enormous. They have inspired thousands of bands and their songs have become alternative rock standards, while they remain an enduringly popular subject for biographers, music journalists and cultural critics. This section delves deep into their resounding impact.

BOOKS

Books by The Velvet Underground

BETWEEN THOUGHT AND EXPRESSION: SELECTED LYRICS

Lou Reed (Penguin Books, 1993; out of print)

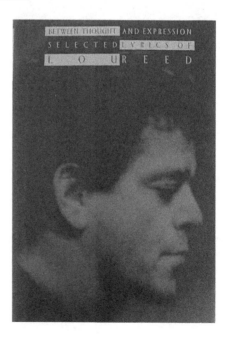

A selection of Reed's lyrics from the Velvet Underground days and his solo work – the latest entries being from *Songs For Drella*. There's a short introduction by Reed, and a smattering of anecdotal footnotes to some of the lyrics, most of which are amusing enough to make tracking a copy of this book down worthwhile. Also included are two poems that first appeared in 1976 in *Unmuzzled Ox* magazine – one of which won an award from the Literary Council For Small Magazines, which was presented to Reed by Senator Eugene McCarthy – and two interviews conducted by Reed, with Czech president Vaclav Havel and novelist Hubert Selby (of *Last Exit To Brooklyn* fame).

8

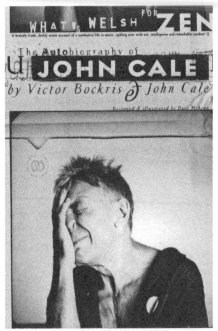

PASS THRU FIRE: THE COLLECTED LYRICS

Lou Reed (Bloomsbury, 2000)

The title is a quote from 'Magic And Loss'. There are a couple of minor works missing, but otherwise this is pretty much Reed's complete lyrical output: all the Velvet Underground material, and his solo work as far as *Ecstasy*. No footnotes this time, but there is a short introduction and several photographs by Reed, plus three unpublished poems and the complete lyrics to *Time Rocker*, his theatrical collaboration with Robert Wilson. The only drawback to this book is the fact that a wide variety of typographical styles are employed, presumably to make it more visually interesting. Unfortunately, some of them are annoyingly difficult to read.

WHAT'S WELSH FOR ZEN? THE AUTOBIOGRAPHY OF JOHN CALE

John Cale and Victor Bockris (Bloomsbury, 1999)

Cale's account of his life is remarkably candid and thoughtful, and eminently readable. Much of the information here had never been available before, and Cale's insights into his relationship with Reed are revealing, to say the least – nor does Cale pull any punches over his own substance abuse and personal shortcomings. An essential read for anyone at all interested in the Velvet Underground or Cale's solo career. The large-format book contains a wealth of rare photographs and was designed by Dave McKean in a style that is both innovative and user-friendly.

'69 ON THE ROAD – VELVET UNDERGROUND PHOTOGRAPHS

Doug Yule (Sal Mercuri/Fierce Pup Productions, 1996)

A signed limited edition of 500 (and thus hard to find), containing photographs of the Velvets taken by Yule in 1969 – though at some point he loans the camera to someone else, since there are shots of the whole band onstage at an outdoor festival in Texas. The photographs themselves are great, but the reproduction and printing isn't – they're very faint and grainy. Yule also contributes very little in the way of text: just an extremely brief introduction and a few comments on the photos.

Books about The Velvet Underground

UP-TIGHT: THE VELVET UNDERGROUND STORY

Victor Bockris and Gerard Malanga (Omnibus, 1983)

The first proper book to be published specifically about the Velvets, and probably the most evocative. A large format paperback illustrated throughout with amazing photographs (though also published in a text-only edition), peppered with hundreds of first-person reminiscences from all concerned and extracts from Malanga's diaries of the period. Sadly, the book is riddled with inaccurate information, much of which Bockris has corrected in his other books (but not here).

TRANSFORMER: THE COMPLETE LOU REED STORY

Victor Bockris (Simon & Schuster, 1995)

Also published under the title *Lou Reed: The Biography*. Reed apparently disliked Bockris's *Uptight* so much that when he learned of the author's plans to write a biography of himself, he demanded of his musical collaborators that no one should co-operate. In fact, Bockris did an amazing job of research, tracking down family friends,

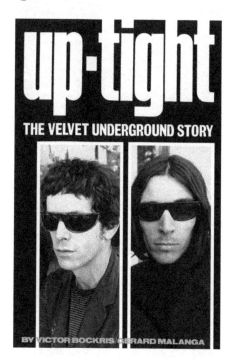

fellow students from Syracuse, Reed's first love Shelley Albin, tour managers and road crew and many more. The cut-off point is shortly after the Velvets' reunion, and the

portrait that emerges is that of a man who is exceptionally talented, extraordinarily complex and very, very messed up. It's a great biography, and one that makes its subject more understandable, though not any more likeable; needless to say, Reed hated it. Bockris updated the book in 2014, to cover Reed's final years. En route he revised many of his opinions, on the grounds that in his eyes Lou's relationship with Laurie Anderson had humanised him, and turned him into a far more rounded and likeable person – a belief shared by many others.

LOU REED & THE VELVET UNDERGROUND

Diana Clapton (Proteus, 1982; out of print)

Large-format illustrated biography that goes up as far as *The Blue Mask*. Some great photos, but the prose style is somewhat florid and breathless – though it does contain one interesting ingredient, in a long interview with Barbara Fulk, who was Reed's tour manager between 1972 and 1975.

THE VELVET UNDERGROUND: AN ILLUSTRATED HISTORY OF A WALK ON THE WILD SIDE

Jim DeRogatis (Voyageur, 2009)

Large-format, scrapbook style history of the Velvets, with contributions from half a dozen writers. The text is pretty slender, but the visuals are stunning: a cornucopia of flyers, posters, ads, record sleeves (including bootlegs) and other memorabilia, plus some incredible photographs, many of which I've never seen anywhere else, such as an amazing colour shot of Andy Warhol working on the 'banana' sleeve. Out of print, but worth tracking down.

8

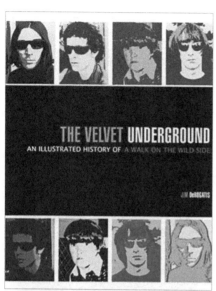

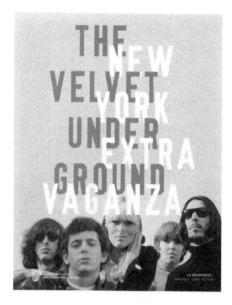

LOU REED: GROWING UP IN PUBLIC

Peter Doggett (Omnibus, 1991; out of print)

The first in-depth Reed biography ends just prior to the Velvets' reunion. Doggett's approach is solid and workmanlike, and he uncovered much hitherto unknown information. However, this book has since been superseded by the Victor Bockris biography.

THE VELVET UNDERGROUND NEW YORK EXTRAVAGANZA

Christian Fevret and Carole Mirabello (Philharmonie de Paris, 2016)

The catalogue for the exhibition of the same name, held in Paris in 2016. A slender volume, with text in French only – but it's crammed full of rare artefacts and photographs of the Velvets and their associates, and is particularly good on the early days. An inexpensive alternative to the more expensive photo books.

THE VELVET UNDERGROUND

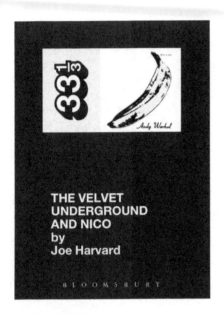

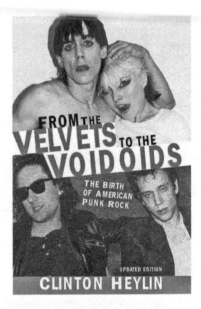

THE VELVET UNDERGROUND AND NICO

Joe Harvard (Continuum, 2004)

A personal appreciation of the Velvets' early days and the recording of their first album. A little breathless and somewhat padded, the book scores on the fact that Harvard (a session musician) unearthed some good new information about the actual recording sessions, most of it the result of an interview with Norman Dolph. Prior to this, the addled memories of some of the participants had made the details of the recording extremely hard to fathom.

FROM THE VELVETS TO THE VOIDOIDS

Clinton Heylin (Penguin, 1993; out of print)

Subtitled "A Pre-punk History For A Post-punk World", Heylin's book traces a line of influence from the Velvets through the MC5 and New York Dolls to Jonathan Richman, Television, the Ramones, Talking Heads, Blondie and beyond. There are only two chapters on the Velvets (though they are well-researched), but it's still a fascinating read, especially if you're interested in the other bands as well.

FANZINES

There have been numerous Velvet Underground fanzines over the years, the most impressive of which being *What Goes On*, founded by Phillip Milstein in 1978. Four issues have appeared and a fifth was promised; for back issues and further details, write to M.C. Kostek, c/o The Velvet Underground Appreciation Society, 5721 SE Laguna Avenue, Stuart, FL 34997-7828 USA.

VELVETOLOGY: **BOOKS**

ALL YESTERDAY'S PARTIES
Edited by Clinton Heylin (Da Capo Press, 2005)

Subtitled "The Velvet Underground In Print 1966-1970", which says it all. Here you'll find contemporary press coverage of the Velvets, plus a smattering of great visuals from the time, such as posters and promotional material. Given that rock journalism as we know it today was in its infancy in the late Sixties, there are still some interesting insights into the mentality of the times: the straight press largely treats the Velvets purely as an inconsequential adjunct of Warhol, comparing them to "Berlin in the decadent Thirties" or calling them the heirs of Baudelaire, while pieces from the underground press and music magazines like *Crawdaddy* vary between incomprehension and semi-incoherent adulation. One the plus side, there's a good interview with Sterling Morrison by Greg Barrios, as well as pieces by Sandy Pearlman, Lester Bangs and Lenny Kaye.

THE COMPLETE GUIDE TO THE MUSIC OF THE VELVET UNDERGROUND
Peter Hogan (Omnibus, 1997)

THE ROUGH GUIDE TO THE VELVET UNDERGROUND
Peter Hogan (Rough Guides, 2007)

Earlier editions of the volume you now hold in your hand (which supersedes them).

THE VELVET UNDERGROUND HANDBOOK
M.C. Kostek (Black spring, 1989; out of print)

An "ultimate book of facts" put together by Mike Kostek, president of the Velvet Underground Appreciation Society. Contains rare photos, a chronological history, a staggeringly comprehensive discography, filmography and bibliography. A good book, and even if some of the information here has since been superseded, still well worth seeking out.

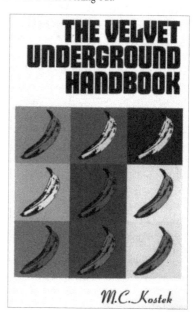

8

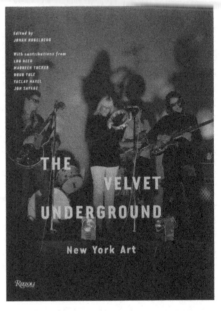

PERFECT DAY: AN INTIMATE PORTRAIT OF LIFE WITH LOU REED

Bettye Kronstad (Jawbone, 2016)

A somewhat breathless account of courtship and marriage by Lou's first wife. Rather sweetly, she still refers to him often as "Lewis". It's heavily padded, and inaccurate in at least some places – Bettye claims to have seen Lou's final gig with the Velvets, but thinks Cale was still in the band. Also, she spends much of the book reconstructing their arguments, and none of it makes for easy reading, as Lou's neediness is truly painful. That the marriage eventually collapsed in a sea of booze and drugs has a tragic inevitability to it, since all those problems were there right at the start. There are some interesting fragments here – such as Lou blaming Warhol for the "failure" of the Velvets, and avoiding him whenever possible – but since she was with him during the creation of his first three solo albums (two of them being among his very best), you would have hoped for a bit more insight. For completists and masochists only.

THE VELVET UNDERGROUND: NEW YORK ART

Edited by Johan Kugelberg (Rizzoli, 2009; out of print)

A massive, lavish coffee-table tome that includes photographs (some of them great), songsheets, memorabilia, posters and promotional material, early interviews and articles (plus a very brief 2009 interview with Lou and Moe). The book covers the Sixties and Seventies only, with nothing about solo work or the band reunion. The tone throughout is sober and respectable, and nowhere near as much fun as the DeRogatis book, which covers similar territory but has much better material. Now out of print, but it's still possible to find secondhand copies for around £30 if you dig deeply enough.

VELVETOLOGY: **BOOKS**

PLEASE KILL ME: THE UNCENSORED ORAL HISTORY OF PUNK

Legs McNeill and Gillian McCain (Little Brown, 1996)

This covers the same territory as Heylin's *From The Velvets To The Voidoids*, with hundreds of first-person accounts of the development of the alternative American music scene between 1967-1992. A great piece of documentation, even if the litany of drug casualties makes for depressing reading. The first chapter concerns the Velvets, with a later chapter on their reunion and the death of Nico.

SEDITION AND ALCHEMY: A BIOGRAPHY OF JOHN CALE

Tim Mitchell (Peter Owen, 2003)

Thorough biography of Cale, which goes up to 2002. It's good on the early avant garde period, and fills in many holes skipped over by Cale's autobiography. There are times that it seems somewhat sketchy, though – and Mitchell's original manuscript is rumoured to have been much longer, but was cut by the publisher simply on the grounds of cost. It's a shame, because Cale is deserving of the fullest biography that could be done. Available in paperback, but the limited edition hardback includes a free CD containing a short story by Cale and a short musical piece called 'Imitating Violin'.

LOU REED: WALK ON THE WILD SIDE

Chris Roberts (Carlton, 2004)

Large format paperback, subtitled 'The Stories Behind The Songs', which takes an analytical album-by-album, track-by-track approach to Reed's solo career (with a brief preamble about the Velvets). A good selection of photographs (but inserted into the text in somewhat haphazard fashion), and the book makes for a lively read even if you disagree with the author.

THE VELVET UNDERGROUND

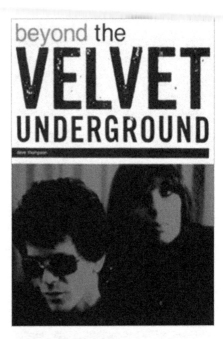

NOTES FROM THE VELVET UNDERGROUND: THE LIFE OF LOU REED

Howard Sounes (Doubleday, 2015)

Easily the best biography of Lou Reed to date. Sounes undoubtedly benefitted from the fact that after Lou's death several major witnesses had already come forward to talk for the first time, notably Reed's sister Bunny and his first wife Bettye – but apart from those two Sounes also managed to track down a host of others, including friends and associates that dated back as far as Lou's days at Syracuse. Not only did he persuade Shelley Albin to talk, he also provides the first photo of her I've ever seen. All of this helps to draw the most rounded picture of this complicated man to date, and while there will undoubtedly be further biographies of him to come in the future, it's hard to imagine how they could better this one.

BEYOND THE VELVET UNDERGROUND

Dave Thompson (Omnibus, 1989; out of print)

This large-format book consists entirely of direct quotes from band members (plus a few journalists and critical reviews), as well as a smattering of photographs. It goes as far as Reed's *New Sensations* and Cale's *Artificial Intelligence*, with a postscript about the death of Nico.

LOU REED & THE VELVETS

Nigel Trevena (White Light, 1973; out of print)

Early, fanzine-style booklet containing a brief chronology, reviews of the Velvets albums and Reed's early solo work, an evaluation of Reed as a writer/performer, a selection of Reed quotes and some nice visual material. What makes this of real interest, however, is the inclusion of not only the words to 'The Gift', but also eleven of Reed's early poems.

8

NICO: IN THE SHADOW OF THE MOON GODDESS

Lutz Graf-Ulbrich (Privately published 2015, available through Amazon)

A brief memoir by Nico's German lover and sometime guitarist. It's a diary-style account of playing gigs and scoring heroin on the road, delivered as a tale of young junkies in love. Pretty dull stuff, in the main, and thus for Nico completists only.

WHITE LIGHT/WHITE HEAT: THE VELVET UNDERGROUND DAY-BY-DAY

Richie Unterberger (Jawbone Press, 2009)

As the sub-title proudly proclaims, this book explores the lives and work of the Velvets and their associates on a chronological basis, in microscopic and mind-boggling detail. Though the solo years and careers are only lightly touched upon, this book covers the Velvets story up as far as 2007; given how evidently exhaustive his research is, one has to assume Unterberger can be relied upon for accuracy – but the Velvets' story is positively rammed with unreliable witnesses, and many stories since discredited are still repeated here. However, if you require more depth than can be found in the book you're currently reading, Unterberger's is undoubtedly the book you seek.

NICO: THE LIFE & LIES OF AN ICON

Richard Witts (Virgin, 1993)

In the late Eighties Nico asked Witts to write her biography, which she wanted to be called *Moving Target*. She thought it should be more like a novel than a biography, "half true, half not." Instead, Witts has done an excellent job of cutting through Nico's addled self-mythologising to paint a vivid portrait

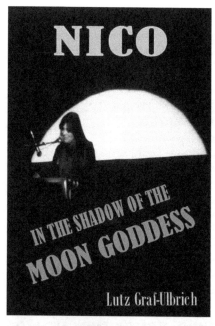

8

of an extraordinary woman who lived an extraordinary life, albeit an extremely depressing one. Even before her plunge into a heroin nightmare, Nico was always a tragedy in search of a place to happen.

LOU REED: BETWEEN THE LINES

Michael Wrenn (Plexus, 1993)

Credited inside to "Michael Wrenn with Glen Marks", this book might as well be called 'Lou Reed In His Own Words', since most of the text consists of direct quotes, linked by short narrative pieces from Wrenn. Apart from the quotes, the strength of this large format paperback (which ends just prior to the Velvets' reunion) lies in the fact that it contains a wealth of truly amazing press cuttings and memorabilia from Glen Marks' own archive.

NICO: SONGS THEY NEVER PLAY ON THE RADIO

James Young (Bloomsbury, 1992)

Also published under the title *Nico: The End*. Young was Nico's keyboard player throughout the Eighties, and his memoir of her declining years is a touching and extremely humorous account of the chaos that surrounded her both at home and on the road. Shored up by third-rate musicians and fourth-rate management, Nico has little to trade except her "legend", and the only thing she's interested in trading it for is heroin. Yet although Young readily acknowledges that Nico was "a monster", his affection for her is evident, and he has enough compassion to concede that junkies are "invalids with criminal tendencies." As a study of rock 'n' roll at its seediest, most unrewarding and unglamorous, this makes for great reading.

THE VELVET UNDERGROUND COMPANION

Edited by Albin Zak III (Schirmer Books, 1997)

Subtitled "Four Decades Of Commentary", this collection is an entertaining ragbag of articles and reviews from the Sixties onwards which veers from the interesting to the inane; writers include Lester Bangs, MC Kostek and Paul Williams. There are interviews with Morrison, Reed, Nico and Tucker, an exhaustive (and exhausting) discography by M.C. Kostek and Phil Milstein, and written tributes to Morrison on his passing by Lou Reed and Doug Yule. Editor Zak is an assistant professor of music at the University of Michigan.

Books about Andy Warhol and the Factory crowd

There are literally hundreds of titles in print about the life, work and world of Andy Warhol. The following are a brief selection of books that may be of particular interest to Velvets fans.

ANDY WARHOL'S PHILOSOPHY: FROM A TO B AND BACK AGAIN
Andy Warhol (Cassell, 1975)

POPISM – THE WARHOL SIXTIES
Andy Warhol & Pat Hackett (Harcourt Inc, 1980)

Andy Warhol's own writings – the rambling 'philosophy' was actually transcribed from Brigid Polk's tape recordings – explore every subject under the sun as well as his own life, and are a wonderfully enjoyable read: childlike, witty and genuinely touching. His memoir of the Sixties is both fragmentary and biased, but nevertheless fascinating, and is – apart from the occasional catty remark – free of the bitchiness that marred his later diaries. For example, although his memoir contains a fair amount of material about his time with the Velvets, he says absolutely nothing about the way that he and Reed parted company.

ANDY WARHOL: THE FACTORY YEARS 1964–1967
Nat Finkelstein (Canongate Books, 1999)

THE VELVET YEARS: WARHOL'S FACTORY 1965–1967
Stephen Shore & Lynn Tillman (Pavilion, 1995)

Two large-format collections of photographs of the Factory era (Shore's in black and white, Finkelstein in black and white and colour). Finkelstein's has a few short prose essays by him and an introduction by David Dalton, while Shore's contains anecdotal prose pieces by some of his subjects, including Morrison, Cale and Tucker. Both books contain otherwise unseen photos of the Velvets and Nico, plus shots of most of the key players in the Factory story, and give fascinating insights into Warhol's world.

EDIE: AMERICAN GIRL
Jean Stein, edited with George Plimpton
(Alfred A. Knopf, 1982)

A riveting account comprised of hundreds of first-person recollections, Stein's book is not only a biography of the troubled

model/actress Edie Sedgwick, but also an extraordinarily vivid portrait of her times and world. Not a great deal of material here about the Velvets, but it's an extremely evocative depiction of Warhol and the whole Factory crowd. Even though Edie's life itself reads like an out-of-control Greek tragedy (which is somewhat depressing), highly recommended.

FACTORY MADE: WARHOL AND THE SIXTIES

Steven Watson (Pantheon, 2003)

A superbly researched – and lengthy – chronicle of Warhol and his world, concentrating mainly on the period 1960-1968. There's nothing about the Velvets in here that you couldn't find elsewhere, but Watson places them in context with the rest of Warhol's activities. Also, if you wanted

one book that would tell you everything you needed to know about the denizens of the Factory, this is the one.

SWIMMING UNDERGROUND: MY YEARS IN THE WARHOL FACTORY

Mary Woronov (Serpent's Tail, 1995)

Whip dancer Woronov's memoir is by turns candid, literary, warm, surreal and harrowing. It evokes the Factory's atmosphere of drug-fuelled desperation better than almost any other book, and despite the rollercoaster ride through her emotional and sexual problems is occasionally laugh-out-loud funny, particularly on the subject of Nico. Not a great deal of material here about the Velvets, but it's still a great read – and contains, according to Lou Reed, the most accurate portrayal of Warhol in print.

THE VELVET UNDERGROUND MAP OF NEW YORK

(Herb Lester Associates, 2015)

Exactly what the title says it is – a map showing the locations of 49 locations in New York that were important in the stories of the Velvet Underground and Andy Warhol. A nicely produced novelty item, stylish enough to pin on your wall and a little bit more comprehensive than the map in this book.

8

FILMS AND VIDEOS

LE BATACLAN

I'm Waiting For The Man/Berlin/The Black Angel's Death Song/Wild Child/Empty Bottles/ Heroin/Ghost Story/The Biggest, Loudest, Heaviest Group Of All/Femme Fatale/I'll Be Your Mirror/All Tomorrow's Parties/Janitor Of Lunacy

French TV; broadcast January 1972; not available

Film of the 1972 Paris reunion of Reed, Cale and Nico. Broadcast once (with a shortened version broadcast several times that year), but unseen ever since. Brief clips have surfaced on several other TV programmes, but the fee demanded by the French government (who own the rights) for the whole show has always been deemed too high by other TV companies. Rumour has it that most of the show may since have been erased.

THE SOUTH BANK SHOW: THE VELVET UNDERGROUND

LWT; broadcast April 1986; not commercially available

A good retrospective evaluation of the band, with 1985 interviews with all of the Velvets,

Nico, Gerard Malanga, Victor Bockris and critic Robert Christgau. Reed was the only one of the Velvets who declined to be interviewed; instead, the show included a brief interview clip taken from another source. There's also archive footage, plus glimpses of both Cale and Nico in solo performance and a few brief clips from the Bataclan gig.

ARSENAL

Catalonian TV3; broadcast May 1986; not commercially available

Spanish documentary about the Velvets, the cornerstone of which is a lengthy interview with Sterling Morrison (the transcript of which can be found in Albin Zak's book *The Velvet Underground Companion*). Rare music can be heard on the soundtrack, including 'Loop' and 'The Ostrich'.

LOU REED AND JOHN CALE: SONGS FOR DRELLA

Warner Music Vision; VHS video released April 1990

Reed and Cale perform their Andy Warhol

THE VELVET UNDERGROUND

song cycle in its entirety, directed and photographed by Ed Lachman using a camera team of four. The staging by Jerome Sirlin is simple, with the two men facing each other amid a bank of instruments, with simple but effective stage lighting by Robert Wierzel, set against back projections of Warhol and his work (and visual interpretations of the lyrics, of varying degrees of success). The film version reinforces the fact that this is the work of two artists at the top of their form, whose communication borders on the telepathic. As per usual, while Reed opts for a simple black turtleneck, Cale's look is more outlandish: a black jacket over a white shirt with one of the widest collars ever seen. Coupled with his physical intensity, the look makes him appear deranged and possibly dangerous. That this performance has never been released on DVD is nothing short of criminal.

THE VELVET UNDERGROUND: VELVET REDUX MCMXCIII

Warner tracklisting

Venus In Furs/Sweet Jane/I Heard Her Call My Name/Femme Fatale/I'm Sticking With

VELVETS ON SCREEN

All contemporary film footage of the Velvet Underground in their first incarnation(s) is of fairly poor quality. Although Warhol and other underground filmmakers, like Barbara Rubin, Jonas Mekas, Ron Nameth and Paul Morrissey – all shot both colour and black and white footage of the Velvet Underground performing and rehearsing during 1966 and 1967, most of these films are seldom (if ever) shown, and virtually all of them are thought to be silent (or are simply overdubbed with recordings from the first album). The only known definite exceptions are:

1. A rehearsal of 'Venus In Furs' (included on the Lou Reed *Rock And Roll Heart* DVD, listed below).

2. *The Velvet Underground: A Symphony Of Sound*. This is a 20-minute film of Warhol's showing the Velvets (with Nico) rehearsing 'Melody Laughter' at the Factory in January 1966 – with the New York police entering at the end to complain about the noise.

The film has rarely been shown, and is not commercially available.

3. A performance of 'Guess I'm Falling In Love' from a January 1967 TV show called *Upbeat*.

4. A short film called 'Sunday Morning' by Rosalind Stevenson – a schoolmate of Lou Reed's – was touted by Channel 4 as showing the Velvet Underground rehearsing that song. In fact, it's simply very moody silent footage overdubbed with the track from the first album – which is how all this silent footage is usually handled when used in documentaries.

5. In 1965, CBS News filmed a feature on underground filmmaker Piero Holiczer which included footage of him jamming (on saxophone) with the MacLise line-up of the Velvets. Holiczer used the soundtrack of this in his film *Venus In Furs*, which also features John Cale, Sterling Morrison, Lou Reed, Angus MacLise and Barbara Rubin in acting roles.

VELVETOLOGY: FILMS AND VIDEOS

You/Rock & Roll/I'll Be Your Mirror/I'm Waiting For The Man/Heroin/Pale Blue Eyes/Coyote/ The Gift/Hey Mr Rain

Rhino tracklisting

Venus In Furs/White Light-White Heat/ Beginning To See The Light/Some Kinda Love/ Femme Fatale/Hey Mr Rain/ I'm Sticking With You/ I Heard Her Call My Name/ I'll Be Your Mirror/ Rock & Roll/ Sweet Jane/ I'm Waiting For The Man/ Heroin/Pale Blue Eyes/Coyote

Warner Music Vision; released 1993, reissued by Rhino 2006; available on Region 1 DVD

The visual version of the reunion live album, filmed at L'Olympia in Paris, directed by Declan Lowney. The filming itself is quite straightforward (using four cameras) but well done, as is the simple stage lighting. While Reed, Morrison and Tucker all opt for a casual/scruffy look in T-shirts and jeans, Cale wears a dark suit over a zip-fronted jerkin, with a floppy hairstyle that makes him look like a 1940s mad scientist. For almost all of their audience, this was the first opportunity to see the Velvets live. Cale's viola playing provides much of the visual action (he also alternates between the viola, bass, and organ), but it's Moe Tucker who commands the attention, whether standing at her kit and playing like she's conducting the entire proceedings or else shyly standing up front to sing with her finger in her ear – a sharp contrast to the solid, impassive figure of Sterling Morrison (who gets a massive cheer when he sings a line on 'I'm Sticking With You').

All of this makes Reed's mannered pose and his expertise in manipulating a concert crowd seem heavy-handed by comparison. For all its musical faults, still an amazing performance.

CURIOUS... THE VELVET UNDERGROUND IN EUROPE

Channel 4; broadcast 1993; not commercially released

A good documentary about the reunion tour, including some live material and extremely revealing interviews with all four Velvets, plus Czech President Vaclav Havel (and a smattering of European fans). There's also a great, bluesy solo version of 'Heroin' from Reed, filmed especially for this. The programme was screened as the opener for Channel 4's Velvet Underground Night in December 1993, which was appropriately titled 'Peel Slowly And See' and hosted by Deborah Harry. Also shown were *Velvet Redux, Songs For Drella*, Warhol's *Chelsea Girls* and *Sunday Morning*. Additionally, there were comments about the influence of the Velvets from Bono, Peter Buck, Kristin Hersh, Peter Hook, Ian McCulloch and Richard Hell. *Chelsea Girls* was introduced by Paul Morley and Paul Morrissey.

JOHN CALE: WORDS FOR THE DYING

Label unknown; released 1993 on video in USA only; currently unavailable

A short and somewhat bizarre documentary by Rob Nilsson about the making of Cale's orchestral adaptation of Dylan Thomas's poetry. The film follows Cale and Brian Eno to Moscow for the recording sessions, and also shows a visit by Cale to his sick and aged mother in Wales. Eno didn't want to be filmed at all, and is uncooperative throughout; at his insistence, the film was only released in the USA.

LOU REED: ROCK AND ROLL HEART

Win Star; released 1998; available on Region 1 DVD

Excellent – if somewhat reverential – 75-minute documentary first shown

THE VELVET UNDERGROUND

on American TV in 1997 in Channel 13's *American Masters* series. Directed by Timothy Greenfield-Sanders, the film features extensive archive footage of Lou, the Velvets and Warhol. There's also live footage taken over the years, and interviews with the man himself and a whole host of people connected with him and/or influenced by him, including John Cale, Maureen Tucker, Mary Woronov, Billy Name, Joe Dallesandro, Holly Woodlawn, Gerard Malanga, David Bowie, David Byrne, Dave Stewart, Patti Smith, Thurston Moore, Suzanne Vega, Philip Glass and Jim Carroll, as well as various rock critics and art historians. The documentary goes up as far as *Magic And Loss*, and also has footage from several scenes of the theatrical production of *Timerocker*. Given how good this film is, it's ironic that it shares its title with one of Reed's worst albums. The DVD extras include a brief clip of the Velvets performing at the Factory in January 1966 and originally shown in the documentary *USA Artists: Warhol* (Channel 13). The band runs through 'Venus In Furs' while Edie Sedgwick, Gerard Malanga and Jack Smith dance. The sound quality is pretty dreadful, the vocals so muffled as to be almost inaudible and the dancing fairly embarrassing... but it's still fascinating. There are also biographies of all the interviewees.

LOU REED: A NIGHT WITH LOU REED

Sweet Jane/I'm Waiting For The Man/Martial Law/Don't Talk To Me About Work/Women/Waves Of Fear/Wild Side/Turn Out The Lights/New Age/Kill Your Sons/Satellite Of Love/White Light-White Heat/Rock 'N' Roll

Eagle Vision; released 2000; available on Region 2 DVD

A live set recorded at The Bottom Line in New York in 1983, produced by Bill Boggs and Richard Baker, directed by Clarke Santee. Filmed with five cameras, none of which intrude on the action, the concert's musicians include: Reed on vocals and guitar; Robert Quine (guitar); Fernando Saunders (bass); Fred Maher (drums).

Unfortunately, although Reed is enthusiastic about the show in the post-concert footage, the reality is that he and the band turn in a pretty laconic performance which is neither involving or exciting – all the 'classics' are treated in a extremely throwaway fashion, and even 'White Light/White Heat' sounds mannered and restrained. They're more alive on the newer material, and there are great versions of 'Women' and 'Waves Of Fear', while Saunders' bass is impressive throughout – but even at its best, this show is merely adequate.

THE END: THE NICO MOVIE THAT NEVER WAS

This biopic of Nico was supposedly in pre-production in 2005, but never materialized. Tilda Swinton was due to star as the model/chanteuse, with David Mackenzie as director. Location shooting was intended to take place in Paris, New York, London and Manchester and the script – by *Blade Runner* writers David and Janet Peoples – was supposedly based partially upon James Young's excellent book *Songs They Never Play On The Radio*, and followed Nico from her early modelling days through to her death.

VELVETOLOGY: **FILMS AND VIDEOS**

NICO: AN UNDERGROUND EXPERIENCE+HEROINE

An Underground Experience:

I'm Waiting For The Man/Vegas/60-40/All Tomorrow's Parties/Femme Fatale/Heroes/Saeta

Heroine:

My Heart Is Empty/Procession/ All Tomorrow's Parties/Valley Of The Kings/The Sphinx/We've Got The Gold/Mutterlein/Afraid/ Innocent And Vain/Frozen Warnings/Fearfully In Danger/Tananore/Femme Fatale

Visionary Communications; released 2000; available on DVD

Two short films of Nico in concert. Malcolm Whitehead's film *Heroine* records a solo performance at Manchester's Library Theatre some time in the Eighties, with the harmonium-playing Nico – accompanied only by a percussionist and a piano player (on 'Femme Fatale' only) – at her most gothic and doom-laden. Even 'All Tomorrow's Parties' – performed a capella – sounds dirge-like. Filmed with only two cameras, the film and sound aren't of the best quality, and nor is the performance.

An Underground Experience is even less fun. Recorded in 1993 in an unnamed small club in Manchester with one camera, Nico – backed by an uncredited but quite good three-piece rock band – looks ancient, haggard and wrecked, wearing a shabby overcoat and chainsmoking cigarettes while she sings. There's also a brief interview with her, though she's fairly dour and uncommunicative, revealing only that she was taking a lot of LSD during her stint with the Velvets. The performance is, ironically, somewhat better than on *Heroine* (although on Bowie's 'Heroes' she sounds like Madeleine Kahn's parody of Marlene Dietrich), but it still makes for uneasy viewing. DVD extras include more interview material from the same gig (more painful viewing), a biography and discography.

NICO: ICON

Éditions À Voir; Released 2001; available on Region 2 DVD

Excellent documentary by Susanne Ofteringer. It opens with passages that concentrate on Nico's later years as a "middle-aged junkie", before backtracking to her childhood and early career. The sequencing makes the contrast between Nico's youth and her decline all the more appalling. There are interviews with her son Ari Boulogne/Delon, her aunt, Niko Papatakis, Alain Delon's mother, Billy Name, Paul Morrissey, Jonas Mekas, John Cale, Sterling Morrison, Viva, Danny Fields, Jackson Browne, Lutz Ullbrich (Nico's accompanist and lover in the Seventies), her Eighties manager Alan Wise and keyboard player James Young. There are amazing photographs and footage from Nico's early modelling career, plus brief clips from *Chelsea Girls*, *An Underground Experience, La Dolce Vita*, Peter Whitehead's promotional video for 'I'm Not Saying' from 1966, and footage of Nico with Iggy Pop. The film closes with John Cale performing a stark, solo version of 'Frozen Warnings' at the piano.

LOU REED: TRANSFORMER

Eagle Vision; released 2001; available on Region 2 DVD

One of a series on 'Classic Albums', this one directed by Bob Smeaton. It's a surprisingly good documentary that re-examines the *Transformer* album track-by-track, and in great depth. There are interviews with Reed, session men Herbie Flowers and John Halsey, producers David Bowie and Mick Ronson and cover photographer Mick Rock, while engineer Ken Scott isolates musical ingredients on the master tape to demonstrate how the tracks were put together, and Flowers demonstrates the twin-bass overdubbing on 'Walk On The

8

THE VELVET UNDERGROUND

Wild Side'. There are also anecdotes from Gerard Malanga, Joe Dallesandro and Holly Woodlawn, and analysis from musicians Dave Stewart and Lenny Kaye, and from journalists David Fricke, Tony Stewart and Timothy Greenfield-Sanders. Throughout his interview, Reed analyses the contributions of Bowie and Ronson, and praises them effusively.

In addition to some archive footage, Reed performs acoustic versions of 'Vicious, 'Satellite Of Love', 'Walk On The Wild Side' and 'Perfect Day', and recites the lyrics of 'Andy's Chest' and 'Hangin' Round' as if they were poetry. He also segues effortlessly between 'Waiting For The Man', 'Vicious' and 'Dirty Blvd.', just to prove they all use the same chord structure ("See? They're brothers."). There are also clips from the video for the all-star charity version of 'Perfect Day' (but sadly, not the whole thing). DVD extras include more interview material about the Velvets and Warhol, and Reed performing an acoustic version of 'Waiting For The Man'.

JOHN CALE: FRAGMENTS OF A RAINY SEASON

On A Wedding Anniversary/Lie Still Sleep Becalmed/Do Not Go Gentle Into That Good Night/Carmen Miranda/Cordoba/Ship Of Fools/Leaving It Up To You/The Ballad Of Cable Hogue/Chinese Envoy/Fear (Is A Man's Best Friend)/Dying Of The Vine/Heartbreak Hotel/Style It Takes/Paris 1919/(I Keep A) Close Watch/Hallelujah

FGL/Revenge; released 2003; available on region 2 DVD

The visual equivalent of Cale's live album of the same name, though three tracks shorter in length and probably recorded at a different venue on the same tour – this was recorded at the Palais des Beaux-Arts in Brussels in April 1992, but the live album gives no details as to its venue. The director was Jacquemin Piel,

assisted by three cameramen. The lighting is simple, the mood intimate, and Cale absolutely riveting as he performs highlights from his back catalogue unaccompanied except for piano (a Steinway) or acoustic guitar, his powerful voice carrying the melody. As might have been predicted, his garb is bizarre – a jacket that makes him look like Ichabod Crane, or an 18th century preacher.

LOU REED: SPANISH FLY – LIVE IN SPAIN

Modern Dance/Why Do You Talk/Venus In Furs/Sweet Jane/Jesus/Romeo Had Juliet/ Satellite Of Love/Ecstasy/The Blue Mask/ Perfect Day/Walk On The Wild Side

Sanctuary Visual Entertainment; released 2005; available on Region 0 DVD

Produced by Rathke and Saunders, executive producer Reed. Recorded at the Benicassím International Festival in Benicassím, Spain on August 7 2004, we see a relaxed-looking Reed (in glasses) and band amble through a truly career-spanning selection of material in front of a Spanish festival crowd. The guitar solos and jamming are somewhat on the self-indulgent side (the world didn't really need a ten-minute version of 'Romeo Had Juliet'), but Reed's vocal delivery is far more thoughtful and less mannered than in recent years. His group here includes: Mike Rathke (guitar); Fernando Saunders (bass); Jane Scarpantoni (cello); Tony 'Thunder' Smith (drums). Scarpantoni's cello adds a dimension missing from simpler guitar-based line-ups, and even though her instrumental histrionics on 'Venus In Furs' aren't really a substitute for Cale's droning viola, it at least seems a nod in the right direction. Saunders' backing vocals are a delight throughout. All in all, a surprisingly enjoyable set. The DVD also contains a gallery of backstage photographs (by Reed).

VELVETOLOGY: **FILMS AND VIDEOS**

LOU REED: LIVE AT MONTREUX 2000

Paranoia Key Of E/Turn To Me/Modern Dance/Ecstasy/Small Town/Future Farmers Of America/Turning Time Around/Romeo Had Juliette/Riptide/Rock Minuet/Mystic Child/Tatters/Twilight/Dirty Blvd./Dime Store Mystery/Perfect Day

Eagle Vision; released 2005; available on Region 2 DVD

Filmed during the Montreux Jazz Festival on July 13 2000, where Reed made an appearance during the course of his *Ecstasy* tour. Joining Reed are Mike Rathke (guitar), Fernando Saunders (bass) and Tony 'Thunder' Smith (drums). Half of this two-hour set is drawn from the *Ecstasy* album. And it's a mess. Reed seems off his stride, and far more interested in playing guitar – which he actually does pretty well – than in sticking to the actual song structure. His vocals are a complete throwaway, meandering all over the place with little regard to the tune involved. 'Rock Minuet' is pretty good, with Saunders playing his bass with a bow like an electric cello – but in the main this is definitely not Reed's finest live recording.

THE VELVET UNDERGROUND UNDER REVIEW

Sexy Intellectual Productions; released 2006; available on Region 0 DVD

Subtitled "an independent critical analysis", this 85-minute long documentary contains no surprises visually, but all the best-known clips of the band are present. The bulk of the film consists of interviews with Moe Tucker and Doug Yule, as well as with Norman Dolph, Billy Name, Velvets expert Sal Mercuri and several rock critics, including Robert Christgau and Clinton Heylin. While it spends the bulk of its time

concentrating on the first album, the film is still an excellent career overview. Also released under the title *The Velvet Underground – Vanishing Point*.

JOHN CALE

Warner Music Vision; released 2007; available on Region 2 DVD

James Marsh's compelling documentary was first broadcast by BBC Wales in 1998, and was timed to tie in to the publication of Cale's autobiography. It follows Cale and his literary collaborator Victor Bockris on a sentimental journey to Garnant in Wales, and to rehearsals of the Scapino Ballet's production of *Nico* in Rotterdam. There's archive footage of the Velvets and Cale's parents, plus shots of Cale and band in rehearsal and in concert, as well as interviews with Lou Reed, La Monte Young, Billy Name, Brian Eno, Chris Spedding and Marian Zazeela. A good overview of the man's career.

LOU REED'S BERLIN

Artificial Eye, 2007; available on DVD

Filmed at St Ann's Warehouse, Brooklyn, in December 2006, it was directed by Julian Schnabel (best known for directing the feature films *Basquiat* and *The Diving Bell And The Butterfly*). It's a fairly lavish production, with a set resembling a cheap but exotic hotel room, and film clips featuring the actress Emanuelle Seigner as 'Caroline'. Reed's core band are augmented by brass and string sections, backing singers and a choir of teenage girls.

The show concludes with encores of 'Candy Says' (featuring Antony, of Antony and the Johnsons), 'Rock Minuet' and 'Sweet Jane' – and it's a pretty great show: the staging is impressive, and the

THE VELVET UNDERGROUND

performances mostly great. If there's a fault here, it lies right at the heart of the matter, because *Berlin* is not a masterpiece, and never was. It's a comparatively minor work that Lou cobbled together out of unused Velvets material and a few new songs during a creative low ebb. When racked up against some of his other 'concept' works, like *Songs For Drella* or even *New York*, it's clear they're in a much higher league.

LOU REED REMEMBERED
BBC 2013; not commercially available

There's a small amount of archive live footage and a few old interviews with Lou himself, but for the most part this hour-long TV programme consists of affectionate tributes from a couple of musicians who'd been influenced by Reed (Boy George and Thurston Moore), and a generous handful of his friends and associates: Lenny Kaye, biographer Victor Bockris, Mary Woronov, Andrew Wylie, Holy Woodlawn, photographer Mick Rock, producer Bob Ezrin, guitarist Steve Hunter, novelist Paul Auster and Maureen Tucker. Nothing new to be learned here, but as tributes go this was nicely done.

THE CHELSEA GIRLS
Released 1967; not commercially available

Warhol and Morrissey's celebrated underground film is virtually two films, since the screen is split vertically down the middle, with two images showing at once. Since none of the people acting here can actually act, the proceedings are almost totally improvised (Warhol's technique was simply to leave the camera running) and the whole thing is pretty tortuous – it plays like a particularly dull home video with terrible sound quality. Of interest to Velvets fans mainly for the lengthy footage

of Nico, shown trimming the fringe of her hair and simply posing for the camera with psychedelic lighting effects. Also featuring numerous Factory stalwarts including Ondine, Ingrid Superstar, Eric Emerson, Brigid Polk, Gerald Malanga, International Velvet and Mary Woronov. There's three and a half hours of this material, and it feels like a lifetime in purgatory.

CIAO! MANHATTAN
Plexifilm; first released 1972; available on Region 1 DVD

John Palmer and David Weisman's underground film is a woolly pile of nonsense that acts as the swansong for its star Edie Sedgwick, who died three months after shooting was completed. It's also the best demonstration of what made this 'femme fatale' so fascinating. The core of the film consists of Edie – lying half-naked on a waterbed at the bottom of an empty swimming pool – reminiscing about her experiences in New York a few years earlier, which are illustrated with black and white footage taken at the time. She also re-enacts her visits to the methedrine-dealing Dr Roberts, and her electroshock therapy. While Sedgwick admittedly looks amazing in the Sixties footage, she's also obviously completely out of it on a cocktail of drugs, and knowing her inevitable fate makes the whole viewing experience somewhat like watching a traffic accident in slow motion – the more so since Edie herself seems completely aware of her own impending doom.

VELVET GOLDMINE
Released 1988; available on DVD

Todd Haynes' glam-rock fantasy is a fable constructed loosely around the early Seventies exploits of David Bowie and Iggy Pop; though it starts out promisingly and has fairly stunning costumes, it soon degenerates into an annoying mess. What makes it of interest here is that the characters who resemble Bowie (played by Jonathan Rhys Meyers) and Pop (played by Ewan McGregor) are both amalgams of the two stars – and McGregor's character also contains elements of a third party, namely Lou Reed. If you know their stories well enough, spotting the way they've all been jumbled up is moderately amusing.

I SHOT ANDY WARHOL

MGM; 1996; available on Region 1 DVD

Former journalist Mary Harron had originally intended to make a documentary about Valerie Solanas for the BBC, but discovered that hardly any footage of Solanas existed, and that there were also very few people willing to discuss her. Instead, Harron made Warhol's would-be assassin the subject of her first feature film as writer and director. Lili Taylor is impressively unlikeable as Solanas, and Jared Harris and Stephen Dorff turn in creditable impressions of Warhol and Candy Darling respectively.

Warhol's Factory is enjoyably and evocatively recreated, even if the party scene makes it all seem like a lot more fun than it probably was. The Warhol Foundation gave their permission to use reproductions of Warhol silkscreens in the film, on the condition that these were destroyed after filming was complete, and Billy Name served as "creative advisor". The party scene features a rock band playing who are obviously intended to be the Velvets, though no actual Velvets music is used. However, John Cale did contribute an orchestral piece to the soundtrack. The film won the special jury award at the 1996 Sundance Festival.

PUNK: ATTITUDE

Fremantlemedia; released October 2005; available on Region 2 DVD

Don Letts' excellent documentary about punk features every major punk band from the Clash and Pistols on down, and is well worth your attention. It includes a brief section on the Velvets as forefathers of punk, with an interview with Cale and fragments of the 'Venus In Furs' rehearsal film. More interestingly, there are also very brief clips of Reed and Nico performing at the 1972 Bataclan gig – the only commercial release of this material to date.

FACTORY GIRL

Released theatrically March 2007; available on DVD

George Hickenlooper's biopic of Edie Sedgwick was attracting flak even before its release, with Lou Reed publicly branding the filmmakers as "whoremongers" and scriptwriter Captain Mauzner as an "illiterate retard". In fact, the film is far better than one might have anticipated, with an amazing degree of visual accuracy, and it paints a fairly rounded portrait of its subject – which means it's also a pretty depressing ride, and probably a dull one if you have no prior knowledge of Warhol's world. Sienna Miller turns in an extremely good performance as Edie, while Guy Pearce's impression of Warhol is positively uncanny. Pearce is now the fourth actor to portray the artist (since David Bowie played Andy in 1996's Basquiat), and easily the best.

On the downside, the chronology is somewhat skewed from reality, Warhol is squarely blamed for Edie's decline (which probably isn't entirely fair) and the romance between Edie and Dylan (here portrayed by Hayden Christensen as 'Billy Quinn') is depicted as being far deeper than it probably

8

was. Dylan threatened to sue for defamation, and one can scarcely blame him, since his character here is both dumber and far more po-faced than the man himself. As for the Velvets and Nico, they're reduced to the briefest of cameos, and the casting is truly bizarre – 'John Cale' being downright short and chubby. Unsurprisingly, no Velvets music is used on the soundtrack. Gerard Malanga acted as one of the film's consultants and is one of several people who actually knew Edie interviewed over the closing credits.

WEBSITES

There is no authorised website for the Velvet Underground. *www.velvetunderground.com* is simply a fan website, and not a particularly good one. Of the numerous Velvet Underground fan sites, easily the best is The Velvet Underground Web Page (*http://olivier. landemaine.free.fr/vu/*) created and maintained by Olivier Landemaine. Here you'll find an extensive discography (including bootlegs), bibliography and filmography, plus classic magazine articles, photo and audio files (including unreleased live material), and much more, including links to further pages on the individual members. Some of the links don't always work, but it's worth returning to this site frequently – there's enough material to keep you occupied for hours.

Maureen Tucker's Taj Moe Hal site (*www. spearedpeanut.com/tajmoehal/*) sadly no longer exists, and she seemingly now has no web presence at all. There used to be a wealth of material at *www.loureed.com*, which was until a few years ago fairly well-maintained,

but many of the links no longer work now. Even so, there are still audio files of music and interviews, and a few video files there. Enrique Miguel's Rock And Roll Animal site (*www.arrakis.es/~e.miquel/rnranimal*), which Lou Reed seemingly considered the best of the Reed fan sites also seems to be defunct now.

The seemingly official *www.john-cale. com* is a major disappointment, containing only promotion and ordering details for the revamped *Fragments Of A Rainy Season*. Hopefully the site will be developed further someday. Meanwhile, an excellent Cale resource can be found at *www.xs4all. nl/~werksman/cale/index.html*. Here you'll find an extensive biography, discography, lyrics and sheet music, photos and much more, including a John Cale quiz.

Finally, the best of the many Nico websites would seem to be the one found at *http:// smironne.free.fr/NICO/*, which has a wealth of material on every aspect of Nico's life and work (including a photo of her grave).

THE LEGACY

8

COVERS, FANS & TRIBUTES

It's almost impossible to overestimate the influence of the Velvet Underground upon rock music. Within a couple of years of the Velvets' demise, both David Bowie and Brian Eno had publicly acknowledged their debt to the band, and both those gentlemen would also influence almost everything else that followed them.

Nor was it just the art rock bands that fell under the Velvet shadow. The Velvets had a direct impact on the Sex Pistols, as did John Cale's production work (which was arguably a continuation of the Velvets' musical methods). The Pistols covered material by both the Stooges and Jonathan Richman (both produced by Cale), and his production work with Patti Smith was also enormously influential on the whole punk/new wave movement. Very few of the late Sixties bands were acknowledged as forebears by the punk bands – chief among them being the Velvets and the Doors. Very few of the indie and grunge outfits that followed them would take Jim Morrison seriously, but the Velvets still counted – and continue to do so. It's no accident that both R.E.M. and Nirvana, neither of whom were known to cover songs by many other artists, recorded Velvets songs.

You can hear echoes of the Velvets' sound everywhere: in Joy Division, Echo & The Bunnymen, Lloyd Cole, Talking Heads, the Smiths, the Cowboy Junkies, Jane's Addiction, Simple Minds, the Cure, the Birthday Party, the Jesus & Mary Chain, the

VELVETS FANS AND TRIBUTES

Jonathan Richman, Iggy Pop, Wayne Kramer of the MC5, Robert Quine of The Voidoids, Ric Ocasek of The Cars and Chrissie Hynde of The Pretenders are all known to have seen the Velvets play live. One of the Velvets' support acts was Chris Stein's first band, many years before he founded Blondie. "You could say everything came from the Velvets," commented one observer. Songs written about, or in honour of, the Velvets include: 'Velvet Underground' by Jonathan Richman; 'Moe Tucker' by the Jesus & Mary Chain; and 'Tugboat' by Galaxie 500 (about the seafaring Sterling Morrison). Nico was – or is generally believed to have been – the inspiration behind the following songs: 'My Eyes Have Seen You' by The Doors; 'Decadence' by Kevin Ayers; 'Take This Longing' and 'Joan Of Arc' by Leonard Cohen; 'We Will Fall' by The Stooges; and 'Song For Nico' Marianne Faithfull.

8

Wedding Present, Nick Cave, the Violent Femmes, the Strokes, the Vines... in pretty much every indie rock band of the last 30 years, whether guitar-based or not. Many of these bands recorded their own versions of Velvets material; many more played it live. The Velvets even impacted visually, their all-black ensemble being adopted almost universally as the de rigeur uniform for any band who wished to be taken seriously; Nico in turn became a Goth icon.

Although it's less obvious, the impact of Lou Reed as a lyricist is also incalculable. Not because he wrote about drugs and sexuality per se, but because in doing so he'd proved that it was possible for rock to embrace any subject matter under the sun or moon, to be literate and ambitious and occasionally witty. As with Bob Dylan, every songwriter since who has aspired to creating something with a degree of intellectual content owes a debt to Reed, whether it's visible (even to them) or not.

It's a fair bet that within the record collections of all interesting lyricists one would find a Velvets album or two (or more), and it seems entirely possible that the Velvets' legend may never fade.

VELVETS COVER VERSIONS

In *The Velvet Underground Handbook* MC Kostek lists over 300 known cover versions of Velvets songs – a sum that's increasing daily, and which doesn't include covers of the solo material by Reed, Cale or Nico. Some place the total at much higher, and there are at least three volumes in the *Heaven & Hell* CD series, all of which are exclusively devoted to cover versions of Velvet Underground songs.

In 1998 the Dutch indie band Bettie Serveert recorded an entire album of Velvets songs, handily titled *Bettie Serveert Plays Venus In Furs And Other Velvet Underground Songs*.

The bizarrest cover version has to be Zeitkratzer's recording of *Metal Machine Music*. This orchestral group transcribed Lou's feedback album for conventional orchestral instruments, and performed it live in Berlin and Venice; the CD was recorded live at performances in Italy. Lou Reed was amazed that anyone would attempt this, and thought it couldn't be done; when he heard a sample, he gave them his blessing, and cried when he heard the piece live. Zeitkratzer obviously took the project very seriously, but although the results are interesting (and even mildly more accessible than Lou's version), it has to be said this is one for devotees of the original piece only.

In 2014 the American singer-songwriter Joseph Arthur recorded an entire album of Lou Reed songs, titled *Lou*. It's very good.

Leaving aside solo versions of Velvets songs by Nico, Reed, Cale and Tucker, a partial list of the most notable cover versions would include:

VELVETOLOGY: **THE LEGACY**

Big Star
'Femme Fatale' (on *Sister Lovers*)

David Bowie
'White Light/White Heat'
(on *Ziggy Stardust: The Motion Picture*)

Nick Cave
'All Tomorrow's Parties'
(on *Kicking Against The Pricks*)

The Cowboy Junkies
'Sweet Jane' (on *The Trinity Sessions*)

Bryan Ferry
'What Goes On' (on *The Bride Stripped Bare*)

James
'Sunday Morning'
(on the compilation *Heaven & Hell Volume I*)

Joy Division
'Sister Ray' (on *Still*)

Lone Justice
'Sweet Jane' (on *I Found Love*)

Thurston Moore
'European Son' (on *The End Of Music As We Know It*)

Mott The Hoople
'Sweet Jane' (on *All The Young Dudes*)

New Order
'Sister Ray' (on the compilation *Like A Girl, I Want You To Keep Coming*)

Nirvana
'Here She Comes Now'
(on the compilation *Heaven & Hell Volume I*)

Rainy Day
'I'll Be Your Mirror' (on *Rainy Day*)

REM
'There She Goes Again', 'Pale Blue Eyes' and 'Femme Fatale' (all on *Dead Letter Office*) and 'Afterhours' (B-side of 'Losing My Religion' single

The Tom Tom Club
'Femme Fatale' (on *Boom Boom Chi Boom Boom*)

Voice Of The Beehive
'Jesus' (B-side of 'I Say Nothing' single)

The Wedding Present
'She's My Best Friend'
(on the compilation *Heaven & Hell Volume I*)

8

8 THERE HE GOES AGAIN: THE WISDOM OF LOU REED

"I'm not tasteful. I never said I was tasteful." (1978)

"I work really hard to make my songs sound like the way people really talk. My concerns are somewhat similar to what Sam Shepard and Martin Scorsese are doing, talking about things that people growing up in a city go through. I'm trying for a kind of urban elegance, set to a beat." (1982)

"I don't know why people give me record deals. I think it's because they at least break even, and I think they even make a few bucks while they're at it. I'm a cult figure, but I sell some records." (1989)

"I'm into this for the long haul. I feel I've just started to get a grip on it, what I can do with it, and who I'd like to take with me when I do it. It's really easy in a sense, because the people who like it will go with me, and the people who don't will say I'm full of shit, and more power to them. They don't want me, and I'm not interested in them either. That's okay. I have no problem with that." (1992)

"Some of the music I like just makes me feel like going out and burning down a house or attacking a politician." (1996)

"I should have been dead a thousand times." (1996)

"You can't walk around with anger in your heart. It causes very negative things." (1992)

"Warhol said that it's too bad in school they don't have a course about love, like practical stuff. Or maybe one on loss, like what do you do with yourself, who do you ask, where do you turn." (1992)

"I was interested in the subject matter that hadn't been covered in rock and pop." (1997)

"Three chords is three chords, but there is a finesse to it." (Date unknown).

"I'd have to sit there with people saying, 'Don't you feel guilty for glamourising heroin, for all the people who've shot up drugs because of you ?' I get that to this day, even though I didn't notice a drop-off in the sales of narcotics when I stopped taking things." (1996)

"Rock 'n' roll for me has no limits. That's one of my points about it." (1997)

"Just say that John Cale was the easygoing one and Lou Reed was the prick." (Date unknown).

THE BIG BANANA: THE VELVET UNDERGROUND'S NEW YORK

8

If ever a band defined the beat of a city, it was the Velvets and New York. Here's a guide to 40 key Velvet Underground sites.

1 Bank Street
La Monte Young lived at #119 during the Sixties.

2 Barrow Street

3 Bleecker Street
John and Risé Cale lived on both these streets in the early Eighties.

4 Broome Street
The Velvets regularly rehearsed in a loft here in 1966.

5 Café Bizarre (West 3rd St)
Where Andy Warhol first met the Velvet Underground.

6 CBGBs (315 Bowery)
Founded by Hilly Cristal in 1973, the club rapidly became the centre of New York's punk movement. It closed on 15 October 2006, with a performance from Patti Smith.

7 The Chelsea Hotel (West 23rd St)
John Cale (with Betsey Johnson) and Nico (for several periods) both lived here.

8 Christopher Street
Reed lived here in the Seventies, and again in the Nineties when Cale also had an apartment here.

9 Church Street
LaMonte Young lived here in the mid-Sixties, and the Theatre Of Eternal Music rehearsed here.

10 Club Baby Grand (125th St)
Cale and Reed busked on the sidewalk in front of here in the summer of 1965.

11 The Delmonico Hotel (502 Park Avenue, at 59th St)
Site of the first performance by the Velvets with Nico, in January 1966. The building is now the Trump Park Avenue apartment complex.

12 The Dom (St Mark's Place)
Venue of the first public gigs of the Exploding Plastic Inevitable show.

13 East 2nd Street
Sterling Morrison lived here in late 1967.

14 East 16th Street
Nico lived here in 1968.

15 East 52nd Street
Lou Reed lived here with Rachel in 1976; Greta Garbo was one of their neighbours.

16 East 63rd Street & Madison Avenue
John Cale lived here with Edie Sedgwick in early 1966.

17 The Factory #1 (231 East 47th St)
The Velvets rehearsed here, and many of Warhol's early films were shot here. The building was demolished in 1968.

18 The Factory # 2 (33 Union Square West)
The Factory occupied the 6th floor. Where Andy Warhol was shot by Valerie Solanas.

19 14th Street
Cale lived here with Jane Friedman in the late Seventies.

20 450 Grand Street
Reed, Cale, MacLise and Morrison shared an apartment on the fifth floor in autumn 1965 with underground filmmaker Piero Heliczer.

21 Jane Street
Nico and Lou Reed lived together in an apartment here in early 1966.

22 Lafayette Street
The Velvets performed here in 1965, playing behind the screen at the Lafayette Street Cinematheque.

23 LaGuardia Place
John Cale lived here while married to Betsey Johnson.

24 Lispenard Street
Cale's first New York apartment, late 1963.

25 Ludlow Street
John Cale had an apartment at #56 during 1964–65. Reed moved in with him in the summer of 1965, and the Velvets rehearsed and recorded demos here.

26 Max's Kansas City
213 Park Avenue South (at 17th Street).

27 Ninth Street & Fifth Avenue
Maureen Tucker briefly lived here in 1967, until poverty forced her to move back in with her parents in Long Island.

28 Perry Street
Lou Reed lived here in 1967.

29 Riviera Café (Sheridan Square)
Here Lou Reed informed Sterling Morrison and Moe Tucker that he wanted John Cale fired from the group.

30 Scepter Records (254 West 54th Street)
The Velvets recorded the bulk of their first album here. The building subsequently housed the club Studio 54.

31 Steve Sesnick's Apartment
East 55th Street.

32 67th Street
Nico and John Cale lived together here (very briefly) in early 1967.

33 30th Street
Cale lived here in 1980.

34 28th Street & 7th Avenue
Reed lived in a loft near Penn Station during 1968-69. According to Morrison, the loft was actually on 31st Street.

35 28th Street
Cale lived in an apartment here (between Madison and Lexington) in 1970.

36 West 3rd Street
Reed, Morrison (and occasionally Cale) lived here during 1966-67, sub-letting an apartment above a firehouse. It was known as 'Sister Ray House'.

37 West 10th Street
John Cale and Sterling Morrison shared an apartment here in 1966; Lou Reed lived in another apartment two blocks over on the same street.

38 West 26th Street
The Velvet Underground rehearsed in a former factory here for their 1993 reunion tour.

39 West 54th Street
Lou Reed lived in the Gotham apartment building here during the Seventies.

40 West 81st Street & West End Avenue
Lou and Sylvia Reed lived here in the Eighties.

Index

THE VELVET UNDERGROUND

the beatles

Ever wished you'd seen The Beatles live?

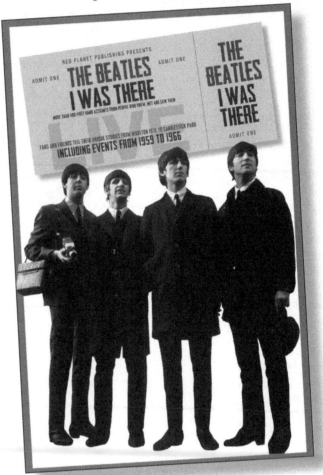

This book provides a fan's-eye account of the Fab Four as they conquered the world. From their skiffle days as The Quarrymen, their thrilling early gigs at the Cavern Club in Liverpool through to the Beatlemania of the Shea Stadium concerts in the USA.

Share in the excitement of over 400 first-hand encounters with The Beatles: the teenagers, kids, twentysomethings, promoters and support bands who can all proudly say 'I was there!'

Featuring anecdotes, stories, photographs and memorabilia that have never been published before, this book is a portrait of an amazing era. It's like being at your very own Beatles gig

ISBN: 9781905959945 Editor: Richard Houghton 400 pages Illustrated

From Me to You

This fascinating book looks at the songs The Beatles wrote for other artists – many of which they never released on record themselves. Author Brian Southall, a long-standing former EMI executive, delivers a unique insight into what The Beatles played live and which of those songs made their way into the studio sessions. The book takes a look at some of the more noteable cover versions of The Beatles songbook – versions The Beatles loved...and hated!

ISBN: 9781 90595923 Author: Brian Southall
160 pages Illustrated

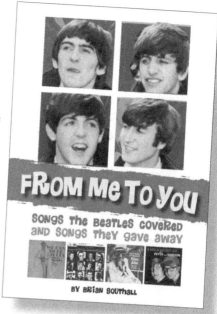

Dead Straight Guide to The Beatles

The Beatles are the most important pop group of all time. It's impossible to imagine modern music without them. This book tells the band's whole story, from their teenage skiffle-group beginnings, through Beatlemania, to global megastardom.

With detailed reviews of all the Beatles albums, solo albums, cover versions, movies and TV appearances, plus in-depth analysis of the greatest 50 Beatles songs and a wealth of Fab 4 trivia, rumours and legends, here is all the Beatles you will ever need.
ISBN: 9781 905959600 Author: Chris Ingham
400 pages Illustrated

Available from ***www.redplanetzone.com***
www.redplanetzone.com, Amazon, HMV and all good bookshops

ROCK ATLAS
UK AND IRELAND SECOND EDITION

*800 great music locations and the
fascinating stories behind them*

Rock Atlas is more than just a guide to over 800 music locations. You can visit many of the places
or simply enjoy reading this extraordinary fact-packed book's fascinating stories. Some are iconic,
others are just plain weird or unusual, such as Bob Dylan turning up unannounced on a public tour
of John Lennon's childhood home or the musical park bench commemorating Ian Dury's life that
plays recordings of his hits and his appearance on Desert Island Discs.

Providing insights into many performers' lives, Rock Atlas includes artists as diverse as The
Beatles, Sex Pistols, Lady Gaga and Lonnie Donegan. Presented in an easy-to-read, region-by-
region format, every entry provides detailed instructions on how to find each location together with
extensive lists of the pop and rock stars born in each county.

Illustrated with hundreds of rare, unseen and iconic colour and black and white photographs,
Rock Atlas is a must for anyone with an emotional tie to contemporary music and the important
places associated with it.

On sale now
For information on Red Planet books visit www.redplanetzone.com

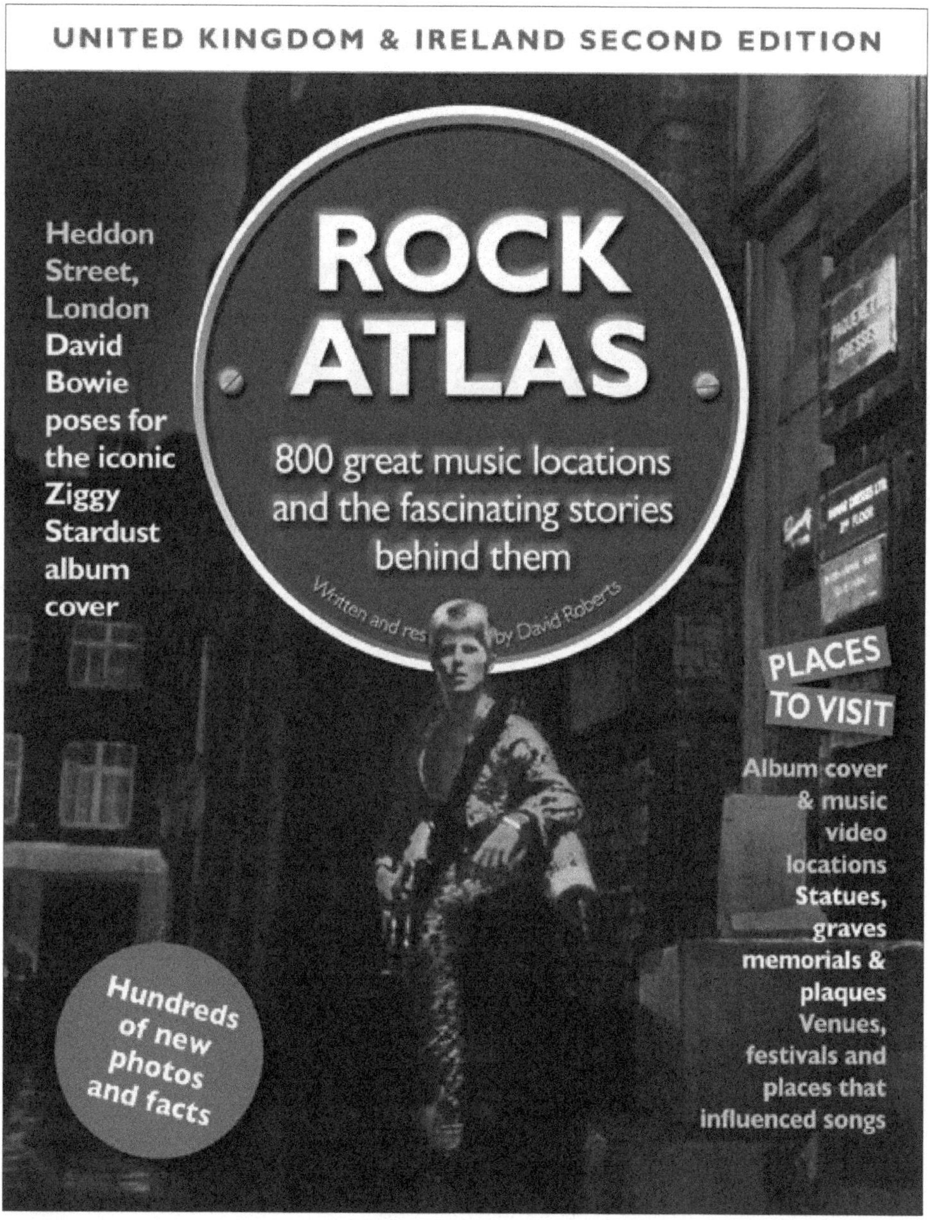

UNITED KINGDOM & IRELAND SECOND EDITION

ROCK ATLAS

800 great music locations
and the fascinating stories
behind them

Written and researched by David Roberts

Heddon
Street,
London
David
Bowie
poses for
the iconic
Ziggy
Stardust
album
cover

PLACES
TO VISIT

Album cover
& music
video
locations
Statues,
graves
memorials &
plaques
Venues,
festivals and
places that
influenced songs

Hundreds
of new
photos
and facts

www.redplanetzone.com

Discover music history and
facts 365 days a year

www.thisdayinmusic.com

Sign up now for the
Red Planet Newsletter
and receive news about our new books and special offers

(its free, it'll save you money, and we promise not to mail you too often or sell your details):

sign up right now at
www.redplanetzone.com

HIS LIFE & MUSIC IN ONE ESSENTIAL BOOK

THE DEAD STRAIGHT GUIDE TO

BOB DYLAN

NIGEL WILLIAMSON